DIGITAL AND DOCUMENT EXAMINATION

PUBLISHED TITLES IN THE *ADVANCED FORENSIC SCIENCE SERIES*

Published

Forensic Fingerprints
Firearm and Toolmark Examination and Identification
Forensic Biology
Forensic Chemistry
Professional Issues in Forensic Science
Materials Analysis in Forensic Science
Forensic Pathology
Forensic Anthropology
Forensic Engineering
Behavioral Analysis
Forensic Toxicology
Digital and Document Examination

DIGITAL AND DOCUMENT EXAMINATION

Advanced Forensic Science Series

Edited by

MAX M. HOUCK, PhD, FRSC

Managing Director, Forensic & Intelligence Services, LLC, St. Petersburg, FL, USA

ACADEMIC PRESS

An imprint of Elsevier

Academic Press is an imprint of Elsevier
125 London Wall, London EC2Y 5AS, United Kingdom
525 B Street, Suite 1800, San Diego, CA 92101-4495, United States
50 Hampshire Street, 5th Floor, Cambridge, MA 02139, United States
The Boulevard, Langford Lane, Kidlington, Oxford OX5 1GB, United Kingdom

Library of Congress Cataloging-in-Publication Data
A catalog record for this book is available from the Library of Congress

British Library Cataloguing-in-Publication Data
A catalogue record for this book is available from the British Library

ISBN: 978-0-12-802717-2
ISSN: 2352-6238

For information on all Academic Press publications visit our website at
https://www.elsevier.com/books-and-journals

Publisher: Mica Haley
Acquisition Editor: Elizabeth Brown
Editorial Project Manager: Kathy Padilla
Senior Production Project Manager: Priya Kumaraguruparan
Designer: Matthew Limbert

Typeset by TNQ Books and Journals

DEDICATION

This volume in the *Advanced Forensic Science Series* is dedicated to the memory of Bryan Found, a scholar, a gentleman, and a true friend. Bryan was a Penfolds Grange 1998 vintage in a sea of plonks. I was lucky enough to be called a friend and colleague by him. He is sorely missed by the profession and his mates.

CONTENTS

SENIOR EDITOR: BIOGRAPHY

Max M. Houck is an internationally recognized forensic expert with research interests in anthropology, trace evidence, education, and the fundamentals of forensic science, both as a science and as an enterprise. He has worked in the private sector, the public sector (at the regional and federal levels), and academia. Dr. Houck has published in a wide variety of areas in the field, in books, book chapters, and peer-reviewed journals. His casework includes the Branch Davidian Investigation, the September 11 attacks on the Pentagon, the D.B. Cooper case, the US Embassy bombings in Africa, and the West Memphis Three case. He served for 6 years as the Chair of the Forensic Science Educational Program Accreditation Commission (FEPAC). Dr. Houck is a founding coeditor of the journal *Forensic Science Policy and Management*, with Jay Siegel; he has also coauthored a major textbook with Siegel, *Fundamentals of Forensic Science*. In 2012, Dr. Houck was in the top 1% of connected professionals on LinkedIn. Dr. Houck is currently the Managing Director of Forensic & Intelligences Services, LLC, St. Petersburg, FL. Dr. Houck is the Director of the Forensic Studies & Justice program at University of South Florida St. Petersburg.

LIST OF CONTRIBUTORS

CL Bird
Forensic Science SA, Adelaide, SA, Australia

E Burton
Greater Manchester Police Forensic Services Branch, Manchester, UK

J Cali
CPA, CFF, CGMA

K Corbin
US Secret Service, Washington, DC, USA

F Crispino
Université du Québec à Trois-Rivières, Trois-Rivières, QC, Canada

J de Koeijer
Netherlands Forensic Institute, The Hague, The Netherlands

J Epstein
Widener University School of Law, Wilmington, DE, USA

T Fritz
IRCGN, Rosny Sous Bois, France

Z Geradts
Netherlands Forensic Institute, Den Haag, The Netherlands

C Grigoras
University of Colorado Denver, Denver, CO, USA

VL Grose
US National Transportation Safety Board, Washington, DC, USA

DL Hammond
U.S. Army Criminal Investigation Laboratory, Forest Park, GA, USA

KC Harris
US Secret Service, Washington, DC, USA

MM Houck
Consolidated Forensic Laboratory, Washington, DC, USA

P Jones
Purdue University, West Lafayette, IN, USA

GC Kessler
Embry-Riddle Aeronautical University, Daytona Beach, FL, USA

RF Lambourn
Transport Research Laboratory, Wokingham, UK

WD Mazzella
Forensic Document Examination Services Inc., Vancouver, BC, Canada; University of Lausanne, Lausanne, Switzerland

J McGinn
Department of Immigration and Citizenship, Perth, WA, Australia; Document Examination Solutions, Perth, WA, Australia

RP Mislan
RP Mislan, DeTour, MI, USA

LA Mohammed
San Bruno, CA, USA

S Nekkache
IRCGN, Rosny Sous Bois, France

DC Purdy
Forensic Document Examination Services Inc., Vancouver, BC, Canada; University of Lausanne, Lausanne, Switzerland

E Quayle
University of Edinburgh, Edinburgh, UK

K Ramsey
Greater Manchester Police Forensic Services Branch, Manchester, UK

LR Rockwell
Forensic and Intelligence Services, LLC, Alexandria, VA, USA

MK Rogers
Purdue University, West Lafayette, IN, USA

W Rosenbluth
Reston, VA, USA

B Saw
Australian Federal Police, Canberra, ACT, Australia

N Scudder
Australian Federal Police, Canberra, ACT, Australia

JA Siegel
Indiana University Purdue University Indianapolis, Indianapolis, IN, USA

JM Smith
University of Colorado Denver, Denver, CO, USA

T Trubshoe
Department of Immigration and Citizenship, Perth, WA, Australia; Document Examination Solutions, Perth, WA, Australia

FOREWORD

Forensic science has much to learn. The breadth of the discipline alone should render any reasonably learned person dizzy with expectations—insects, explosives, liver functions, DNA, firearms, textiles, adhesives, skeletons...the list goes on forever. That is because anything, truly *anything*, can become evidence, from a single fiber to an entire ocean liner. Forensic science does not lack for specialized knowledge (some might stay too specialized) but what it is wanting is knowledge that is comprehensive, integrated, and foundational. Introductions to forensic science abound and many highly specialized texts are also available but a gap exists between the two: A bridge from novice to practitioner. As the 2009 NRC report noted,

Forensic science examiners need to understand the principles, practices, and contexts of scientific methodology, as well as the distinctive features of their specialty. Ideally, training should move beyond apprentice-like transmittal of practices to education based on scientifically valid principles. NRC (2009, pp. 26–27)

The *Advanced Forensic Sciences Series* seeks to fill that gap. It is a unique source, combining entries from the world's leading specialists who contributed to the second edition of the award-winning *Encyclopedia of Forensic Sciences* and organizing them by topic into a series of volumes that are philosophically grounded yet professionally specialized. The series is composed of 12 volumes that cover the breadth of forensic science:

1. Professional Issues
2. Biology
3. Chemistry
4. Fingerprints
5. Firearms
6. Materials Analysis
7. Pathology

8. Anthropology
9. Engineering
10. Behavioral
11. Digital and Document Examination
12. Forensic Toxicology

Each volume contains sections common to all forensic sciences, such as professionalism, ethics, health and safety, and court testimony, and sections relevant to the topics in that particular subdiscipline. Pedagogy is included, providing review questions, discussion questions, the latest references in additional readings, and key words. Thus, each volume is suitable as a technical reference, an advanced textbook, or a training adjunct.

The *Advanced Forensic Science Series* provides expert information, useful teaching tools, and a ready source for instruction, research, and practice. I hope, like learning, it is the only thing for you.

M.M. Houck, PhD
Series Editor

Reference

National Research Council, 2009. Strengthening Forensic Science in the U.S.: A Path Forward. National Academies of Science, Washington, DC.

INTRODUCTION

Despite the digital world we live in, documents still surround us and dictate our lives. We start with birth certificates and end with final certification of our demise. In between, documents from doctors, schools, universities, governments, banks, insurance companies, businesses, and many other sources determine our activities and authenticity. Whether stored on paper or electrons, these documents provide proof that we are who we say we are and that we can do what we are allowed to do.

Ever since the invention of writing,[1] there have been attempts to alter documents or create entirely fake ones. Forgery is the process of making or altering objects or documents with the intent to deceive. This intended deception can be about many things, including source, authorship, age, or content. A forged check could

Figure 1 Computer files used to be stored on thin strips of plastic film that had a magnetized coating. Over time, the binder in the plastic tape hydrolyzes, making it unusable ("sticky-shed syndrome").

---

[1] Writing is thought to have been invented independently at least three times: China, around 7000years before the current era (BCE); Mesopotamia, around 3300 BCE; and ancient Mexico, around 2300 BCE.

contain many possible deceptions, such as the date it was written, the amount it was written for, the account from which the money is to be drawn, the signer of the check, among others. Money is not the prime motivator for forging documents—although it is usually in the top three[2]—it figures in one degree or another in many document cases, paper, or digital.

Much has and continues to be made about the future and a "paperless" society. Digital does do some things far better than physical documents; editing, sharing, and size come to mind. Paper, however, as the popular example of documents, is an old technology. Although wood, bone, or stone came first, paper as a technology is about 2200years old. By comparison, the first word processor was invented a scant 50years ago (about the same time the editor of this series was invented) and the printer as a peripheral soon after (1968). As a civilization, we have lived with paper over 40 times longer than we have lived with computers. As a modern society, we will probably never be rid of physical documents.

Some documents require a physical presence (imagine showing a police officer a *photo* of your driver's license). Standards are necessary to access digital files. Computer file formats come and go, as do media (have you ever seen a floppy disk?). The editor remembers a time when, prior to giving an invited talk at a NASA facility, during a tour, he saw a box of old computer tapes (digitized files used to be saved on long magnetized, plastic tapes stored on spools like ribbon…no, really; see **Figure 1**). When he asked his tour guide what they were, he was told they were the schematics for the first lunar lander from the 1969 Apollo 11 mission. No one could use or copy them, however, because there was no computer in existence that could read the code from that medium. Over time, the binder in the plastic hydrolyzes and the tapes become useless. The point is, even if you can't read Japanese, you can still go to a library and find a *legible* binding of *The Tale of Genji*, the oldest novel in history. In the game of rock—paper—computer media, paper almost always wins.

As a computerized, digital world, we cannot escape information, regardless of its form. Most of us in our daily lives leave a digital trail a mile wide and decades long. Try Googling yourself. Anyone with a modicum of activity in the current world of social media, smartphones, and instant communication has a presence discoverable by anyone with access to the Internet. And the Internet never forgets. Our private documents once held in dark filing cabinets or tall government shelves can now be discerned by nearly anyone with a computer and a credit card.[3] Digital media make it easy for anyone to alter documentation. Although altering documents and photographs predates the computer (see **Figure 2**), the combination of digital cameras and image processing software makes it a simple matter to significantly alter documents and images.

---

[2] The editor's personal contention is that the top three, in fact, would be (1) money, (2) sex, and (3) revenge. Police, criminals, and mystery writers are free to disagree.
[3] 5 tips for finding anything, about anyone, online: https://www.cnet.com/how-to/5-tips-for-finding-anything-about-anyone-online/.

Figure 2   The act of altering photos predates the computer. (Top left) Kliment Voroshilov, Vyacheslav Molotov, Stalin, and Nikolai Yezhov at the shore of the Moscow-Volga canal. After Yezhov was tried and executed, he vanished from this image sometime after 1939 (bottom left).[4] Computers and digital cameras have made it so easy to alter documents and images, anyone can do it. A bored film crew scouting locations in Colorado made this image to have some fun with friends and family (right).[5]

Images notwithstanding, most of our daily lives, personal, professional, and financial, are wrapped up in the digital world. Given that criminals live there as well, it seems that forensic digital and document examiners have a rich and busy future.

[4] By unknown: http://www.tate.org.uk/tateetc/issue8/erasurerevelation.htm; public domain: https://commons.wikimedia.org/w/index.php?curid=4802378.
[5] Hogan, M., February 28, 2016 (Sunday). Hoaxes that went viral. The Observer. Online at: https://www.theguardian.com/technology/2016/feb/28/hoaxes-that-went-viral-kanye-west-donald-trump.

Section 1. Introduction

Forensic science has a perception problem: We are not CSI but we are not chopped liver, either. The real issue may stem from a lack of core scientific philosophical principles from which to work. Even relatively young disciplines such as chemistry (the recognizable form of which developed in the early 1600s) have established fundamental philosophies from which to work. Forensic science is only about 100 years old, give or take; we have much to work on to rediscover our philosophical base and make it explicit.

One of the obstacles in the process of redefining forensic science as a science is that so much of what gets done is task based, that is, methods. The emphasis on technique distracts from a deeper understanding of not just the *how* but the *why*. The philosopher William Barrett in his book, *The Illusion of Technique*, discussed that, while technicians know what to do, scientists know what to do when something goes wrong because they understand the process more completely:

> The technician is called upon to handle the instrument he is assigned to without having necessarily to know how it works...So the biologist need not know the laws of optics on which his microscope has been constructed. The characteristic of technical organization is the subdivision of labor at the specificity of the task assigned. Within science this begets the common situation where one scientist borrows and uses the results of another scientist without having to know clearly on what they are based, or what their finer meaning may be. Now imaging this procedure carried out to the farthest degree. Each link in the chain does what it does without knowing what the whole chain is about. We would end by building a tower of Babel[1] where each layer of the structure cannot communicate with the next. Barrett (1978, pages 121–122).

As Barrett points out, this problem expands as science becomes more specialized (biologists do not understand optics, chemists do not understand electrical engineering, etc.). This is, in a nutshell, the trouble with forensic science to a large degree. We have a bag of tools but not a wealth of knowledge about how they work.

Digital and documents examination suffers from this perhaps more than other forensic disciplines, the former more than the latter. Recent research in handwriting has lead to great gains in our understanding of how this method works and when it does not, why.

Principles of Forensic Science

F Crispino, Université du Québec à Trois-Rivières, Trois-Rivières, QC, Canada
MM Houck, Consolidated Forensic Laboratory, Washington, DC, USA

Glossary

Abduction Syllogism in which one premise is certain whereas the other one is only probable, generally presented as the best explanation to the former. Hence, abduction is a type of reasoning in which we know the law and the effect, and we attempt to infer the cause.

Deduction Process of reasoning that moves from the general to the specific and in which a conclusion follows necessarily from the stated premises. Hence, deduction is a type of reasoning in which, knowing the cause and the law, we infer the effect.

---

[1] The Tower of Babel is a Near Eastern story in the Book of Genesis. In the story, at one time, all humanity spoke one language. They agree to build a tower—together—tall enough to reach heaven. God, seeing this attempt to reach him, confounds their speech into many languages and scatters the people across the globe. Thus, humanity could not understand each other and could not finish the Tower. By one account, the tower received its name from the Hebrew word *balal*, meaning to jumble or to confuse.

Forensic intelligence Understanding on how traces can be collected from the scene, processed, and interpreted within an holistic intelligence-led policing strategy.

Heuristic Process of reasoning by rules that are only loosely defined, generally by trial and error.

Holistic Emphasizing the importance of the whole and the interdependence of its parts.

Induction Process of deriving general principles from particular facts or instances, i.e., of reasoning that moves from the specific to the general. Hence, induction is a type of reasoning in which, knowing the cause and the effect (or a series of causes and effects), we attempt to infer the law by which the effects follow the cause.

Linkage blindness Organizational or investigative failure to recognize a common pattern shared on different cases.

Science The intellectual and practical activity encompassing the systematic study of the structure and behavior of the physical and natural world through observation and experiment. It is also defined as a systematically organized body of knowledge on a particular subject.

Given that it identifies and collects objects at crime scenes and then treats them as evidence, forensic science could appear at first glance to be only a pragmatic set of various disciplines, with practitioners adapting and developing tools and technologies to help the triers of fact (juries or judges) interpret information gained from the people, places, and things involved in a crime. The view could be—and has been—held that forensic science has no philosophic or fundamental unity and is merely the application of knowledge generated by other sciences. Indeed, many working forensic scientists regard themselves mainly as chemists, biologists, scientists, or technicians, and rarely as practitioners of a homogeneous body of knowledge with common fundamental principles.

Even the 2009 National Academy of Sciences National Research Council Report failed to recognize such a concept, certainly blurred by a semantic gap in the terminology itself of field practitioners, who confuse words such as "forensic science(s)," "criminalistic(s)," "criminology," "technical police," "scientific police," and so on, and generally restrict the scientific debate on analytical techniques and methods. An independent definition of forensic science, apart from its legal aspects, would support its scientific status and return the expert to his or her domain as scientist and interpreter of his analyses and results to assist the lay person.

What Is Forensic Science?

In its broadest sense, forensic science describes the utility of the sciences as they pertain to legal matters, to include many disciplines, such as chemistry, biology, pathology, anthropology, toxicology, and engineering, among others. ("Forensic" comes from the Latin root *forum*, the central place of the city where disputes and debates were made public to be solved, hence, defining the law of the city. Forensic generally means of or applied to the law.) The word "criminalistics" was adopted to describe the discipline directed toward the "recognition, identification, individualization, and evaluation of physical evidence by application of the natural sciences to law-science matters." ("Kriminalistik" was coined in the late nineteenth century by Hans Gross, a researcher in criminal law and procedure to define his methodology of classifying investigative, tactical, and evidential information to be learned by magistrates at law schools to solve crimes and help convict criminals.) In the scheme as it currently stands, criminalistics is part of forensic science; the word is a regionalism and is not universally applied as defined. Difficulties in differentiating the concepts certainly invited the definition of criminalistics as the "science of individualization," isolating this specific epistemologically problematic core from the other scientific disciplines. Individualization, the concept of determining the sole source of an item, enthroned a linear process—identification or classification onto individualization—losing sight of the holistic, variable contribution of all types of evidence. Assessing the circumstances surrounding a crime, where the challenge is to integrate and organize the data in order to reconstruct a case or propose alternative propositions for events under examination, requires multiple types of evidence, some of which may be quite nuanced in their interpretation. This is also true in the use of so-called forensic intelligence, which feeds investigative, police, or security needs, where one of the main reasons for failures is linkage blindness. Nevertheless, it seems that the essence of the forensic daily practice is hardly captured within the present definitions of both terms.

Forensic science reconstructs—in the broadest sense—past criminal events through the analysis of the physical remnants of those activities (evidence); the results of those analyses and their expert interpretation establish relationships between people, places, and objects relevant to those events. It produces these results and interpretations through logical inferences, induction, abduction, and deduction, all of which frame the hypothetico-deductive method; investigative heuristics also play a role. Translating scientific information into legal information is a particular domain of forensic science; other sciences must (or at least should) communicate their findings to the public, but forensic science is often required by law to communicate their findings to public courts. Indeed, as the Daubert Hearing stated, "[s]cientific conclusions are subject to perpetual revision as law must resolve disputes finally and quickly." This doubly difficult requirement of communicating to the public and to the law necessitates that forensic scientists should be better communicators of their work and their results. Scientific inferences are not necessarily legal proofs, and the forensic scientist must recognize that legal decisions based, in part, on their scientific work may not accord with their expert knowledge. Moreover, scientists must think in probabilities to explain evidence given possible causes, while jurists must deal in terms of belief beyond reasonable doubt. As Inman and Rudin state: "Because we [the scientists] provide results and information to parties who lack the expertise to independently understand their meaning and implications, it is up to us to furnish an accurate and complete interpretation of our results. If we do not do this, our conclusions are at best incomplete, at worst potentially misleading."

The Trace as the Basic Unit of Forensic Science

The basic unit of forensic science is the trace, the physical remnant of the past criminal activity. Traces are, by their very nature, semiotic: They represent something more than merely themselves; they are signifiers or signs for the items or events that are its source. A fiber is not the sweater it came from, a fingerprint is not the fingertip, soot in the trachea is not the victim choking from a fire, blood droplets are not the violence against the victim, but they all point to their origin (source and activity) to a greater or lesser degree of specificity. Thus, the trace is a type of proxy data, that is, an indicator of a related phenomenon but not the phenomenon itself. Traces come from the natural and manufactured items that surround us in our daily lives. Traces are, in essence, the raw material available at a crime scene, which becomes forensic intelligence or knowledge. Everyday items and their traces become evidence through their involvement in criminal activities; the activities add meaning to their existing status as goods in the world; a fireplace poker is transformed into "the murder weapon" by its use as such. The meaning added should also take into account the context of the case, the circumstances under which the criminal activities occurred, boarding the trier of fact mandate.

Traces become evidence when they are recognized, accepted as relevant (if blurred) to the past event under investigation, and collected for forensic purposes. Confusing trace, sign, and evidence can obscure the very process of trace "discovery," which lies at the root of its interpretation. Evidence begins with detection by observation, which is possible because of the available knowledge of the investigator or scientist; unrecognized traces go undiscovered and do not become evidence. When the investigator's or scientist's senses are extended through instrumental sensitivity, either at the scene or in the laboratory, the amount of potential evidence considerably increased. Microscopes, alternate light sources, instrumental sensitivity, and detection limits create increases in the number of traces that can be recognized and collected. More evidence, and more evidence types, inevitably led to increases in the complexity not only of the search for traces but also to their interpretation. Feeding back into this system is the awareness of new (micro)traces that changed the search methods at scenes and in laboratories, with yet more evidence being potentially available.

Traces are ancillary to their originating process; they are a by-product of the source activity, an accidental vestige of their criminal creation. To be useful in the determination of associations, traces whose ultimate sources are unknown must be compared to samples from a known source. Comparison is the very heart of the forensic science process; the method is essentially a diagnostic one, beginning with Georges Cuvier, and is employed by many science practitioners, including medical professionals. (Including, interestingly, Arthur Conan Doyle, a medical doctor and author, whose Sherlock Holmes character references Cuvier's method in *The Five Orange Pips*.) Questioned traces, or items, may have a provenance (a known location at the time of their discovery) but this is not their originating source; a few examples may help:

Trace (questioned)	Source (known)
Fiber on victim	Sweater
Gunshot residue	Ammunition discharge
Blood droplet	Body
Tool marks in door jamb	Pry bar used to open door
Shoeprint in soil	Shoe from suspect
Fingerprint on glass	Finger from suspect

The collection of properly representative known samples is crucial to accurate forensic analyses and comparisons. Known samples can be selected through a variety of legitimate schemes, including random, portion, and judgment, and must be selected with great care. Thus, traces are accidental and known samples are intentional.

Some of the consequences of what has been discussed so far induce the capacities and limitations of a forensic investigation based on trace analysis. A micro- to nanolevel existence allows forensic scientists to plan physical and chemical characteristics in their identifications and comparisons with other similar data. This allows forensic science to be as methodologically flexible as its objects of study require. Because time is asymmetric and each criminal action is unique, the forensic investigation and analysis in any one case is wedded, to a certain degree, to that case with no ambition to issue general laws about that event ("In all instances of John Davis being physically assaulted with a baseball bat …"). Inferences must be drawn with explicit uncertainty statements; the inferences should be revised when new data affect the traces' relevancy. Therefore, the search for traces is a recursive heuristic process taking into account the environment of the case at hand, appealing to the imagination, expertise, and competency of the investigator or scientist to propose explicative hypotheses.

Two Native Principles

With this framework, two principles can be thought of as the main native principles that support and frame philosophically forensic science. In this context, principles are understood as universal theoretical statements settled at the beginning of a deduction, which cannot be deduced from any other statement in the considered system, and give coherence to the area of study. They provide the grounds from which other truths can be derived and define a paradigm, that is, a general epistemological viewpoint, a new concept to see the natural world, issued from an empiricist corroborated tradition, accepted by the community of practitioners in the field. Ultimately, this paradigm can even pilot the perception itself.

Although similar but nonequivalent versions are used in other disciplines, Locard's exchange principle exists as the central tenant of forensic science. The principle that bears his name was never uttered as such by Locard, but its universal statement of "every contact leaves a trace" stands as a universally accepted short-hand phrasing. Locard's principle embraces all forms of contact, from biological to chemical to physical and even digital traces, and extends the usual perception of forensic science beyond dealing only with physical vestiges.

One of its corollaries is that trace deposition is continual and not reversible. Increases in the number of contacts, the types of evidence involved, and cross-transfers (A–B and B–A) also increase the complexity of determining the relevance of traces in short duration and temporally close actions.

Even the potentially fallacious rubric of "absence of evidence is not evidence of absence" leads to extended discussions on the very nature of proof, or provable, that aims to be definitive, notwithstanding the explanations for the practical aspects of the concept (lack of sensitivity, obscuring

of the relevant traces, human weakness, actual absence, etc.). Applying Locard's principle needs to address three levels. First is the physical level, which deals with ease of transfer, retention, persistence, and affinity of materials, which could better support the exchange of traces from one source to another. Second is the situational or contextual level, which is the knowledge of circumstances and environments surrounding criminal events and sets the matrix for detection, identification, and proximate significance of any evidence. Third is the intelligence level, which covers the knowledge about criminal behavior in single events or series, specific problems related to current trends in criminal behavior, and communication between relevant entities (police, scientists, attorneys, etc.); these components help the investigator in the field to focus on more meaningful traces that might otherwise go undetected.

The second, and more debated, principle is Kirk's individuality principle; again, Kirk did not state this as such beyond saying that criminalistics is the science of individualization. In its strongest form, it posits that each object in the universe can be placed demonstratively into a set with one and only one member: Itself. It therefore asserts the universal statement, "every object in our universe is unique." Philosophers such as Wittgenstein have argued that without defined rules or limits, terms such as "the same" or "different" are essentially meaningless. There is little question that all things are unique—two identical things can still be numerically differentiated—but the core question is, can they be distinguished at the resolution of detection applied? Simply saying "all things are unique" is not useful forensically. For example, each fingerprint left by the same finger is unique, but to be useful, each print must also be able to be traced back to its source finger. Uniqueness is therefore necessary to claim individualization, but not sufficient. Thus, it is the degree of association that matters, how similar, how different these two things being compared are. Referring to Cole, "What distinguishes … objects is not "uniqueness"; it is their diagnosticity: our ability to assign traces of these objects to their correct source with a certain degree of specificity under certain parameters of detection and under certain rules governing such assignments," or as Osterburg stated, "to approach [individualization] as closely as the present state of science allows." Statistics, typically, is required to accurately communicate levels of comparison that are reproducible. In fact, Kirk noted that individualization was not absolute. ("On the witness stand, the criminalist must be willing to admit that *absolute identity is impossible to establish*. … The inept or biased witness may readily testify to an identity, or to a type of identity, that does not actually exist. This can come about because of his confusion as to the nature of identity, his inability to evaluate the results of his observations, or because his general technical deficiencies preclude meaningful results" (Kirk, 1953; emphasis added).)

Nonnative Principles

Numerous guiding principles from other sciences apply centrally to forensic science, several of which come from geology, a cognate historical science to forensic science. That these principles come not from forensic science but from other sciences should not imply that they are somehow less important than Locard's or Kirk's notions. The first, and in many ways the most important, of the external principles is that of uniformitarianism. The principle, proposed by James Hutton, popularized by Charles Lyell, and coined by William Whewell, states that natural phenomena do not change in scope, intensity, or effect with time. Paraphrased as "the present is the key to the past," the principle implies that a volcano that erupts today acts in the same way as volcanoes did 200 or 200 million years ago and, thus, allows geologists to interpret proxy data from past events through current effects. Likewise, in forensic science, bullets test fired in the laboratory today do not change in scope, intensity, or effect from bullets fired during the commission of a crime 2 days, 2 weeks, or 2 years previously. The same is true of any analysis in forensic science that requires a replication or reconstruction of processes in play during the crime's commission. Uniformitarianism offers a level of objectivity to historical sciences by posing hypotheses or relationships generally and then developing tests with respect to particular cases.

Three additional principles from geology hold as applicable to forensic science. They are as follows:

- *Superposition*: In a physical distribution, older materials are below younger materials unless a subsequent action alters this arrangement.
- *Lateral continuity*: Disassociated but similar layers can be assumed to be from the same depositional period.
- *Chronology*: It refers to the notion of absolute dates in a quantitative mode (such as "10:12 a.m." or "1670–1702") and relative dates in a relational mode (i.e., older or younger).

These three principles are attributed to Nicolaus Steno but were also formalized and applied by William Smith. A forensic example of applying the principle of superposition would be the packing of different soils in a tire tread, the most recent being the outermost. A good case of lateral continuity would be the cross-transfer of fibers in an assault, given that the chances of independent transfer and persistence prior to the time of the incident would be improbable. An example of absolute chronology in forensic science would be the simple example of a purchase receipt from a retail store with a time/date stamp on it. Examples of relative chronology abound but could range from the *terminus post quem* of a product no longer made to something hotter or colder than it should be.

See also: **Foundations:** Forensic Intelligence; History of Forensic Sciences; Overview and Meaning of Identification/Individualization; Semiotics, Heuristics, and Inferences Used by Forensic Scientists; Statistical Interpretation of Evidence: Bayesian Analysis; The Frequentist Approach to Forensic Evidence Interpretation; **Foundations/Fundamentals:** Measurement Uncertainty; **Pattern Evidence/Fingerprints (Dactyloscopy):** Friction Ridge Print Examination—Interpretation and the Comparative Method.

Further Reading

Cole, S.A., 2009. Forensics without uniqueness, conclusions without individualization: the new epistemology of forensic identification. Law, Probability and Risk 8, 233–255.

Crispino, F., 2006. Le principe de Locard est-il scientifique? Ou analyse de la scientificité des principes fondamentaux de la criminalistique. Editions Universitaires Européennes No. 523, Sarrebrücken, Germany. ISBN 978-613-1-50482-2 (2010).

Crispino, F., 2008. Nature and place of crime scene management within forensic sciences. Science & Justice: Journal of the Forensic Science Society 48 (1), 24–28.

Dulong, R., 2004. La rationalité spécifique de la police technique. Revue internationale de criminologie et de police technique 3 (4), 259–270.

Egger, S.A., 1984. A working definition of serial murder and the reduction of linkage blindness. Journal of Police Science and Administration 12, 348–355.

Giamalas, D.M., 2000. Criminalistics. In: Siegel, J.A., Saukko, P.J., Knupfer, G.C. (Eds.), Encyclopedia of Forensic Sciences. Academic Press, London, pp. 471–477.

Good, G. (Ed.), 1998. Sciences of the Earth, vol. 1. Garland Publishing, New York.

Houck, M.M., 2010. An Investigation into the Foundational Principles of Forensic Science (Ph.D. thesis). Curtin University of Technology, Perth.

Inman, N., Rudin, K., 2001. Principles and Practice of Criminalistics: The Profession of Forensic Science. CRC Press, Boca Raton, FL, pp. 269–270.

Kirk, P.L., 1953. Crime Investigation: Physical Evidence and the Police Laboratory. Interscience, New York, p. 10.

Kirk, P.L., 1963. The ontogeny of criminalistics. Journal of Criminal Law, Criminology and Police Science 54, 235–238.

Kuhn, T., 1970. La structure des révolutions scientifiques. Flammarion, Paris.

Kwan, Q.Y., 1976. Inference of Identity of Source (Ph.D. thesis). Berkeley University, Berkeley.

Mann, M., 2002. The value of multiple proxies. Science 297, 1481–1482.

Masterman, M., 1970. The nature of a paradigm. In: Lakatos, I., Musgrave, A. (Eds.), Criticism and the Growth of Experimental Knowledge. Cambridge University Press, Cambridge, pp. 59–86.

Moriarty, J.C., Saks, M.J., 2006. Forensic Science: Grand Goals, Tragic Flaws, and Judicial Gatekeeping. Research Paper No. 06-19. University of Akron Legal Studies.

National Research Council Committee, 2009. Identifying the Needs of the Forensic Science Community, Strengthening Forensic Science in the United States: A Path Forward. National Academy of Sciences Report. National Academy Press, Washington, DC.

Osterburg, J.W., 1968. What problems must criminalistics solve. Journal of Criminal Law, Criminology and Police Science 59 (3), 431.

Schuliar, Y., 2009. La coordination scientifique dans les investigations criminelles. Proposition d'organisation, aspects éthiques ou de la nécessité d'un nouveau métier (Ph.D. thesis), Université Paris Descartes, Paris. Université de Lausanne, Lausanne.

Sober, E., 2009. Absence of evidence and evidence of absence: evidential transitivity in connection with fossils, fishing, fine-tuning, and firing squads. Philosophical Studies 143, 63–90.

Stephens, C., 2011. A Bayesian approach to absent evidence reasoning. Informal Logic 31 (1), 56–65.

US Supreme Court No. 92–102, 1993. William Daubert, et al., Petitioners v Merrell Dow Pharmaceuticals, Inc. Certiorari to the US Court of Appeals for the Ninth Circuit. Argued 30 March 1993. Decided 28 June 1993.

Wittgenstein, L., 1922. Tractacus Logico-philosophicus. Gallimard Tel 311, Paris.

Relevant Websites

http://www.all-about-forensic-science.com—All-About-Forensic-Science.COM, Definition of Forensic Science.
http://www.forensic-evidence.com—Forensic-Evidence.com.
http://library.thinkquest.org—Oracle ThinkQuest – What is Forensics?

Forensic Classification of Evidence

MM Houck, Consolidated Forensic Laboratory, Washington, DC, USA

Glossary

Set Any group of real or imagined objects.
Taxonomy The science of identifying and naming species with the intent of arranging them into a classification.

Taxon (pl. taxa) A group of one or more organisms grouped and ranked according to a set of qualitative and quantitative characteristics; a type of set.

Introduction

Evidence is accidental: Items are transformed into evidence by their involvement in a crime regardless of their source or mode of production. By becoming evidence, their normal meaning is enhanced and expanded. Evidence is initially categorized much as the real world; that is, based on the taxonomy created by manufacturers. Forensic science adds to this classification to further enhance or clarify the meaning of evidence relevant to the goals and procedures of the discipline.

Methods of Classification

Set Theory

Any collection of objects, real or imagined, is a set; set theory is the branch of mathematics that studies these collections. Basic set theory involves categorization and organization of the objects, sometimes using diagrams, and involves elementary operations such as set union and set intersection. Advanced topics, including cardinality, are standard in undergraduate mathematics courses. All classification schemes are based on set theory, to a greater or lesser degree.

The notion of "set" is undefined; the objects described as constituting a set create the definition. The objects in a set are called the members or elements of that set. Objects belong to a set; sets consist of their members. The members of a set may be real or imagined; they do not need to be present to be a member of that set. Membership criteria for a set should be definite and accountable. The set, "All people in this room are over 5'5" tall," is a well-defined, if currently unknown, set—the height of the people in the room would have to be measured to accurately populate the set. If the definition is vague, then that collection may not be considered a set. For example, is "q" the same as "Q"? If the set is "The 26 letters of the English alphabet," then they are the same member; if the set is, "The 52 uppercase and lowercase letters of the English alphabet," then they are two separate members.

Sets may be finite or infinite; a set with only one member is called a single or a singleton set. Two sets are identical if and only if they have exactly the same members. The cardinality of a set is the number of members within it, written |A| for set A. A set X is a subset of set Y if and only if every member of X is also a member of Y; for example, the set of all Philips head screwdrivers is a subset of the set of all screwdrivers. Forensic scientists would term this a "subclass" but that is a terminological and not a conceptual difference. Two more concepts are required for the remainder of our discussion. The union of X and Y is a set whose members are only the members of X, Y, or both. Thus, if X were (1, 2, 3) and Y were (2, 3, 4), then the union of X and Y, written $X \cup Y$, would contain (1, 2, 3, 4). Finally, the intersection of two sets contains only the members of both X and Y. In the previous example, the intersection of X and Y would be (2, 3), written $X \cap Y$.

Taxonomy

Natural items, such as animals, plants, or minerals, often occur as evidence. These items are classified according to schemes used in other sciences such as biology, botany, or geology. It is incumbent on the forensic scientist to be knowledgeable about the classification of naturally occurring items.

In biology, taxonomy, the practice and science of classification, refers to a formalized system for ordering and grouping things, typically living things using the Linnaean method. The taxa (the units of a taxonomic system; singular "taxon") are sufficiently fixed so as to provide a structure for classifying living things. Taxa are arranged typically in a hierarchical structure to show their relatedness (a phylogeny). In such a hierarchical relationship, the subtype has by definition the same constraints as the supertype plus one or more additional constraints. For example, "macaque" is a subtype of "monkey," so any macaque is also a monkey, but not every monkey is a macaque, and an animal needs to satisfy more constraints to be a macaque than to be a monkey. In the Linnaean method of classification, the scientific name of each species is formed by the combination of two words, the genus name ("generic" name), which is always capitalized, and a second word identifying the species within that genus. Species names (genus species) are either italicized or underlined, for example, *Homo sapiens* (humans), *Sus scrofa* (pigs), *Canis familiaris* (domesticated dogs), and *Rattus rattus* (rats).

The term "systematics" is sometimes used synonymously with "taxonomy" and may be confused with "scientific classification." However, "taxonomy" is properly the describing, identifying, classifying, and naming of organisms, while "classification" is focused on placing organisms within groups that show their relationships to other organisms. Systematics alone deals specifically with relationships through time, requiring recognition of the fossil record when dealing with the systematics of organisms. Systematics uses taxonomy as a primary tool in understanding organisms, as nothing about the organism's relationships with other living things can be understood without it, first being properly studied and described in sufficient detail to identify and classify it correctly.

In geology, rocks are generally classified based on their chemical and mineral composition, the process by which they were formed, and the texture of their particles. Rocks are classified as igneous (formed by cooled molten magma), sedimentary (formed by deposition and compaction of materials), or metamorphic (formed through intense changes in pressure and temperature). These three classes of rocks are further subdivided into many other sets; often, the categories' definitions are not rigid and the qualities of a rock may grade it from one class to another. The terminology of rocks and minerals, rather than describing a state, describes identifiable points along a gradient.

Manufacturing

Manufactured evidence is initially categorized by the in-house or market-specific system created by one or more manufacturers. Manufacturers of economic goods create their classifications through product identity or analytical methods. Set methods of production ensure a quality product fit for purpose and sale; the classification is based on the markets involved, the orientation of the company production methods, and the supply chain. Explicit rules exist on categories recognized by manufacturers and consumers, as either models or brands. Materials flow downstream, from raw material sources through to a manufacturing level. Raw materials are transformed into intermediate products, also referred to as components or parts. These are assembled on the next level to form products. The products are shipped to distribution centers and from there on to retailers and customers.

Forensic Approaches to Classification

The supply network of raw materials, intermediate steps, production methods, intended consumer end use, and actual end use all contribute to the characteristics available for forensic taxonomic classification. While the forensic taxonomies are unique to that discipline, they are based on the production taxonomies used in manufacturing. These characteristics form the basis for statements of significance, that is, the relative abundance or rarity of any one particular item in a criminal context. Some objects are common but have a short-entrance horizon (e.g., iPods), but are essentially identical at the outset while others are common with long-entrance horizons (denim blue jeans), but have a high variance (regular, stone washed, acid washed, etc.). It is in the best interest of forensic scientists to understand the fundamental manufacturing processes of the items that routinely become evidence. This understanding can form the basis for statistical significance statements in courts and may provide the foundations for a more quantitative approach to testimony.

Forensic analytical methods create augmented taxonomies because the discipline uses different sets of methods and forensic scientists have different goals. Their taxonomies are based on manufactured traits, but also aftermarket qualities, and intended end use, but also "as used." The "as-used" traits are those imparted to the item after purchase through either normal or criminal use. Forensic science has developed a set of rules through which the taxonomies are explicated. For example, forensic scientists are interested in the size, shape, and distribution of delustrants, microscopic grains of rutile titanium dioxide incorporated into a fiber to reduce its luster. The manufacturer has included delustrant in the fiber at a certain rate and percentage with no concern for shape or distribution (but size may be relevant). The forensic science taxonomy is based on manufacturing taxonomy but is extended by incidental characteristics that help us distinguish otherwise similar objects.

Natural, manufacturing, and forensic classifications lead to evidentiary significance because they break the world down into intelligible classes of objects related to criminal acts. Forensic science has developed an enhanced appreciation for discernment between otherwise similar objects but has yet to explicate these hierarchies to their benefit.

Class Level Information

Identification is the examination of the chemical and physical properties of an object and using them to categorize it as a member of a set. What the object is made of, its color, mass, size, and many other characteristics are used to identify an object and help refine that object's identity. Analyzing a white powder and concluding that it is cocaine is an example of identification; determining that a small translucent chip is bottle glass or yellow fibrous material and determining that they are dog hairs are also examples of identification. Most identifications are inherently hierarchical, such as classification systems themselves: In the last example, the fibrous nature of the objects restricts the following possible categories:

- Hairs
- Animal hairs
- Guard hairs
- Dog hairs
- German shepherd hairs

As the process of identification of evidence becomes more specific, it permits the analyst to classify the evidence into successively smaller classes of objects. It may not be necessary to classify the evidence beyond dog hairs if human hairs are being looked for. Multiple items can be classified differently, depending on what questions are asked. For example, the objects in **Figure 1** could be classified into "fruit" and "non-fruit," "sports related" and "nonsports related," or "organic" and "inorganic."

Sharing a class identity may indicate two objects that come from a common source. Because forensic science reveals and describes the relationships among people, places, and things involved in criminal activities, this commonality of relationship may be critical to a successful investigation. Commonality can show interactions, limitations in points of origin, and increased significance of relationships. What is meant by a "common source" depends on the material in question, the mode of production, and the specificity of the examinations used to classify the object. For example, the "common source" for an automotive paint chip could be the following:

- the manufacturer (to distinguish it from other similar paints),
- the factory (to determine where it was made),

- the batch or lot of production (to distinguish it from other batches at the same factory),
- all the vehicles painted with that color paint, or
- the vehicle painted with that color paint involved in the crime in question.

All of these options, and they are not exhaustive, could be the goal in an investigation of determining whether two objects had a "common source."

Uniqueness and Individualization

If an object can be classified into a set with only one member (itself), it can be said to be unique. An individualized object is associated with one, and only one, source: It is unique. Uniqueness is based on two assumptions. The first assumption is that all things are unique in space and, thus, their properties are nonoverlapping. The assumption of uniqueness of space is considered axiomatic and, therefore, an inherently non-provable proposition for numerous reasons. The population size of "all things that might be evidence" is simply too large to account. In addition, conclusive evidence is not readily available in typical forensic investigations. Because of this, as Schum notes, statistics are required:

> Such evidence, if it existed, would make necessary a particular hypothesis or possible conclusion being entertained. In lieu of such perfection, we often make use of masses of inconclusive evidence having additional properties: The evidence is incomplete on matters relevant to our conclusions, and it comes to us from sources (including our own observations) that are, for various reasons, not completely credible. Thus, inferences from such evidence can only be probabilistic in nature (Schum, 1994, p. 2).

Figure 1 A range of objects may be classified in a variety of ways, depending on the question being asked. For example, given the objects in this figure, the sets would differ if the question was, "What is edible?" rather than "What is sporting equipment?".

A statistical analysis is therefore warranted when uncertainty, of either accounting or veracity, exists. If an absolutely certain answer to a problem could be reached, statistical methods would not be required. Most evidence exists at the class level, and although each item involved in a crime is considered unique, it still belongs to a larger class. In reality, the majority of forensic science works at a class level of resolution. Indeed, even DNA, the argued "gold standard" of forensic science, operates with classes and statistics.

It has been argued that the concept of uniqueness is necessary but not sufficient to support claims of individualization. If it is accepted that uniqueness is axiomatic, then

> What matters is whether we have analytical tools necessary to discern the characteristics that *distinguish* one object from all others or, in the forensic context, distinguish *traces* made by each object from traces made by every other object ... Every object is presumably unique at the scale of manufacture. The question is whether objects are distinguishable at the scale of detection. Since all objects in the universe are in some respects 'the same' and in other respects 'different' from all other objects in the universe, according to Wittgenstein, what really matters is not uniqueness but rather what rules we articulate by which we will make determinations of 'sameness' and 'difference' (Cole, 2009, pp. 242–243).

Although things may be numerically unique at the point of *production*, this does not help to distinguish between otherwise similar objects at the point of *detection* or *interpretation*. This is where forensic science adds value to the investigative and legal processes.

Relationships and Context

The relationships between the people, places, and things involved in crimes are central to deciding what items to examine and how to interpret the results. For example, if a sexual assault occurs and the perpetrator and victim are strangers, more evidence may be relevant than if they live together or are sexual partners. Strangers are not expected to have ever met previously and, therefore, would have not transferred evidence before the crime. People who live together would have some opportunities to transfer certain types of evidence (e.g., head hairs and carpet fibers from the living room) but not others (semen or vaginal secretions). Spouses or sexual partners, being the most intimate relationship of the three examples, would share a good deal of more information (**Figure 2**).

Stranger-on-stranger crimes beg the question of coincidental associations, that is, two things that previously have never been in contact with each other have items on them, which are analytically indistinguishable at a certain class level. Attorneys in cross-examination may ask, "Yes, but could not [insert evidence type here] really have come from anywhere? Are not [generic class level evidence] very common?" It has been proven for a wide variety of evidence that coincidental matches are extremely rare. The enormous variety of mass-produced goods, consumer choices, economic factors, biological and natural diversity, and other traits create a nearly infinite combination of comparable characteristics for the items involved in any one situation.

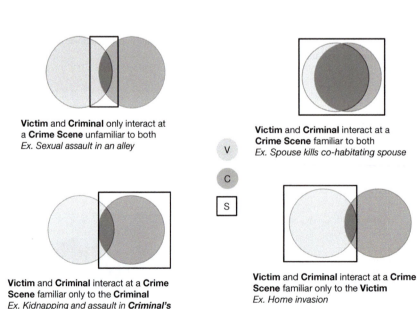

Victim and Criminal only interact at a Crime Scene unfamiliar to both
Ex. Sexual assault in an alley

Victim and Criminal interact at a Crime Scene familiar to both
Ex. Spouse kills co-habitating spouse

V

C

S

Victim and Criminal interact at a Crime Scene familiar only to the Criminal
Ex. Kidnapping and assault in Criminal's house

Victim and Criminal interact at a Crime Scene familiar only to the Victim
Ex. Home invasion

Figure 2 The relationships between suspect, victim, and scene influence what evidence is collected and what its significance is.

See also: **Foundations:** Evidence/Classification; Statistical Interpretation of Evidence: Bayesian Analysis; The Frequentist Approach to Forensic Evidence Interpretation.

Further Reading

Cole, S., 2009. Forensics without uniqueness, conclusion without individualization: the new epistemology of forensic identification. Law, Probability, and Risk 8 (3), 233–255.

Devlin, K., 1993. The Joy of Sets. Springer, Berlin.

Haq, T., Roche, G., Parker, B., 1978. Theoretical field concepts in forensic science. 1. Application to recognition and retrieval of physical evidence. Journal of Forensic Sciences 23 (1), 212–217.

Houck, M.M., 2006. Production Taxonomies as the Foundation of Forensic Significance. European Academy of Forensic Sciences, Helsinki, Finland.

Johnson, P., 1972. A History of Set Theory. Weber & Schmidt, New York.

Kwan, Q.Y., 1977. Inference of Identity of Source. University of California (Ph.D. thesis).

Schum, D.A., 1994. Evidential Foundations of Probabilistic Reasoning. John Wiley & Sons, New York.

Thornton, J., 1986. Ensembles of class characteristics in physical evidence examination. Journal of Forensic Sciences 31 (2), 501–503.

Underhill, P., 2000. Why We Buy: The Science of Shopping. Simon & Schuster, New York.

Interpretation/The Comparative Method

MM Houck, Consolidated Forensic Laboratory, Washington, DC, USA

Glossary

Alignable differences Differences that are connected to the hierarchical system of relatedness of two or more things.

Analogous trait A characteristic that is similar between two things, which is not present in the last common ancestor or precedent of the group under comparison.

Analogy A cognitive process that transfers information or meaning from one subject (the analog or source) to another subject (the target).

Diagnosticity The degree to which traits classify an object.

Homologous trait A characteristic shared by a common ancestor or precedent.

Nonalignable differences Differences with no correspondence at all between the source and the target.

Introduction

Analogy, and its more specific relative comparison, is a central component of human cognition. Analogy is the process behind identification of places, objects, and people and plays a significant role in many human mental operations, such as problem solving, decisions, perception, memory, and communication. Some researchers, including Hofstadter, have even argued that cognition is analogy. Likewise, the cognitive process of analogy and the method of comparison lie at the heart of the forensic sciences. The ability to compare is predicated on some sort of classification (more properly, a taxonomy) that results in classes, groups, or sets.

Aristotle is considered the first to approach comparison as a way to arrange the world. His attempt to codify the process raised, however, an intractable problem that would only be addressed later: the classification of living things. Comparison, by itself, is a minimal technique, at best. A classification system—a taxonomy—is a prerequisite to a fuller comparative methodology. Comparative anatomy, one of the earliest formal applications of the method, goes beyond mere representation (mere comparison, that is) to explain the nature and properties of each animal.

The French naturalist Pierre Belon (1517–1564) compared the skeletal structures of birds to humans in his book *L'Histoire de la Nature des Oiseaux* (*History of the Nature of Birds*, 1555; **Figure 1**) and, along with the Flemish naturalist Andreas Vesalius (1514–1564), was one of the first naturalists to explicitly apply the comparative method in biology. Georges Cuvier (1769–1832) was the first to use comparative anatomy and taxonomy as a tool, not an end in itself, in his studies of animals and fossils. Cuvier was frustrated that biological phenomena could not be reconfigured into experimental conditions that would allow controlled testing, a difficulty common to many sciences (e.g., see Diamond). The intimate integration of a living organism's physiology with its anatomy created obstacles in teasing out and relating function to structure: Once an organism was dead and prepared for dissection, its function had ceased, thus confounding the relationship of form to function. Cuvier considered that careful examinations and the interrelating of structures between specimens might also prove to be useful in revealing principles of observation and comparison. Perhaps the original scientist-as-detective, Cuvier, used scattered, fractured bits of information to reconstruct the prehistory of the Earth and its animals. In a 1798 paper, Cuvier wrote on his realization of the form and function of bones as it relates to the overall identifiable anatomy of an animal, leading to the recognition of the creature from which the bone originated:

> This assertion will not seem at all astonishing if one recalls that in the living state all the bones are assembled in a kind of framework; that the place occupied by each is easy to recognize; and that by the number and position of their articulating facets one can judge the number and direction of the bones that were attached to them. This is because the number, direction, and shape of the bones that compose each part of an animal's body are always in a necessary relation to all the other parts, in such a way that—up to a point—one can infer the whole from any one of them, and vice versa (Rudwick, 1998, p. 36).

This has been called "Cuvier's Principle of Correlation of Parts" and is a central tenet in biology and paleontology. It is

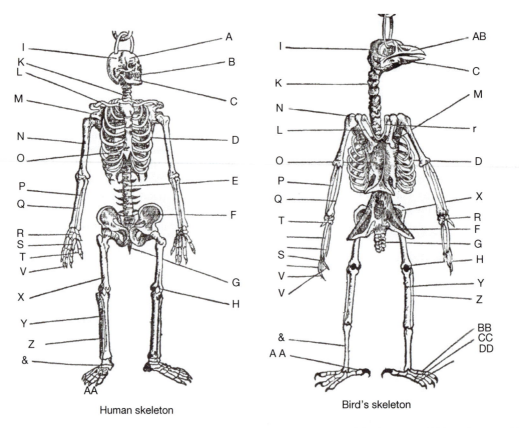

Human skeleton

Bird's skeleton

Figure 1   A drawing from Pierre Belon's 1555 book, *History of the Nature of Birds*, comparing the skeletal anatomy of birds to humans, which is one of the first books using the science of comparative anatomy. Source: Wikimedia Commons, open source.

important to note that Cuvier claimed to be able to *identify* an animal taxonomically from a single bone, but not completely *reconstruct* it, as the above quote might imply. The reconstruction would only be possible with a sufficient number of bones representing the animal in question. The comparative method has been a successful cornerstone of science ever since, with new or emerging sciences, such as ecology, moving from the purely observational or descriptive approach to that of comparison through experimental or analytical methods.

A short discussion of terms in biology will help clarify concepts used in biological comparisons. The concept of homology, the same structure under every variety of form found in different animals, is the organizing foundation for comparative anatomy. Animals share homologous traits because they also share a common ancestor with the same or related trait. By contrast, analogous traits are similarities found in organisms that were not present in the last common ancestor of the group under comparison; that is, the traits evolved separately. The canonical example of the difference between homologous and analogous traits is the wings of birds and

bats: They are homologous as forearms but analogous as wings; the latter structures evolved their functions separately. A homologous trait is termed a homolog. In biology, evolution and natural selection formed the system within which these relationships developed and were maintained, homogenized, or differentiated.

In manufacturing, other external and internal constraints form the basis for homologous and analogous traits through design, function, form, and costs. Design follows from the product's intended end use, aesthetic concerns, and cost limitations. The function and form of an object tend to correlate and variances in design cluster around necessary and sufficient criteria. In **Figure 2**, for example, although the hammer heads, opposite sides, handles, materials, weight, shape, and components all vary, they are nonetheless identifiable as hammers. If **Figure 2** were finches, as Darwin studied in the Galapagos in his historic voyage with the *Beagle*, the base process of taxonomy would be the same but the criteria and foundations—the history and causes—would obviously vary because of the vastly different processes that produce hammers and finches.

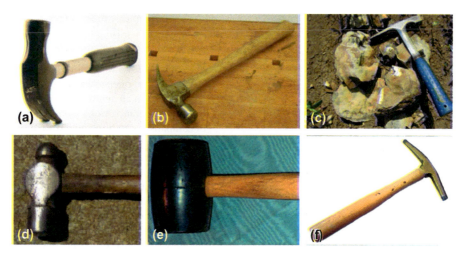

Figure 2 Hammers. All of the objects (A–F) are recognizable as hammers even though their components vary. (A) Claw hammer; (B) framing hammer; (C) geological hammer; (D) ball-peen hammer; (E) rubber mallet; and (F) upholstery hammer. Source: Wikimedia Commons, open source.

Broadly speaking, the supply chains and distribution networks of material goods are like the phylogenetic trees based on evolutionary descent. Regardless of whether the items are biological or manufactured, the independence of traits should not be assumed. Comparative studies that do not control for historical relationships through phylogeny or supply chains may imply spurious relationships (coincidences). Forensic science is unique in its use of the comparative method to reconstruct past criminal events and sourcing of evidence, either biological or manufactured (in essence, reverse engineering to a level of distribution or manufacturing resolution).

Analogy and Comparison within a Forensic Process

Analogy is a cognitive process that transfers information or meaning from one subject (the analog or *source*) to another subject (the *target*); it thus implies at least two things: situations or events. The source is considered to be the more complete and more complex of the two, and the target is thus less informative and incomplete in some way. The incompleteness may be due to any of several factors, alone or combined, such as damage, fracture, deterioration, or size. The elements or traits—including their relationships, such as evolutionary or supply chains—between the source and the target are mapped or aligned in a comparison. The mapping is done from what is usually the more familiar area of experience and more complete repository of information, the source, to the typically more problematic target.

Salience of the elements or traits is of prime importance: There are an innumerable number of arbitrary differences in either elements or relations that could be considered but are not useful given the question at hand ("Are both items smaller than the Empire State Building? Are they redder than a fire truck?"). Ultimately, analogy is a process to communicate that the two comparators (the source and the target) have *some* relationship in common despite any arbitrary differences. Some notion of possible or hypothetical connection must exist for the comparison to be made. As a forensic example, consider trace debris removed from the clothing of a suspect and the body of a victim: Although there may be no physical evidence (hairs, fibers, glass, soil, etc.) in common, the suspect's clothing and the victim's body have, at least prima facie, a common *relationship* (the victim is the victim and the suspect is a person of interest in the crime) until proven otherwise. Thus, common relations, not common objects, are essential to analogy and comparison.

The comparison process as a method makes several assumptions. First, the space in which the comparators are mapped is assumed to be Euclidean. Second, the method embeds the comparators in a "space of minimum dimensionality" (Tversky) based on all observed salient similarities. Each object, a, is detailed and described by a set of elements or traits, A. Any observed similarities between a and another object b, denoted as $s(a, b)$, are expressed as a function of the salient traits they are determined to have in common. The comparison and any observed familiarity can be expressed as a function of three arguments (**Figure 3**):

- $A \cap B$, the features shared by a and b
- $A - B$, the features of a that are not shared by b
- $B - A$, the features of b that are not shared by a

Psychological studies show that people tend to pay more attention to the target (the comparator with less information)

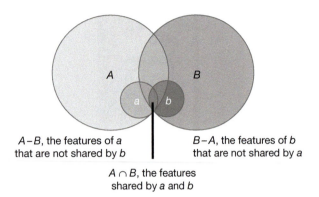

$A - B$, the features of a that are not shared by b

$B - A$, the features of b that are not shared by a

$A \cap B$, the features shared by a and b

Figure 3   A comparison of observed familiarities can be expressed as a function of three arguments, visualized here.

than to the source. In forensic science, this means that analysts would pay more attention to the samples from the crime scene or actors than to the known samples collected. This is true even though the known has more salience, because arguably it has more information and a documented provenance than the questioned sample. For example, a toy ship is quite similar to a real ship because most of the main features of the real ship are expressed in the toy (otherwise it might not be recognized as a simulacrum of its referent). A real ship, however, is not as similar to the toy ship because many of the features of a real ship are not expressed in the toy (due to function, scale, or safety, among other factors). The reason for paying more attention to the target is, first and foremost, to determine if there is sufficiency of salient information in the target for the comparative process to occur (see Vanderkolk for a discussion on this).

The main determinant of feature salience for comparative purposes is the degree to which they classify an object, that is, their diagnosticity. A feature that serves as the basis to reassign an object from one class to another class with fewer members is more salient than one that does not. Salience is hierarchical and is based on how many members of a class share that feature; the goal is thus to place an object, by successive comparative features, into classes with increasingly fewer members. Salience of a feature, therefore, should increase inversely with the number of members of a class into which it places an object; $A \cap B$ increases and may be thought of as an expression of diagnosticity. A comparative process that does not maximize diagnosticity or exploit features that do so will have low forensic utility.

The Comparative Method within Forensic Science

The comparative method involves the aligning of the relational structures between one or more targets (items of questioned

source; Qs) and one or more sources (items of known provenance or source; Ks). This alignment, to work as a method, has three constraints or requirements:

- The alignment has to be *structurally consistent*, that is, it has to observe a one-to-one correspondence between the comparators in an argumentative structure that is the same between the comparisons (*parallel connectivity*). One point of comparison can be aligned with at most one other point of comparison in the target or source. Similarly, matching relationships must have matching arguments to support them (the reason for the proposed relationship cannot be based on an unrelated argument).
- The comparison has to involve *common relations* but does not have to involve common object descriptions. All the evidence that came from the crime scene, for example, need not have originated from only one source.
- Finally, comparisons are not made merely between the objects at hand but also include all of the higher order "constraining relations" that they may share (*systematicity*). In biology, this would relate to the evolutionary and genetic connections; for manufactured materials, this would be the design factors and the supply chain of raw materials and intermediate processes that lead to a finished consumer good. The deeper the relational history, the more higher order classes that two objects share, the stronger the relationship they share, and, therefore, the greater the chance of a shared origin. This obviates the significance of coincidental matches between otherwise similar but unrelated objects: A series of coincidences between two objects are not a salient relationship, no matter how many of them exist. Type I and type II errors stem from these coincidences.

A comparison results in a type of cross-mapping of analogous traits or phenomena that have differential relational roles in two situations (e.g., victim's clothing and crime scene). A systematic mapping between source and target is a natural method for differentiating potentially ambiguous relationships. This relates to the classification of the target and source and the identification of traits or features each has, which place them in one or more sets (classes) of items. The cross-mapping is of these traits within a class. Once a source has been aligned to a target, *candidate inferences*, based on the source, can be projected onto the target, such as a shared source or history. A handgun with blood on it, for example, can be compared to a bullet removed from a victim (through test firings of similar ammunition) and determined to have been the source (to some degree of certainty) of the bullet while the blood can be tested through DNA typing with the victim's known sample and be shown to have the victim as its source (again, to some degree of certainty); the fact that the victim's blood is on the handgun indicates a shared history of occurrence (lateral contemporaneity).

Comparison is selective. The requirement of systematicity is predicated on the idea that classes or sets are flexible and hierarchical. Higher order connections predict lower order relations, and commonalities that are not a part of the aligned system of relationships are considered inconsequential: A blue shoe and a blue car have little in common other than the stated color category; likewise, the fact that the source shoe and the target print might have the same kind of outsole design recedes in importance to the fact than none of the individual traits on the sole appears in the print. Differences that are connected to the hierarchical system of relatedness are called *alignable differences*; those differences with no correspondence at all between the source and the target are called *nonalignable differences*. Alignable differences are more meaningful and salient than nonalignable ones because they exist within the same relationship system making them more relevant to each other. The strange conclusion this observation leads to is that there should be more meaningful differences for comparators that are very similar (*toy train–real train*) than for ones that are less similar (*toy train–toy ship*) because the more similar comparators will have or be derived within more common systems of relationships and will have more alignable differences. As an example, consider all the possible differences for the pair *automobile–truck* and for the pair *duck–baseball*. More alignable differences could be found for the first pair than the second: After a few differences ("You don't play sports with a duck. You don't hunt baseballs."), the list seems pointless because the two are not aligned. The details that could be elicited by comparing *automobile* with *truck*, however, could go on for some time, depending on the level of detail desired. Most sets of comparators in the world are dissimilar (which is why forensic comparisons tend to be stronger in exclusion than inclusion) and this "nonconsideration" heuristic makes sense given humans' cognitive load: "Intuitively, it is when a pair of items is similar that their differences are likely to be important"

(Genter and Markman). Psychological experiments support this statement and it seems to be an integral part of human cognition. Related to this idea is Wittgenstein's proposal 5.5303 in his work *Tractatus logico-philosophicus*: "Roughly speaking, to say of two things that they are identical is nonsense, and to say of one thing that it is identical with itself is to say nothing at all." This points to the need for a statistical evaluation of the *strength* of a comparison, either inclusive or exclusive.

See also: **Foundations:** Forensic Intelligence; Overview and Meaning of Identification/Individualization; Semiotics, Heuristics, and Inferences Used by Forensic Scientists.

Further Reading

Diamond, J., Robinson, J.A. (Eds.), 2010. Natural Experiments of History. Cambridge University Press, Cambridge, MA.

Gentner, D., Markman, A.B., 1997. Structure mapping in analogy and similarity. American Psychologist 52 (1), 45–56.

Hofstadter, D., 2001. Analogy as the core of cognition. In: Gentner, D., Holyoak, K., Kokinov, B. (Eds.), The Analogical Mind: Perspectives from Cognitive Science. MIT Press/Bradford Book, Cambridge, MA, pp. 499–538.

Markman, A.B., Genter, D., 2000. Structure mapping in the comparison process. American Journal of Psychology 113 (4), 501–538.

Pellegrin, P., 1986. Aristotle's Classification of Living Things. University of California Press, Berkeley, CA.

Rudwick, M., 1997. Georges Cuvier, Fossil Bones, and Geological Catastrophes. University of Chicago Press, Chicago.

Tversky, A., 1977. Features of similarity. Psychological Review 84, 327–352.

Vanderkolk, J., 2009. Forensic Comparative Science. Academic Press, New York.

Wittgenstein, L., 1922. Tractatus Logico-philosophicus. (Translated by C.K. Ogden (1922), prepared with assistance from G.E. Moore, F.P. Ramsey, and Wittgenstein). Routledge, London.

Key Terms

Analogy, Classification, Comparison, Crime, Epistemology, Evidence, Forensic, Kirk, Locard, Metho, Paradigm, Science, Set, Taxon, Taxonomy.

Review Questions

1. If the "basic unit of forensic science is the trace," how does digital evidence fit within this conceptual framework? What would they be a "physical remnant" of? Are they even "physical"?
2. What are the three levels that Locard's principle needs to address?
3. Besides Locard's principle, what else do Crispino and Houck consider to be a "native" forensic principle?
4. What are the nonnative principles that forensic sciences uses? Give an example of each one in action.
5. What is the difference between uniqueness and individualization?
6. What is a digital evidence sample compared to?
7. Name the three reasons documents are submitted to a forensic laboratory.
8. What is forensic intelligence?

9. Why does forensic science's role in the criminal justice system require scientists to be better at communicating?
10. What do Crispino and Houck mean when they say traces are an "accidental vestige of their criminal creation"?
11. Who was Charles Lyell? What role does the principle of uniformitarianism have in digital or document examinations?
12. When Houck says, "[e]vidence is initially categorized much as the real world", what does that mean?
13. How can a set be infinite?
14. What does "common source" mean? Why does it matter?
15. Houck mentions that, "for a wide variety of evidence that coincidental matches are extremely rare." What does "extremely rare" mean? Can a number be applied to that phrase? Why or why not? What is the utility of forensic science if the answer is "No"?
16. Why is comparison, by itself, a minimal technique?
17. How does Georges Cuvier, a paleontologist, figure into forensic science?
18. Why should the independence of traits not be assumed?
19. Define "diagnosticity."
20. Distinguish alienable differences from nonalignable differences. Give an example of each.

Discussion Questions

1. Forensic laboratories are specialized to analyze a typical range of evidence types (biological materials, drugs, firearms, etc.). Accreditation schemes reinforce this specialization and support standard approaches to analysis.
2. If, as Crispino and Houck note, forensic science "identifies objects at crime scenes," what objects are identified in digital crime scenes? If a single document, such as a will, is the evidence, what is the crime scene?
3. Think of a signed, initialed, and notarized document. What "traces" would be available to the expert for examination and analysis? List at least five.
4. Using the idea of the document in Question 3 and assuming it is a last will and testament, create a taxonomic hierarchy (list or visual) of it under the starting category of "All Documents."
5. Kirk is quoted as saying, "On the witness stand, the criminalist must be willing to admit that *absolute identity is impossible to establish*. … The inept or biased witness may readily testify to an identity, or to a type of identity, that does not actually exist." What are the implications for the interpretation of forensic evidence if absolute identity is impossible to establish? If forensic scientists cannot speak of absolute identity, what can they use?

Additional Readings

Barrett, W., 1978. The Illusion of Technique. Anchor Press/Doubleday, New York.
De Alcaraz-Fossoul, J., Roberts, K.A., 2017. Forensic intelligence applied to questioned document analysis: a model and its application against organized crime. Science & Justice 57 (4), 314–320.
Dror, I.E., Morgan, R., Rando, C., Nakhaeizadeh, S., 2017. The bias snowball and the bias cascade effects: two distinct biases that may impact forensic decision making. Journal of Forensic Sciences 62 (3).
Lancaster, M.J., 2016. An Exploration of statistical issues in forensic science related to document Examination. CHANCE 29 (1), 44–48.

Section 2. Digital Devices

Stretch your arms out as wide as they will go. Now turn in a circle. Somewhere in that space circumscribed by your fingertips is a digital device, a cell phone, computer, tablet, watch, or even a computer embedded in a device of some sort. They are ubiquitous in our modern world. The amount of information able to be stored and processed on these devices outstrips anything in human history; in fact, the amount that can be stored and processed this very *minute* will be exceeded only the next minute. In terms of crime scenes, digital devices pose many challenges, only some of which have been or are being addressed.

For example, police in Bentonville, AR, received a call from James Bates about the death of his friend, Victor Collins. Bates, Collins, and some work associates had spent the previous night watching a football game and drinking. Bates' story was that two of the attendees had drunk too much and Bates let them sleep over. In the morning, Collins' body was discovered in the hot tub. Police suspected foul play (there were signs of a struggle). Obtaining a warrant, one of the items police saw in the home was an Amazon Echo. The Echo is a digital device connected to Amazon, the online retailing giant. The Echo has seven microphones and responds to a "wake word," typically the name of the software assistant, Alexa. When the device detects the wake word, it instantly begins streaming audio to Amazon, where it is logged and stored in the application. So, if you said, "Alexa, what is the weather like?", the time of the request would be logged and stored. The police collected the Echo in hopes that it would have collected some information or conversation at the time of the incident. The police were apparently under the impression that the Echo was listening constantly (true) and recording some amount of any sounds in the vicinity (not true; it only records after detecting the "wake word"). Unless someone said, "Alexa" during the incident, nothing would be recorded. Amazon refused to release any information or data, citing its customers' privacy. Police turned to another smart source for their investigation: the home's water meter that measures and records the exact consumption of electricity and water. The home used 140 gallons of water between 1 and 3 a.m. The police contended that the water was used to hose down the patio area, which was still wet when police arrived at the scene. Bates has since allowed Amazon to turn over his data to the police, saying Collins' death was an accident, not murder.

Regardless of the outcome, this type of case—and the attendant use and misunderstanding of technology—is a bellwether for what is to come in the forensic laboratory: the digital crime scene.

Digital Imaging and Photography: An Overview

P Jones, Purdue University, West Lafayette, IN, USA

Glossary

Charged coupled device The sensor that acts "sees" the image and records it to magnetic media.

IR Infrared light.

Jpg or jpeg Joint Photographic Experts Group. A lossy compression format.

Lossless A compression format that allows the exact original data to be reconstructed from the compressed file.

Lossy A compression encoding format that compresses data by losing some of the data.

Meter A meter equals 39.37 inch. The meter is the length of the path traveled by light in vacuum during a time interval of $1/299\,792\,458$ of a second.

Nanometer $1/1\,000\,000\,000$ of a meter.

Single-lens reflex (SLR) SLR camera. A camera that has a moving mirror system that allows the photographer to see exactly what the lens "sees."

tif or tiff Tagged image format. A lossless compression format.

UV Ultraviolet light.

Visible spectrum 400–750 nm.

History of Images in Forensic Science

The use of images to reconstruct a crime scene goes back to the early days of photography. In the 1880s, Jack the Ripper was active in London, England. In 1888, photography was used to document and record both victims and crime scenes (**Figures 1 and 2**). There were no "rules" or "best practices"; in fact, there were no "forensic photographers." The local newspaper photographers were summoned by the police to take the picture. There was no complete coverage taken; in most cases, just one or two images were taken. It is only possible to image the level of reconstruction of the Whitechapel murders that could be done today if a complete set of images were taken.

What is photography and digital photo imaging? Reducing it to its most basic definition, it is the capturing of an image of a person, place, or thing at a specific time and place. Photography and digital photo imaging are synonymous.

Figure 1   The mortuary photo of Elizabeth Stride, one of two prostitutes who was murdered in the Whitechapel district of London on September 30, 1888 by Jack the Ripper.

Figure 2   Mary Jane Kelly was found lying on a bed in a single room at 13 Miller's Court on Friday, November 9, 1888.

Photography has been identified with film cameras, while digital photo imaging has been associated with using digital media as an image storage device. Both record an image of a person, place, or thing, and they differ only as far as to the media on which the image is stored. This is similar to moonshiners' still and professional brand makers' still. They both end up with whiskey; each uses a different method to get to the end product.

When the image of a person, place, or thing is "captured," the object is not actually captured, but rather the reflected light from that object. Photons from a light source are projected toward an object of interest or are in the path of an existing photon producing light source such as the sun. The object of interest, the moon, does not generate energy or photons; therefore, only the reflected light (from the sun) is seen when one looks at the moon.

Human eyes work the same way as the camera. The eyes see the reflected light from objects. The human eye is much more complicated than any camera, allowing us to see in low, normal, and intense light. Human eyes and brain make adjustments so that one sees effectively color balanced, proper contrast, and brightness—all, automatically.

Forensic

The term "forensic" is often misunderstood. As a result of the many "CSI" shows on television and the movies, it has come to mean anything from murder investigations, crime scene work, to laboratory analysis. Breaking it down to the most basic, it means "as pertains to a court of law." For example, if an individual is a plumber, and he testifies in a court concerning plumbing, be it a criminal or a civil court, he has acted as a "forensic plumber." Forensic science is applying a specific discipline of science to a court or legal proceeding. Forensic imaging or forensic digital imaging is applying photography to a court or legal action.

Technical Photography versus Creative Photography

Technical photography reconstructs a person, place, or thing with exacting accuracy without distortion. It has to show, in many cases to a juror, exactly what a scene, a victim, or perhaps a weapon looked like without distorting distance, perspective, and, in some cases, lighting. Forensic photographers have to be able to answer in the affirmative when asked, "Does this picture, taken by you, truly and accurately depict the scene on the date and time in question?"

Forensic photographers are not creative photographers who will photograph a person on his or her "best side," but rather on all sides so that the scene is accurate and not misleading. Photographs are taken to assist in reconstruction of the scene, not for beauty. It is necessary when a forensic photographer photographs an item for record that the object be photographed with the camera at 90° to the object so that the object is not distorted. This is important. Perception can be skewed. Draw a circle on a sheet of paper. Look at it at 90°. One sees a circle. View the same circle at 10°. The circle appears to be an oval. If the picture is taken at this angle, what is the answer to the question: "Does this picture, taken by you, truly and accurately depict the scene on the date and time in question?"

The Film Camera

The film camera records images on film. There are many different types of films. Black and white negative, color negative (both of these used to make positives or photographic pictures), color reversal (slides), and many special-purpose films, as well as infrared (IR), ortho, and the like. The film is currently made of cellulose acetate originally introduced by Kodak (1908). Black and white film has a single emulsion of silver halides, which is sensitive to light. Once "exposed" to light, it must be developed in chemicals to produce a negative, which can then be "printed" to photographic paper. Color film has a minimum of three emulsion layers, and films such as Kodacolor II (**Figure 3**), a color negative film, have as many as 12 emulsion layers.

The Polaroid camera, while not a film camera, is also not a digital camera either. It was used in years past in forensic photography, when a positive image was needed immediately (**Figure 4**)—immediately was a minimum of 60 s. It produced a developed positive photo image. While the camera did produce a good picture, usually measuring 3″ × 3″, it did not have a negative. If additional copies were needed, one would have to rephotograph the positive Polaroid image with a 35-mm or other camera, which produced a negative, and then have that negative printed. This resulted in degradation of the copy. A "generation" was lost when the copy was made. Since the advent of digital imaging, obtaining an "instant image" is truly instant. Not only can the images be seen and checked for

Figure 4 Polaroid picture shot at a crime scene. A positive image only, no negative is produced. It can only be duplicated by rephotography or scanning.

quality in less than a second, but also an exact duplicate of the original can be copied, enlarged, and sent to the other side of the world instantaneously with no loss of resolution from the original. The other issue has always been cost. Each 3″ × 3″ image costs over a dollar each.

The "speed" of the film or, more properly, the sensitivity of the film to light measured in a scale "ISO" (former scales such as ASA—American Standards Association, now ANSI and DIN—Deutsches Institut fur Normung) must be part of the calculation to determine a properly exposed picture. Other parts of the calculation are shutter speed and aperture. The higher the film's ISO rating, the more sensitive the film is to light.

The Digital Camera

The "Point-and-Shoot" Digital Camera

The digital "point-and-shoot" camera has significantly improved over the past several years. Modeled after the "instamatic" 126 and the "disposable" 35-mm cameras, these cameras have sufficient quality to be used in forensic photography (**Figure 5**). They have many features of the digital single-lens reflex (SLR), yet are somewhat inexpensive. Many of their features are equal to those of the digital SLR. The Nikon Coolpix, for example, is 14 MP (megapixel) and can take 720p videos. Their limitations are the fixed lens and limited controls on the camera. Composing the image is done through the camera's image sensor seen on the LCD view screen on the back of the camera.

Figure 3 Kodacolor 35-mm film.

Figure 5   Nikon Coolpix 3100 point-and-shoot camera.

Digital Imaging

The term "digital imaging" is very often confused with photo digital imaging. Digital imaging refers to the material stored on a computers' hard drive and data stored on memory cards and other types of storage media and on other various computer-like devices such as iPhones, iPads, cell phones, and pagers. SWGDE, the Scientific Working Group on Digital Evidence, is the working group tasked with the creation of "best practices" associated with digital evidence stored on magnetic media. This includes memory cards, CDs, DVD, and hard drives. The entire SWGDE document is available on the Web at http://www.swgde.org/.

Digital SLR

The digital SLR is similar in concept to the film camera. It is focused on an object and light is allowed to flow through the lens when its shutter is opened and it is then recorded on the film (**Figures 6 and 7**). The digital SLR's adjustment knobs are "read"

Figure 7   Nikon digital single-lens reflex (SLR) camera rear view.

on an LED screen instead of increments marked on the dials. One of the major differences is in how the image is recorded. In the film camera, the shutter is opened and reflected light from the object of interest is allowed to show on the sensor. In most digital cameras, this sensor is a CCD or charged coupled device. In more expensive digital SLRs, the sensor is a c-mos.

The digital SLR differs from the point-and-shoot camera in that one looks through the lens, which is used to record the image onto the magnetic media (**Figure 8**). This is accomplished by the use of a mechanical mirror system and a pentaprism to direct light from the lens to the sensor in the camera (**Figure 9**).

Scientific Working Group on Imaging Technology

SWGIT is the Scientific Working Group on Imaging Technology. The Technical Working Group on Imaging Technology was formed by the Federal Bureau of Investigation in December

Figure 6   Nikon digital single-lens reflex (SLR) camera front view.

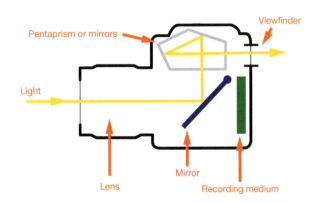

Figure 8   Diagram of a single-lens reflex (SLR) camera.

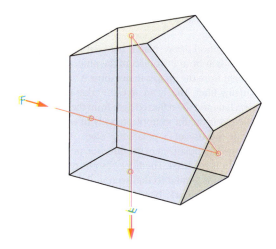

Figure 9 This is a pentaprism. Used inside single-lens reflex (SLR) cameras so the photographer can see exactly what the lens sees.

Figure 10 Logo of SWGIT—Scientific Working Group on Imaging Technology.

1997. In 1999, the name of the group was changed to the SWGIT. The group has been comprised of individuals from federal, state, and local law enforcement agencies, the American military, academia, foreign law enforcement agencies, and other researchers. Those selected for membership in the group are experienced professionals working in the field of imaging technology or a related field and demonstrate the willingness to participate by consulting on the release of best practices and guidelines for the use of imaging technology in the Criminal Justice System (**Figure 10**). Because SWGIT is so interwoven with forensic digital photo imaging, individual sections have been listed:

Section	Title
Section 1	Overview of SWGIT and the use of imaging technology in the criminal justice system
Section 2	Considerations for managers migrating to digital imaging technology
Section 3	Field photography equipment and supporting infrastructure
Section 4	Recommendations and guidelines for using closed-circuit television security systems in commercial institutions
Section 5	Guidelines for image processing
Section 6	Guidelines and recommendations for training in imaging technologies in the criminal justice system
Section 7	Best practices for forensic video analysis
Section 8	General guidelines for capturing latent impressions using a digital camera
Section 9	General guidelines for photographing tire impressions
Section 10	General guidelines for photographing footwear impressions
Section 11	Best practices for documenting image enhancement
Section 12	Best practices for forensic image analysis
Section 13	Best practices for maintaining the integrity of digital images and digital video
Section 14	Best practices for image authentication
Section 15	Best practices for archiving digital and multimedia evidence (DME) in the criminal justice system
Section 16	Best practices for forensic photographic comparison
Section 17	Digital imaging technology issues for the courts
Section 18	Best practices for automated image processing
Section 19	Issues relating to digital image compression and file formats
Section 20	Recommendations and guidelines for crime scene/critical incident videography—DRAFT; open for public comment until September 23, 2011
Section 21	Procedure for testing scanner resolution for latent print imaging—DRAFT; open for public comment until September 23, 2011
Section 22	Procedure for testing digital camera system resolution for latent print photography—DRAFT; open for public comment until September 23, 2011

Admissibility in Court of Digital Photo Images

Since the word "forensic" is defined as "as relates to a court of law," there has been much discussion concerning the admissibility of digital photo images in court proceedings. Several of these untruths are discussed here.

● Digital images can be manipulated, film images cannot. This is false. Film images can also be altered. It is just more difficult. Both altered film and digital images can be examined and discovered to be altered or not altered.
● Film has a higher resolution than digital images. This is false. As technology progresses (it seems on a daily basis), digital cameras are available that produce 25-MP images. This surpasses the much-used 100-speed (ISO) film used in crime scene photography.
● Digital cameras do not accurately depict color. No again. The sensor in the digital camera is no more or no less accurate in recording color.
● All digital images must be electronically authenticated in order to be admissible in court. Digital images, film images, and other evidence as well as authenticated by TESTIMONY. The courtroom authentication of images must be able to pass the scrutiny of the question, "Does the image in front of you truly and accurately represent the scene on the date and time in question?"

In the past, when color was an issue as to whether it should be shown to a jury, our question, "Does the image in front of you truly and accurately represent the scene on the date and time in question?" must be answered "No." This is because the scene was in color and the black and white photo is not. Eventually, color is now a commonly accepted medium to use in court.

Additional and more detailed "myth and facts" can be reviewed in the SWGIT Document, Section 17, on the Web site http://www.theiai.org/guidelines/swgit/.

Official Images

The official images of a crime scene are the first one's take. This statement is actually very logical. If an image is taken 5 min after a murder, another taken 30 min after the murder, and a third is taken 60 min after the murder, which is most accurate? It again comes down to the question, "Does the image in front of you truly and accurately represent the scene on the date and time in question?" The image taken 30 min after the murder could be significantly different from the one taken 5 min after the murder. Likewise, the image taken 60 min after the murder could be significantly different from both the 5- and 30-min pictures. Other than having images of a crime scene appear on the evening TV news, this is another good reason to ensure the media do not get photo images before the police photographer takes his or her forensic images.

Photographic Filters

A filter is an optical device placed between the camera lens and the reflected light from the object of the photo. They modify the reflected light from the images in question. A very helpful filter is the polarizing filter. This is an accessory that is placed between the camera lens and the reflected light from the object of interest. Light reflected from, for example, a body of water can be minimized with the use of a polarizing filter. When the filter is rotated, only light polarized in the direction perpendicular to the reflected light is reflected. The filter absorbs much of the reflection. This effect is similar to that seen in Polaroid sunglasses.

There are band-block, band-pass, and special effects filters. Special effects filters are soft focus, star or cross screen (they make all light points into stars), kaleidoscope, and many others.

These special effects filters have little or no use in forensic photo imaging.

Visible light (to the human eye) covers the spectral region of approximately 400–750 nm (**Figures 11–13**).

The band-pass filter allows a specific bandwidth to pass through to the camera's sensor and rejects others outside this bandwidth. This is important when doing IR and UV (ultraviolet) photography.

UV light technologies are used for multiple purposes in forensic investigations, including authenticating paintings and other fine art, authenticating signatures, analyzing questioned documents, illuminating latent fingerprints at crime scenes and trace evidence on clothing, analyzing ink stains, and revealing residual stains of body fluids.

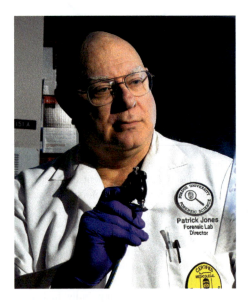

Figure 11   This image is to be hidden in an e-mail or word processing document.

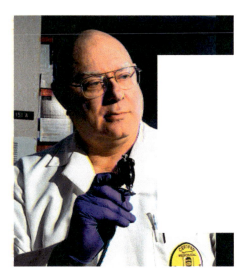

Figure 12   This shows the same image as **Figure 11** but with a white rectangle placed over the picture image. This rectangle can be enlarged to cover the entire picture rendering it virtually invisible.

Fuji IS Pro

The Fuji IS Pro is a digital SLR camera designed for specialty work using IR and UV light.

The camera is designed by Fuji and built around a Nikon frame and using Nikon lenses. It has unique software and modifications developed and designed by Fuji. It does not have a "hot filter." The "hot filter" is a UV/IR band-block filter present in almost all digital cameras (**Figure 14**). The Fuji IS Pro can have a UV/IR band-block filter attached on the front of the lens to allow it to operate as a regular digital SLR, blocking much of the UV and IR wavelengths.

It has some very unique features. One of the best is the "live image preview." In the past with film cameras, when using IR film, one would focus on the subject matter, then "adjust" the focus using the "little red dot" on the lens. This is because the IR spectrum is slightly out of focus as one looks at it in the visible spectrum. The live preview gives a 20-s window in which you can actually focus the camera, while viewing in the IR spectrum.

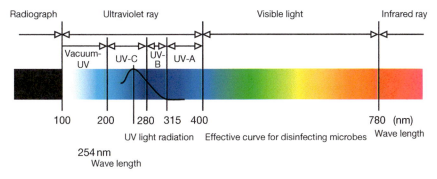

Figure 13   The electromagnetic spectrum.

Figure 14   Fuji IS Pro camera is designed to see light from the infrared, ultraviolet, and visible light spectrum. It has features that are used in law enforcement, forensic lab, and research applications.

Conclusion

This chapter is an overview of digital forensic photo imaging. It is definitely not all-inclusive and is meant to address only some of its characteristics. Being in an era of technology, one should expect to see extreme leaps in technology relating to the photo imaging process. Film photo imaging had come a long way since the 1990s. As the world migrates to digital photo imaging from film photo imaging, one cannot even imagine what is on the horizon. From the author's first digital camera, 1/2 MP, to his current Nikon D300 and its 12.3 MP is a long way to come in just 10 years. Applying this and other digital photo imaging technology to forensic work is a great pleasure. The courts do and will accept new technology as long as one uses good science and operates under rules and standards.

> *See also:* **Digital Evidence:** Cellular Phones; Child Pornography; **Digital Imaging:** Enhancement and Authentication; **Documents:** Handwriting; Ink Analysis; Paper Analysis; **Engineering:** Accident Investigation – Determination of Cause; Forensic Engineering/Accident Reconstruction/Biomechanics of Injury/ Philosophy, Basic Theory, and Fundamentals; **Forensic Medicine/Clinical:** Airplane Crashes and Other Mass Disasters; Suicide; Traffic Injuries and Deaths; **Forensic Medicine/ Pathology:** Autopsy; External Postmortem Examination; Postmortem Imaging.

Further Reading

Geberth, V., 2011a. Practical Homicide Investigation, fourth ed. CRC Press, Boca Raton, FL.

Geberth, V., 2011b. Sex Related Homicide and Death Investigation, second ed. CRC Press, Boca Raton, FL.

Jones, P., 2009. Forensic Digital Photo Imaging. In: James, S., Nordby, J. (Eds.), Forensic Science, third ed. CRC Press, Taylor and Francis Group, Boca Raton, FL, pp. 185–202.

Jones, P., 2010. Practical Forensic Digital Imaging: Applications and Techniques. CRC Press, Taylor and Francis Group, Boca Raton, FL.

Jones, P., Williams, R.E., 2009. Crime Scene Processing and Laboratory Workbook. CRC Press, Boca Raton, FL.

Redsicker, D., 2001. The Practical Methodology of Forensic Photography. CRC Press, Boca Raton, FL.

Robinson, E., 2007. Crime Scene Photography. Academic Press, San Diego, CA.

Weiss, S., 2008. Forensic Photography: The Importance of Accuracy. Prentice Hall, Englewood Cliffs, NJ.

Relevant Websites

http://www.swgde.org/—Scientific Working Group on Digital Evidence.

http://www.theiai.org/guidelines/swgit/—Scientific Working Group on Imaging Technology.

Cellular Phones

GC Kessler, Embry-Riddle Aeronautical University, Daytona Beach, FL, USA
RP Mislan, RP Mislan, DeTour, MI, USA

Glossary

Code Division Multiple Access (CDMA) A digital cellular phone technology employing spread spectrum, where users are assigned a code and hop between frequencies in a prearranged fashion.

Faraday box (or bag) Named for scientist Richard Faraday, a *Faraday cage* is an enclosed space surrounded by a material that blocks electromagnetic signals, such as radio transmissions. A Faraday box or Faraday bag is merely a small version of such an enclosure and, like *flight mode*, ensures that a mobile device is isolated from the mobile carrier network. If *flight mode* is not available on a phone, a Faraday box is another option to secure the phone from receiving incoming network signals.

Flight mode Also known as *airplane mode*, an operational mode of a mobile phone where the radio is turned off, thus allowing the user to access all features of the phone except the ability to place and receive calls. This is ideal for investigations and analysis because the phone is isolated from the network.

Global System for Mobile (GSM) communications A TDMA technology used for cellular telephones. GSM is in growing use in North America and widely used throughout the rest of the world.

Integrated Digital Enhanced Network (iDEN) A Motorola-developed TDMA mobile telecommunications technology. iDEN phones allow normal two-way telephone conversations as well as a walkie–talkie capability.

Short message service (SMS) The protocol for cell phone text messages. SMS messages are limited to 1120 bits or 160 7-bit (ASCII) characters, 140 8-bit (ASCII) characters, or 70 16-bit (Unicode) characters.

Subscriber identity module (SIM) A smart card that provides storage and other features for some types of cell phones, such as contact names and SMS messages (sometimes including deleted SMS messages). Always found in GSM and iDEN phones.

Time Division Multiple Access (TDMA) One of the digital cellular phone technologies, where multiple users share one frequency range, but each only gets a preassigned fraction of the time. TDMA is the underlying technology used in GSM and iDEN phones.

Wideband Code Division Multiple Access (WCDMA) A newer, third-generation (3G) mobile device technology for voice and data. WCDMA is not compatible with CDMA.

Introduction

Cellular phones—a term that encompasses a wide array of mobile devices that include simple cellular telephones, personal digital assistants (PDAs), and smartphones (which are essentially portable Internet terminals)—represent that fastest growing specialty in the realm of digital forensics. It has often been observed that computers have been the fastest growing instrument, target, and/or record keeper of criminal activity over the last two decades. This observation is even more true for cell phones and devices that are pervasive in society worldwide and are present at nearly every arrest and crime scene. The worldwide rate of adoption of cell phones has occurred at a rate faster even than adoption of the Internet.

In some ways, cell phones provide better opportunities for finding probative evidence than traditional computers. First, cell phones are generally single-user devices, and it is often easier to place a suspect's finger on the phone than on a computer's keyboard. Second, because of their compactness and constant use for communications—everything from phone calls and photographs to text messages and electronic mail (e-mail)—there is more probative information per byte examined on a cell phone than on a typical computer.

This all said, cell phone forensics is different than traditional computer forensics in several fundamental ways. First, in most cases, forensics examiners cannot make a forensic copy (i.e., an image) of the cell phone as they would a computer hard drive. Second, many cell phone forensic tools make analysis of phones, which appear to be simple, and therefore, many untrained (or undertrained) examiners fail to properly and completely examine phones. Finally, the information on cell phones is fragile and is often lost due to mishandling during seizure, storage, and examination.

There is a process for acquiring and examining cell phone data, but it is very different from the procedures for handling computers. The sections below address some of the high-level issues related to forensically processing mobile phones.

Mobile Phone Network Technology

Cell phones are so called because they utilize radio technology over a small geographic area called a *cell*. Cells are defined by the presence of towers at the edge of the cell; it usually requires the antenna on three towers to cover the area of a cell. The geographic size of a cell is governed by the topology, capacity of the communication channels, placement of antenna, and network architecture; cells can be as small as a few square kilometers to several hundred square kilometers.

There are three basic technologies used to allow multiple users to share radio frequencies on mobile phone networks:

- *Frequency Division Multiple Access* (*FDMA*): Each call is on a different assigned frequency.
- *Time Division Multiple Access* (*TDMA*): Multiple calls are each assigned a time slot on a shared frequency band.
- *Code Division Multiple Access* (*CDMA*): Calls are assigned a code and hop through the given set of frequencies (spread spectrum).

These technologies are the basis for the primary types of cell phone networks used around the world today.

- The Advanced Mobile Phone Service (AMPS) was an analog network that employed FDMA. This technology, originally introduced in the early 1980s, is no longer deployed. FDMA was the basis of so-called first-generation (1G) cell phone networks.
- CDMA One and CDMA 2000 are the second-generation (2G) and third-generation (3G) networks, respectively, deployed in North America.
- The Global System for Mobile (GSM) communication network is widely used throughout the world but only in the late 2000s introduced in North American networks. GSM 2G uses TDMA technology and GSM 3G uses wideband CDMA (WCDMA); this is also referred to as the Universal Mobile Telecommunications System (UMTS).
- Motorola's Integrated Digital Enhanced Network (iDEN) employs TDMA technology for two-way voice calls, as well as a walkie–talkie mode.

Table 1   Evolution of network technologies

Generation	3GPP family	3GPP2 family	Other
1G			AMPS
2G	GSM	CDMA One	iDEN
2G transition	GPRS, EDGE	CDMA 2000 1xRTT	WiDEN
3G	WCDMA/UMTS	CDMA 2000 1xEV-DO	
3G transition	HSDPA, HSPA, LTE	CDMA 2000 1xEV-DO	Mobile WiMAX (IEEE 802.16e)
4G	LTE advanced	LTE advanced	IEEE 802.16m

EDGE, Enhanced data for global evolution; *IEEE*, Institute of electrical and electronics engineers; *EV-DO*, Evolution—data optimized; *RTT*, Radio transmission technology; *GPRS*, General packet radio service; *WiDEN*, Wideband iDEN; *HSDPA*, High-speed downlink packet access; *WiMAX*, Worldwide interoperability for microwave access; *HSPA*, High-speed packet access.

A final classification of cell phone networks and devices is by "generation" (**Table 1**):

- First-generation networks employed analog (FDMA) technology.
- Second-generation networks employed digital communication over TDMA and CDMA.
- Third-generation networks utilized technologies to offer enhanced data services, such as support for multimedia and data rate greater than 200 kbps. In most cases, 3G data networks are overlaid over the voice network. 3G standardization and development efforts are being led by the Third-Generation Partnership Project (3GPP) group, while North American 3G efforts are being led by the 3GPP2 group.
- Fourth-generation networks will be Internet Protocol (IP)-based, offering Voice over IP (VoIP) services and truly integrating the voice and data infrastructures (much as what has happened to the landline networks). 4G networks will employ long-term evolution (LTE) technology, merging the efforts of the 3GPP and 3GPP2 bodies.

Although there is a merging of the technologies used by mobile phones, it should be noted that the radio frequencies used by various countries vary widely. The 800 and 1900 MHz bands are widely used in North America and some other countries, while 900, 1800, and 2100 MHz bands are used in most of the rest of the world.

The text message and multimedia capabilities of mobile devices are also related to the phone's technology. The original text message protocol was the short message service (SMS). SMS supports short messages of up to 1120 bits in length, which can comprise 160 7-bit characters, 140 eight-bit characters, or 70 16-bit unicode characters. The enhanced message service (EMS) was an extension to SMS that allowed for the exchange of ringtones and simple graphics. EMS supported limited size attachments but required no infrastructure change to the cell phone network. SMS and EMS messages are sent over the cell phone network's out-of-band signaling network.

The multimedia message service (MMS) is the current protocol for sending true audio, image, and video attachments to "text" messages. MMS was designed for GSM and CDMA networks.

Mobile Phone Hardware Components

There are three possible hardware components in a mobile phone that can contain probative data. Each component has its own method of identification, type of data content, and methods for processing. This section discusses those three components, namely the handset, subscriber identity module (SIM), and memory expansion card.

The Phone Handset

The mobile phone handset is what most people think of as *cell phone*. The handset is the physical housing that contains the radio transceiver, memory chip for the operating system and data, screen, camera (if present), a SIM card (if present), memory expansion card (if present), battery, and other hardware components. Handsets generally have a label under the battery that will list the manufacturer, handset model number, serial number, and other identifying numbers.

CDMA handsets are identified by an electronic serial number (ESN) or mobile equipment identifier (MEID). An ESN is a 32-bit number that is provided in decimal and/or hexadecimal format. (Because of the way in which the ESN and MEID are interpreted, the hexadecimal value is not a direct representation of the decimal value.) Because of the way in which the ESN and MEID are interpreted, the hexadecimal value is not a direct representation of the decimal value. Because of the exhaustion of the 32-bit ESN number space, most new CDMA handsets have an MEID, which is a 56-bit value. The ESN and MEID values contain a field that identifies the handset manufacturer.

GSM and iDEN handsets are identified by an international mobile equipment identifier (IMEI). The IMEI is a unique 15-digit value that is specific to the handset.

Phone numbers assigned to CDMA phones are called the mobile identification number (MIN) and mobile directory number (MDN). The MIN is a carrier-specific 10-digit number. The MIN is the carrier's internal reference to the handset. The MDN is the actual globally unique telephone number of the device that would be used to call this phone. The MIN and MDN are generally the same when a user first acquires a phone.

Wireless number portability rules, however, allow a subscriber to change carriers yet keep their old telephone number; in that case, the MDN would stay the same but the MIN would change on changing carriers.

Phone numbers are not assigned to GSM and iDEN phones but are contained in the SIM card.

Subscriber Identity Module

A SIM card is a form of read-only memory with a usual capacity of 16–128 kb. A SIM card will contain a phone number and can also store contact lists, call history, last number dialed, location information, and SMS messages (including deleted SMS messages). GSM and iDEN phones have SIM cards, although they are not interchangeable. A Universal SIM (USIM) card is a SIM card for 3G phones, allowing for multiple phone numbers to be assigned to a single card. A Removable User Identity Module (R-UIM) provides GSM SIM capabilities to CDMA handsets; an extension of the GSM SIM standard, R-UIMs, generally contains the same kind of user information as a GSM SIM.

A SIM card usually has an integrated circuit card identification (ICCID) printed on it, along with the logo of the network service provider. The ICCID is a 19- to 20-digit number that includes a country code, network code, and SIM serial number.

GSM and iDEN SIM cards contain two numeric identifiers. The first is the international mobile subscriber identity (IMSI), a 15-digit code that identifies the country, network, and SIM card. The second number is the mobile station international subscriber directory number (MSISDN), a 15-digit globally unique telephone number. SIMs in iDEN phones also contain a direct connect number to facilitate the walkie–talkie mode.

SIM cards—and their handsets—can be protected using a personal identification number (PIN). A PIN1 code, if defined by the user, protects access to the SIM card and the handset. After some number of incorrect PIN entries—usually between 3 and 10—will lock the SIM card. A PIN2 code, if defined, is used to protect a small number of network settings on the card and do not affect handset features protected by the PIN1 code.

A PIN-locked SIM can be unlocked with a personal unlocking key (PUK), which can be obtained by the service provider issuing the SIM. The PUK1 code is used to bypass a PIN1-locked SIM; after 10 incorrect entries of the PUK1 code, the SIM will be permanently locked. The PUK2 code is required to unlock a PIN2-locked SIM.

It is worth noting that some newer phones have slots for two or more SIM cards. This allows a single phone to have multiple personalities without requiring the user to swap out SIM cards. These phones are more common today in Asia than in North America or Europe.

Memory Expansion Cards

The most common form of memory expansion card in mobile phones is that of a microSD card, usually with a capacity of up to 16 GB. These cards are generally formatted to use the FAT16 file system. From a digital forensics perspective, then, these can usually be processed as if they were a hard drive, using traditional computer forensics imaging and analysis methods.

In older phones, the memory expansion card usually just stores media files, such as images and video files. Newer smartphones actually use the memory expansion cards as an extension of the handset's internal memory. To that end, the memory card may contain system and user files.

Mobile Phone Software

The cell phone's radio technology will drive several aspects of the examination of a mobile device; some of these aspects are described below when seizure identification is discussed. The other major factor in the data acquisition and analysis of cell phones, however, is the operating system (OS) of the phone. While computers today generally use one of three operating systems (Linux/Unix or a variant, MacOS, or a version of Windows), there are no fewer than six major OSs found on cell phones:

- *Android*: Although a major initiative of Google, development is under the control of the open handset alliance, which includes Google, HTC, Intel, LG, Motorola, Qualcomm, Samsung, and many more hardware and software developers. Android is built around a lightweight Linux kernel and an open app marketplace.
- *Blackberry OS*: Developed by research in motion, the Blackberry runs a proprietary OS. Version releases of the OS are carrier specific.
- *iPhone OS (iOS)*: Developed and distributed solely by Apple Corp., iOS is evolving into the universal OS for Apple's mobile devices, including the iPad and iPod Touch. iOS is a Unix-like system. Apple manages and closely monitors the app store.
- *PalmOS/WebOS*: The PalmOS was developed by Palm Computing, renamed WebOS when Palm was acquired by HP, and then discontinued in 2011. PalmOS was a leader in PDA devices and software. WebOS, in particular, is based around a Linux kernel.
- *Symbian*: Nokia's OS was inspired by OpenVMS, which itself derived from Digital Equipment Corporation's virtual memory system (VMS) OS. Nokia accounts for ~40% of smartphones worldwide, although the OS is not widely seen in North America.
- *Windows CE*: This is Microsoft's mobile OS, which is also found on the PocketPC, Windows Mobile, and Smartphone products. Although similar to Windows, Windows CE is optimized for devices with a small amount of storage.

The OS will directly affect how the examiner can access the handset; for example, the examiner can gain direct terminal access to the Linux-based OSs above. The OS will also affect the capabilities of the device as well as what data elements are available for download. Consider that even low-end cell phones might include any or all of the following types of data: contact list, call history, text messages, multimedia (images, audio, and video) files, ringtones, calendar entries, and alarm information. Smartphones, of course, will generally contain all of those, plus global positioning system (GPS) data, e-mail, Web browser history, cache, and cookie files, music files, documents, and a variety of applications and their log files.

The Mobile Phone Forensics Hierarchy

Standard computer tools operate essentially the same on all hard drives in order to create forensics images and allow analysis of the contents. Such is not the case with cell phones. In fact, the tools for cell phone forensics will be largely dependent on the technology of the handset and the phone's OS.

Sam Brothers first described a hierarchy of cell phone forensic analysis. The higher up in the hierarchy that the examination takes places will yield the greatest amount of information; those steps are also the most technically challenging and time-consuming:

1. *Manual extraction*: This is the easiest—and least complete—method of acquiring data from a phone. A manual extraction merely refers to accessing data on the phone via the device's interface and preserving any such information by taking notes and/or photographs of the screen. This method is prone to error, by either missing certain data due to unfamiliarity with the interface and/or inadvertently modifying handset data.
2. *Logical analysis*: This method involves a physical connection to the phone via a data cable and access to the contents of the phone that the processor allows. In many cases, data that are known to be on the phone (e.g., SMS messages) may be inaccessible to the analysis software. In addition, deleted data are almost never accessible. Some level of logical analysis can be employed on nearly all phones on the market today and nearly all computer forensics tools can perform a logical extraction on some number of phones.
3. *Hex dump*: A hex dump of memory can be achieved by using a data cable to the handset and sending commands to the phone's processor in order to download the contents of memory. This method allows the examiner to access contents of memory that would not be accessible via the phone's handset and also allows access to deleted data (as do the methods above, as well). Information is downloaded in a raw format and has to be parsed, decoded, and interpreted. This is the most superficial level of physical analysis;

a number of tools are currently able to physically acquire a large range of cell phones—particularly smartphones.

4. *Memory read*: This method requires removing the memory chip from the handset and extracting all the contents by a direct connection. This method requires specialized equipment in order to make the physical connection to the memory chip. As above, the information comes out of memory in a raw format and has to be parsed, decoded, and interpreted.

5. *Micro read*: A micro read provides access to the handset's memory chip so that it can be read it with an electron microscope. With this method, the examiner can view the actual state of memory, thus being able to extract and verify all the data from the handset's memory. This method obviously requires highly specialized equipment in a specialized laboratory and would generally be reserved for very high-value items. As above, information comes out of memory in a raw format and has to be parsed, decoded, and interpreted.

Seizing and Handling Cell Phones

When a cell phone is physically obtained as part of a criminal or civil investigation, it should be treated just as any other item so as to maintain evidentiary integrity. The circumstances surrounding the seizure should be described, such as the specific location where the device was found and the physical condition of the device. A chain-of-custody form should be completed to document the transfer and photographs of the device taken. Any manipulation or use of the device after being seized should be documented. If possible, also seize any manuals, chargers, or cables associated with the device.

There are other actions that should be taken with cell phones that can help to preserve the information on the phone. It is of utmost importance that the phone be isolated from the network as soon as possible. There are a number of services and applications that can be employed to remotely wipe a cell phone under a variety of circumstances. To avoid this eventuality, the phone should be placed into *airplane mode* (which shuts telephone and 3G/4G data services) and all other network communications, such as IEEE 802.11 Wi-Fi, Bluetooth, and infrared, turned off.

If the phone is protected with a password and/or PIN, it is a good idea to ask the owner for this information. If that information is provided, attempt to use it to access the phone; if successful, it is also a good idea to actually disable those protections. It is important to be careful with multiple attempts or guesses at a password as for many phones, especially the smartphones, there are limits to incorrect attempts or guess. Failure to get the right code results in permanent locking or deletion of all data. Under no circumstances should the device be returned to the owner once it has been seized.

Table 2 Mobile phone forensics tools

General device tools	Specific Operating System tools
BitPim	Elcomsoft Blackberry Backup Explorer
Cellebrite UFED and Physical Analyzer	Lantern for iOS
FinalMobile	WinMoFo (Windows Mobile)
MicroSystemation XRY and XACT	viaExtract (Android)
Oxygen Software Forensic Suite	
Paraben Device Seizure	
Radio Tactics Aceso	
Susteen Secure View	

In most instances, the best way to transport the phone is to power it down, keeping in mind that powering it back on may result in a handset or SIM lock code. At this point, the phone label (usually found under the battery) should be photographed and all identifying information (e.g., make, model, serial number, and ESN/MEID/IMEI) documented in the case notes.

Mobile Phone Forensic Tools

There are a variety of tools currently available that a mobile phone forensic examiner can employ. At a high level, they can be sorted into two categories, namely, those tools that cover numerous phones and other personal digital devices (such as PDAs, GPS systems, or even satellite phones) and those tools that cover a specific OS. **Table 2** lists some of the more popular tools for each category.

All the tools have their strengths and weaknesses, and it is a fundamental truth that no one tool is sufficient for all purposes. Indeed, many tools "support" a given device but will only be able to acquire a subset of the available data from the device; it is often the case where multiple tools will have to be used in order to reliably acquire a phone. In addition, there are a variety of specialty programs that can process raw data after it is downloaded from a phone, such as software to carve images or SMS messages from raw memory dumps or editors to read the database files that many phones use to store information.

Further Reading

Ayers, R., Jansen, W., Cilleros, N., Danielou, R., 2005. Cell Phone Forensic Tools: An Overview and Analysis. National Institute of Standards and Technology (NIST) Interagency Report (IR) 7250, Gaithersburg, MD. Retrieved from: http://csrc.nist.gov/publications/nistir/nistir-7250.pdf.

Brothers, S., 2008. How cell phone "forensic" tools actually work (proposed leveling). In: Mislan, R. (Ed.), Proceedings of Mobile Forensics World. Purdue University, Chicago, IL.

Daniels, K., Wagner, W., 2009. Creating a Cell Phone Investigation Toolkit: Basic Hardware and Software Specifications. SEARCH, Sacramento, CA. Retrieved from: http://www.search.org/files/pdf/celldevicetoolkit101309.pdf.

Hoog, A., 2011. Android Forensics: Investigation, Analysis and Mobile Security for Google Android. Syngress, Waltham, MA.

Hoog, A., Strzempka, K., 2011. iPhone and IOS Forensics: Investigation, Analysis and Mobile Security for Apple IPhone, IPad and IOS Devices. Syngress, Waltham, MA.

Jansen, W., Ayers, R., 2007. Guidelines on Cell Phone Forensics. National Institute of Standards and Technology (NIST) Special Publication (SP) 800-101, Gaithersburg, MD. Retrieved from: http://csrc.nist.gov/publications/nistpubs/800-101/SP800-101.pdf.

Jansen, W., Delaitre, A., Moenner, L., 2008. Overcoming Impediments to Cell Phone Forensics. In: Proceedings from the Hawaii International Conference on System Sciences (HICSS). IEEE Computer Society, Waikoloa, HI. Retrieved from: http://csrc.nist.gov/groups/SNS/mobile_security/documents/mobile_forensics/Impediments-formatted-final-post.pdf.

Mellars, B., 2004. Forensics examination of mobile phones. Digital Investigation 1 (4), 266–272.

Mislan, R.P., Casey, E., Kessler, G.C., 2010. The growing need for on-scene triage of mobile devices. Digital Investigation 6 (3–4), 112–124.

Relevant Websites

http://www.e-evidence.info/cellarticles.html—The Electronic Evidence Information Center: Cellular/Mobile Phone Forensics.

http://www.e-evidence.info/cellular.html—The Electronic Evidence Information Center: Cellular/Mobile Phone Forensic TRools.

http://www.garykessler.net—GCK's Cybercrime and Cyberforensics-related URLs: Mobile Device Forensics.

http://csrc.nist.gov/groups/SNS/mobile_security/—National Institute of Standards and Technology (NIST), Computer Security Division, Computer Security Resource Center, Mobile Security and Forensics.

http://www.ssddfj.org—Small Scale Digital Device Forensics Journal.

Digital Imaging: Enhancement and Authentication

C Grigoras and JM Smith, University of Colorado Denver, Denver, CO, USA

Abbreviations

BMP	Bitmap or Bitmap Image File, a raster graphic image format
CFA	Color filter array, a mosaic of tiny color filters (e.g., red, green, blue) placed over the camera sensor to filter and capture color information
CLA	Compression level analysis, a numerical method to assess the lossy compression effects of a finite sequence
DCT	Discrete Cosine Transform, a numerical algorithm to decompose a finite sequence in a sum of cosine functions
DFT	Discrete Fourier Transform, a numerical algorithm to decompose a sequence of values into different frequency components
DLFC	Digital light field camera, a camera that captures the color, intensity, and direction of all the light in one exposure
ELA	Error level analysis, a numerical algorithm to assess traces of editing on JPEG files
FFT	Fast Fourier Transform, a mathematical algorithm to compute the Discrete Fourier Transform
JPEG, JPG	Joint photographic experts group, a common lossy compression algorithm for images
MAC	Modified, Accessed, Creation time stamps of a digital file
RAW	A minimally processed data from an image sensor
TIFF, TIF	Tagged image file format, a file format to store images

Glossary

Artifact A visual/aural aberration in an image, video, or audio recording resulting from a technical or operational limitation. For example, speckles in a scanned picture, "blocking" in JPEG compressed images, unnatural "birdy" noises as a result of MP3 audio compression.

Aspect ratio The width to height ratio of an image.

Authentication The process of substantiating that the data are an accurate representation of what it purports to be.

Cognitive image analysis The process used to extract visual information from an image.

Deblurring A type of image restoration used to reverse image degradation, such as motion blur or out-of-focus blur. It is accomplished by applying algorithms based on knowledge or an estimate of the cause of the original degradation.

Deinterlacing Separating an interlaced frame into two discrete fields.

Demonstrative comparison A method of presenting the similarities and/or differences among images and/or objects without rendering an opinion regarding identification or exclusion.

Digital image An image that is represented by discrete numerical values organized in a two-dimensional array. When viewed on a monitor or paper, it appears like a photograph.

Field An element of a video signal containing alternate horizontal lines. For interlaced video, the scanning pattern is divided into two sets of spaced lines (odd and even) that are displayed sequentially. Each set of lines is called a field, and the interlaced set of the two sets of lines is a frame.

Frame Lines of spatial information of a video signal. For interlaced video, a frame consists of two fields, one of odd lines and one of even lines, displayed in sequence. For progressive scan (noninterlaced) video, the frame is written through successive lines that start at the top left of the picture and finish at the bottom right.

Image An imitation or representation of a person or thing, drawn, painted, photographed, etc.

Image analysis A subdiscipline of digital and multimedia evidence, which involves the application of image science and domain expertise to examine and interpret the content of an image and/or the image itself in legal matters.

Image averaging The process of averaging similar images, such as sequential video frames, to reduce noise in stationary scenes.

Image comparison (photographic comparison) The process of comparing images of questioned objects or persons to known objects or persons or images thereof, and making an assessment of the correspondence between features in these images for rendering an opinion regarding identification or elimination.

Image content analysis The drawing of conclusions about an image. Targets for content analysis include, but are not limited to, the subjects/objects within an image; the conditions under which, or the process by which, the image was captured or created; the physical aspects of the scene (e.g., lighting or composition); and/or the provenance of the image.

Image enhancement Any process intended to improve the visual appearance of an image or specific features within an image.

Image output The means by which an image is presented for examination or observation.

Image processing Any activity that transforms an input image into an output image.

Multiplexer/demultiplexer A device used to combine multiple video signals into a single signal or separate a combined signal. These devices are frequently used in security and law enforcement applications for recording and/or displaying multiple camera images simultaneously or in succession.

Noise Variations or disturbances in brightness or color information in an image, which do not arise from the scene. Sources of noise include film grain, electronic variations in the input device sensor and circuitry, and stray electromagnetic fields in the signal pathway. It frequently refers to visible artifacts in an image.

Quantitative image analysis The process used to extract measurable data from an image.

Sharpening A process used to emphasize edge detail in an image by enhancing the high-frequency components.

Video The electronic representation of a sequence of images, depicting either stationary or moving scenes. It may include audio.

Video analysis A subdiscipline of digital and multimedia evidence, which involves the scientific examination, comparison, and/or evaluation of video in legal matters.

Video enhancement Any process intended to improve the visual appearance of video sequences or specific features within video sequences.

Video stabilization The process of positioning individual frames so that a selected object or person will remain in the same location as the video is played.

Introduction

Digital images (considered to be both still photographs and video) play a key role in civil and criminal cases, law enforcement investigations, and extrajudicial inquiries. Its application areas include closed-circuit television systems, surveillance operations, media, Internet, crime scene investigations, etc. Digital technology is everywhere and it can both enable criminal activity and be the medium that captures and stores events related to a crime. When seized, analyzed, and interpreted according to best practices, this kind of digital evidence can be extremely useful for criminal investigation. Additionally, digital images created by law enforcement during a crime scene investigation or during laboratory analyses represent digital evidence as well and must be handled properly to maintain integrity.

Digital images open new frontiers for modern types of analysis and enhancement that were not available for classic photography. Still, the proper choice of a filter, for instance, for a specific type of noise or the chain of processes for video enhancement can be crucial to obtain optimal results to help solve a case.

Digital images also raise new challenges for forensic scientists who are asked to authenticate this kind of evidence because counterfeiting tools are freely available and easy to use.

Digital Imagery: Legal Constraints

With digital and multimedia evidence, the collection, preservation, analysis, and any other kind of evidence handling are crucial for a forensic investigation. According to the forensic science principle concerning evidence recovery, nothing should be modified during the recovery process, and digital media and evidence shall not be contaminated at all, by any digital, chemical, mechanical, or any other mean. In special cases, where there is no possibility to seize digital evidence without modifying the original data, the appropriate experts should be called in who have the training and proficiency to introduce the least possible contamination of evidence, document their activities, and assume the responsibility. It is also recommended that forensic experts inform the investigators or representatives of the Court about the risks of and necessity to irreversibly modify digital evidence, clearly state the scientific limitations and the reason that there is no other nondestructive solution, assume responsibility for them, and request written permission.

For instance when labeling digital cameras or digital media, special attention shall be taken to not destroy fingerprints, DNA, or any other traces. A wire with a label indicating the evidence ID may be preferred to write or stick an ID on a camera's body, while a paper bag can be used for media cards to avoid contaminating trace evidence. For mobile phones containing digital image evidence, a special shield bag or case should be used to isolate the equipment against any network or electromagnetic source that can contaminate the evidence.

Just like other forms of digital evidence, photos and videos shall be duplicated through bitstream image from the media unto which they were created to a working medium using write blockers and forensic software. Analysis should be carried out on working copies while safe backups are kept for archival. Appropriate safety measures should also be taken when transporting and preserving digital evidence to the laboratory or archive to avoid their contamination or degradation.

Furthermore, analysis of digital images in the lab should be based on scientific methods to ensure accuracy, repeatability by the same scientist, and reproducibility by other scientists of the entire set of functions applied on the digital image working copy.

Digital Image Enhancement

Digital imaging technology is commonly embedded in equipment for applications such as video surveillance systems, high-definition TV, mobile communications, Internet, social networks, commercial digital cameras, and crime scene investigations.

Digital image enhancement is needed in different forensic sciences, and its goal is to filter out the unwanted noises and fix the distortions or other unwanted phenomena by introducing the fewest possible artifacts on the analysis image.

Following the digital evidence collection and seizure of the original evidence, any subsequent enhancement functions shall be documented and their results should be compared with the working copy of evidence. In order to respect the requirement for repeatability and reproducibility, enhancements are commonly performed using software that can generate audit trials. Alternatively, print screens of function menus and their settings can also be an option.

Digital Image Authentication

In forensic imagery, the primary image consists of the data first recorded onto digital media from which the digital signal or file can be transferred in the native format or exported to another one. The digitally recorded information is stored as a finite set of binary values, and exact duplicates or clones can be further made. Each stage of copying is exact, there is no loss of information between generations of digital copies or multiplications and it becomes impossible to assess which is a first generation or original, and the implications are that any digital image copy or clone can be thought of as being "the original" even if it is produced from a copied set of data, unless it is tagged in some way to identify it as the first-generation made.

Special attention should be paid to the distinction between an original file containing a digital image and the visual image represented therein. If an original image is not bit-to-bit transferred but rather copied/pasted from the original media, it will leave the original Modified/Accessed/Created (MAC) time stamp irreversibly modified. In this case, we deal with a nonauthentic file that is in fact a copy of the original digital image file, containing exactly the same visual image like the original. In another scenario, the copy of the original image can be opened with an image editor, tampered with or edited using commonly known techniques in order to create an illusion or deception, and saved back on the same or different format. Ideally the forensic image analysis shall detect all the editing traces, and their interpretation shall allow the expert to assess the tampering processes applied on the image. In real cases, it is known that some tampering techniques are difficult or even impossible to be detected, and their quality depends on the operator's skills. Even so, an ideal or "perfectly counterfeited image" is also known to be difficult or even impossible taking into consideration the time and skills needed to do it.

When the forensic analysis reveals no traces of image manipulation, prudence is recommended in drawing conclusions with a general finding being stated as such: "the evidence is consistent with an authentic image."

Other reported techniques for establishing digital image integrity consist of watermarking, encryption, and proprietary methods (proposed by different producers of digital cameras) to check the digital image authenticity. Each of them can be useful unless a reversible solution or access to encryption key is reported by third parties and the authentic procedure is compromised.

Digital Image Enhancement Techniques

As presented previously, digital image enhancement is necessary to reveal data that would be imperceptible or distorted to the human eye. The results of any enhancement are dependent on the quality and quantity of the original imagery and the types of noise and distortions. These limitations will further dictate the optimum type of enhancement tools used. A typical digital enhancement system has facilities such as enlarge, crop, brightness/contrast adjustment, histogram equalization, fix out-of-focus or motion blur, average frames, and deinterlace. It is also possible to combine different systems or plug-ins to reach optimal results. It is not possible to cover all filters in this chapter; a representative collection is discussed below.

Enlargement

The most common enlargement filters are based on pixel expansion, near or natural neighbor, bilinear interpolation, and cubic convolution with the last two being most common in forensic applications.

The bilinear interpolation algorithm is based on a weighted average of neighboring pixels surrounding the pixel location of interest. With this system of enlargement, it may be possible to completely eliminate pixelation artifacts.

Cubic convolution is a more complex interpolation algorithm. It is also based on a special averaging of the pixels surrounding the pixel location of interest. With cubic convolution, pixel breakthrough is eliminated and the system maintains the integrity of the object with respect to its background, irrespective of the degree of enlargement. The limitations are, therefore, the same as those of lens-based optical enlargement systems, that is, the degree of enlargement is limited only by the resolution of the picture (**Figure 1**).

Sharpening

Sharpening may be required because the process of capturing digital images often produces stills lacking definition due to the optics, sensor, or settings. Sharpening high-frequency detail can enhance the edges in a digital image, while the image focus and clarity can be adjusted by increasing the contrast between adjacent pixels.

Edge detection filters produce sharp edge definition and can be used to enhance edges with both positive and negative brightness slopes. All algorithms used for edge detection work on a weighting system for the value of the pixels surrounding the pixel of interest. In a 3×3 filter, the system diagnoses the eight pixels around the main pixel. The system applies a weighting to maintain a balance where the sum of all the weights equals zero.

Edge sharpening uses a subtractive smoothing methodology by applying an average spatial filter that retains the frequency data but reduces high-frequency edges and lines. The averaged image is subtracted from the original image to leave the edges and linear features intact. Once the edges are identified in this way, the difference image is added to the original. This method provides clearer edges and linear features but has the disadvantage that any system noise is also enhanced. Examples of detail and edge enhancement are presented in **Figure 2**.

Brightness and Contrast Adjustments

Because images may be captured with nonideal settings or in nonideal conditions, it may be necessary to adjust their brightness or contrast. These are the most commonly applied enhancement tools and will help to enhance differences between image details by bringing them into the accommodation range of the human eye. A full grayscale 8-bit monochromatic image will have up to 256 grayscale steps. However, the human eye can only "see" up to 26 of these. Furthermore, an observer's visual perception is improved when color is introduced (e.g., red, green, and blue layers). By subjectively shaping these ranges, one can make details more clearly to the human eye.

Figure 1   Original image (left), bilinear interpolation (center), and cubic convolution (right).

Figure 2 Original image (left), detail enhance (center), and edge enhance (right).

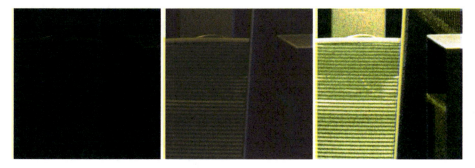

Figure 3 Original image (left), brightness/contrast adjustment (center), and 12 equalization (right).

Histogram Equalization

Histogram operations modify the brightness response curve of an image and alter the distribution of contrast within the spectrum of dark to bright pixels. One of the most important operations is histogram equalization, which modifies the response curve nonlinearly by distributing the total pixel dynamic range in a balanced and uniform manner. This emphasizes contrast in bright areas where it is increased the most. Also, histogram operations allow the operator to change the material from a positive image to a negative image. In complex and difficult images, the eye can sometimes appreciate contrast better in the negative domain and vice versa (**Figure 3**).

Blur

Out-of-focus blur makes the image unclear, less distinct, and it is a common phenomenon in photography. The digital image is blurred the same amount in all directions, and mathematical deconvolution can be applied to recover a part of the lost details. **Figure 4** shows an example using deblur.

Motion blur is another common problem in photography where the image is blurred in one direction only due to motion in either the subject or the camera. It is important to correctly differentiate this from out-of-focus blur. Usually, the length of blur in pixels is provided to the motion deblur algorithm where

the more accurately the color of each pixel is defined, the better the results (**Figure 5**).

Color Deconvolution

Color deconvolution allows the separation of different features from an interfering background or foreground or the extraction of a specific color within an image. This is also known as a type of color separation in various forensic science disciplines including digital images, questioned documents, and fingerprint examination. The color deconvolution algorithm uses

Figure 4 Original out-of-focus blurred image (left) and deblurred image (right).

Figure 5   Original motion blurred image (left) and motion deblurred image (right).

subtle color differences that are invisible to the naked eye in a nondestructive way. There are advantages of this method against other physical/chemical methods such as thin-layer chromatography, high-performance liquid chromatography, and capillary electrophoresis. These include nondestructive, higher speed, direct visual contact with the digital image, higher resolution even then IR/UV visual spectral comparators, and less color artifacts after processing. **Figure 6** shows the color separation of a questioned document, whereas **Figure 7** shows a fingerprint separation.

Noise Reduction

Noise is unwanted data in a digital image. Two of the most common noises are "salt-and-pepper" and periodic noise. Salt-and-pepper can be defined as a distribution of black-and-white pixels over the digital image as seen in **Figure 8**. Periodic noise

can be described as a distribution of unwanted equidistant forms, usually lines or segments, over the entire image as seen in **Figure 9**. It is recommended to apply the noise reduction filters at the beginning of the enhancement stage because many other enhancement techniques enhance the noise as well as the required signal. It should be noticed that most enhancement filters also affect the desired image information so caution shall be taken to remove as much noise and introduce the fewest artifacts on the desired image information.

Deinterlacing

Deinterlacing is a procedure applied to analog and digital video to remove artifacts due to the interlacing of fields within a frame. Analog video (which is captured on a Video Home System (VHS)) is composed of a series of frames with each frame being made up of two interlaced fields. It is important to

Figure 6   Scanned region of interest (left), the handwriting ink separation (second to the left), the stamp ink separation (second to the right), and the form ink separation (right).

Figure 7   Scanned evidence (left), ink separation (center), and fingerprint separation (right).

Figure 8   Salt-and-pepper noisy image (left), filtered image (center), and the removed noise (right).

Figure 9   Periodic noisy image (left), filtered image (center), and the subtracted periodic noise (right).

know that these fields represent two distinct images. This phenomenon is a result of the helical scan technology employed in VHS systems. If still images from this system without deinterlacing are reproduced, quickly moving objects will have jagged or stepped edges as a result of the composite image being from two fields representing two distinct moments in time.

Multiplexed video, which is commonly acquired in forensic investigations, exploits interlaced VHS technology by recording separate video channels to each field. The most common VHS recording solution in security CCTV systems has four or more video channels multiplexed to one VHS tape periodically interlacing images from the cameras to adjacent fields. Upon playback in a standard VHS player, a convoluted series of unrelated images will greet the examiner.

Therefore, when working with this medium, it is necessary to separate the fields through a deinterlacing process in order to reconstitute separate video channels from one recorded tape or to remove motion artifacts. Once digitized and deinterlaced, it is necessary to interpolate the missing fields in order to maintain the native resolution and proper aspect ratio. Alternatively, if working with nonmultiplexed video, a process called video field alignment can be applied where it is possible to shift an

odd field's position relative to the even (or vice versa) rather than removing a field in order to reduce the interlacing artifacts for objects in motion. This approach may be preferred in some circumstances as it maintains a higher resolution than deinterlaced images with subsequent interpolation. In **Figure 10**, see an example of deinterlacing applied to a still from multiplexed video.

Because modern digital technology has fewer limits especially with regard to the equipment necessary to capture it, interlaced digital video is not common but the procedure remains the same.

Frame Averaging

Frame averaging can be considered a special type of noise reduction for digital video. Not only does each frame of a video contain scene content relevant to the action being filmed but also dynamic noise that is captured by the imaging sensor with a random distribution across the entire image and between exposures. By averaging a series of frames to produce one still image, the intended details of stationary objects are enhanced while the overall noise is reduced (**Figure 11**).

Figure 10   Original image (left), deinterlaced image—odd fields (right).

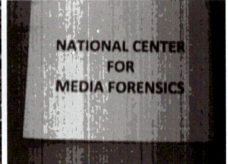

Figure 11   One original frame (left) and averaged frames (right).

Super Resolution

Super-resolution techniques produce one or a set of higher-resolution images from a sequence of lower-resolution frames. There are single-frame and multiple-frames algorithms used to improve the image fusing information from low-resolution stills producing images that contain clearer details of the scene (see **Figure 12**).

Image Stabilization

Image stabilization is a set of techniques applied to reduce the motion effects on depicted stills. It can be incorporated within a digital camera capturing a single image or video or applied to video during postprocessing using specific software (see **Figure 13** for frames from a stabilized video).

Lens Distortion Correction

The most common distortions for rectilinear lenses are pincushion distortion and barrel distortion. In pincushion distortion, the edges curve away from the center. For barrel distortion the edges of the image curve toward the center. Both types of distortions can be corrected by image processing, as it is exemplified in **Figure 14**.

Perspective Correction

Perspective correction allows user to transform an oblique image into a perspective different from that which was originally captured. This procedure maintains the object's original scale whereby dimensions can be geometrically derived. This is usually applied to flat field surfaces and traces (see **Figure 14** for a perspective correction example).

3D Modeling

In some situations, it may be useful to model an environment for courtroom demonstration, usually to reconstruct a crime scene. This approach can be costly in terms of time and money and may require building plans or specific equipment that uses lasers for precise measurements. Special software will be required and operated by adequately trained personnel to model the space and animate the crime scene.

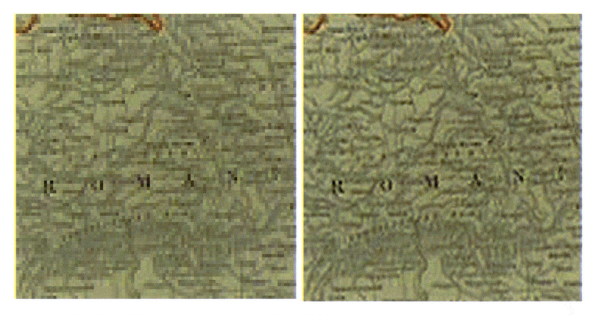

Figure 12 One original frame (left) and super-resolution processed frame (right).

Holograms

Holograms are images created by a technique that records and reconstructs the light scattered by an object. The resulting holographic images appear in three dimensions, while the position and orientation of the viewing system change in the same manner as if the objects were still in the same place. With advances in the technological development and a decrease in price for the end user, holograms are suitable for more realistic crime scene reconstructions than 3D modeling.

Figure 13 Original shaking frames (upper row) and stabilized frames (lower row).

Figure 14   Original image with barrel distortions (left), barrel corrected image (center), and perspective corrected image (right).

Digital Light Field Cameras

Digital light field cameras (DLFCs) represent a solution to the long-standing problems related to focusing images accurately and compensating for out-of-focus objects during post-processing. While conventional analog and digital cameras do not record the amount of light traveling along individual rays that contribute to the image, DLFCs sample the total geometric distribution of light passing through the lens in a single exposure. The resulting information can be image processed to refocus on the intended details. As DLFCs capture the color, intensity, and direction of all the light, investigators can much more quickly depict the details of a crime scene, with much more information in one exposure than conventional analog or digital cameras.

Digital Image Authentication Techniques

Owing to the widespread availability of image processing software, it has become easier to produce visually convincing image forgeries. To overcome this issue, there has been considerable work in the digital image analysis field to determine forgeries when no visual indications exist. However, while certain manipulation techniques can elude one or more analyses, it may be difficult to elude them all. For the most part, a digital image is composed of a finite set of numbers, arranged by a series of mathematical algorithms to create a digital image file. Like all mathematical functions, these algorithms operate in a predefined, predictable way. If the output of one algorithm is altered, the alteration will most likely affect the output of other algorithms. In some cases, when the authenticity of this kind of evidence is questioned, it is necessary to perform forensic analysis.

Forensic image authenticity is defined by SWGIT as "the application of image science and domain expertise to discern if a questioned image or video is an accurate representation of the original data by some defined criteria." Furthermore, the authenticity of a digital image can be defined as "an image made simultaneously with the visual events it purports to have

recorded and in a manner fully and completely consistent with the method of recording claimed by the party who produced the image, an image free from unexplained artifacts, alterations, additions, deletions, or edits."

Different techniques have been developed for forensic image analysis, and this chapter presents some of them.

Scene Inconsistencies

Scene inconsistencies such as shadows, eye reflections, object positions or sizes, and event mismatches can be extremely important in a forensic image analysis. The visual analysis of image evidence can reveal these kinds of scene inconsistencies and can be extremely important, especially in cases when other techniques cannot be applied or their results are not relevant.

File Structure Analysis

File structure analyses investigate the format of the digital information such as the file type, EXIF, hex data, and MAC stamps. Digital cameras create files in a particular way, each with its own unique structure. Information is embedded into image files, which can be distinct between manufacturers and cameras. When computers, or image processing software, interact with the file, this structure could be altered in some way. While this type of alteration does not necessarily mean that image content has been altered, it can raise concern about the authenticity of the file.

The information indicated by the MAC time stamps can reveal useful information about the history of a file if it is consistent with the claimed recording procedure, if it is the original or a copy of it, if it was modified, and if it may be correlated with information in the EXIF. Structure analysis can also reveal the presence of joint photographic experts group (JPEG) thumbnail and preview images, which should be investigated for their properties and consistency with a camera.

The EXIF represents the metadata located in the digital photo's header, and, on authentic files, it stores information about the make, model, camera settings, image size, and

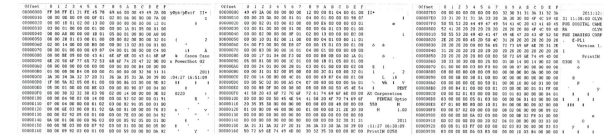

Figure 15 EXIF fragments of a JPG (left), TIF (center), and an ORF file (right).

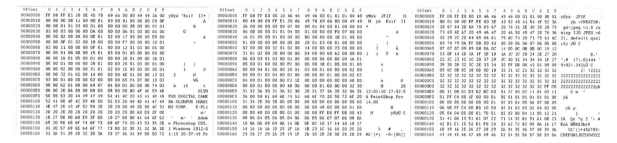

Figure 16 EXIF traces left by Adobe Photoshop (left), Corel PaintShop Pro (center), and Facebook (right).

resolution, as well as GPS coordinates and user's ID in some cases. **Figure 15** shows examples of EXIF fragments from three authentic files: one JPEG from a Canon PowerShot G2, one tagged image file format (TIF) from a Pentax Optio 550, and one ORF from an Olympus E-PL1.

The EXIF analysis can also reveal traces of image processing, left by image editors or conversion engines (e.g., social networks), as it is shown in **Figure 16**.

Image editors can also leave traces in the body of an image's data. Again, the name of the software used to process the images in **Figure 17** is seen in each image's hex data. As cameras do not introduce these kinds of traces in the original files, the

detection of specific words can indicate previous edits with a specific software.

Quantization Table

The JPEG compression algorithm employs one or more quantization tables that define the amount of compression achieved. Various camera producers and their camera settings typically embed different quantization tables. Some of them can be fixed per camera and setting, while others may depend on the camera settings and image content. Software image editors also use their own quantization tables when saving

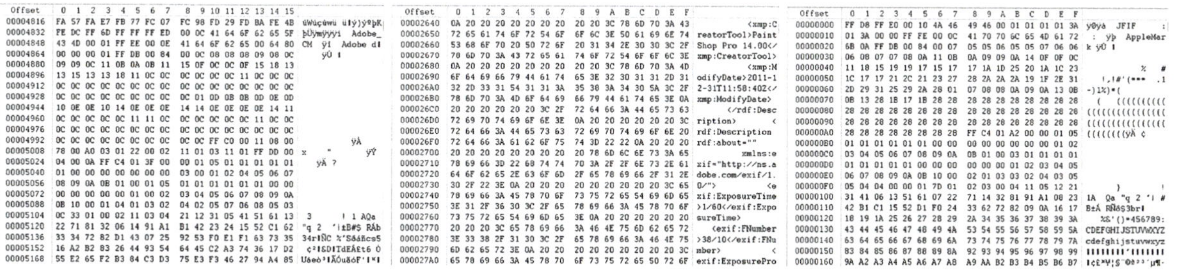

Figure 17 Traces left by Adobe Photoshop (left), Corel PaintShop Pro (center), and QuickTime PictureViewer (right).

Luminance								Chrominance								Luminance								Chrominance							
9	6	5	9	13	22	29	35	9	9	12	20	15	26	79	79	6	4	7	11	14	17	22	17	7	9	19	34	20	20	17	17
6	6	8	11	15	33	34	30	9	10	12	10	26	26	79	79	4	5	6	10	14	19	12	12	9	12	19	14	14	12	12	12
8	7	9	13	22	33	39	31	12	12	10	10	26	79	79	79	7	6	8	14	19	12	12	12	19	19	14	14	12	12	12	12
8	9	12	16	28	49	45	34	20	10	10	26	79	79	79	79	11	10	14	19	12	12	12	12	34	14	14	12	12	12	12	12
10	12	21	32	39	61	58	42	15	26	26	79	79	79	79	79	14	14	19	12	12	12	12	12	20	14	12	12	12	12	12	12
13	19	31	36	45	58	63	51	26	26	79	79	79	79	79	79	17	19	12	12	12	12	12	12	20	12	12	12	12	12	12	12
28	36	44	49	58	68	66	55	79	79	79	79	79	79	79	79	22	12	12	12	12	12	12	12	17	12	12	12	12	12	12	12
41	52	54	55	62	56	57	54	79	79	79	79	79	79	79	79	17	12	12	12	12	12	12	12	17	12	12	12	12	12	12	12

Figure 18   Quantization tables of two JPEG files: Canon PowerShot G2 (left) and Adobe Photoshop (right).

JPEG files with specific quality settings. A quantization table is an 8 × 8 matrix, as it is exemplified in **Figure 18**.

Color Filter Array

A color filter array (CFA) consists of three color filters (red, green, and blue) placed on the camera's sensor. Each pixel records one single color sample, and the other two colors have to be estimated through a CFA interpolation algorithm, which introduces a specific statistical periodic correlation between subsets of pixels, per color channel. This can be estimated as a digital signature of a camera model and, when a JPEG image is resaved with an image editor, the original CFA correlation is changed too. The CFA analysis can reveal inconsistencies with an original JPEG and/or indicate traces of image recompression.

Resampling

One digital image manipulation technique involves copying and resampling an area from one image and pasting it into another. Resampling changes the original structure of pixels and the correlation between neighboring blocks and can therefore be detected.

Discrete Cosine Transform Coefficients

The JPEG compression algorithm involves using the Discrete Cosine Transform (DCT) that converts data from the spatial domain into the frequency domain, where it can be more efficiently encoded. The resultant values from the DCT transformation are sets of 64 signal-based amplitudes referred to as the DCT coefficients. The DCT coefficients are separated into two types of signals, DC and AC components. The DC coefficient refers to the mean value of the data and represents the average of the input samples. The DC components typically contain a significant portion of the total energy for the image. The remaining 63 coefficients are referred to as the AC coefficients. Each JPEG recompression operation involves irreversible modifications to the DCT coefficients that can be very important information in forensic image authentication.

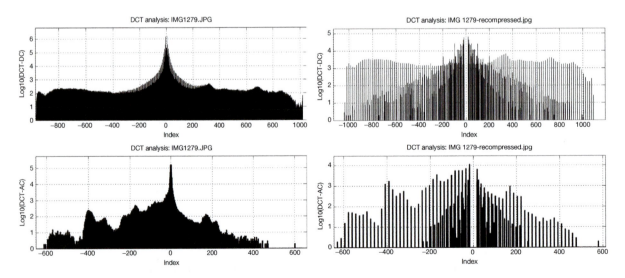

Figure 19   DCT histograms of two JPEG files: original (left) and JPEG recompressed (right).

Figure 20   Original image (left), tampered image (second to the left), DCT map (second to the right), and ELA (right).

Figure 21   Original image (left), tampered image (center), and clone detection results (right).

Figure 19 shows the DCT histograms of an original compared with second-generation recompression of a JPEG image.

The DCT map technique is also based on DCT coefficients, by displaying the values per 8 × 8 sample blocks, for DC or AC coefficients, as shown in **Figure 20**.

Error Level Analysis

Alterations in JPEG images can be identified using the quantization and rounding errors inherent in the JPEG compression process. The error level analysis (ELA) technique consists in the conversion of an image from the spatial domain into the frequency domain using the DCT. A quantization table then quantizes the resulting DCT frequency coefficients. The main loss of information is due to the quantization error or rounding of decimal values to the nearest integer. JPEG ELA focuses on the quantization and rounding error caused by the quantization and dequantization process in the DCT coefficients of a JPEG compressed file, as shown in **Figure 20**.

Photo-Response Nonuniformity

Pattern noise is a systematic distortion inherent in the operation of a particular electronic sensor. The pattern of this noise is consistent from one image to the next and consists of dark current noise and photo-response nonuniformity (PRNU).

PRNU is the dominant part of the pattern noise and is caused by imperfections in the manufacturing process, sensor components, as well as the nonhomogeneity of the silicon wafer that is used in the sensor. These slight imperfections affect a pixel's ability to convert photons to electrons, causing minor variations to exist between pixels, so that some pixels are more sensitive to light while others are less sensitive. This imprints a fingerprint, so to speak, onto each image produced by the sensor. PRNU is light dependent, and the strength of the fingerprint amplifies as the intensity of light hitting the sensor increases. Characteristics exhibited by the PRNU make this component of the digital image a unique and helpful tool in identifying the "fingerprint" of digital sensors. The PRNU is inherent in all imaging sensors, which makes it a universal identifier.

Clone Detection

The clone detection technique allows the detection of identical pixels or groups of pixels as a result of the copying and pasting of areas inside the image, as shown in **Figure 21**.

See also: **Digital Evidence/Audio Forensics:** Audio Enhancement and Authentication; **Digital Evidence/ Photography and Digital Imaging**: Digital Imaging and Photography: An Overview; **Investigations:** Recording.

Further Reading

Bayram, S., Sencar, H.T., Memon, N., Avcibas, I., 2005. Source camera identification based on CFA interpolation. In: Proceedings of the 2005 IEEE International Conference on Image Processing, pp. 69–72.

Conotter, V., Boato, G., Farid, H., 2010. Detecting photo manipulation on signs and billboards. In: Proceedings of the 2010 IEEE International Conference on Image Processing.

Fridrich, J., Soukal, D., Lukas, J., 2003. Detection of copy-move forgery in digital images. In: Proceedings of the 2003 Digital Forensic Research Workshop.

Gallagher, A.C., 2005. Detection of linear and cubic interpolation in JPEG compressed images. In: Proceedings of the 2nd Canadian Conference on Computer and Robot Vision.

Geradts, Z.J., Bijhold, J., Kieft, M., Kurosawa, K., Kuroki, K., Saitoh, N., 2001. Methods for identification of images acquired with digital cameras. In: Proceedings of the International Society for Optics and Photonics, 4232.

Kee, E., Johnson, M.K., Farid, H., 2011. Digital image authentication from JPEG headers. IEEE Transactions on Information Forensics and Security 6 (3), 1066–1075.

Luo, W., Haung, J., Qiu, G., 2010. JPEG error level analysis and its applications to digital image forensics. IEEE Transactions on Information Forensics and Security 5 (3), 480–491.

Mahdian, B., Saic, S., 2009. Detecting double compressed JPEG images. IET Seminar Digests 2, 12–17.

Petre, A., Grigoras, C., 2010. Inregistrarile Audio si Audio-Video. C.H. Beck, Bucharest, Romania.

Popescu, A.C., Farid, H., 2005. Exposing digital forgeries by detecting traces of re-sampling. IEEE Transactions on Signal Processing 53 (2), 758–767.

Popescu, A.C., Farid, H., 2005. Exposing digital forgeries in color filter array interpolated images. IEEE Transactions on Signal Processing 53 (10), 3948–3959.

Relevant Websites

www.swgde.org—Documents of the Scientific Working Group on Digital Evidence.
www.swgit.org—Documents of the Scientific Working Group on Imaging Technology.

Audio Enhancement and Authentication

C Grigoras and **JM Smith,** University of Colorado Denver, Denver, CO, USA

Glossary

Artifact A visual/aural aberration in an image, video, or audio recording resulting from a technical or operational limitation. For example, speckles in a scanned picture, "blocking" in JPEG compressed images, unnatural "birdy" noises as a result of MP3 audio compression.

Audio enhancement Processing of recordings for the purpose of increased intelligibility, attenuation of noise, improvement of understanding the recorded material, and/or improvement of quality or ease of hearing.

Dynamic range The ratio of the strongest nondistorted signal to that of the weakest discernible signal in a unit or system as expressed in decibels (dB); a way of stating the maximum signal-to-noise ratio.

Forensic audio A subdiscipline of digital and multimedia evidence, which involves the scientific examination, analysis, comparison, and/or evaluation of audio.

Media Physical objects on which data can be stored.

Media authentication The process of substantiating that the data in an image, video, or audio recording are an accurate representation of what they purport to be.

Multimedia evidence Analog or digital media, including, but not limited to, film, tape, magnetic and optical media, and/or the information contained therein.

Introduction

Audio forensics is a discipline within the digital and multi-media evidence (DME) field of forensics. DME includes digital evidence such as computers and mobile phones as well as recorded evidence in the form of audio, video, or still images. This confluence comes as a result of the ubiquity of digital technology and the commonality of media used to store digital data. For example, an external hard drive that is collected at a crime scene may contain audio recordings relevant to a case while the digital video recorder-based security system in the next room recorded audio and video to a hard disk drive during the events being investigated. Or, a cell phone found on a suspect may have been used to record voice notes and videos all related to a case under investigation. Because these items of evidence coexist in a digital realm that is not tangible as most other forensic sciences are known to be, the necessities of handling digital evidence must be respected throughout the DME discipline.

Audio evidence is commonly found during the course of investigation when circumstances such as these arise: a victim records audio for their protection, perpetrators use recordings to carry out their crimes, or phone call logging systems such as emergency assistance record a violent crime that occurred during a call. Similarly, investigators employ audio recording technology in covert operations or with a cooperative subject during an interview. The possible scenarios are too numerous to list here, but it is obvious that recorded audio evidence can be an important part of both criminal and civil proceedings where recordings of speech or other acoustic events can be very useful.

Because most forensic audio recordings are made in nonideal environments, the circumstances under which they are made are hard to control, quality, and intelligibility often suffer. The details that have been recorded are often hard to understand or not clear enough to make confident decisions. This is when it may be necessary to enhance or clarify the recorded audio by removing interfering noises and distortions or adjusting the amplitude of low-level information. Likewise, the authenticity of audio recordings must be established if they are to be given any weight in criminal prosecution or in the settlement of a civil dispute. This is necessary in order for the trier of fact to be assured that the recorded information accurately represents the events under investigation. A brief background on the topics of forensic audio enhancement and authenticity is provided in the sections below.

Technology

There are many elements to consider when presented with audio evidence before processing or conducting an analysis. Chiefly, is the recorded audio analog or digital? If dealing with analog recorded sound, it is imperative to understand analog media in order to choose the proper playback equipment. Once identified, all equipment used for the playback, analysis, and digitization of analog material should be properly maintained and calibrated according to the manufacturer's specifications. If working with recorded audio that is digital, it is no less imperative to understand the equipment and media used to record the audio digitally. It is also crucial to understand the variety of digital audio formats that are available and the difference between those that are native uncompressed and those that are compressed using either lossy or lossless compression algorithms. While an in-depth description of these principles will not be presented here, the following outline will give one a basic understanding.

Sound can be described as the compression and rarefaction of a medium (in most cases air) as a result of an acoustic impulse or vibration. In a relevant example, one can imagine the human mechanism that produces speech where air is forced through the larynx by the lungs causing the vocal folds to vibrate. The periodicity of this vibration produces sound with a perceived pitch, while the modulation of this sound by the tongue and teeth establishes language communication. Further modulation to the sound is caused by the acoustic space in which the sound is made by either absorbing or reflecting certain frequencies lending greater or lesser energy to the speech impulses. The acoustic space can obviously vary; it could be an office, auditorium, stairwell, or, an extreme example, an anechoic chamber, which absorbs all frequencies of sound resulting in reverberant energy close to zero. Acoustic impulses such as speech are fleeting and unless recorded, last no longer than a fraction of a second.

The ability to record and playback sound has been around since Thomas Edison perfected the phonograph in 1878. The principles of sound have obviously not changed since this time, but methods to record sound have undergone many technical advances and every day we see innovations in sound recording technology. In the broadest and most basic sense, recording technology can be summarized as a microphone that acts as a transducer converting the acoustic energy into an electrical signal, which may be recorded on some sort of medium. Once an acoustic sound is represented in this way, it may be referred to as audio and recorded in one of two ways: as an analog or a digital signal. Although becoming more and more obsolete, the medium used to record analog audio is most commonly in the form of a cassette or microcassette tape. On tape-recorded medium such as this, the analog waveform is recorded as varying fluctuations of magnetic energy representing the original compression and rarefaction of sound. When played back, variation of the stored magnetic flux is converted back to an electrical signal and, in a process opposite that of a microphone transducer, the speaker driver acts as a transducer converting electricity back into a series of acoustic impulses. While digital audio may be played back in a similar fashion, it is recorded onto media as a representation of the acoustic waveform as a finite set of binary values or samples. In this case, sound is quantized at a specific sample rate and bit depth. The sample rate refers to the number of samples per second used to quantize the waveform, and the bit depth is the number of bits per sample available to represent the amplitude of the waveform. Once sampled and stored in some sort of file format, digital audio is no different than any other file on a computer and may be saved for later use and playback. Digital audio may be saved as a common file format such as WAV or AIFF or bit compressed in some manner to reduce the size of the recorded file. Compression algorithms used to achieve smaller file sizes or bit rates vary but will either be lossless such as the Free Lossless Audio Codec or lossy such as MP3, AAC, WMA, and many more. With lossy encoding algorithms, the digital audio is typically limited in its frequency range and/or perceptually encoded resulting in the permanent degradation of the original, uncompressed digital waveform. It is crucial when working with digital audio to understand the principles behind audio sampling and encoding.

Competency and Proficiency

In order to work in the field of audio forensics, as with all forensic sciences, a level of education and training must be met. This is crucial because of the role the forensic expert plays in the courtroom and in the litigation process. It is common for an examiner to prove competency with a relevant educational background and up-to-date training and/or scientific research in order to conduct examinations. Once deemed competent and approved by either a court or by their agency, the analyst may work with evidence and provide scientific and unbiased opinion in matters related to their field.

The foundation of knowledge one should possess regarding the science of sound, audio technology, and laboratory practices is broad and may be garnered through various avenues including but not limited to training in audio production and recording or electrical engineering and signal processing. For an inclusive list of the minimum areas that one should know and demonstrate competency and proficiency in, refer to documents from working groups such as the Scientific Working Group on Digital Evidence, European Network of Forensic Science Institutes—Forensic Speech and Audio Analysis Working Group, etc. A summarized list of these areas would include audio recording technology, audio evidence collection and handling, audio laboratory configuration to include analog and digital signals, the repair and recovery of analog and digital audio media, and a working knowledge of the ethical and legal issues surrounding the processing, analysis, and interpretation of audio evidence.

Evidence Handling

As stated earlier, the handling of audio evidence is crucial. Thorough documentation at each stage of analysis is important to establish and maintain the provenance of recorded media on seizure and throughout the term in which it is in possession. Some important considerations follow. A chain of custody or audit trail shall be initiated and maintained for all items of evidence. Digital evidence media shall be bitstream imaged to ensure provenance and integrity of data. Digital analyses and processing shall be carried out on a working copy of recordings so that the original unprocessed files may remain unchanged. All actions taken to enhance or process evidence shall be logged so that a similarly trained examiner may reproduce results. The audio as it was originally recorded must be provided to the examiner for analysis. In cases where this is not possible, the examiner should be aware of and make others aware of limitations including those related to enhancement and authentication.

Forensic Audio Enhancement

Forensic audio recordings are typically made in nonideal environments in circumstances that are hard to control, leading to poor fidelity and intelligibility. The details that have been recorded are often hard to understand or not clear enough to make confident decisions. This is when it may be necessary to enhance or clarify the recorded audio by removing interfering noises and distortions or adjusting the amplitude of low-level information. This can either be done in real time while monitoring the audio of events or in a postprocessing phase after the recorded events have taken place. Either way, the application of signal processing in the digital domain is standard practice. There is often a trade-off where one can increase intelligibility by increasing the signal-to-noise ratio only to a certain point before the artifacts created by signal processing algorithms themselves interfere. Therefore, care should be taken to not overprocess material and abide by a general "less-is-more" rule of thumb.

A simplistic approach to enhancing forensic audio can be followed as such: file preparation, critical listening and analysis, audio processing, and preparation of output file for distribution.

File Preparation

It is necessary to prepare audio for analysis and enhancement prior to examination. This means taking steps necessary to digitize, transfer, or convert recordings into an uncompressed format (most commonly WAV) and at a relevant sample rate, bit depth, and channel configuration (mono or stereo). Before describing this process, a brief introduction

will be given on digital sampling with regard to sample rate and bit depth.

Digital audio represents an acoustic sound wave as a finite set of binary values or samples. When an analog signal is received by an analog to digital converter, the acoustic waveform is quantized at a specific sample rate and bit depth. The sample rate refers to the number of samples per second used to quantize the waveform, and the bit depth is the number of bits per sample available to represent the waveform's amplitude at that moment in time. The resolution of the recording, then, is a function of the rate at which the waveform is sampled according to Nyquist's theorem that defines the upper bound of a sampling system. As two discrete sample points are required to represent the waveform of a specific frequency, the sampling rate must be twice that frequency. In other words, an 8 kHz audio recording only represents frequencies up to 4 kHz. Thus, the higher the sample rate, the more accurately the acoustic waveform is represented. See **Figure 1** demonstrating one period of a 1 kHz sine wave sampled at two different sample rates.

For analog media such as cassette and microcassette tapes, it is necessary to digitize the audio so that it may be processed, distributed, and played back more conveniently. For this process, all analog playback equipment shall be maintained and calibrated regularly according to the manufacturer's specifications and the analog to digital converter used should be external from the host computer and connected via Firewire, USB, or similar. The sample rate and bit depth used to digitize analog tape should be a minimum of 44.1 kHz, 24 bits (or 16 bits in the unlikely event that 24 bits are unavailable).

It is also possible to receive recordings on digital media that will require a transfer. These types of legacy media include digital audio tapes, Minidisc, and others. As the recordings that reside on these devices are native digital, it is best to digitally transfer the audio to the host computer using digital outputs on the media player. This maintains the originally quantized waveform and avoids redigitizing a quantized waveform if one were to use analog outputs on the digital media player. When performing a digital transfer, the original sample rate and bit depth should be used rather than resampling during the process in order to preserve the originality of the recordings.

The third general type of recording submitted would be one that was recorded as a digital audio file. There are many devices capable of recording digital audio files with the most common being handheld recorders and cell phones. The digital audio files may be recorded in an uncompressed format such as WAV or AIFF. More commonly, however, recorded files are bit compressed in some manner to reduce the size of the recorded file. This process employs compression algorithms in order to achieve a smaller file size or bit rate and will either compress the audio waveform losslessly, causing no detrimental effect to the sound when played back, or in a way that causes permanent degradation of the original digital waveform. The term "lossy"

(a)

(b)

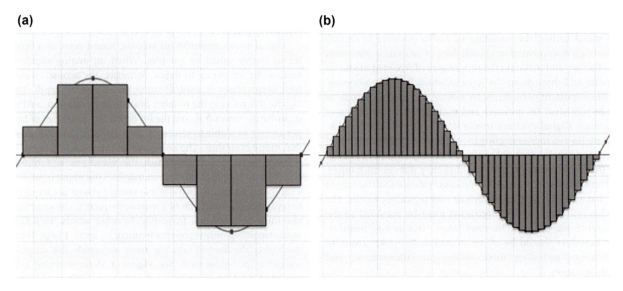

Figure 1   1 kHz sine wave sampled at 8 kHz (a) and at 44.1 kHz (b).

(a)

(b)

(c)

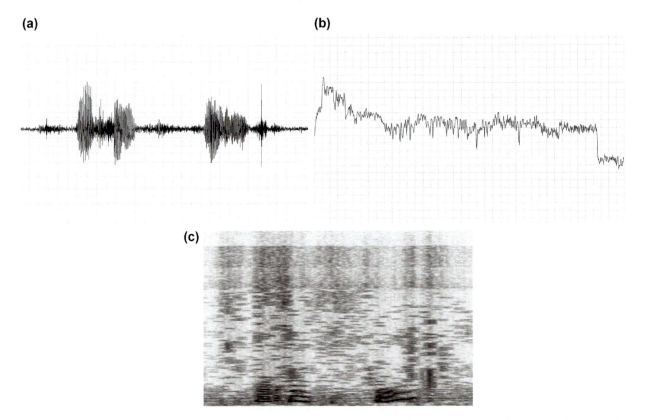

Figure 2   Waveform (a) with time on the x-axis and amplitude on the y-axis. Fast Fourier transform spectrum (b) with frequency on the x-axis and amplitude on the y-axis. Spectrogram (c) with time on the x-axis, frequency on the y-axis, and intensity of color (or gradient of grayscale) representing amplitude.

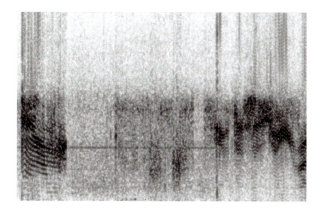

Figure 3 Spectrogram showing speech with tonal noise (the vertical line at ~1.6 kHz).

is used for these codecs (short for compression/decompression) where the digital audio is typically limited in its frequency range and/or perceptually encoded. Audio codecs include AMR, MP3, WMA, ADPCM, etc. If the digital audio being submitted is in a digital format that is compressed, it is necessary to convert it to an uncompressed format such as WAV in order to achieve the best possible results. In this case, the original sample rate should be maintained and bit depth maximized for processing. When it is submitted to a laboratory for enhancement or clarification and prepared in these ways, it can be easily processed to clarify the content as much as possible.

Critical Listening and Analysis

The second step to enhancing audio material is to listen to the recording while analyzing the time, frequency, and amplitude content in order to characterize the types of noises or distortions that are masking the target signal (most commonly speech). For this process, software should be used which is

not only capable of audio playback and displaying the digital waveform (**Figure** 2) but also capable of displaying the fast Fourier transform (FFT) spectrum (**Figure** 2) and spectrogram (**Figure** 2). The FFT is the algorithm employed to convert the time-based audio signal to the frequency domain for frequency analysis. By listening to the material while conducting visual analyses, interfering noises and distortions masking the intended material can be observed and measured.

Generally, an interference masking the target signal can be characterized as either a noise or a distortion. These differ in that "noises" are acoustic or electromagnetic events captured while the recording was made. "Distortions" on the other hand are changes to the content of an audio signal during transmission or recording, which disrupt the original waveform, much like a reflection on water distorted by ripples that would otherwise be accurate. In this same example, noise would be leaves floating on the surface of the water masking the reflection itself. Once noises and distortions are classified and measured, digital processing can be applied to remove them as much as it is possible.

Common types of noise in forensic audio recordings can be grouped into four categories: tonal, continuous broadband, variable broadband, and convolved. Tonal noise commonly comes from mains power hum, when an audio signal is not properly shielded, or acoustic noises come from machines that oscillate at a specific frequency or set of frequencies (**Figure 3**). Continuous broadband noise (**Figure 4**) occupies a broad range of frequencies with little spectral change in time, for instance, tape hiss, machine or channel noise, or building ventilation systems. Variable broadband noise is a term used to describe interferences that occupy a broad range of frequencies with variable spectral content, for instance, wind, rain, and speech other than the target signal (**Figure 5**). Lastly, convolved noise is excessive reverberation interfering with the source signal (**Figure 6**).

Distortions disrupt a signal and prevent the acoustic waveform from being accurately recorded due to interference or

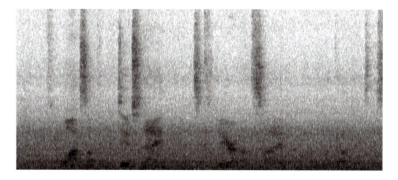

Figure 4 Spectrogram showing speech in the presence of continuous broadband noise.

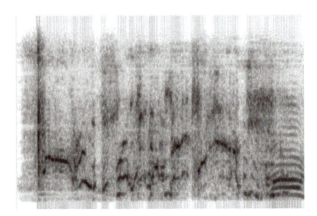

Figure 5   Spectrogram showing speech in the presence of variable broadband noise.

faulty equipment. One common example includes mobile phone interference (GSM bursts shown in **Figure 7**). In another example, **Figure 8** shows artifacts due to the application of aggressive lossy compression.

Audio Processing

Once the various interfering noises and distortions are identified, specific filters and algorithms can be applied in an attempt to remove or attenuate them. At this stage, the recorded audio may be enhanced for increased intelligibility or ease of listening. Not all noises can be removed nor all distortions fixed. In cases where the ratio of target signal amplitude to noise amplitude is too small, content in the waveform representing the target signal is not adequately represented. Therefore, it must be noted that some audio is recorded so poorly and with such compromising conditions that speech is not recoverable. In these instances, the submitter of the recording must be made aware of the limitations when working with forensic audio. Specific filters and algorithms designed to remove noises and fix distortions are provided here. While this section is not entirely exhaustive, the elements provided represent commonly employed techniques. In most cases, distortions should be fixed before attempting to remove noise.

- Clipped audio may be repaired manually or by using a *declipping* algorithm that analyzes the distorted waveform

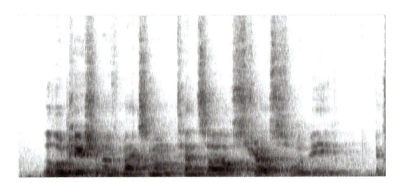

Figure 6   Spectrogram showing speech recorded in excessively reverberant conditions. The clarity of speech formants is smeared in time due to reflections from the environment.

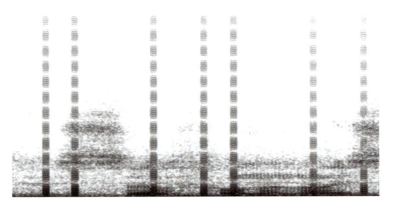

Figure 7   Spectrogram showing speech obscured by GSM burst interference.

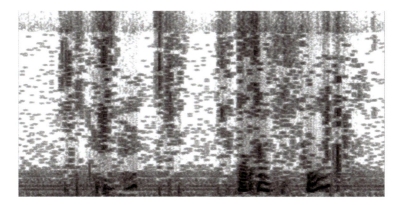

Figure 8 Spectrogram showing speech recorded with lossy WMA compression.

with flattened or clipped peaks and interpolates the waveform that should otherwise be sinusoidal in nature.

- *Mobile phone interference* is induced into audio equipment electromagnetically, as mobile devices transmit packets of data in very short bursts. These bursts are tonal in nature, but use of notch or comb filters is not typically successful because the interference has multiple harmonics of very high amplitude. It is possible to remove the bursts by determining the fundamental frequency of the distortion (based on the carrier network) and removing them with an adaptive filter. Modern filters built for this purpose will then interpolate the information obscured by the bursts.
- *Time domain distortions*, such as tape wow and flutter, can be compensated for by applying time compression or expansion on appropriate segments of recorded audio.
- *Lossy compression artifacts* can in some cases be removed and the missing information reconstructed using algorithms designed for musical recordings. However, with forensic audio where speech is typically the target signal

and other noises are present, these solutions are not very useful.

- *Notch, comb, and band-pass filters* are digital filters that are designed to attenuate or remove a specific frequency or frequencies. They are therefore useful in the removal of tonal noises. While a notch filter can be used to attenuate one specific frequency (such as 1.6 kHz in **Figure 3**), comb filters are designed to attenuate a fundamental frequency and its harmonics. This is especially useful in the case of induced mains power hum (at 60 or 50 Hz depending on the country) where harmonics at multiples of the fundamental are present.

Figure 9 (a) 1 kHz sine wave imaged using a magneto-optical system. (b) 1 kHz sine wave imaged using freon-based ferrofluid. Photo courtesy of Jonathan Broyles, www.iasforensics.com.

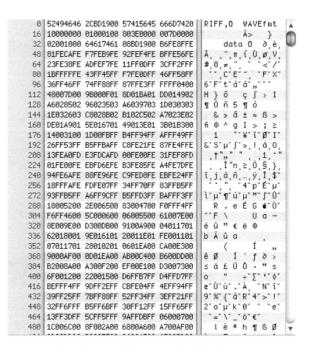

Figure 10 Hexadecimal display of audio data.

By selecting the fundamental frequency, harmonics are automatically calculated and attenuated. Band-pass filters on the other hand will attenuate a range of frequencies. For instance, a high-pass filter can easily be applied to attenuate frequencies from 0 to 150 Hz in order to reduce low-frequency rumble and make speech more intelligible.

- *Spectral subtraction* is very useful in removing continuous broadband noise where the spectral content of noise does not vary greatly over time. In a simple arithmetic procedure, this algorithm subtracts an input noise profile from recorded audio to effectively remove noise and enhance intelligibility.
- *Adaptive filters* can work in both the time and frequency domains and achieve spectral subtraction on short time windows that change, as the noises in the environment change. These filters develop predictive coefficients to continually update the input noise profile to be subtracted and can therefore be useful in dealing with variable broadband noise such as outdoor environments where background conversations, rain, etc. may be present.
- *Convolved noise*, or excessive reverberation, can be removed with some success using algorithms designed for this purpose. While many methods have been proposed, typical techniques that are commercially available use adaptive dereverberation algorithms where spectral subtraction of convolved elements is achieved based on predictive coefficients.
- *Stereo source separation* can be very powerful when available. In this situation, a stereo recording is provided that has speech in the presence of, most likely, variable broadband noise. If the target speech signal is present on only one channel, the second channel can be used to inform the algorithm of the noise profile to be removed. For example, for a stereo recording of a noisy bar where the background voices, music, and other acoustic impulses are captured in relatively equal amplitude on both channels and speech is

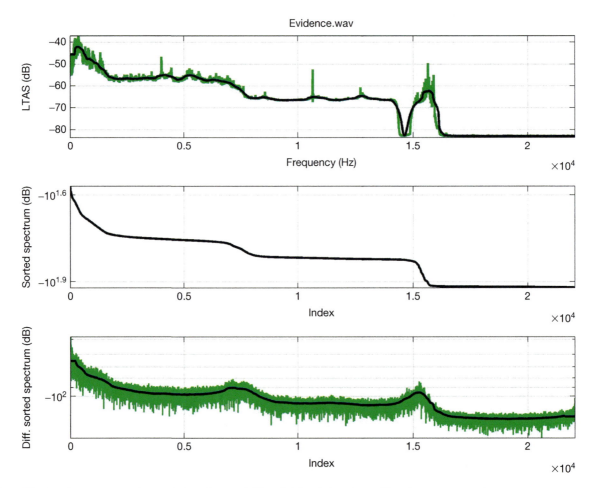

Figure 11   Long-term power spectrum, sorted spectrum, and differentiated sorted spectrum of long-term average spectrum.

on one. Alternatively, when dealing with mono recordings, it is possible to provide the algorithm with the second reference channel containing identical noise information as that which is present on the source. For instance, when presented with a mono recording of speech obscured by commercially released music or a media broadcast, the music or broadcast can be obtained to build the reference channel for subtraction.

- In some cases, conversations are recorded in which one person is at a higher amplitude than another. This situation is referred to as *near-party/far-party* and can easily be compensated for by either manually adjusting the volume of the digital file during quiet portions or by applying amplitude compression/limiting to bring loud and quiet material to within the same range of volume. Some systems provide an automatic gain control feature that will expand and compress portions of audio to achieve a more balanced overall level.

A forensic audio recording that requires enhancement may be processed with one or many of the above techniques. Depending on the noises and distortions present, it is up to the examiner which ones will be appropriate and in which order. This is done by comparing and contrasting the audio before and after each step of processing. It is advised to save each iteration of processing as an independent audio file to maximize efficiency if any alterations to previous steps must be taken. For any processing that is applied, it is necessary to document filters and settings used so that identical results may be achieved at a later time by the same examiner or by another adequately trained examiner. This helps to establish the provenance of the original material and can demonstrate, if necessary, that the content or meaning of the audio was not changed during the course of enhancement.

Preparation of Output File

Once noises and distortions have been compensated for satisfactorily, further processing may be needed to make the recording appropriate for playback in a courtroom: adjusting the overall amplitude of the audio, for example. Or it may be desired to further shape the frequency response of the recording by applying equalization. Once complete, it is necessary in this last stage of the forensic audio enhancement procedure to

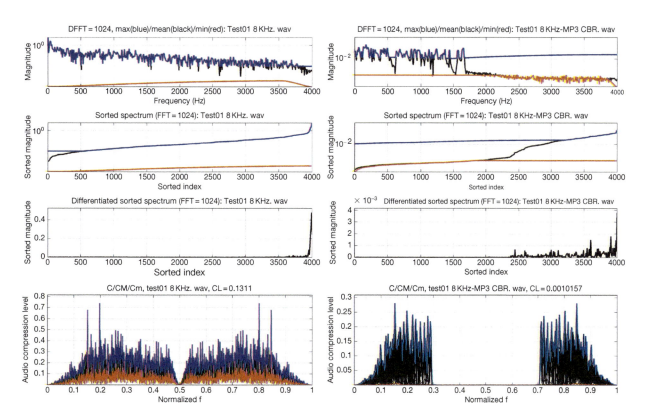

Figure 12   Compression level analysis, original WAV PCM recording (left column), MP3 CBR (right column).

prepare the audio in a format as deemed appropriate by the analyst and the submitter of evidence. For example, due to technology limitations of the contributor or the court, it may be requested to provide an audio CD that can be played back in a CD player requiring the output audio to be at 44.1 kHz, 16 bits. If the file is to be converted in any way from the resolution that it was processed at, the unconverted output file should be also provided, as it represents the most original form of the enhanced evidence. Finally, the original unprocessed audio should also be provided to the contributor especially in cases where the originally supplied recording is not in a format useful for the contributor or the courts.

Forensic Audio Authentication

Commonly, a review of audio authenticity is requested to determine whether the material presented accurately represents the events recorded with requests coming either through investigation or as a request from the court or its advocates. An audio authenticity examination, as defined by the Scientific Working Group on Digital Evidence, seeks to determine if a recording is original, unaltered or continuous, and/or consistent with the manner in which it is alleged to have been produced. Many elements from a recording may be analyzed, and the methodology employed will depend on whether the recording was made digitally or on analog media. In either case, the questioned original recording on its original media must be analyzed and, if available, the original recording device must be obtained. This is crucial in establishing the provenance of the recording; otherwise analyses and conclusions are compromised. If the original recorder is not available, a recorder of the same model and brand may be used to produce test recordings. Test recordings are necessary to produce known data from which comparisons to the questioned recording can be made.

Analog Tape Authentication

Analysis methods in tape authentication examinations first began with the Watergate Scandal of 1972. Since that time, the methodology employed to analyze analog tape recordings has not changed greatly nor have the tools for analysis. Once the questioned recording has been obtained, an analysis of the

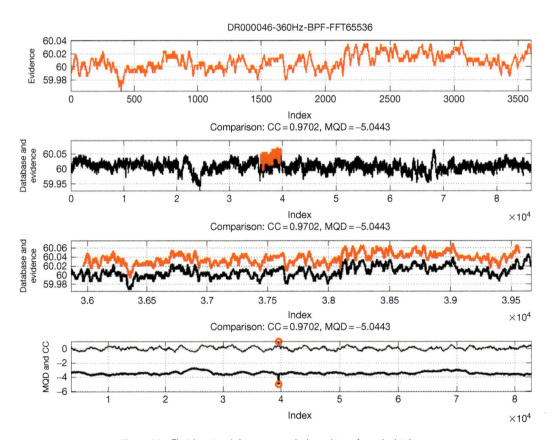

Figure 13 Electric network frequency analysis against a forensic database.

magnetic material on the tape is conducted along with digital analysis of the audio material. In essence, the examiner must analyze any inconsistencies in the questioned recording and make comparisons with test recordings in order to determine whether they are a result of normal operation or possible editing.

Bruce Koenig published a paper in 1990 describing a formal methodology for conducting analyses of analog recordings, which employs freon-based ferrofluid to conduct visual examinations of the magnetic waveform stored on the tape (**Figure 9**). An alternative method of visualizing magnetic flux that provides higher frequency resolution and less physical contact with the tape itself employs a magneto-optical imaging system (**Figure 9**).

Digital Audio Authentication

An analysis of digitally recorded audio does not differ in scope from an analog examination in that the examiner seeks to explain observed anomalies, through the analysis of test recordings, as a result of normal recorder operation or inconsistencies, which may indicate alteration or editing. However, the techniques employed vary greatly. These should include but

not be limited to analysis of header and file structure, waveform, FFT spectrum, spectrogram, compression level, and electric network frequency (ENF). Koenig and Lacey provide a formal methodology for the authentication of digital audio recordings while information regarding analysis can be found in the References section as well. Different techniques have been developed for forensic audio authenticity analysis, and this chapter presents some of them.

MAC, header, and file structure analysis can be carried out checking the MAC (Modify, Access, Creation time stamp of a file and/or digital media) and using software capable of viewing the individual bits and bytes that make up a file represented as hexadecimal, or hex, data (**Figure 10**). In viewing the hex data of a digital audio file, comparisons may be made between a questioned recording and test recordings to observe recorder and file write behavior. The internal arrangement of proprietary files can be confirmed as well as the header structure. Header information may also include the date/time of the recording, recording duration, make/model/serial number of the recorder, file type, and compression scheme and rate. Any observed inconsistencies in this information may be a result of alteration or editing.

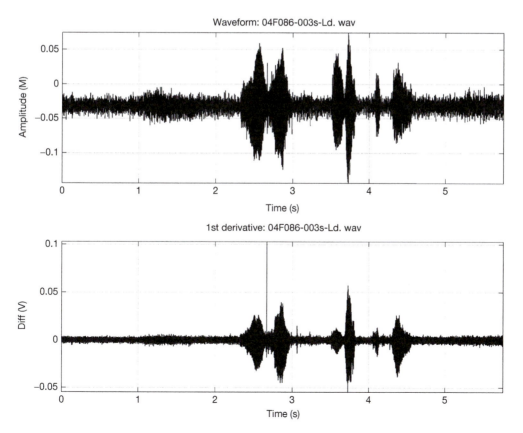

Figure 14 Butt-splice detected at 2.665 s.

Power spectral analysis may be useful in identifying traces of file recompression or inconsistencies between the recording and the claimed recorder. If present, inconsistencies can be easily detected by comparing the long-term power spectrum, sorted spectrum, and differentiated sorted spectrum of unknown and test recordings as well as comparing histograms of their spectral power (**Figure 11**).

Compression level analysis may also be useful in identifying traces of file recompression or inconsistencies between the recording and the claimed recorder. This function, proposed by Grigoras, applies the discrete FFT on the second derivative of consecutive frames to produce a plot of the compression level. By comparing an unknown recording's compression level with test recordings of the claimed recorder, inconsistencies may be found if present (**Figure 12**).

ENF analysis involves the detection, extraction, and comparison of the ENF trace induced onto recording from mains power. If present, ENF may help an examiner do many things in addition to identifying the presence of edits, insertions, and deletions. With a reference database of ENF, it is possible to determine the date/time a recording was made, how the device was powered, and gross geographical location, all of which can further corroborate the authenticity of a recording (**Figure 13**).

Butt-splice detection can be useful in identifying the insertion or deletion of material without the application of cross-fades (**Figure 14**).

DC level analysis may be used to determine the insertion of material or to compare an unknown recording to the recorder claimed to have made it (**Figure 15**).

In the examination of digital audio for authenticity, a sound methodology should be used that is based on validated methods and principles. While the specific analyses will depend on the situation, the examiner should not rely on one

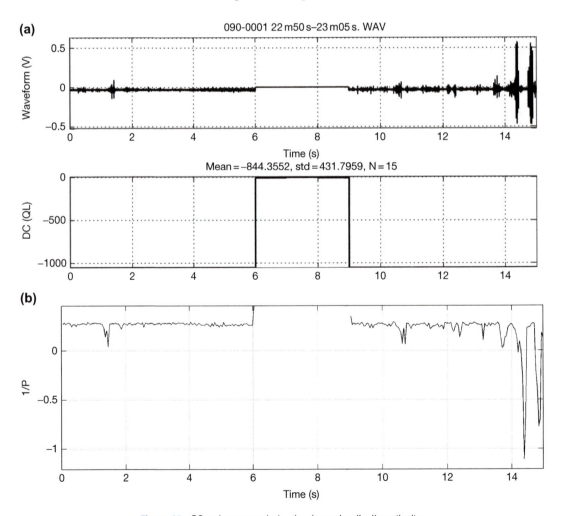

Figure 15 DC and power analysis, showing a signal's discontinuity.

specific element or tool but seek to exhaust all possible techniques because an inconsistency observed through one analysis may not be present in another. Specific determinations from analyses will also vary depending on the situation but will generally conclude that the recording is consistent with an authentic recording, inconsistent with an authentic recording, or inconclusive.

See also: **Behavioral**: Forensic Linguistics; Forensic Phonetics; **Digital Evidence**: Digital Imaging: Enhancement and Authentication; **Digital Evidence/Photography and Digital Imaging**: Digital; Imaging and Photography: An Overview; **Investigations**: Recording.

Further Reading

Bouten, J., van Rijsbergen, M., Donkers, S., 2007. Derivation of a transfer function for imaging polarimetry used in magneto-optical investigations of audio tapes in authenticity investigations. Journal of the Audio Engineering Society 22, 257–265.
Brixen, E.B., 2011. Audio Metering: Measurements, Standards, and Practice, second ed. Focal Press, Burlington, MA.

Cooper, A., 2010. Detecting butt-spliced edits in forensic digital audio recordings. In: Proceedings of the 39th International Conference of the Audio Engineering Society: Audio Forensics. Denmark.
Grigoras, C., 2009. Applications of ENF analysis in forensic authentication of digital audio and video recordings. Journal of the Audio Engineering Society 57, 643–661.
Grigoras, C., 2010. Statistical tools for multimedia forensics. In: Proceedings of the 39th International Conference of the Audio Engineering Society: Audio Forensics. Denmark.
Harris, C.M., 1998. Handbook of Acoustical Measurements and Noise Control, third ed. Acoustical Society of America, Woodbury, NY.
Koenig, B.E., 1990. Authentication of forensic audio recordings. Journal of the Audio Engineering Society 38, 3–33.
Koenig, B.E., Lacy, D., 2009. Forensic authentication of digital audio recordings. Journal of the Audio Engineering Society 57, 663–695.
Loizou, P.C., 2007. Speech Enhancement: Theory and Practice. Taylor and Francis Group, Boca Raton, FL.
Pohlmann, K.C., 2005. Principles of Digital Audio, fifth ed. McGraw-Hill, New York, NY.

Relevant Websites

www.enfsi.eu—Documents of the ENFSI Expert Working Group Forensic Speech and Audio Analysis.
www.swgde.org—Documents of the Scientific Working Group on Digital Evidence.
www.aes.org—The EOB Tape of June 20, 1972 by the Advisory Panel on White House Tapes.

Analysis of Digital Evidence

MK Rogers, Purdue University, West Lafayette, IN, USA

Glossary (SWGDE, 2011)

Bit Short for binary digit. Fundamental unit in computing. It has two possible values: 1 or 0.

Bitstream image A bitstream image is a sector-by-sector/ bit-by-bit exact copy of a hard drive or other storage device.

Data Information in analog or digital form that can be transmitted or processed.

Hash or hash value Numerical values, generated by hashing functions, used to substantiate the integrity of digital evidence and/or for inclusion/exclusion comparisons against known value sets.

Hashing function An established mathematical calculation that generates a numerical value based on input data. This numerical value is referred to as the hash or hash value.

Integrity verification The process of confirming that the data presented are complete and unaltered since the time of acquisition.

Metadata Data, frequently embedded within a file, that describe a file or directory, which can include the locations where the content is stored, dates and times, application-specific information, and permissions.

Partition User-defined section of electronic media.

Storage media Any object on which data are preserved.

Work copy A copy or duplicate of a recording or data that can be used for subsequent processing and/or analysis.

History/Background

Digital evidence is an emerging area in the field of forensic science. As society becomes more dependent on technology, more of daily lives are reflected in the world of cyberspace. The notion of a carbon footprint has become popular in the media, what is equally as important is the digital footprint. Technologies such as Facebook, Twitter, Google+, and text messaging allow one to record and share almost all facets of daily lives. One has friend-finding applications on GPS-enabled cell phones, security cameras that monitor daily travels, and Internet companies that record one's Web browsing activities and predilections. One's health records, phone conversations, and even book or magazine reading habits are monitored and recorded. These days most people conduct their banking online, with little or no interaction with the physical bank. The end result of all this is that digital evidence is poised to surpass the volume of physical evidence, such as paper documents or paper receipts.

The term digital evidence is bandied about in the vernacular and often highlighted in movies and the popular media. But what exactly does this term mean? While there are several definitions available, the more common definition of the term is

Digital data that establish that a crime has been committed can provide a link between a crime and its victim, or can provide a link between a crime and the perpetrator.

Like physical evidence, digital evidence exists in a crime scene. To be more accurate, digital evidence exists in two crime scenes, the physical and the cyber or digital realm. An example would be e-mail evidence. This evidence could be stored on a laptop that exists in the physical world, but the actual content of the e-mail is in the digital world. Thus, one needs to define this second type of crime scene, the digital crime scene. A digital crime scene is defined as

The electronic environment where digital evidence can potentially exist.

Digital evidence falls within the larger category of digital forensic science. Digital forensic science is defined as

The use of scientifically derived and proven methods toward the preservation, collection, validation, identification, analysis, interpretation, documentation, and presentation of digital evidence derived from digital sources for the purpose of facilitating or furthering the reconstruction of events found to be criminal or helping to anticipate unauthorized actions shown to be disruptive to planned operations.

As a field, digital forensics is relatively new to the forensic sciences. The American Academy of Forensic Sciences (AAFS) added a Digital and Multimedia Sciences section in February 2008. Prior to this time, practitioners and scientists engaged in digital forensics belonged to other sections such as the General Section or Engineering Sciences section.

Apart from the establishment of its own section within the AAFS, digital forensics as a concept first appeared in the 1970s as a result of the efforts of law enforcement in the United States, Canada, and Europe to have laws passed to deal with technology-related crimes. In the 1980s, police agencies in North America and Europe started to create dedicated computer crime units such as the FBI's Computer Analysis Response Team, which lead to international conferences in the 1990s designed to begin the work of harmonizing efforts at the international level.

In the late 1990s, the International Organization for Computer Evidence (IOCE, European) and the Scientific Working Group for Digital Evidence (SWGDE, USA) began formal discussions on standardizing investigative approaches for dealing with digital evidence.

In 2000, the FBI opened their first Regional Cyber Forensics Laboratory (RCFL). The goal of the RCFL program was to provide computer forensic resources to state and local law enforcement. The program has expanded to 16 RCFLs covering the majority of the United States.

In 2003, the American Academy of Crime Laboratory Directors/Laboratory Accreditation Board (ASCLD/LAB) included specific certification criteria for laboratories handling digital evidence. The inclusion of these criteria mirrored the European efforts related to ISO 17025 requirements for international laboratories.

As was previously mentioned, the AAFS in 2008 recognized its first new subsection in over 25 years. The Digital and Multimedia Sciences section is the current home for digital forensics and digital analysis in the context of a forensic science.

Current Context

Evidence that is digital in nature is an integral part of most modern-day investigations (**Figure 1**). Digital evidence has been used as corroborative evidence in cases that range from homicides to cyber stalking, extortion, and child custody cases. Dennis Rader, the BTK killer, was eventually caught as a result of digital evidence found on a diskette. Investigations relating to intellectual property (IP) or fraud and embezzlement rely more heavily on digital evidence than on document-based evidence. In the business setting, the volume of digital documents has surpassed paper-based documents. The paper documents that exist are commonly printouts of digital or electronic documents.

E-mail-based evidence has been the proverbial "smoking gun" in numerous high-profile cases such as Enron and the antitrust investigation involving Microsoft. The sheer volume of e-mails produced daily (estimated to be in the billions worldwide) make this kind of evidence common to any investigation. Some federal law enforcement agencies estimate that at least 80% of their current and future investigations involve or will involve digital evidence.

Standards

Given the recent emergence of digital analysis, there are no standards that are recognized as being definitive. Several organizations such as the SWGDE, American Society for Testing and Materials (ASTM), the IOCE, the National Institute of Justice (NIJ), and the Association of Chief Police Officers (ACPO) are developing guidelines and best practices. However, most of these works are in progress and are not intended to be checklists or formal standards at this time.

The development of standards and certifications is further complicated due to the diverse communities that are enveloped by the field of digital forensics and digital evidence analysis. These communities include (1) law enforcement, (2) private sector, (3) government/military, and (4) academia. These communities have subtly different objectives and thus different requirements for practitioners in their area.

Digital Evidence Life Cycle

Similar to other forms of evidence, digital evidence has a life cycle. The digital evidence life cycle parallels the flow from data to information to knowledge. Digital evidence begins its life cycle in the domain of data. Once the data have been located, the context of the investigation as well as the content of the data moves it into the domain of information. This information is then used to make decisions, test hypotheses, or legal theories and to provide opinions—the knowledge realm.

The National Institute for Standards and Technology (NIST) in the United States has developed a diagram that illustrates the progression of the digital evidence life cycle in the context of the Digital Evidence Process Model (**Figure 2**).

Digital Evidence Process Model

The digital forensics process model consists of five phases: identification, collection/acquisition, transportation, analysis/ examination, and report.

Identification

Prior to any collection, the evidence or potential evidence must first be identified. Unlike with physical evidence, digital evidence is latent. One cannot see bits and bytes or data flowing through the airways via wireless transmissions. Humans are dependent on technology to assist in abstracting and

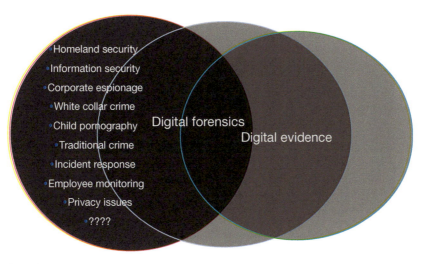

Figure 1 Context of digital evidence.

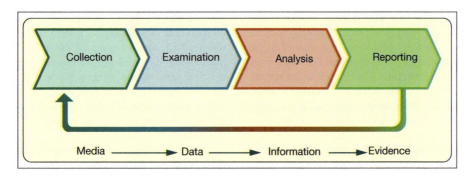

Figure 2 National Institute for Standards and Technology model.

representing the data in a way that is human readable (e.g., computer monitor displaying the data, directory trees listing files on a hard drive). This latent characteristic of digital evidence makes it difficult to identify and requires that investigators take a very methodical approach.

Investigators commonly look for well-established "containers" of data. These include hard drives, thumb drives, digital versatile discs (DVDs), mobile phones, external USB drives, laptops, etc. Unfortunately, due to the rapid changes in technology, unconventional containers must also be searched for. These can include digital video recorders, MP3 players, and even Internet-connected televisions.

Another factor that complicates the identification phase is that containers of data can have very small form factors such as USB thumb drives or SD memory cards. These devices can be as small as a quarter or a person's thumbnail and still hold gigabytes of data. These small devices are easily hidden by someone and are easily destroyed by breaking the connector or the device in half.

Similar to the steps for collecting physical evidence, the entire identification process must be well documented and recorded. The basic foundation for a chain of custody must be established at this phase and maintained throughout the entire process. It is preferable to use a digital video camera and record the crime scene.

Collection/Acquisition

Once digital evidence and/or the containers that contain the data are identified, the data must be acquired in a manner that is consistent with the precepts of the chain of custody and ensure that the evidence will be admissible in a legal proceeding. This usually entails taking steps to ensure that the data are not modified or altered and if changes must be made, to thoroughly document what has been changed. In this phase, there are actually two major considerations: is the device/system still powered on and will remain so—live system or is the device/system powered off and/or could be powered off—dead system or autopsy approach. Devices/systems that are powered off or can be powered off without disrupting the integrity of the evidence are the easiest to deal with. An example would be a computer system such as laptop or workstation that is powered off.

The standard procedure for powered off systems is to remove the storage device using a write blocker (preferably a physical or hardware write blocker) and create an electronic copy of the drive or device. This electronic copy is referred to as a forensic copy or forensic bitstream image. There are two types of images that can be made, physical copy or a logical copy. A physical copy contains all the data on the storage device, from the very first sector to the last sector. A logical copy only captures the data in the defined volume or partition on the device/hard drive (e.g., the "C" drive on a windows system). If possible, a physical copy is preferable, as it captures all the data and helps to place evidence in the correct context.

The approach for collecting evidence from a live system is more complicated than the autopsy approach. One of the fundamental concepts in forensics is to avoid altering the crime scene or at least keeping any disturbances or changes to a minimum. With live systems, it is necessary to execute some tool on the suspect system in order to make a copy of all the volatile data. Volatile data or evidence here refers to information that is lost when the electrical power is cut to the system. These volatile data can include contents in random access memory (RAM), process tables, connection logs, and network connections. In this situation, an investigator would use a piece of forensic software that is stored on an external device such as USB thumb drive, DVD, or some other externally connected disk. The external device contains all the necessary code to run the application without having to use any of the software resources on the suspect device other than the RAM. Here is where potential problems can occur. When the forensic software is executed, it will use a portion of the RAM on the suspect system, and this will push out or replace whatever data were in the area of the RAM that is now being used by the forensic software. The digital crime scene has now been altered, albeit in a minimal manner. However, despite altering the evidence, the courts have allowed this procedure, as it is the only viable method available at this time. Of course, extensive documentation of the process and how it may have impacted the suspect system is required. The forensic software run on the suspect system will collect an image of the RAM, running processes, and other such volatile data.

While the current trend is to have investigators to create an image (block device image) of a physical device, there are certain circumstances where a physical-to-physical device acquisition is preferable. To elaborate, in the case of physical-to-physical device acquisitions, there is a direct one-to-one relationship. In these instances, there are advantages and disadvantages. With a physical-to-physical copy, the drive that the image will be copied to must be at least the same storage capacity or larger. For every drive/device that is being copied, there will be a corresponding physical drive for the copy to be stored on. Drive-to-drive copies have the advantage of being very fast, and it is straightforward to determine whether it is an exact copy or not. The determination that the copy is an exact or valid copy is done using hash functions. Hash functions allow one to take an arbitrary-sized data input and produced a fixed sized output, a hash total of the data in our case. In the case of MD5, the output is a hash function represented by 128 bits (**Figure 3**). The hash function is very sensitive to bit-wise changes. This means that if any bit of the data is changed, the resultant 128-bit hash total is completely different.

The use of hash functions to ensure integrity and validity of the forensic copies is not practical with live systems. Since the system is powered on and running, numerous changes and updates are occurring during the imaging process. If the desired image is a physical copy, then using hash functions is useless, as the state of system when the original hash total is calculated will be different by the time the forensic copy is made. If a logical image is being acquired on a nonactive volume (not the partition or volume that system was booted from), then using a hash total to compare the image to original is fine, nothing will have changed on the nonactive partition during the time span of the imaging process. If an image is being acquired that included the boot volume on a live system then it is the same situation as with the physical, the state of the system will be changing during the process, making a hash total comparison meaningless.

The common practice is to compute the hashes before the drive is imaged and then calculate the hash of the image and compare the outputs. If the hash totals match, this is sufficient for the copy to be considered an exact duplicate of the original drive. In some jurisdictions, the forensic image or copy qualifies as "best evidence," and it can be stipulated that the original is no longer required. This is more common in large organizations that may wish to wipe the drive and repurpose it back into operations.

A second copy of the original can be made. The forensic image is copied, and the subsequent computed hash total of this copy is calculated and compared to the total of the forensic image. If they match, then the second copy is considered an exact copy of the original as well. This process can be used to prepare numerous copies of the original if required, without touching the original again.

The original drive or device can be placed in secure storage or as mentioned, wiped, and repurposed. The first copy is

---

MD5 (Evidence.rtf) = d0221be1afb9af6dc1bd6e41243ce658

Figure 3   MD5 hash.

deemed the library copy and is used to make further copies if required. The second copy is the working copy and is used in the subsequent stages of the process model.

It should be noted that the acquisition process as described could also include encrypting all the forensic images. Compressing the image(s) to save on storage space can also be conducted without impacting the integrity or validity of the images.

Transportation

Given the volatile and fragile nature of digital evidence, care must be taken to ensure that evidence is not altered or damaged during the stage of transporting from the scene to the laboratory or more secure environment. Digital evidence is very sensitive to changes in temperature, humidity, and any type of magnetic field, radiofrequency field, or static charge. The common practice is to place devices such as hard drives, thumb drives, and so on into antistatic bags and then place these into shock-resistant and water-resistant containers.

The storage of digital evidence can also be problematic, as evidence (e.g., last numbers dialed) on some devices such as mobile phones can be lost if the battery is depleted. Other storage devices such as DVDs must be protected from sunlight or other natural lighting, as this will degrade the compounds used to store the data. Magnetic-based storage hard drives start to decay the minute they are manufactured, so any long-term storage (>5 years) can result in areas of the drive demagnetizing, and the data stored in these areas become inaccessible.

Analysis and Examination

The next step in the process is to begin examining the data in order to determine what if anything is of evidentiary value. An analogy for this phase in the process is that of a funnel (**Figure 4**). Raw data are entered into the large end of the funnel. These data are filtered based on the context of the investigation. Data that are determined to be important (in

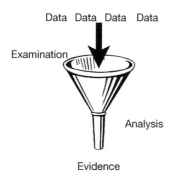

Figure 4 Examination and analysis.

order to either confirm a legal theory or negate another) become evidence. This evidence is further filtered and interpreted by the analyst until a decision or decisions are made, which are directly supported by the derived evidence.

The extremely large capacity of storage devices (e.g., hard drives) makes it impractical to examine all the data that are contained on the device. Therefore, an examination plan is required. The plan weighs the context and goals of the investigation. Context can refer to the type of the investigation (e.g., threatening e-mails, theft of IP, possession of contraband images). Understanding this context allows the investigator to develop a decision tree to guide the exploration of the data.

Digital Evidence Artifacts

Since the analysis of the data must be somewhat focused, certain artifacts are routinely examined during the course of the analysis phase. These artifacts include e-mails, Web browsing histories, chat and texting logs, deleted files, and time lines. Other secondary artifacts consist of documents, pictures, and spreadsheets.

The sheer volume of e-mails that are sent and received in any given day makes e-mail a target-rich item for investigators. E-mails contain various metadata items such as the IP address of the system sending the e-mail, the IP addresses of all the mail systems it passed through (as well as time stamps), and in some cases, the type of e-mail client used to create the message. These metadata are contained in the header portion of the e-mail that is human readable. However, e-mails can have the source address tampered with to make it look like it came from somewhere or someone else (this is referred to as "spoofing"), and the header information can be stripped out by anonymous remailers.

The use of graphical Web browsers such as Safari, Internet Explorer, and Mozilla has lead to the popularity of the Internet. Since Web browsing is such a common activity, a detailed history of what sites were visited and when what was downloaded from these sites and what terms were searched for in the common search engines are important sources of evidence. In many cases, the history of search terms (e.g., buying guns, cleaning a crime scene, chloroform) has been vital in the successful prosecution or exoneration of an accused person.

The explosion of social networking and the need to be in constant communication with one's friends and family have resulted in there being an increase in evidence related to texting, chatting, and other social media technologies. Most texting and chat programs have the ability to record a log of the conversation, and many providers for this media store the conversations on their servers. Depending on the case, these records of the communications can provide a link between the suspect and the victim, the suspect and the activity, or in the case of civil disputes and IP cases, the intent of the party in question. In several criminal cases, individuals have bragged about their crimes on their social network pages or texted their accomplices or friends to discuss the criminal activity.

Files and data that have been deleted or placed in the recycle or trash bin on the system are of special interest since these are items that in some cases, a person wants to hide or get rid of (i.e., delete). Modern operating systems (e.g., Windows 7, OS X Lion) and file systems (e.g., NTFS, HFS+) allow for files to be deleted or placed in the trash without actually removing the data from the system. These files still exist, but the location in the file system that they occupy is flagged as being available to store new data. Unless and until new data are written to these areas, the deleted files are recoverable.

As with physical investigations, reliable time lines are important in digital evidence analysis. A reliable reconstruction of events and cause–effect relationships can be the difference between a determination of guilt or innocence. Time lines allow for the examination of alibis and can place an individual at certain critical locations at a particular time (mobile phone evidence is often used for this purpose, as most phones log their positions relative to cell towers and wireless telecommunication companies store tower records). Unfortunately, developing a reliable and accurate chronology of events can be difficult with digital evidence. While most modern operating systems and file systems record the time a file was modified, accessed, or created/copied, these time stamps depend on the system's clock and the operating system clock. Users usually have access to their clock/time applications, which they can use to modify their system's time. This modification would alter the time stamps on files and impact their reliability. Even if the system's clock is not tampered with, computer systems do not have accurate clocks. Research has shown that over the course of a day, the system clock can drift anywhere from minutes to hours out of sync with the actual time.

Electronic documents, spreadsheets, and pictures in relation to digital evidence are for the most part identical to their physical counter parts. Most individuals store their documents, spreadsheets, and pictures within default locations as determined by their operating system and file system. Unlike physical copies of documents and spreadsheets, digital versions contain metadata such as version changes, comments, and authorship and time stamps such as creation and modification. An investigator could readily determine when the document in question was created or deleted and who created the original document and could see all the different versions of the document from when it was first created to when it was last modified.

With pictures, digital images can contain information about the type of camera that was used to take the picture and if the camera or device (e.g., mobile phone) has a GPS function, the exact geographical location where the picture was taken at (i.e., geopositioning).

Conclusion

Digital evidence investigation and analysis are a relatively new field/activity within the forensic sciences. As the field matures, it will develop a standardization of methods, tools, processes, and certifications as well as a common corpus of knowledge. In its present state, the most that can be said is that the five-step process of identification, collection, analysis, examination, and reporting mirrors the phases used in the other physics-based forensic sciences are compliant with basic crime scene investigation procedures.

Society's ongoing dependence on technology increases the importance of analyzing digital evidence. Today and into the foreseeable future, individuals live in two realities, the physical and the virtual or cyber. Hence, the need to effectively deal with evidence that is digital in nature is paramount, as this category of evidence surpasses the physical in terms of volume. This field is somewhat unique, as it deals with a human-made science (computers and technology) and not a natural science (e.g., biology and chemistry) as the other forensic sciences do. Technology is constantly changing; therefore, tools, techniques, and processes that worked yesterday may not work tomorrow.

The legal justice system is also less comfortable in dealing with digital evidence than it is in dealing with more traditional scientific evidence (e.g., physical, biological, and chemical). To some, the Internet and technology are still rather magical, and therefore, evidence derived from this media is either believed at face value or classified as being suspect and incomprehensible. As the current judiciary ages out and is replaced with a newer generation, this uncertainty and fear will naturally be reduced.

Digital evidence analysis, while representing a different mode of evidence than the physical, still must be held to the same scientific and legal standards as the other forensic sciences.

> See also: **Digital Evidence:** Child Pornography; **Digital Evidence/Photography and Digital Imaging:** Digital Imaging and Photography: An Overview; **Foundations:** Principles of Forensic Science; **Investigations:** Collection and Chain of Evidence.

Further Reading

ASCLD/LAB, 2005. Laboratory Accreditation Manual.
Carrier, B., Spafford, E.H., 2003. Getting physical with the digital forensic process. International Journal of Digital Evidence 2 (2), 1–19.

Casey, E., 2000. Digital Evidence and Computer Crime. Academic Press, New York.

Ciardhuáin, S.Ó., 2004. An extended model of cybercrime investigations. International Journal 3, 1–22.

Digital Evidence: Its True Value, 2009. Tech Beat (Vol. Winter 2009). National Law Enforcement and Corrections Technology Center.

Garfinkel, S.L., 2010. Digital forensics research: the next 10 years. Digital Investigation 7, S64–S73. http://dx.doi.org/10.1016/j.diin.2010.05.009.

ISO/IEC, 2005. General Requirements for the Competence of Testing and Calibration Laboratories. Switzerland.

Jones, K., Bejtlich, R., Rose, C., 2005. Real Digital Forensics: Computer Security and Incident Response. Addison Wesley, New York.

Kanellis, P., Kiountouzis, E., Kolokotrinics, N., Martakos, D., 2006. Digital Crime and Forensic Science in Cyberspace. Idea Group Publishing, London.

Kent, K., Chevalier, S., Grance, T., Dang, H., 2006. Guide to Integrating Forensic Techniques into Incident Response. NIST NIST Special Publications, Gaithersburg, MD.

Meyers, M., Rogers, M., 2004. Computer forensics: the need for standardization and certification. International Journal of Digital Evidence 3, 1–11.

Palmer, G., 2001. In: Report, D.T. (Ed.), A Road Map for Digital Forensic Research. Digital Forensic Research Workshop, Utica, New York.

Rogers, M., 2004. The future of computer forensics: a needs analysis survey. Computers and Security 23, 12–16. http://dx.doi.org/10.1016/j. cose.2004.01.003.

Rogers, M., Mislan, R., Goldman, J., Wedge, T., Debrota, S., 2006. Computer forensics field triage process model. Journal of Digital Forensics, Security, and Law 1 (2), 27–40.

SWGDE, 2011. SWGDE and SWGIT Glossary of Terms. Retrieved from. http://www.swgde.org/documents/current-documents/SWGDE-SWGIT%20Glossary%20v2%204.pdf.

Relevant Websites

http://www.cybercrime.gov/—Computer Crime and Intellectual Property Section.
http://www.DCFB.org—Digital Forensics Certification Board.
http://www.forensicswiki.org—Digital Forensics Wiki.
http://www.ioce.org/—International Organization on Digital Evidence.
http://www.cftt.nist.gov/—NIST Cyber Forensics Tool Testing Project.
http://www.swgde.org—Scientific Working Group for Digital Evidence.

Key Terms

Analog tape authentication, Android, Audio enhancement, Audio forensics, Best practices, BlackBerry, Cell phones, Computer forensics, Cyber forensics, Digital audio, Digital audio authentication, Digital evidence, Digital forensic sciences, Digital forensics, Digital image, Digital image authentication, Digital image enhancement, Digital photo, Digital photo authentication, Digital photo enhancement, Digital photo imaging, Digital video, Digital video authentication, Digital video enhancement, E-discovery, Electronically stored information, Forensic, Forensic audio, iOS, iPhone, ISO, Lossless, Lossy, Mobile devices, Mobile phone forensics hierarchy, Mobile phones, Multimedia evidence, Official images of a crime scene, Photo imaging, Photography, Point-and-shoot cameras, Recorded evidence, SIM cards, Single-lens reflex (SLR), Smartphones, Steganography, SWGIT, Symbian, Windows mobile.

Review Questions

1. When were the first images used to reconstruct crimes? Who were the first photographers at crime scenes?
2. What is the difference between a photograph and an image?
3. What is ISO in relation to photography?
4. Why is it necessary to still understand film in a digital world?
5. What does "SLR" stand for?
6. Why is there more probative information per byte examined on a cell phone than on a typical computer?
7. What are the three basic technologies used to allow users on mobile phone networks?
8. What is the GSM?
9. What is VOIP?
10. What is an ESN? Why is it important?
11. List the five steps in cell phone forensic analysis. Briefly describe each.
12. Why should cell phones be put in airplane mode when seized?
13. What does it mean to authenticate a digital image?
14. List five types of digital image enhancement.
15. What is frame averaging? How does it work?
16. What is photo-response nonuniformity?
17. What does it mean that most forensic audio recordings are made in "nonideal environments"?
18. What is lossy compression?
19. What is a band-pass filter?
20. What is the "digital evidence life cycle"?

Discussion Questions

1. Review Jones' example of a circle viewed at 10° tilt. How does the expert answer the question, "Does this picture, taken by your, truly and accurately depict the scene on the data and time in question?"
2. What is a "smart phone"? Why is that a difficult term to define?
3. Why is a perfectly counterfeited image very difficult or even impossible to produce?
4. Why would it be necessary to understand analog audio recordings in a digital age? When would they ever be encountered?
5. Do some internet research on Dennis Rader, the "BTK Killer." How was he caught? What does the "vintage" of the technology involved say about the nature of digital evidence? List five types of digital evidence currently available that you may not encounter in 10 years' time.

Additional Readings

Anwar, N., Riadi, I., Luthfi, A., 2016. Forensic SIM card cloning using authentication algorithm. International Journal of Electronics and Information Engineering 4 (2), 71–81.

Kamenicky, J., Bartos, M., Flusser, J., Mahdian, B., Kotera, J., Novozamsky, A., Saic, S., Sroubek, F., Sorel, M., Zita, A., Zitova, B., 2016. PIZZARO: forensic analysis and restoration of image and video data. Forensic Science International 264, 153–166.

Nikkel, B., 2016. Practical Forensic Imaging: Securing Digital Evidence with Linux Tools. No Starch Press.

Samy, G.N., Shanmugam, B., Maarop, N., Magalingam, P., Perumal, S., Albakri, S.H., April 2017. Digital forensic challenges in the cloud computing environment. In: International Conference of Reliable Information and Communication Technology. Springer, Cham, pp. 669–676.

Taimori, A., Razzazi, F., Behrad, A., Ahmadi, A., Babaie-Zadeh, M., 2017. A novel forensic image analysis tool for discovering double JPEG compression clues. Multimedia Tools and Applications 76 (6), 7749–7783.

Wang, A., December 28, 2016. Can Alexa Help Save a Murder? Police Think so—But Amazon Won't Give Up Her Data. Washington Post, Online at: https://www.washingtonpost.com/news/the-switch/wp/2016/12/28/can-alexa-help-solve-a-murder-police-think-so-but-amazon-wont-give-up-her-data/?utm_term=.899f3fadb721.

Watt, A., 2017. The challenges of interpreting digital evidence in the courtroom. Precedent (Sydney, NSW) (139) 43.

Section 3. Transportation

Data are collected everywhere, even in cars. Even the most basic new car model has *at least 30* computers on board, controlling dozens of functions, from cruise control to door locks. Starting in 1977 with a single computer that controlled spark plug timing, today's modern vehicles are more akin to a box of computers on four wheels. Cables and mechanical connections were long ago replaced by "throttle-by-wire" technology,

a series of sensors and controllers that make the car work and respond. Those who claim that people should be able to fix their own cars have not looked under the hood lately.

Other forms of transportation are also heavily computerized, from onboard computers to those systems that coordinate travel and safety. Modern global travel would not be possible without computerized systems and digital information.

Aircraft Flight Data Recorders

VL Grose, US National Transportation Safety Board, Washington, DC, USA

Glossary

Adversary truth Pursuit of truth in the law involving a process of confrontation between opposing parties, which eliminates voluntary disclosure of uncertainties, must be certain, must be known firsthand, and excludes hearsay, rumors, and guesses.

Air Line Pilots Association International (ALPA) Representing more than 53 000 pilots at 37 US and Canadian airlines, it is chartered by the AFL-CIO and the Canadian Labour Congress and is a member of the International Federation of Air Line Pilot Associations.

Analog information Continuous phenomena with no quantized or discrete variances whose recorded result is subject to interpretation as to meaning and significance.

Bureaud'Enquêtesetd'Analysespourla sécurité de l'aviationcivile (BEA) The French authority responsible for safety investigations into accidents or incidents in civil aviation.

Coalition of Airline Pilots Associations (CAPA) A trade association comprised of over 28 000 professional pilots in five individual member unions.

Cockpit voice recorder (CVR) An electronic device used to record conversation in the cockpit, radio communications between the cockpit crew and others (including conversation with air traffic control personnel), as well as ambient sounds.

Collision Safety Institute (CSI) An independent traffic collision research, training, and crash consulting organization with a mission to provide state-of-the-art training and technology transfer to both public and private entities involved in the analysis and evaluation of motor vehicle collisions.

Digital information Discrete values of quantized time, frequency, and amplitude that are not subject to interpretation as to content.

Event data recorder (EDR) An electronic device used to record information related to vehicle (automobile, truck, locomotive) performance that can be retrieved and analyzed following an accident.

Federal Aviation Administration (FAA) The national aviation authority of the United States. An agency of the Department of Transportation, it has authority to regulate and oversee all aspects of civil aviation.

Flight data acquisition unit (FDAU) A junction box that receives various discrete, analog, and digital parameters from a number of sensors and avionic systems, then routes them to a flight data recorder.

Flight data recorder (FDR) An electronic device used to record hundreds of specific aircraft flight performance parameters, including control and actuator positions, engine information—all on a time basis.

National Transportation Safety Board (NTSB) An independent US federal agency charged with determining the probable cause of transportation accidents, promoting transportation safety, and assisting victims of transportation accidents and their families. It has five Board Members, each nominated by the President and confirmed by the Senate to serve 5-year terms.
Probable cause Conclusions reached by an investigating body as to the factor or factors that caused an accident.
Proximate cause An event directly related to a loss and legally held to be its cause.

Technical truth Pursuit of truth in scientific work that includes not only what is known but also open admission of uncertainties, assumptions, suppositions, and hunches—all of which are probabilistic; that is, never certain and always subject to reversal should new findings disprove them.
Underwater locator beacon (ULB) A device fitted to both CVRs and flight data recorders that, when triggered by water immersion down to depths of 14 000 ft, emits an ultrasonic pulse of 37.5 kHz at once per second.

Introduction

Commercial aircraft crashes arouse wide public interest for several reasons. They generally involve massive, unexpected death and destruction. The flying public easily correlates an airliner crash with its own perceived risk beyond any possible personal control. Even though the probability of a crash per flight is one in every 19 000 years, it is one of the six most feared causes of death. So such disasters appear mysterious—but demand a raison d'etre. Aircraft flight data recorders (FDRs) help to answer that demand.

Pursuit of Truth

Airliner crashes and criminal acts both provoke public concern for their avoidance—focused on what needs to be eliminated or corrected. Crash-free airliners and crime-free society are admirable goals but never likely to be fully achieved.

Approaches to perfection for both goals are similar but not identical. Truth in airliner technology involves traditional scientific freedom to look anywhere at any time under unrestricted rules. In contrast, truth sought under rules of criminal law is bound by restrictions as to its relevance. These two types of truth may lead to contrasting use of recorders.

Adversary versus Technical Truth

Adversary truth pursued in the law involves a process of confrontation between opposing parties. That eliminates the voluntary disclosure of uncertainties. To be admissible in court, information must be certain and known firsthand. Hearsay, rumors, and guesses are not allowed.

Technical truth sought in scientific work includes not only what is known but also open admission of all uncertainties. So assumptions, suppositions, and hunches have a large role in

science. In contrast to public perception, science is probabilistic—never certain and always subject to reversal and should new findings disprove it. **Figure 1** illustrates these two types of truth.

These two truths are not competitive because they have different truth objectives. However, digital recordings may play contrasting societal roles in providing information. Law enforcement's use of recorded automobile data (e.g., velocity and location) does not enjoy the same public endorsement that recorded aircraft data used in postcrash analysis does.

Immediately after an airliner catastrophe, the public expects someone to determine not only what happened but also why it happened. In the United States, the National Transportation Safety Board (hereinafter NTSB) pursues both.

That process consists of nine steps:

- On-scene fact finding
- Collection of physical evidence

Two truths	
Vernon L. Grose, DSc	
Adversary truth	Technical truth
Only what has been elicited as *known*	What is *known* plus full disclosure of all *uncertainties*
Fault-finding, blame assessment	Accident-preventing
Protection of deficiencies	Openness to deficiencies
Reaction to events	Foreseeability
Post-facto review	"A priori" projection
Involuntary, screened data	Voluntary exposure
First-hand facts	Hunches, possibilities

Figure 1   Two truths.

- Interrogation of witnesses
- Conduct of public hearings for sworn expert testimony
- Analysis of all obtained evidence (including FDR readouts)
- Formulation of conclusions
- Determination of causation
- Creation of recommendations to preclude a similar accident
- Summary and publication of the determinative process

This evidentiary pursuit can often require a year. All nine steps revolve around history—dealing with what has already been transpired but was unplanned and unforeseen. Most require human judgment that is subjective rather than objective.

Compounding that search is the likely disintegration of the aircraft and its contents because of their velocity at impact and release of onboard energy sources, which frequently results in wide distribution of wreckage.

What is being sought? Accurate knowledge of something that can never be fully replicated. That airliner crash knowledge deficiency likewise exists in criminal situations that forensic sciences attempt to solve. Therefore, pursuit of what, how, and why of airliner crashes—utilizing FDR data—is explored for its application to forensic sciences.

Desired Knowledge

Knowledge about past events—regardless of nature—is always limited. Airline disasters suffer this limitation in several ways.

First, a limit exists because there are seldom any surviving on-scene witnesses. So knowledge can only be inferred by deduction.

Second, even if witnesses survive, humans are not accurate observers. They have limited sensory capacity at best. Eyewitnesses of any accident are rarely unanimous in recalling what happened.

Third, human recollection of major disasters often atrophies over time as testimonies disagree. Therefore, individual witness memory is quite unreliable.

Fourth, there can be motivational conflict in obtaining truth of what has transpired. On one hand, desire for revenge, emotional resolution, justice, future prevention, or historical accuracy stimulates intensity to pursue such knowledge. But on the other hand, witnesses of tragedies often desire to suppress or purge painful recollection of them.

Despite these limitations, postevent knowledge is essential to understanding how both airline crashes and major criminal acts occur.

Seeking Causation

A force for obtaining knowledge of past events is the belief that they were caused. This emanates from the philosophical concept of causality—where one event is believed to produce a responding subsequent event. An airliner crash thereby becomes an outcome of an initial cause or causes that enabled the disaster to occur.

Single versus Multiple Causes

Seldom are catastrophes due to a singular cause. The NTSB, initially part of the Department of Transportation (DOT), was separated in 1974 from DOT by Congress as an independent agency and charged with determining the probable cause(s) of aircraft accidents. However, for many years thereafter, controversy and political pressure within the NTSB forced it to promote singularity of causation.

On one hand, advocates of adversary truth favored a sharp, singular focus on defining fault that would facilitate legal action following a crash. Underlying this position was blame assessment but thereby subordinating loss prevention (the prime NTSB objective).

On the other hand, proponents of technical truth insisted that causality is never singular. Being forced to discard the known causes (or list them only as contributory to a single cause in order to select only one) needlessly fragmented the causality search.

Testimony before the US Senate on October 22, 1985 resolved this controversy in favor of the scientific position that retains pursuit of causation plurality and assures focus on maximizing safety.

Approximate versus Proximate Cause

There are two types of causation in the law: cause-in-fact and proximate or legal cause. Cause-in-fact says, "But for this, the accident would not have occurred…" while proximate cause is an event directly related to a loss and held to be its cause.

Given that aircraft crashes have several causes, the purpose of seeking causation is to (1) define, (2) isolate, and (3) remove or control all factors believed to have contributed to the crash.

The US Air Commerce Act uses "probable cause" to define aircraft accident causation. This term stops short of "proximate cause" to remove any stigma of blameworthiness. This distinction allows investigators to freely discuss anything related to an accident without fear of legal action.

This contrast between proximate and probable cause may likely affect digital recording in forensic science. Beyond that distinction, two contrasting—negative and positive—concepts regarding accident causation in **Figure 2** may also influence forensic data recording.

First, the public believes that most airliner crashes somehow occur in spite of all countermeasures incorporated to prevent them—much like a snake mysteriously slithering with diabolical intent through a maze of preventive measures.

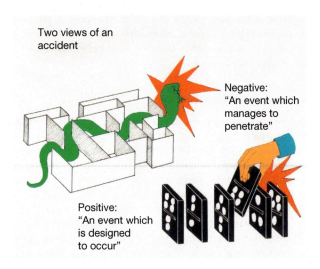

Two views of an accident

Negative:
"An event which manages to penetrate"

Positive:
"An event which is designed to occur"

Figure 2 Contrasting views of causation.

A second view—proposed by Dr. Nestor B. Kowalsky—is that an aircraft crash is a positive, successful event—inevitable when preceded by a series of committed or omitted acts. It is created by decisions. Thereby, FDRs identify some of the dominoes to be eliminated to preclude future crashes.

Role of Evidence in Establishing Truth

Knowledge of truth about the past—whether pursued by adversary or technical means—ultimately becomes classified as evidence. It has different meanings in the law (adversary truth) and in airliner crash investigation (technical truth).

Evidence produced by FDRs is generally objective (free from human manipulation) and can be interpreted by experts in science, engineering, psychology, sociology, management, and operations.

Digital versus Analog Evidence

The FDR evidence is either digital or analog. Digital information consists of discrete values of quantized time, frequency, and amplitude. Those signals are not subject to interpretation as to content (although there may be interpretive disagreement regarding raw data conversion into engineering units). Analog information consists of continuous phenomena with no quantized or discrete variances. Its recorded output is therefore subject to interpretation as to meaning and significance.

Multiengine, turbine-powered aircraft carrying over ten passengers must have an FDR. A cockpit voice recorder (CVR) is required for multiengine aircraft with two pilots, which carry over six passengers. FDR inputs are digital, while CVR inputs

are analog. When both recorders are recovered and their outputs can be correlated on a common time line, unique evidence of what has transpired is available.

Validity of FDR digital data—being virtually free of interpretation—is universal, giving it objectivity over CVR analog evidence. CVRs record more than cockpit conversation. All audio data in the cockpit, including switch clicks, wind noise, control equipment operation, and ambient acoustics such as engine pitch, are available. However, translating, interpreting, analyzing, and affirming recorded conversation require excellent linguistic and cultural skills.

Aircraft FDR History

The genesis of FDRs was a series of mysterious crashes in 1953 of the world's first jet airliner—the British "Comet." The Comet revolutionized commercial flight in altitude, speed, quietness, and freedom from vibration—until several of them crashed inexplicably.

Cause of Comet disasters was not soon determined. Dr. David Warren (1925–2010), a principal research scientist for the Aeronautical Research Laboratories in Melbourne, Australia, was engaged to investigate the crashes.

Dr. Warren early proposed recording flight crew voices in the cockpit. Initially, his idea raised little interest. He built an experimental device to store 4 hours of speech and flight instrument readings. He then published a report "A Device for Assisting Investigation into Aircraft Accidents." But it took 5 years for the device to be accepted.

Warren's first recorder was produced in 1958. It was about the size of an adult hand but was rejected by Australian aviation experts who said it had "little immediate direct use in civil aircraft." Pilots joined opposition by calling it "a spy flying alongside." Warren then took it to England where their aviation experts endorsed it—urging its installation in all British civil aircraft.

Before long, aircraft flight recorders were adopted—for both cockpit sounds and aircraft performance—by 1964, the US Federal Aviation Administration (hereinafter FAA) mandated them in commercial aircraft.

"Black Boxes"

News media early began to call FDRs "black boxes." This designator may be traced to its use in technology as "a device, system, or object viewed solely for its input, output, and transfer characteristics without concern about its internal workings." In that sense, how black boxes function may be unknown—even unnecessary to be understood but only to be useful—and thereby opaque or black.

However, FDRs are never black in color. In stark contrast, they are painted International Orange or Yellow (per US

Federal Standard 595) to increase their visibility for recovery from amidst wreckage.

CVR Hostility

From the beginning, pilots opposed recorders in a cockpit based on their reduction of the pilot's personal privacy.

No other profession endures the surveillance, oversight, and potential for second guessing—particularly after death—that CVRs represent. Voice recordings cannot fully provide rationale for past human behavior, especially under stressful circumstances. CVRs personify George Orwell's "1984" Big Brother syndrome to pilots.

On the other hand, airline passengers totally surrender their lives to pilots when the door closes, and the aircraft departs the terminal. This unusual transfer of life-and-death responsibility to someone unknown seems to justify unusual accountability and oversight.

Beyond this pilot–passenger trust relationship is the larger issue of maintaining airline safety. Obtaining recorded cockpit audio following a fatal crash enhances prevention of future disasters—invaluable in advancing flight safety.

Thus, tension between pilot freedom and airline passenger dependence on the pilot is likely to continue.

Evolution of Recording Processes

Flight recording technology has progressed in parallel with commercial aircraft development. The first generation of recorders—installed in early jet airliners such as B-707, DC-8, and Caravelle—recorded five analog aircraft parameters (heading, altitude, airspeed, vertical accelerations, and time).

To survive high impact velocity and sustained postimpact fire, the readouts of five parameters were embossed onto a metal foil (Incanol Steel) used only once (i.e., not recorded on a repeatable loop). Although the recording foil was nearly indestructible, crash survival of these recorders was a serious problem. By 1965, the original 100 g (100 times the accelerative force of impact by simply being dropped) requirement was upgraded to 1000 g.

A second FDR generation emerged after aircraft performance data proved insufficient for determining accident causation. Magnetic tape technology (recording data in digital format) was adopted for FDRs, replacing metal foil. These upgraded FDRs covered additional parameters such as engines, flight controls, and flaps. Use of magnetic tape, however, required even more complex fire and crash protection. This second class of FDRs was installed in B-747, DC-10, L-1011, and A300 wide-body aircraft during the late 1960s and early 1970s.

Based on Dr. David Warren's earlier work, advanced audio recording technology enabled capture of a wider range of cockpit sounds, including crew conversation, air traffic control communications, and aircraft noises. By 1965, all US commercial airlines carrying over 20 passengers had a CVR retaining the latest 30 min of cockpit sounds.

A third generation of solid-state recorders was available by 1990. These recorders store data in semiconductor memories or integrated circuits—replacing electromechanical techniques. One of its advantages is that such memory does not require scheduled maintenance or overhaul. At present, solid-state recorders provide vastly expanded data while also saving airline operational costs when the aircraft is in service. Stored flight data in these recorders can be readily evaluated for aircraft flight performance or whether a device requires maintenance.

Adaptation of solid-state recorders for the CVR occurred later than for the FDR—primarily because more memory capacity was required for audio data. In 1992, a 30-min CVR became available. By 1995, a 2-h CVR was introduced.

Most current FDRs receive inputs via specific data frames from a flight data acquisition unit (FDAU) that records many flight parameters—including control and actuator positions, engine information, and time of day. A minimum of 88 parameters are currently required (only 29 were required until 2002), but some systems today monitor even thousands of variables. Most parameters are recorded a few times per second, but some data are stored at a much higher frequency. FDRs record a minimum time frame of 25 h of data in a continuous loop.

Recorder Survivability

Two simultaneous and violent forces are unleashed on recorders when an aircraft crashes—high impact velocity and sustained high-temperature fire. As technically sophisticated as a recorder may be, it is useless unless it survives those forces generated by the very event it is designed to record. Therefore, recorder survival is fundamental.

First, if the aircraft is integral when impacting the ground, recorders must survive not only that initial blow but also a possible secondary impact if they are launched by explosion of jet fuel. Early recorders were installed in the forward avionics bay of the aircraft and required to survive a 100 g impact. After several crashes, recorders failed to survive. At present, the acceleration requirement has been raised from 100 g to the current 3400 g for 6.5 ms.

The second survival factor for recorders is fire generated by Jet A or Jet A-1 fuel with open air burning temperatures of 1000 °C. This fuel can ignite other aircraft materials surrounding the recorders, resulting in even higher ambient temperatures. Damage by fire is dependent on not only temperature but also time at temperature. So, at present, recorders must survive 1100 °C for 1 h.

Additional recorder requirements exist for penetration resistance, static crush, deep-sea pressure, sea water immersion, and fluid immersion.

Installed Location of FDRs

After increasing recorder impact requirement to 1000 g, the FAA also required relocation of both CVR and FDR recorders to the rear of the aircraft where survival was believed to be higher. **Figure 3** shows the position of both recorders and their recording pickup instrumentation.

Relocation rationale was that most crashes occur while the aircraft is moving forward and considerable energy is absorbed before the tail impacts the ground. Further, as the aircraft breaks apart, the tail is often separated from remaining wreckage and fuel sources in the wings. Of course, this reasoning does not apply when the aircraft disintegrates in the air before hitting ground or water, for example, following an airborne explosion.

Underwater Locator Beacons

Both CVR and FDR have an underwater locator beacon (ULB) to assist in locating them following an overwater airliner crash. The ULB—called a "pinger"—is activated once it is immersed in water. Therefore, it never emits a signal following crashes on land. The pinger transmits a 37.5-kHz acoustical signal detected only with a special receiver. It can transmit from depths down to 14 000 ft.

Recorder manufacturers install pingers as part of their individual recorder models. The airline owning and installing

a recorder is required to replace its pinger batteries to keep them operational. Required pinger life is 6 years.

Government Regulation

The Air Line Pilots Association International (ALPA), founded in 1931, currently represents 59 000 pilots of 39 US and Canadian airlines. The ALPA was an early and vocal opponent of the CVR.

An initial ALPA-NTSB compromise stipulated (1) 30-min duration of retained recorded information, (2) flight crew erasure of recording once on the ground, and (3) disclosure of recorded information only for accident investigation. CVR acceptance by airline pilots is thereby viewed as a reasonable, needed component of aircraft crash investigation.

However, political pressure occasionally arises to expand CVR use beyond accident investigation to disciplinary enforcement of pilot behavior that violates the "sterile cockpit" rule. That rule prohibits, below 10 000 ft, any cockpit conversation not directly related to flight operation.

The source of such pressure is generally public reaction—stimulated by dramatic news media coverage—to obtained CVR recordings that reveal bizarre or irrelevant chatter or behavior in the cockpit.

In February 2010, the US Senate Pilot Professionalism Act (S.3048) was introduced "to improve air safety by authorizing the limited use by air carriers of information collected through

Figure 3 Flight data recording and storage.

CVRs and FDRs, to prohibit tampering with such devices, and for other purposes."

Both the ALPA and the Coalition of Airline Pilots Associations (CAPA) representing over 28 000 pilots objected seriously to this bill because it could allow airlines to administer discipline—even terminate or require a pilot to pass a proficiency check in a simulator—based on CVR and FDR findings.

Ultimately, S.3048 was not adopted.

Public Access to Voice Recordings

Interest in listening to final minutes of a fatal aircraft crash occasionally arises. On some occasions, families of deceased pilots have demanded to listen to those final moments of life. News media also seek recordings to satisfy public interest after crashes. Increasing electronic capability and exposure via the Internet have made recordings available—although a large percentage of alleged recordings are created artificially.

Historically, the NTSB has exercised tight discipline in permitting cockpit voice recordings to be heard only by parties engaged in translating and converting conversation to written format. The recorders are the property of the involved airline. Once a transcription of the CVR has been officially documented, the recorder is released back to its airline owner who is responsible for whatever public access is subsequently obtained.

The US Congress has imposed reasonable restrictions on the use of CVR materials. It exempts CVR data from Freedom of Information Act requests. In the Transportation Safety Act, Congress limited public disclosure of CVR data involving aircraft crash investigations. However, that Act allows the NTSB to publicize any transcript segment believed relevant to a crash—provided it holds a public hearing or if it is discussed along with other factual reports at the same time. The Board is also allowed to refer to CVR recordings in its safety recommendations.

A court may allow discovery of a CVR recording or transcript without prior public release of the information. If the CVR transcript is publicly released, the transcript becomes discoverable. Each CVR audio transcription released to the public by the NTSB carries the warning shown in **Figure 4**.

The Bureau d'Enquetes et d'Analyses (hereinafter BEA) is the French equivalent to NTSB. Citing Article 14 of the European Regulation of 20 October 2010 as its policy standard governing public release of CVR transcripts, it came into effect on December 2, 2010 following the crash of Air France Flight 447.

Current Recorder State of the Art

Recorder technology continues to expand. At periodic intervals, the FAA upgrades performance requirements as shown in **Figure 5**. These revisions result from technological, operational, and financial forces that demand increasing knowledge of truth about the past to advance airline safety.

NTSB warning on cockpit recording transcription

- The reader of this report is cautioned that the transcription of a CVR tape is not a precise science but is the best product possible from an NTSB group investigative effort.

- The transcript, or parts thereof, if taken out of context, could be misleading.

- The attached CVR transcript should be viewed as an accident investigation tool to be used in conjunction with other evidence gathered during the investigation.

- Conclusions or interpretations should not be made using the transcript as the sole source of information

Figure 4   Cockpit voice recorder transcript protection.

Image Recorders

Superiority of visual and aural images over oral recordings to obtain knowledge of the past is undeniable. Therefore, video technology increases to be considered to augment CVR output. Cockpit video recorders are not yet required in commercial airliners, but they are installed in smaller aircraft and helicopters.

Cultural Repercussion of Recorders

Two airliner crashes are summarized to illustrate the significant role recorders have played in international, political, cultural, and business controversies, thereby highlighting the influence that recorders can contribute to ascertaining truth.

EgyptAir Flight 990

On October 31, 1999, the Boeing 767 en route from JFK airport in New York to Cairo crashed into the Atlantic Ocean about 60 miles south of Nantucket Island, Massachusetts, killing all 217 people on board. As the crash occurred in international waters, the Egyptian Civil Aviation Authority (ECAA) had investigation responsibility. But since ECAA lacked adequate technical resources, the Egyptian government asked the NTSB to conduct the investigation.

Within two weeks, NTSB proposed transferring the investigation to the US Federal Bureau of Investigation (FBI) since evidence suggested that (1) a criminal act had taken place and (3) the crash was intentional rather than accidental. The Egyptians rejected this proposal. So the NTSB continued to lead the investigation.

As evidence of the deliberate crash increased, the Egyptian government reversed itself, and the ECAA began its own investigation. The two investigations reached conflicting

FAA proposed revisions of aircraft recorders 24 February 2005	
Cockpit voice recorders (CVRs)	
Proposed	Current
Two hours recording time	15–30 min recording time; valuable communications can be taped over
No magnetic tape recorders	Magnetic tape OK; can sustain damage in crash
10-minute independent backup power supply	Recorder stops if aircraft electrical power fails
Standardized recording start: Begins when pilots start checklist	Variable requirements for recording start
Mounted in box separate from FDR (except helicopters)	Separate box is FAA policy but not a regulation
No single electrical failure can disable both CVR and FDR	Both CVR and FDR can stop working if aircraft electrical power fails
Flight data recorders (FDRs)	
Proposed	Current
Measurement of control surface (rudder, ailerons, elevators, etc.) movements every 0.0625 s	Measurements every 0.25 or 0.5 s; may not permit accurate reconstruction of movements in all circumstances
Measurement of pilot inputs on control wheel, control column, rudder pedals (airplanes aircraft) every 0.0625 s	Measurements every 1 s; may not permit accurate reconstruction of forces in all circumstances
Measurement of cockpit controls and flight control surfaces (helicopters) 4X per second	Measurements 2X per second; may not permit accurate reconstruction of movements in all circumstances
Mounted in box separate from CVR (except helicopters)	Separate box is FAA policy but not a regulation
No single electrical failure can disable both CVR and FDR	Both CVR and FDR can stop working if aircraft electrical power fails

Figure 5 Aircraft recorder updating.

conclusions. NTSB concluded that the cause was a deliberate action of the EgyptAir's relief first officer (RFO). ECAA found the cause to be the mechanical failure of the airplane's elevator control system.

Both CVR and FDR provided determinative evidence that (1) the RFO had committed suicide by deliberately diving the aircraft into the ocean and (2) no mechanical failure scenario could have produced the aircraft movements recorded by the FDR.

An international firestorm erupted. Egypt's state-owned *Al Ahram Al Misai* called RFO Al-Batouti a "martyr." The Islamist *Al Shaab* newspaper even accused US officials of secretly recovering the FDR, reprogramming it, and throwing it back into the water to be publicly recovered.

Given strong Egyptian cultural aversion to suicide, the possibility of a common NTSB–ECAA agreement on probable

cause evaporated. The NTSB probable cause, however, avoided discussing suicide.

> The airplane's departure from normal cruise flight and subsequent impact with the Atlantic Ocean was a result of the relief first officer's flight control inputs. The reason for the relief first officer's actions was not determined.

Air France Flight 447

On June 1, 2009, the Airbus A330-200 aircraft crashed in the Atlantic Ocean en route from Rio de Janeiro to Paris, killing 228 persons. After 30 months of investigation, BEA had not determined probable cause—as CVR and FDR were not recovered for 23 months. CVR and FDR unavailability allowed widespread and conflicting speculation—overshadowed by several factors seldom acknowledged publicly.

First, intensive worldwide competition in the commercial aircraft market between Airbus and Boeing meant that US markets were pitted against those in Europe—even free enterprise (Boeing) challenging government enterprise (Airbus).

Second, these two aircraft giants employ contrasting approaches to the pilot–aircraft interface. To summarize: Boeing designs aircraft control around the pilot as primary, augmented by automation while Airbus reverses those roles—automation prime, pilot as secondary. While the Airbus approach eases the piloting load, its automation is more complex and less intuitive.

Third, where Boeing has continued to use the traditional control yoke in front of the pilot, Airbus employs a control sidestick beside the pilot. Advocates for both approaches abound, but controversy remains—primarily because the "feel" or feedback to pilot varies considerably.

Air France announced 3 days after the crash that an onboard monitoring system had transmitted—before crashing—a 4-min series of electronic messages concerning failures and warnings in navigation, autoflight, flight controls, and cabin air-conditioning. These sketchy data—while insufficient for cause determination—ignited extensive but unresolved prognosis about both crew and aircraft performance that persisted for over 2 years.

On June 7, 2009, the AF447 vertical stabilizer was recovered (confirming crash location), so initial search for the recorders ensued. Three more independent recovery attempts occurred before May 2, 2011, when both CVR and FDR were found in about 13 000 ft of water. Amazingly, data on both recorders were recovered.

During the years since the crash, recorders have remained the prime focal point. Their recovery, however, failed to resolve its probable cause even after nearly 3 years likely because of two unique factors—the responsibility for investigation and anticipated legal culpability. In contrast to NTSB investigations in the United States, the French government opened two independent and simultaneous investigations of AF447.

Technical Investigation

BEA was charged with the investigation since the aircraft was of French registration and crashed over international waters. Representatives from Brazil, Germany, UK, and the United States were directly involved. In addition, observers were appointed from China, Croatia, Hungary, Ireland, Italy, Lebanon, Morocco, Norway, South Korea, Russia, South Africa, and Switzerland because their citizens were onboard.

Criminal Investigation

French law requires—for any accident involving loss of life (but implying no presumption of foul play)—that manslaughter be charged against Air France and Airbus. This investigation has been overseen by the Gendarmerie nationale, which conducted it through its aerial transportation division (Gendarmerie des transports aériens or GTA) and its forensic research institute (Institut de Recherche Criminelle de la Gendarmerie Nationale or FR).

Expanded Employment of Recorders

As data recorders gain acceptance, aviation is not the only transportation mode utilizing them. In 1993, the Federal Railroad Administration (FRA) required event data recorder (EDR) in locomotives.

An EDR is also being installed in automobiles to record vehicle information immediately before and/or during a serious crash. Police and crash investigators download EDR data to learn what happened to the vehicle and how its safety features are performed. In some cases, those data help establish culpability.

Most EDRs are built into a vehicle's airbag control module and record data on airbag deployment. Some vehicles also record precrash data, such as engine throttle and vehicle speed from the engine control module. Certain airbag and engine control modules store only diagnostic trouble codes and whether there was a signal to deploy supplemental restraint systems (i.e., airbags and belt tensioners).

Built-in vehicle modules are not considered to be an EDR. Therefore, they are not governed by federal regulations, as are EDRs that record vehicle speed before a crash or speed change during impact.

In summary, there is no way that David Warren could have foreseen how aircraft flight recorders would impact both civil and criminal litigation. They also affected economics of the expert witness field. The Collision Safety Institute reports that expert testimony based on EDR data has increased both criminal convictions and death penalty sentences, as well as high-dollar verdicts in civil cases.

See also: **Engineering:** Analysis of Digital Evidence; Human Factors Investigation and Analysis of Accidents and Incidents; **Forensic Medicine/Clinical:** Airplane Crashes and Other Mass Disasters; **Investigations:** Explosions; Major Incident Scene Management; Recording; **Legal:** History of the Law's Reception of Forensic Science.

Further Reading

Craig, M.W., 2008. Thinking Outside the Black Box: How an Electronic Security Device Became a Police Informant. http://works.bepress.com/mary_craig/1.

Grose, V.L., 1987a. Managing Risk. Prentice Hall, Englewood Cliffs, NJ.

Grose, V.L., 1987b. Commercial Airline 'Margin of Safety'. Presidential Aviation Safety Commission. Aviation Safety Commission Report. ISBN-13: 9780160032875.

Grose, V.L., 1987c. Coping with Boredom in the Cockpit before It's Too Late. Presidential Aviation Safety Commission. Aviation Safety Commission Report. ISBN-13: 9780160032875.

Grose, V.L., 1995a. Your Next airline flight: Worth the risk? Risk Management 42 (4), 47–56.

Grose, V.L., 1995b. Technology's impact on human risk. Proceedings of the Marine Safety Council 52, 57–63.

Electronic Data Recorders (Black Boxes)

W Rosenbluth, Reston, VA, USA

Abbreviations

Accel	Accelerator	EDR	Event data recorder
ECU	Electronic control unit	VUT	Vehicle under test

Glossary

A/D Analog/digital (converter used in D/A processes).

ABS Antilock braking system, which prevents wheel lockup on mixed-friction road surfaces, thereby enhancing vehicle stability during braking.

AE Algorithm enable, also called algorithm wakeup, the acceleration threshold value (x time) that triggers the ECU software to start considering whether the cumulative crash pulse can be predicted to reach a value for which one or more passive restraints should be deployed.

ALDL Assembly Line Diagnostic Link, a historic term created by G.M., referring to a common diagnostic connector on a vehicle in the era before the common SAE J1962 (OBD-II) connector was in use. However, this term is now common in automotive jargon.

Algorithm wakeup Also called algorithm enable, the acceleration threshold value (x time) that triggers the ECU software to start considering whether the cumulative crash pulse can be predicted to reach a value for which one or more passive restraints should be deployed.

APS Accelerator position sensor, a sensor of the accelerator pedal that presents a position-analog voltage to an engine electronic control computer (engine control ECU).

CAN Controller area network (data bus), an advanced and robust intravehicle communications media for data transfer between various on-vehicle system control ECUs.

D/A Data acquisition, a system whereby various vehicle parameters can be recorded on a common time line for use in later analyzing vehicle performance.

DAWN Data acquisition with vehicle networks (HEM Data Corp).

Delta-V The (abrupt) change in velocity during a particular event (such as would be caused by an impact event). This distinguished from the approach velocity (vehicle velocity just before an impact event).

DLC Diagnostic Link Connector, see ALDL.

DPID Data packet identification number, usually for multiple data values (per SAE J 2190, p 4).

DUT Device under test refers to a specific component, which is the subject of a particular test step.

ECU Electronic control unit. A typical on-board automotive computer assembly with a dedicated functional purpose.

EDR Event data recorder. Typically, a control ECU that incorporates nonvolatile memory (EEPROM), which records vehicle and system parameters in the event of a significant event (such as a crash that causes airbag deployment).

EEPROM Electrically erasable read-only memory (typical NVRAM implementation). Memory that saves its contents via a physical charge-storage property so that it retains its data even if removed from system power. Thus when system power is removed (as in a crash event), the EEPROM memory contents are saved.

ESC Electronic stability control, a system that can modulate engine output and/or apply individual wheel braking when it senses vehicle acceleration anomalies. Usually implemented in conjunction with ABS functions.

J1962 SAE J1962 connector. Refers to SAE J1962. The standard diagnostic port on all US domestic sold vehicles since 1996. Also referred to as the OBD-II connector (on-board diagnostics, version II) and the ALDL (Assembly Line Diagnostic Link).

KAM Keep alive memory, random access memory (or a subportion thereof) that is forced to retain its data while energized with system power. When system power is removed, the KAM memory contents are lost.

ms Millisecond, 1/1000 s.

NVRAM Nonvolatile random access memory (see EEPROM).

OBD-II On-board diagnostics connector, version II, a now federally mandated common diagnostic connector for use in diagnosing on-board systems DTCs (originally purposed for emissions-related DTCs).

PCB Printed circuit board, insulating substrate with plated wires that form interconnects between various integrated circuit components and discrete components (resistors, capacitors, diodes, etc.).

PCM Powertrain control module. The engine electronic control computer (engine control ECU).

PID Parameter identification number, usually for a single data value (per SAE J 2190, p4).

RAM Random access memory, memory in an ECU, which is writable to save in-process values during the ongoing function of a control ECU. Such memory typically operates only when system power is applied and thus loses its contents when the vehicle key is turned off, or in a significant crash event.

ROM Read-only memory, memory in an ECU, which has fixed contents (such as a control program and/or default calibration constants). Such memory is fixed and not writable by the normal production ECU.

SLOT SLOT factors are defined by SAE J2178-2 to be scaling, limit, offset, and transfer function specifications that allow hexadecimal encoded engineering data to be interpreted or mapped into engineering units such as DTCs, RPM, mph, lbf, psi, seconds, volts, amps, and Gs.

SRS Supplemental restraints system. The passive restraints system in a vehicle, which operates without operator intervention, typically controlling frontal airbags, side airbags, curtain airbags, and seatbelt pretensioners.

Thrott Throttle. Typically in EFI (electronic fuel injection) vehicles, an air valve. Fuel is adjusted by the PCM (engine computer, engine control module, ECM) to achieve an optimum mixture for the air input.

TPS Throttle position sensor, a sensor on the throttle body of an engine, which presents a position-analog voltage to an engine electronic control computer.

VSS Vehicle speed sensor (usually on the transmission output shaft). Usually a reluctance or Hall effect device, which presents a voltage pulse train whose frequency is directly proportional to the rotational speed of the transmission output shaft (and thus directly related to the speed of the vehicle). A reluctance device is a wire coil in a magnetic circuit, which produces a voltage output as the magnetic field changes. A Hall effect device is a semiconductor element, which produces a resistive change in its properties in response to a transverse magnetic field, thus producing a voltage difference when a constant current is flowing in that device.

WSS Wheel speed sensor (associated with each wheel, used for ABS/ESC functions). Usually a reluctance or Hall Effect device that presents a voltage pulse train whose frequency is directly proportional to the rotational speed of the wheel on which it is mounted and thus can be used for comparison to other wheels having similar sensors, thereby allowing an ABS ECU to determine if there is excessive braking slip on any particular wheel.

Background of Electronic Data in Ground Vehicles

Superceding a long tradition of analog and mechanical technology for control of vehicle functional systems, current ground vehicle control technology is dominated by pervasive use of electronic controllers. Electronic control is achieved by using small-package in-vehicle-mounted dedicated real-time computers (electronic control units, ECUs) to accomplish the logic and magnitude control of vehicle system parameters. Such controllers allow for increased calibration accuracy and enhanced diagnostics and serviceability when compared with their traditional analog forebears. Typical ECUs consist of a controller (computing) device, memory, sensor input circuits, and actuator power driver circuits. ECU memory is used to save diagnostic information, which often includes diagnostic trouble codes (DTCs) and information about the status of inputs (representing vehicle parameters) to that ECU at historical moments in the operating life of that ECU. When the ECU memory is used to save data triggered by a crash event and that data can be later accessed for investigation purposes, that ECU is often referred to as an event data recorder (EDR).

Typical ECUs incorporate a controller (computing) device, memory, sensor input circuits, and actuator power driver circuits. (Often computational, memory, and analog/digital conversion functions are integrated onto a single integrated circuit device. Such devices are identified as a microcontroller unit (MCU) device.) ECU (MCU) memory can be broadly characterized into three categories.

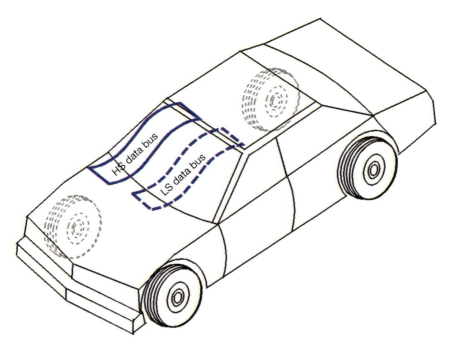

Figure 1 A generic wireframe vehicle with a dual data bus implementation, a high-speed bus (HS data bus), and a low-speed data bus (LS data bus).

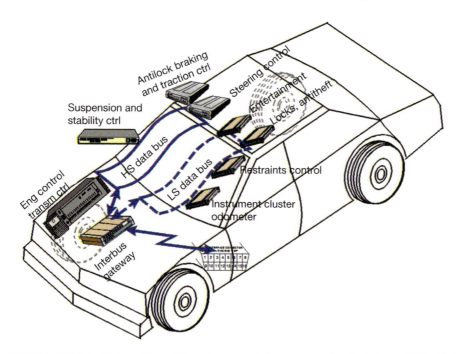

Figure 2 Vehicle operating system controllers requiring real-time intercommunication are grouped on the high-speed (HS) data bus and how other systems controllers, not requiring real-time intercommunication, are grouped on the low-speed (LS) data bus. (However, individual LS data bus controllers certainly act independently in real time. For instance, the restraints controller must autonomously act within 50 ms of the inception of a crash event to calculate the potential magnitude of such a crash event and then deploy passive restraints if appropriate. However, once it has acted with respect to restraints deployment, the need to communicate with other controllers can take 1000 ms or more.) This figure also shows how inter-bus communications are typically accomplished by using an interbus communications controller, often called gateway.

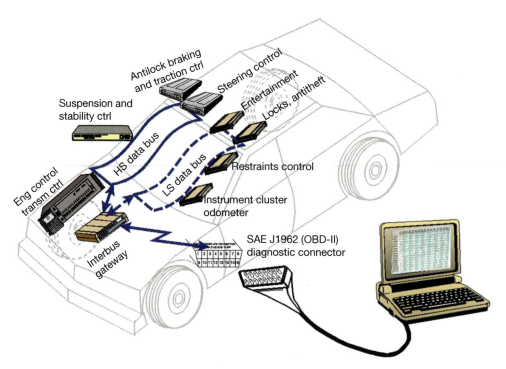

Figure 3 Vehicle diagnostics may be accomplished using a standard diagnostic data port directly accessing the gateway, which then allows indirect access to both high-speed (HS) and low-speed (LS) data buses. Laptop-based diagnostics are shown in the illustration, but other small specialized computer terminals called scanners or code scanners can also be used in this manner. The standard diagnostic port is defined by SAE J1962 and has been mandated on US sale vehicles since 1996.

1. ROM (read-only memory)—a fast read-only technology, which has fixed contents and is typically used to store application program code and base (default) calibration data.
2. RAM (random access memory)—a fast read–write technology, which is used as a calculation scratchpad for the algorithms in the computing element.
3. NVRAM (nonvolatile random access memory)—a usually slower read–write technology, which is used to save update or adaptive calibration data and diagnostic information. NVRAM can be battery dependent (KAM, keep alive memory, usually a part of RAM), or it can be a different technology, which retains data even when the ECU is disconnected from a vehicle electrical system (EEPROM, electrically erasable programmable read-only memory). (EEPROM data retention times are often specified for periods of 10–20 years.)

Diagnostic information almost always includes DTCs and often includes information about the status of inputs (representing vehicle parameters) to that ECU at historical moments in the operating life of that ECU. (A common use of KAM is the storage of freeze frame data in powertrain control module (PCM) ECUs to assist in the diagnosis of emissions-related PCM DTCs.)

Current vehicle systems now typically relying on electronic control mechanisms, with the inherent ability to save selected data in NVRAM, include electronic fuel injection, engine emissions feedback, antilock braking, traction control, stability control, antitheft, occupant safety protection, and rollover protection. These various ECUs are invariably communicating with each other on one or more internal vehicle data bus(es). To give the reader an immediate reference, a series of stepped-complexity symbolic representations of distributed control ECUs and vehicle diagnostic data bus(es) are shown in **Figures 1–4**. Since some, or all, of the ECUs may contain NVRAM data, there can be crash-related event data in more than one ECU and this is clearly shown in **Figure 4**.

Retrieving ECU NVRAM Data for Use in Crash Investigations

A Word about the Data

EDR data exist as binary bits stored in the nonvolatile memory of a particular ECU. Such data must be accessed via electronic

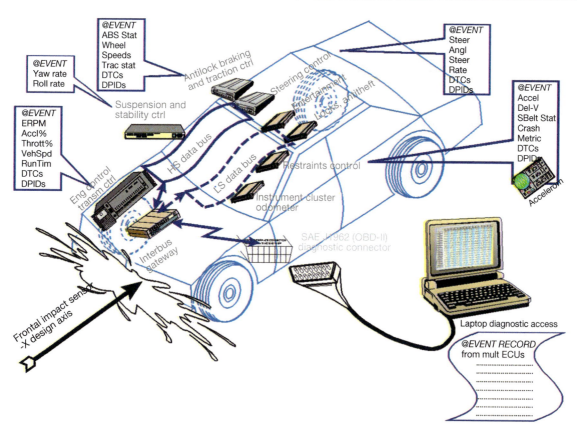

Figure 4 Vehicle operating parameters may be stored in different ECU system controllers and how these parameters, if captured at an event, may be accumulated to form an EVENT RECORD which may be retrieved via a specialized laptop access. If one ECU is designated as a central point to save the various parameter data in its nonvolatile memory, that ECU is typically designated as the event data recorder.

data retrieval methods. Additionally, since binary bit representations can be long and are nearly impossible to assimilate, such data are normally represented in its most economical human readable form, hexadecimal notation. Hexadecimal notation is a base 16 arithmetic notation, with characters (0–9, A–F) corresponding to decimal values of 0–15 of the original binary value. Hexadecimal notation is most often represented with a leading dollar sign, "$." Hexadecimal notation typically considers "byte" quantities, which consist of 8 bits of data. Each byte consists of two ½ bytes, each containing a hexadecimal character representing 4 bits (a "nibble"). For example, a binary value of "1001" = $9 = 9decimal, and a binary value of "1110" = $E = 14decimal. Just as in decimal arithmetic, when the maximum digit count is achieved ($F = 15dec for hexadecimal), the next count is a carry to the left column. The first carry in decimal arithmetic (the next count after 9) gives a representation of 10; the decimal quantity, ten. The first carry in hexadecimal arithmetic (the next count after $F) gives

a hexadecimal representation of $10; the decimal quantity, 16. As a last example, the binary value "0011 0101," represented as hexadecimal byte = $35, stands for a decimal quantity of 53 ($3 \times 16 + 5$).

Post-crash event investigations involving those vehicles now typically utilize such data, as translated into standard engineering units, and such investigations now commonly reference data stored in various EDRs in both bullet- and target-involved vehicles.

Retrieving the Data

The most common method to access EDR data on passenger vehicles and light trucks is via a standard vehicle network interface, the SAE J1962 port (aka the OBD-II port, the DLC or the ALDL) as shown in **Figure 3**.

However, other, equally valid, methods can include direct umbilical-to-ECU interrogation and direct umbilical-to-EEPROM

Figure 5   A typical CDR connection to the vehicle J1962 Data Port (aka the OBD-II port or the ALDL port).

interrogation. If the objective of EDR data retrieval is its use in a litigation process, with either method, a key consideration is the reliability and consistency of output data and the preservation of the source data for other investigators.

With respect to passenger vehicles and light trucks, there are public and proprietary retrieval tools, which can retrieve EDR data and present that data both as hexadecimal bytes and as translated engineering values. The most common data retrieval tool specifically designed for impact data retrieval from select supplemental restraints system (SRS) ECUs and from select engine ECUs is the Bosch/Vetronix CDR® (crash data retrieval tool), and this tool is employed by most vehicle crash investigators. The CDR operates using a serial data interface to the vehicle diagnostic network (see **Figure 2**), and the CDR capabilities are available for specific vehicle application sets. There are CDR options for data retrieval from the J1962 port (OBD-II connector) or from an ECU directly, both employing a serial data interface.

While the CDR presents an orderly and tested means of EDR data retrieval, there are many vehicle models with

NVRAM-incorporated ECUs (EDRs) not covered in the CDR application set. Many investigators, when confronted with non-CDR-covered vehicle, do not pursue EDR data retrieval. Many manufacturers and EDR suppliers can access such non-CDR-coverage data with proprietary data retrieval tools; however, there is little if any public access to such proprietary tools. Additionally, when manufacturers and EDR suppliers provide data to other parties, that data can be seriously incomplete (or incompletely translated). For succeeding discussions, vehicles contained within the CDR application set are referred to as CDR vehicles, and vehicles outside of the CDR application set are hereafter referred to as non-CDR vehicles.

There are three options to retrieve EDR/ECU data.

Method 1: Via a vehicle serial data link communication path to the vehicle diagnostic communication port

Method 1 serial communications operate through the vehicle diagnostic connector (SAE J1962, OBD-II connector) as described above. Often, the data retrieved via this method are data packet identification number (DPID) data, which is a representation of the actual raw NVRAM data, but not the actual NVRAM data itself. For direct access of the actual NVRAM data, there is usually a special mode and security feature incorporated into the serial access protocol—and this prevents general public access to the actual raw stored event data (**Figures 5–7**).

Method 2: Via a serial data link communication path connected via a direct umbilical cable to the target ECU

Alternative serial communications operate via a direct umbilical cable to the EDR/ECU itself (also incorporating the security access feature). The direct ECU umbilical method is invariably nonforensically neutral and can be nonconforming with ASTM E2493-07. That is because direct connections to the EDR/ECU generally present an incomplete system environment to the EDR/ECU and will often lead to test-induced data changes (e.g., generating DTCs for nonexisting sensors, and squibs). Such violations of ASTM E2493-07 practices, when the investigation involves a litigation context, can lead to conditions considered as "data spoliation" in that context (**Figure 8**).

Method 3: Via a direct umbilical to the EEPROM component on the printed circuit board within the EDR assembly

This method requires disassembly of the ECU to access the printed circuit board (PCB), cleaning the EEPROM component contacts with a solvent, and operates by using a direct electrical connection of the EEPROM device and an EEPROM reader. This process retrieves the raw binary

Hexadecimal Data

Data that the vehicle manufacturer has specified for data retrieval is shown in the hexadecimal data section of the CDR report. The hexadecimal data section of the CDR report may contain data that is not translated by the CDR program. The control module contains additional data that is not retrievable by the CDR system.

```
$01   B2 3C 00 E6 64 69
$02   00 00 00 E0 18 00
$03   00 00 00 00 00 00
$04   70 88 40 00 00 00
$05   3F 00 00 06 C0 E2
$06   3F 00 00 06 C0 E2
$07   00 00 C0 00 22 00
$08   00 08 08 50 50 00
$09   04 64 04 64 7F 00
$0A   00 00 00 00 00 00
$0B   08 F6 00 00 FE 00
$12   FF 7F 00 84 40 00
$17   03 03 03 02 00 00
$18   03 03 00 00 00 00
$19   00 00 00 00 00 00
$1A   00 00 00 00 00 00
$1B   00 00 00 00 00 00
$1C   4F 4F 00 4F 00 01
$1D   32 C1 00 00 00 00
$1E   00 00 00 00 00 00
$1F   0C 0D 31 32 5C 5C
$20   20 93 03 00 00 00
$21   7F 7F 7E 7F 7F 7E
$22   01 00 00 00 00 00
$23   00 FF FF 1E 59 00
$24   00 FF 1E 59 F9 00
$25   82 C0 00 00 00 00
$26   41 4F 4F 4F 4F 00
$27   00 01 01 01 01 01
$29   26 26 26 26 26 00
$2A   46 46 46 46 46 00
$2B   00 00 00 00 00 80
$2C   01 01 00 01 00 40
$2F   00 00 00 00 00 80
$30   00 00 00 00 00 80
$36   8C 00 00 00 00 00
$37   00 A5 00 00 00 00
$38   00 00 00 00 00 00
$39   00 FF FF 1E 58 00
$3A   FF 1E 58 00 00 00
$3B   FF FF FF FF FF FF
$3C   FF FF FF FF FF FF
```

Figure 6 Virtual hexadecimal data (i.e., DPID data) as retrieved by the CDR.

data in hexadecimal notation format. This process, while far more tedious and time-consuming than methods 1 and 2, overcomes the serial security access controls (by avoiding it entirely), retrieves the actual raw NVRAM binary data (in hexadecimal representation), and also avoids the problem of test-induced data changes. Thus this process (as is method 1) is forensically neutral and in conformity with ASTM E2493-07. As this methodology works independently of serial data communications, it is especially valuable for non-CDR vehicles. It has been demonstrated for retrieval of crash event data in EDRs on vehicles from domestic, European, and Asian manufacturers (**Figures 9 and 10**).

The Use of ECU NVRAM Data in Crash Investigations

Post-crash event investigations involving those vehicles now typically utilize such EDR engineering data, and such investigations now commonly reference data stored in various EDRs in both bullet and target involved vehicles. It is incumbent on the investigator wishing to introduce such data as "evidence" in the litigation process to be able to confirm to the Court that such "evidence" is stated with reasonable engineering certainty and that it meets certain clear tests for such admission. These tests are typically lumped under the umbrella terms, "Frye Criteria" or "Daubert Criteria." These tests require that the retrieval, resultant translation, and interpretation of EDR data must:

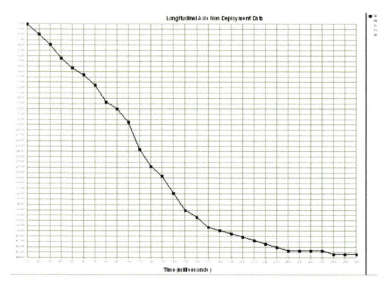

Figure 7   Typical integrated longitudinal Delta-V data as produced by the CDR postprocessing software, which translates the retrieved DPID data.

Figure 8   A data retrieval using a CDR direct connection to an SRS ECU.

1. Be founded on an underlying methodology of scientific tests, documentation of test results (charts, graphs, etc.), which have been reviewed by peers who have confirmed the reliability and acceptance of test methods. This can include refereed publication of tests and methods.

2. Be repeatable by any peer scientist/engineer using the conditions and/or data recorded in the subject tests. This means that other investigators must be able to repeat the subject tests and derive the same test results from the EDR at issue.

3. Have a reasonable error rate. This means that the error rate for the method employed is consistent and that is accepted by other practitioners in the field.

4. Be consistent with industry or commonly accepted standards that define or direct the tests and results postulated. This means that the procedures (methodology) must be compatible with applicable sections of ASTM E860, ASTM E1188, and ASTM E2493.

5. Pass a test of relevance and linkage to the facts at issue in the subject litigation. Obviously, the essence of the tests used must be consistent with the conditions of the accident under investigation, and the results presented must be relevant to the issues under consideration by the trier of fact (the Jury).

Figure 9   ECU disassembly and the direct EEPROM data retrieval process.

Figure 10   A portion of the raw hexadecimal data retrieved through a typical direct EEPROM data retrieval process. Note that in this case, the immediate ASCII translation shows the vehicle VIN as written to the EEPROM. (The VIN was correct for the donor vehicle.)

Acknowledgments

The author wishes to acknowledge Mr Fred Chandler, Chandler & Sons Automotive, Herndon, VA, who contributed to many aspects of the testing and raw data retrieval work described herein.

> *See also:* **Engineering:** Analysis of Digital Evidence; Forensic Engineering/Accident Reconstruction/Biomechanics of Injury/ Philosophy, Basic Theory, and Fundamentals; Human Factors Investigation and Analysis of Accidents and Incidents; Investigation and Analysis of Structural Collapses.

Further Reading

Note: It is hoped that this introduction to EDRs encourages the reader to continue his or her research on the subject. To assist with that, several references for further reading are presented below.

American Society for Testing and Materials E1188–95, 1995. Standard Practice for Collection and Preservation of Information and Physical Items by a Technical Investigator. ASTM International, West Conshocken, PA, 19428–2959.

American Society for Testing and Materials E860–97, 1997. Standard Practice for Examining and Testing Items that Are or May Become Involved in Litigation. ASTM International, West Conshocken, PA, 19428–2959.

American Society for Testing and Materials E2493–07, 2007. Standard Guide for the Collection of Non-volatile Memory Data in Evidentiary Vehicle Electronic Control Units. ASTM International, West Conshocken, PA, 19428–2959.

Bosch/Vetronix. CDR® Data Retrieval Tool Vehicle Coverage Information, Can Be Found at Vetronix Corporation, 2030 93103–101716, Alameda Padre Serra, Santa Barbara, CA, USA, 1 800 321-4889. http://www.boschdiagnostics.com/testequipment/diagnostics/cdr/Pages/CDRHome.aspx.

Chidester, A., Hinch, J., Roston, T., 2001. Real world experiences with event data recorders. In: Proceedings of the 17th International Technical Conference on the Enhanced Safety of Vehicles (ESV) Conference. Amsterdam, The Netherlands, 4–7 June 2001. Washington, DC: National Highway Traffic Safety Administration, DOT HS 809 220. Paper Number 247, 11pp.

Chidester, A., Hinch, J., Mercer, T., Schultz, K., May 3–5, 1999. Recording automotive crash event data. In: National Highway Traffic Safety Administration Paper, International Symposium on Transportation Recorders, Arlington, VA, USA.

Gabler, H.C., Hampton, C.E., Hinch, J., 2004. Crash Severity: A Comparison of Event Data Recorder Measurements with Accident Reconstruction Estimates. Rowan University; National Highway Traffic Safety Administration, Washington, DC, Glassboro, NJ, 8 p. Accident reconstruction 2004. Warrendale, SAE, 2004, pp. 81–88. Report No. SAE 2004–01–1194. UMTRI-98091.

Gabler, H., Hinch, J., Steiner, J., 2008. Event Data Recorders – a Decade of Innovation. SAE International, Warrendale, PA, ISBN 978-0-7680-2066-3. Product Code: PT-139.

Ishikawa, H., Takubo, N., Oga, R., et al. Study on Pre-crash and Post-Crash Information Recorded in Electronic Control Units(ECUs) Including Event Datra Recorders, National Research Institute of Police Science Japan, Paper Number 09–0375.

Kowalick Thomas, 2004. Fatal Exit: The Automotive Black Box Debate. Wiley.

Murthy, S.K., Satish, D.A., (n.d.). Diagnostics for Automobiles – A Snapshot. Bengaluru: Dearborn Electronics. http://www.deindia.com/images/downloads/whitepapers/Diganostcs_for_Automobiles-A_Snapshot.pdf.

Niehoff, P., Gabler, H., Brophy, J., Chidester, A., Hinch, J., Ragland, C., 2005. In: Evaluation of Event Data Recorders in FullSystems Crash Tests. National Highway Traffic Safety Administration, United States, Paper No: 05–0271.

Reust, T.J., 2004. The Accuracy of Speed Captured by Commercial Vehicle Event Data Recorders. Accident Science, Newhall, CA, 8 p. Accident reconstruction 2004. Warrendale, SAE, 2004, p. 115–122. Report No. SAE 2004–01–1199. UMTRI-98091.

Riling, J., 1995. Sensing and Diagnostic Module for Airbags. SAE Technical Paper, 952682. http://dx.doi.org/10.4271/952682.

Rosenbluth, W., 2001. Investigation and Interpretation of Black Box Data in Automobiles: A Guide to the Concepts and Formats of Computer Data in Vehicle Safety and Control Systems. The American Society for Testing and Materials (ASTM) and the Society of Automotive Engineers (SAE).

Rosenbluth, W., 2009. Black Box Data from Accident Vehicles, Methods for Retrieval, Translation and Interpretation, ASTM Monograph 5. ASTM International, West Conshocken, PA.

Rosenbluth, W., 2010. Collecting EDR Data for Crash Investigations, Forensic Magazine. Vicon Publishing, Amherst, NH.

Ruth, R., Daily, J., 2011. Accuracy of Event Data Recorder in 2010 Ford Flex during Steady State and Braking Conditions. SAE 2011– 01–0812, Detroit, MI.

Ruth, R., West, O., Nasrallah, H., 2009. Accuracy of Selected 2008 Ford Restraint Control Module Event Data Recorders. SAE_2009– 01–884, Detroit, MI.

Takubo, N., Ishikawa, H., Kato, K., et al., 2009. Study on Characteristics of Event Data Recorders in Japan; Analysis of J-NCAP and Thirteen Crash Tests. SAE Technical Paper 2009-01-0883. http://dx.doi.org/10.4271/2009-01-0883.

Gaasbeck, Van, Stephen, February 1, 2007. How to Challenge Black Box Data, Trial Magazine.

Relevant Website

http://www.cdr-system.com—Crash Data Group: Crash Data Retrieval Tool.

Analog Tachograph Chart Analysis

RF Lambourn, Transport Research Laboratory, Wokingham, UK

Glossary

Odometer A device that displays the total distance traveled by a vehicle since its manufacture, usually incorporated in its speedometer.
Rolling road A set of rollers on which the wheels of a vehicle may be placed in order to test its speedometer.
Tachograph Device that records speed and distance traveled by a vehicle, primarily for the purpose of regulating a driver's hours of work and also of use in determining speeds, etc. in incidents.
Tachograph chart A stiff paper chart, usually circular, on which traces recording speeds, distances, and modes of work are scribed.

Introduction

The tachograph is a device fitted to motor vehicles, which makes a recording of the speed traveled and distance driven, together with details of the driver's periods of work and rest. Although found in vehicles worldwide, it is particularly used in the countries of the European Union (EU), where it is a requirement in most larger goods and passenger-carrying vehicles. Analog tachographs make this recording on a paper chart. However, in the EU, these devices are obsolescent, with vehicles registered from 2006 having to be fitted with digital tachographs that store the data electronically.

A note on digital tachographs will be found at the end of this chapter, but otherwise it is concerned only with analog tachographs and lays particular emphasis on the instrument, as it is specified in EEC Regulations. However, the principles of chart analysis and the use of tachograph data described here are applicable to all types of analog device. In any case, the user of tachograph data must be aware of the characteristics of the particular make and model from which it comes, in order to appreciate the amount of information available and its limitations. The range of models is large, and this chapter cannot therefore cover every detail of every instrument that may be encountered.

The Forensic Use of Tachograph Data

Tachograph data have two main forensic applications:

1. in road accident investigation, to determine the speed at and immediately before an incident, the rate of braking, and the manner of driving;
2. in general criminal investigation, to find the route traveled and the time when a vehicle was at a particular location.

The Tachograph Chart

Figure 1(a) and 1(b) shows typical paper tachograph charts and illustrates the information provided by the instrument. The shape and design are not specified by the EEC Regulations, but the chart pattern shown here has become the standard for the industry. Other designs do exist, but the instruments that require them are obsolete.

The chart is a disk (123 mm in diameter) coated with a material that blackens under pressure. In the center is an area where the driver writes his or her name, the starting and finishing places for his or her day's driving, the date, vehicle number, and odometer readings.

Printed around the edge of the chart, and repeated further in, is the time scale of 24 h. Between these is the field where the speed is recorded, usually with a maximum of 125 km h^{-1}. Further in is the work mode field, where the driver indicates whether he or she is driving, engaged on other work, or resting. The indication is made by either the track in which the recording line runs (**Figure 1(a)**) or the thickness of the line (**Figure 1(b)**). It is sometimes possible to extract useful information from the mode-of-work line when the vehicle has been moving very slowly.

The innermost recording is of distance, shown by a zigzag line. One stroke of this line is made during 5 km of travel; a complete V indicates 10 km of movement, whereas other distances will create partial strokes.

The Tachograph Instrument

Older models of tachograph combine their function with that of a speedometer in a single unit and are therefore designed to

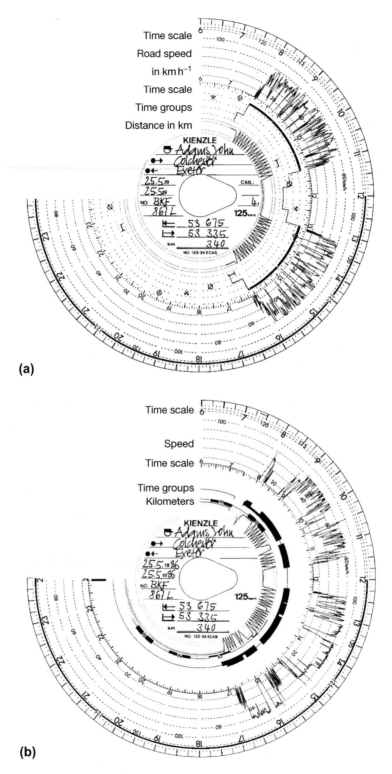

(a)

(b)

Figure 1 Tachograph chart showing recordings with (a) "manual" time group recordings and (b) "automatic" time group recordings. Continental Automotive Trading UK Ltd.

Figure 2 The face of a Veeder Root model 8400 tachograph.

Figure 4 An opened Kienzle model 1318 tachograph showing the insertion of a chart.

be mounted on a vehicle's dashboard in front of the driver. **Figure 2** shows such an instrument. More recent models, which are called "modular," have an appearance akin to a car radio or CD player and are located elsewhere in the cab, while being linked to a conventional speedometer. **Figure 3** shows an example of a modular tachograph.

Externally the older instruments (as in **Figure 2**) have the usual speedometer features—a speed dial and an odometer display—together with a clock and knobs with which the driver and a colleague can indicate their modes of work. (Most instruments hold two charts to cater for there being two drivers crewing the vehicle.)

In these instruments, the chart usually lies behind the face, which is hinged to open downward to allow insertion and removal. **Figure 4** shows an open instrument with a chart about to be inserted. The spindle on which it is mounted

Figure 3 The Kienzle MTCO1324 modular tachograph. The lower part is the drawer onto which the chart is placed.

rotates once in 24 h. When the instrument is closed, the chart bears against three styluses that move up and down to make the recordings. The spindle and the hole in the center of the chart are oval to ensure the correct orientation of the chart with respect to time.

With the modular instrument in **Figure 3**, the charts are placed on a tray where, when it is pushed into the body of the instrument, they are brought into contact with the recording styluses. **Figure 5** shows a modular instrument with the tray open and a chart in place.

Tachographs may operate either mechanically or electronically. Mechanical types, in which a rotating cable from the vehicle gearbox drives a cup-and-magnet system, are now rarely seen. Typical models are the VDO Kienzle TCO1311 and the Veeder Root 1111. Electronic types receive a train of pulses from a transducer at the gearbox, the frequency of which is translated as speed. There are many models: examples of the unitary type are Motometer EGK100, Jaeger G.50, VDO Kienzle TCO1314 and TCO1318, and Veeder Root 8300 and 8400, and examples of the modular type are Kienzle MTCO1324 and Stoneridge (Veeder Root) 2400.

The Principles of Chart Analysis

Figure 6 shows a schematic tachograph trace and the quantities to be measured in an analysis. The speed trace is thought of as a series of points connected by straight lines. The speed at each point (v_1, v_2, v_3) is measured, as are the time intervals between them (t_1, t_2, t_3). This provides a plot of speed against time, which can then be integrated to yield a plot of speed against distance. **Figure 7** shows a real tachograph trace, **Table 1** shows the tabulated analysis, and **Figure 8** shows the resulting plot. (This trace and analysis is used for the case example at the end of this chapter.)

Figure 5 An opened Kienzle MTCO1324 tachograph with a chart placed on the drawer.

There are various approaches to making these measurements. Taking the speed from the chart is relatively straightforward and can be done from a photographic enlargement or with a traveling microscope. Allowance has to be made for the

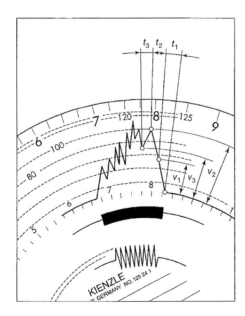

Figure 6 Schematic speed trace showing time intervals and speeds.

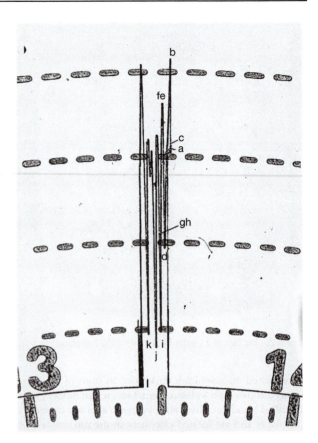

Figure 7 A real tachograph speed trace with analysis points.

accuracy of the speed recordings. Measurement of the time intervals is, however, not at all easy. Because the chart rotates just once in 24 h, 1 min occupies only 0.25°, and in 1 s it turns through only 15 s of arc. It is usual to mount the chart beneath a microscope on a rotating table that is turned by a micrometer.

Table 1 Data from tachograph chart shown in **Figure 7**: the analysis points a, ..., i run backward from the end of the driving

Point	Speed (km h^{-1})	Time (s)	Distance (m)
a	–	0	0
b	81	0	0
c	61	32	630
d	38	67	1110
e	71	83	1355
f	71	87	1435
g	40	111	1805
h	39	116	1860
i	19	122	1905

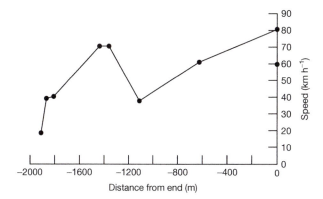

Figure 8 Plot of speed data from **Figure 7** against distance.

Figure 9 shows one such microscope, as produced by VDO Kienzle. A glass plate etched with a vertical cursor line, 3 μm wide, lies over the chart, and this combines with a horizontal line in one eyepiece to form a "crosswire" in the field of view. Points for measurement are brought successively under the crosswire by rotating the chart table and moving it backward and forward, and transducers are attached to these two movements. Signals from the transducers, which are interpreted as time and speed, are fed to a microcomputer, where listings of these quantities and graphs of speed versus time and distance are produced.

It is very important to recognize, when measuring time intervals, that the line along which the recording stylus moved was unlikely to have passed exactly either through the center of rotation of the chart when mounted on the microscope or when mounted in the tachograph instrument, or through the

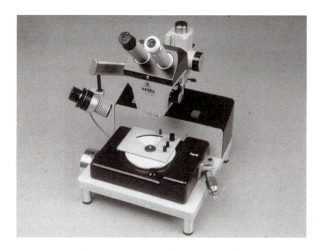

Figure 9 The Kienzle microscope with computer-linking modifications.

geometric center of the chart itself. This is illustrated in an exaggerated form in **Figure 10**. If the vertical cursor is not arranged such that it lies along the line on which the stylus moved, any time intervals measured between points at different speeds will be in error. In the VDO Kienzle microscope, the glass plate carrying the cursor line can be swiveled about a point at the outer edge of the chart, and this adjustment is used to set the line in what the analyst judges to be the correct position.

The Accuracy of the Speed Record

The EEC Regulations require that having been installed and calibrated, the analog tachograph record may not have an error in its speed figures greater than ± 6 km h^{-1}. The analyst may be content to use this as a probable error figure, but the author's

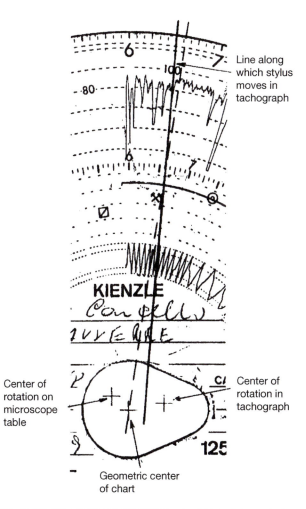

Figure 10 The need for an adjustable cursor when analyzing a chart.

experience is that although the error is generally not greater than ± 3 km h^{-1}, there are occasional cases where it is substantially more than ± 6 km h^{-1}. It is therefore desirable that the calibration in each case be checked, and various methods have been devised for this.

Calibration Checks on the Tachograph Installation

The most straightforward method of checking the accuracy of a tachograph system is to employ a "rolling road" of the sort used when tachographs are installed in vehicles. A chart is placed on the instrument, and the vehicle is then effectively driven through a range of known speeds. The chart will then show how each speed is recorded, from which the amount of error is found.

Some agencies find the rolling road method quite inconvenient and instead use a method that requires no special facilities and that can be employed in any open space. The procedure is performed in two stages: first, the signal sent from the vehicle's gearbox is measured (either as pulses per kilometer in electronic systems or turns per kilometer in mechanical ones) in one of two ways, and the second, the way the tachograph instrument responds to a known set of input signals is found.

The first of the two ways of measuring the signal is called the 20-m track and is one that may actually be used by some installers. It is fully described in manuals produced by tachograph manufacturers for the guidance of their agents. It is appropriate for vehicles that can be moved slowly in a straight line; thus, they need not be fully mobile and may have, for example, accident damage to the steering gear or the engine coolant system. The test can even be performed by towing the vehicle.

In this method, the drive to the tachograph is either disconnected and a turn or pulse counter is attached to it, or, with later electronic models, a pulse counter is plugged into a socket in the head itself. The vehicle itself is then driven slowly on a straight and level surface for 20 m, the distance being measured exactly. From the number of pulses and the distance, the rate per meter is calculated: this is usually referred to as the w figure.

The second way is called the static method and is appropriate for vehicles that cannot be moved, either through accident damage or through restriction of space. In this method, a turn or pulse counter is attached in the same way as in the 20-m track method. One of the driven wheels of the vehicle is then lifted off the ground, and its circumference is measured with a tape; later, the other driven wheels are also measured. The raised wheel is then rotated manually 10 times and the resulting turn or pulse reading is noted. From these data, the w figure can be calculated, remembering to take account of the effect of the axle differential, which averages the rotation of the wheels at each end: thus, with one wheel being stationary and the other wheel being turned, 10 turns of the single wheel are

equivalent to 5 turns of the two wheels together and therefore of the whole axle.

If the accident damage is so great that neither of these methods can be used, then the investigator may have to resort to examining gear trains and counting gear teeth.

Having determined w, the response of the tachograph instrument itself is found by driving it in steps through its speed range with a sequence of signals generated by a specially constructed test unit. These units are produced by the tachograph manufacturers for the use of their installation agents and display either the mechanical rotation rate or the electronic pulse rate (in units of min^{-1}). A new tachograph chart is put in the instrument, and a test chart similar to that in **Figure 11** is produced.

The sequence of tests in **Figure 11** is given as follows:

1. The instrument is taken up to its maximum speed (140 km h^{-1} in this example) and then very quickly back to zero to check the straightness of the recording stylus movement.
2. This is repeated three times.
3. Next, the instrument is taken to an indicated speed of 60 km h^{-1}: at this speed the input figure (in min^{-1}) is known as the characteristic coefficient or k figure and should be, in a correctly calibrated system, approximately equal to the w figure of the vehicle.
4. The speed is taken from zero up to the maximum in 20 km h^{-1} steps, holding each step for 2 min, and then back down to zero at the same speed between the steps (130 km h^{-1}, 110 km h^{-1}, etc.).
5. Finally, the instrument is run at 60 km h^{-1} for as long as it takes 1 km to be recorded on its odometer, and the actual number of turns or pulses delivered is noted: this should equal the κ figure. During the last test, the activity mode switch is also changed through its four settings.

The information from part (4) of the test can now be used, together with the w figure, to construct a graph of how the recording on the chart at any point relates to the true speed. This can be done manually or by using the software associated with the Kienzle computer-linked microscope.

The "Route Trace" Method of Calibration

An alternative to the direct methods of calibration is the so-called route trace method. This can only be used when the route the vehicle has taken is known and is particularly appropriate when the vehicle is unavailable for testing or has been so seriously damaged as to make the other methods impossible. The tachograph record can also be used to find the route that a vehicle has taken (see Route Tracing section). The calibration method is an inversion of this procedure and briefly involves attempting to match the recorded pattern of driving to the known route. A system that is in calibration will give an

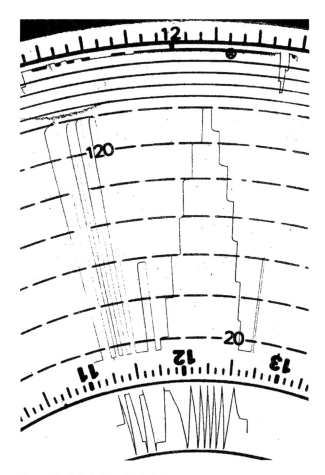

Figure 11 A typical head test chart.

between two points, the precision can therefore never be greater than ±2 s. In any case, the edge of the speed-recording trace is insufficiently smooth for these steps to be resolved. With a good trace, a confidence of ±2 s can probably be assumed, but in some instruments an unsteadiness will be evident, which means that wider uncertainty must be accepted. It is found that although some manufacturers' instruments yield consistently good traces, other manufacturers produce tachographs that are invariably poor.

Figure 12 shows an example of a poor trace. The drive train from the clock to the chart is somewhat loose, and allowing a generally unsteady speed trace as the stylus moves up and down, it permits the stylus, as it falls after rising to a maximum, to track back along the groove it has made on the chart instead of drawing a new line. This effectively drives the clock backward for a few seconds (20 s being typical) until the slack is taken up, and only then the stylus will start to follow a new track.

immediate match, whereas one that is out of calibration will require an adjustment of its speed by some factor before the match is found. Thus, the calibration method is one of the findings what this adjustment factor is.

Problems of Interpretation

Once the cursor on the analyzing microscope has been correctly aligned and the errors, if any, in the speed record have been determined, the chart can be analyzed. However, the limitations of the recording and the individual instruments must be recognized.

Time Intervals

The clock in most tachograph instruments advances the chart in 1-s step, and it is, therefore, not possible in principle to measure the time at a particular point on the chart with a precision greater than ±1 s. When measuring the interval

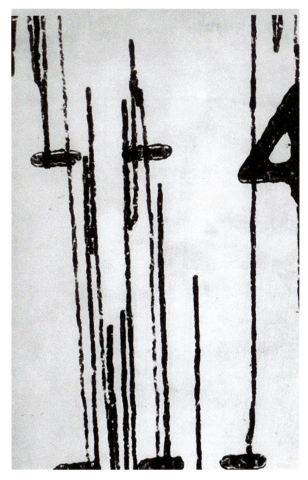

Figure 12 An unsteady trace from a Jaeger mechanical instrument.

In some tachographs, severe steering or swerving may cause the recording trace to deviate, and a likely example appears in **Figure 13**, where the period of perfectly constant speed, which can be seen just before the final descent of the trace to zero speed, was probably caused by a swerving action that made to chart shift slightly within the instrument.

Impacts to the Vehicle

A severe impact to the vehicle will generally produce a disturbance of the tachograph recording traces (**Figures 7 and 13**). When such a disturbance is apparent on the speed trace, it is obviously an indication of the speed of the vehicle at the moment of impact and is an item of the information easily read from the chart. However, some caution is needed before interpreting it. The disturbance was properly caused by a shock to the tachograph itself, and its magnitude therefore depends on the proximity of the impact to the instrument. A collision with a pedestrian, where the pedestrian meets the vehicle very close to the instrument panel, can cause a clear disturbance, whereas a severe impact from another vehicle to the rear of an articulated lorry may have little or no effect on the recording.

If heavy braking is taking place at the time of the impact, the speed at which the disturbance appears may be affected by other factors.

Finally, a severe impact will often derange the instrument for at least a few seconds, such that little or no reliance can be placed on any features that may immediately follow it.

Response of the Instrument

The EEC Regulations require tachograph instruments to be able to follow "acceleration changes" of $2\,\text{m s}^{-2}$. Since during braking the deceleration of a vehicle may well be as much as $7\,\text{m s}^{-2}$, there is the possibility that the speed-recording stylus may not be able to keep up with the changing speed. This does not, in fact, appear to be a problem in Kienzle, Motometer, Jaeger, and mechanical Veeder Root tachographs, but there is a difficulty with older electronic Veeder Root instruments.

Earlier Veeder Root 1200 and 1400 series tachographs only just met the $2\,\text{m s}^{-2}$ requirement; early 8300 series models had a response of $2.5\,\text{m s}^{-2}$, whereas later 8300 series and all 8400 series models have a response of $5.7\,\text{m s}^{-2}$. The consequence of a response of 2 or $2.5\,\text{m s}^{-2}$ is that during heavy braking, the speed being recorded at any moment will be greater than the true speed, and any event recorded during the braking, for example an impact, will be shown at too high speed. It also means that it is not possible for an analyst to give an opinion as to whether a particular piece of braking was at a normal or an emergency rate.

A response of $5.7\,\text{m s}^{-2}$, however, is much closer to the braking rate, which can be expected of a lorry in an emergency, and will generally allow a reasonable speed for an impact to be recorded.

An even higher response rate leads to a difficulty where there has been a wheel slip during braking.

Tire Slip Effects

The tachograph records the speed of rotation of the wheels to which it is connected, almost always the driven wheels of the vehicle. Therefore, if for some reason those wheels slip, that is, rotate at a speed that does not correspond to the speed of the vehicle over the ground, then the recording will be in error.

Wheel slip particularly occurs during heavy braking, notably when the driven wheels lock. An instrument with a fast response will react to wheel locking as though the vehicle had instantaneously come to a halt: the stylus will fall very quickly to its base position even though the vehicle is still traveling forward, and an impact may even appear to have been at zero speed. An example is shown in **Figure 13**, where, because the vehicle has skidded, the prominent impact feature will certainly

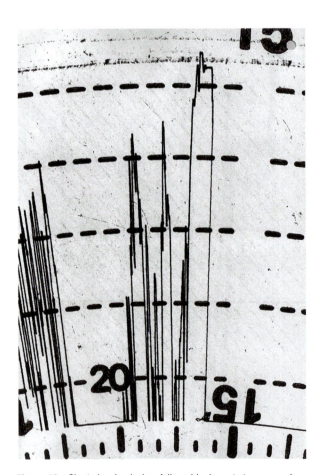

Figure 13   Chart showing lockup followed by impact at zero speed.

be at a level much lower than the true speed. The operation of an antilock braking system will also cause the speed of the wheels to be less than the road speed of the vehicle.

The opposite can occur if one of the driven wheels lifts off the road, allowing it to spin. This typically occurs as a vehicle starts to roll onto its side. In **Figure 14**, the speed at C would appear to be that at which the accident has occurred. In fact, the correct speed is at B, from which the trace has jumped to C, as the wheels on one side of the lorry lifted from the road.

Low-Speed Behavior

Incidents at low speed cause particular problems in the interpretation of tachograph data because all instruments have a level below which they do not record speed. In all current models, this is about 5 km h^{-1}, although in some older instruments it is somewhat higher, up to 16 km h^{-1}. Therefore, it can neither be said, for example, whether a vehicle that has slowed before entering a main road actually stopped or merely reduced its speed to, say, 5 km h^{-1} before proceeding nor may it be possible to say whether or not during an apparent stationary period the vehicle was moved a small distance.

Some information can, however, be gained from the mode-of-work trace. Movement of the vehicle generates a thicker line, made by an oscillation, or an increased oscillation, of the recording stylus (see the examples in **Figure 1**). A small gap in the thick line can be taken as a brief stationary period. The threshold for this thick line depends on the model. Mechanical instruments will produce a noticeable movement in the stylus only when the vehicle has moved for about 20 m or more. Electronic instruments have a critical speed at which the line is made. The mode trace in Kienzle 1318 and 1319 instruments, however, operates during driving in the same way as the zigzag distance trace, making one stroke over a distance of 50 m.

Falsifications and Diagnostic Signals

Tachographs have always been prone to attempts by drivers to falsify the recordings, to show either lower speeds or shorter hours of work. Most falsifications are readily apparent on careful examination, for example, by comparing the apparent average speed during a journey with the recorded distance and the time taken, or by comparing the total recorded distance for the day's driving with the difference in the handwritten odometer figures. **Figure 15** shows a commonly attempted falsification, where driving has stopped at 1736, the clock has been rewound, and driving has resumed, apparently earlier, at 1623.

The scope for such tampering is greatly increased with electronic instruments, and therefore, various "diagnostic" features are incorporated in them to show when certain irregularities occur. These depend on the individual models of instrument, and a full account of them is beyond the scope of this chapter. However, two examples are as follows.

If the pulse sender is disconnected in an attempt to make it appear that the vehicle is not being driven, the speed stylus will oscillate between zero and, typically, 30 km h^{-1} to make a broad band (**Figure 16**).

If the electrical supply to the instrument is interrupted, in an attempt to halt recording for a period, then, on reconnection, the speed stylus will execute a characteristic movement, for example, a full-scale deflection or a dip to zero speed.

Other attempts at falsification, which can be more difficult to detect, include connecting the wires from the pulse sender to earth; reducing the voltage to the tachograph, such that the clock continues to operate but the other electronic systems fail; and connecting certain spare terminals on the back of the instrument together, again to cause some of the electronic functions to fail.

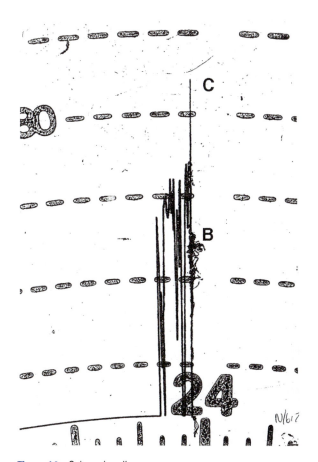

Figure 14 Spin up in roll-over.

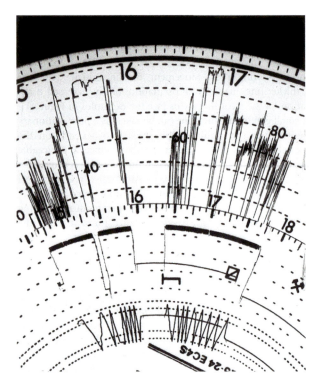

Figure 15 Fraudulent rewinding of tachograph clock. The overlapping traces show that the time was turned back from 1736 to 1623 h.

Case Example

Figure 7 is an enlarged section of a tachograph recording made by a tourist bus that came into collision with a pedal cycle. The bus had been on a slip road, approaching a main dual-carriageway road. The pedal cyclist was traveling on the main road and appears to have cut suddenly across the path of the bus. The bus driver braked hard and swerved to his right. **Figure 17** shows the route the bus had taken to the scene of the accident.

The results of the detailed analysis, given in **Table 1** and plotted in **Figure 8**, indicate that (point i) about 120 s before the accident the speed of the bus was at a minimum of 19 km h^{-1} and that it was about 1900 m from the scene of the accident. Its speed then increased to a maximum (points f and e) of 71 km h^{-1} before falling to another minimum (point d) of 38 km h^{-1}. It was then about 67 s and 1110 m from the end.

Again the speed increased, reaching its final maximum (point b) of 81 km h^{-1} immediately before the collision. There was then heavy braking to a sudden disturbance of the trace (point a), which on the chart is at an indicated speed of 60 km h^{-1}. However, the time interval between a and b is too small to measure, and at the scene, locked wheel skid marks were found from the rear wheels on one side of the vehicle. The

Figure 16 Broad trace generated when speed transducer is disconnected.

rapid fall of the recording trace between the last two points has clearly occurred as a result of the locking of these driven wheels, which accounts for the immeasurably small time interval and also means that the figure of 60 km h^{-1} (because of the characteristics of the particular instrument) is probably significantly less than the speed at which the disturbance occurred.

The disturbance itself consists of a thickening of the trace, caused by a small shock to the stylus, followed by a step to the left (i.e., "backward" in time). The shock would have been caused by the impact at the front of the bus with the pedal cycle, whereas the sudden swerve would have brought about some sideways movement of the components of the tachograph instrument, to create the step to the left.

Route Tracing

The two minima of speed in **Table 1** lie at distances from the end, which, on an accurate map, can be readily identified with a roundabout (point d) and an intersection (point i). When the analysis is extended back to the start of the driving, two further minima and the start of the journey itself can be matched to a complex road junction and two more roundabouts (points j, k, and l in **Figure 7**). Some very slow driving before point i indicates that the bus started its driving from a place just before the roundabout.

In the context of a road accident, the matching of the trace to a known route serves to confirm the accuracy of the analysis process and of the calibration of the tachograph installation. If it had not been possible to check the calibration independently, this matching, with any necessary adjustment of the speed figures, could have been used as a calibration procedure in itself.

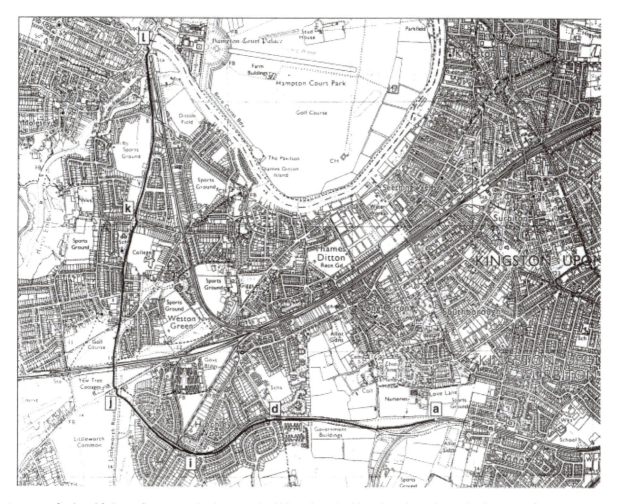

Figure 17   Section of Ordnance Survey map showing route of vehicle as determined from the tachograph recording in **Figure 7**. Crown copyright reserved.

However, if it is imagined that, in different circumstances, the route of the vehicle was unknown, and there was a need for it to be found, it can be seen that working back from the known end point (a), it would be possible to do so by comparing distances between speed minima with distances on a map between road junctions. A typical case where this method is applied would be where a vehicle carrying a valuable load is stolen from a known location X, driven to an unknown place Y and unloaded, and then driven to a third place Z and abandoned. From its tachograph record, it may be possible to locate Y by tracing back from Z or forward from X. The success of this method depends on traffic conditions; in heavy traffic, the vehicle may have had to stop so many times at places other than road junctions, where following its route becomes impossible.

Digital Tachographs

EEC Regulations now require that from May 2006, all tachographs fitted to vehicles that fall within their scope be of the digital rather than analog type. Digital tachographs make their recording on a removable "smart card" rather than a paper chart, although a printer within the instrument also provides a summary of some of the data on a paper strip. Digital tachographs have similarities with the event data recorders (EDRs) fitted to some vehicles. Current models of digital tachograph include Siemens VDO DTCO1381, Stoneridge SE5000, and Actia SmarTach L2000.

The specifications to which they all conform require, among other things, that speed is recorded with a resolution of 1 Hz and that the smart card holds the record for the last 24 h of driving (not simply the last 24 h of time). The 1 Hz record of earlier driving is deleted, although simplified data are still held on times and distances traveled and maximum speeds. But manufacturers may choose to exceed the specifications, and, for example, the Siemens VDO DTCO1381 holds a record of the speed at 4 Hz for the *xx* seconds preceding the last stop made by the vehicle.

The reader is referred to EEC Regulation 1360/02, manufacturers' literature, and the chapter on EDRs for further information.

See also: **Engineering:** Accident Investigation—Determination of Cause; Electronic Data Recorders (EDRs, Black Boxes).

Further Reading

EEC, 1985. Council regulation (EEC) no. 3821/85. Official Journal of the European Communities L370, 8–21.

EEC, 2002. Council regulation (EEC) no. 1360/02. Official Journal of the European Communities L207, 1–252.

Lambourn, R.F., 1985. The analysis of tachograph charts for road accident investigation. Forensic Science International 28, 181–199.

Lehmann, H., 1992. Die mikroskopische Diagrammscheibenauswertung für die Unfallrekonstruktion (Microscopic analysis of tachograph charts for accident reconstruction). Verkehrsunfall und Fahrzeugtechnik 1, 2–4.

Lowe, D., 1989. The Tachograph, second ed. Kogan Page, London.

Needham, P., 1988. Tachograph chart computer-linked microscopic analysis. Forensic Science International 36, 211–218.

Wach, W., Unarski, J., Duś, A., 2005. Tachograph Chart – Analysis of Intensive Braking Recording. Technical Paper 2005-01-1185. Society of Automotive Engineers, Warrendale, PA.

Key Terms

Adversary truth, Air France 447, Audio recording, Black box data, Black boxes, Causation, CVR, Digital vs. Analog, EgyptAir 990, Electrically erasable programmable read-only memory (EEPROM), Event data recorders, Evidence, FAA, FDR, Nonvolatile memory (NVM), Nonvolatile random access memory (NVRAM), NTSB, Probable versus proximate cause, Recorded data disclosure, Recorder color, Recorder hostility, Recorder survivability, Route tracing, Speed, Tachograph chart analysis, Tachograph chart falsification, Tachographs, Technical truth, Traffic accident investigation, Video recording.

Review Questions

1. What is the probability of an airplane crash?
2. What is the NTSB? What is its role? How is it unique?
3. Why is causality never singular?
4. What is the difference between proximate and approximate causes?
5. What is the relevance of the world's first jet airliner, the Comet, to crash investigations?
6. What color are "black boxes"?
7. What are CVRs and FDRs? Why are they located in the rear of the plane?
8. What has delayed the results from analysis of the CVR and FDR in Air France Flight 447?
9. In a black box, what is the ECU?
10. What is NVRAM?
11. What is an EEPROM?
12. List the three ways data can be extracted from EDR/ECU data.
13. List the requirements for the retrieval, translation, and interpretation of EDR data.
14. What is a digital tachograph? What does it do?
15. What is a speed trace?
16. What is wheel slip and how can it effect accident reconstructions?
17. Why are low-speed incidents difficult to interpret with a tachograph?
18. What is the precision (acceptable error range) of a tachograph?
19. What is a "route trace"?
20. How long do digital tachograph devices hold information?

Discussion Questions

1. When Grose says, "In contrast to public perception, science is probabilistic—never certain and always subject to reversal should new findings disprove it," how does that apply to forensic science? The law wants a specific answer within a set timeframe (usually a trial). How can science meet the needs of the law if it is "subject to reversal"?
2. How would you correlate black box data with any eye witness accounts? Which you give greater weight to?

3. Why is black box data encrypted? What is the point? What would be the consequences of it not being encrypted?
4. Consider a car–train collision. What factors would you consider to determine if it was an accident or a suicide? Could you rule out homicide? What evidence would you want to collect and examine to rule out your multiple hypotheses?
5. What additional considerations would there be for a large-scale scene, such as an airplane crash or a train derailment, over a smaller scene? What kind of planning do you think would be necessary or prudent?

Additional Readings

Barbosa, H.C., Lima, D.A., Neto, A.M., Vitor, G.B., Martinesco, A., Rabelo, G., Etgens, V.H., 2016. November. The new generation of standard data recording device for intelligent vehicles. In: IEEE 19th International Conference on Intelligent Transportation Systems (ITSC), 2016. IEEE, pp. 2669–2674.

Chen, G., Wang, Y.C., Perronnet, A., Gu, C., Yao, P., Bin-Mohsin, B., Hajaiej, H., Scully, M.O., 2017. The advanced role of computational mechanics and visualization in science and technology: analysis of the Germanwings Flight 9525 crash. Physica Scripta 92 (3), 033002.

Khan, M.K., Zakariah, M., Malik, H., Choo, K.K.R., 2017. A novel audio forensic data-set for digital multimedia forensics. Australian Journal of Forensic Sciences 1–18.

Lebkowski, A., 2017. Electric vehicle data recorder. Measurement 1050, 35.

Oliver, N., Calvard, T., Potočnik, K., 2017. Cognition, Technology, and Organizational Limits: Lessons from the Air France 447 Disaster. Organization Science. http://dx.doi.org/10.1287/orsc.2017.1138.

Section 4. Documents

Documents are complex materials. Don't think so? Check out how paper is made[1]:

1. Typically, trees used for papermaking are specifically grown and harvested like a crop for that purpose. Forest products companies and private landowners plant millions of new seedlings every year.
2. To begin the process, logs are passed through a debarker, where the bark is removed, and through chippers, where spinning blades cut the wood into 1″ pieces. Those wood chips are then pressure-cooked with a mixture of water and chemicals in a digester. Used paper is another important source of paper fiber. Thanks to curbside recycling programs in many communities, 40% of all paper used in America for recycling and reuse. The paper is shredded and mixed with water.
3. The pulp is washed, refined, cleaned, and sometimes bleached, then turned to slush in the beater. Color dyes, coatings, and other additives are mixed in, and the pulp slush is pumped onto a moving wire screen. Computerized sensors and state-of-the-art control equipment monitor each stage of the process.
4. As the pulp travels down the screen, water is drained away and recycled. The resulting crude paper sheet, or web, is squeezed between large rollers to remove most of the remaining water and ensure smoothness and uniform thickness. The semidry web is then run through heated dryer rollers to remove the remaining water. Wastewater is carefully cleaned and purified before its release or reuse. Fiber particles and chemicals are filtered out and burned to provide additional power for the mill. Papermakers carefully test for such things as uniformity of color and surface, water resistance, and ink holding ability.
5. The finished paper is then wound into large rolls, which can be 30 feet wide and weigh close to 25 tons. A slitter cuts the paper into smaller, more manageable rolls, and the paper is ready for use.

And that is just the *generic* description of the overall process. There are literally hundreds if not thousands of commercially available paper types, and that excludes those used for classified or government use, such as currency and passports. From flashy cases such as supernotes, where excellent counterfeit $100 bills were circulated worldwide from the late 1980s to the early 2000s, to the simplest signature on a contract, document analysis requires the expert to know a dizzying array of technologies and materials, including paper, polymers, inks, dyes, pigments, oils, solvents, physics, and optics (for detection and analysis), among many others. Perhaps the complexity of the training, as well as the reduction of requests for document analysis in criminal cases (it still thrives in civil suits), is why many laboratories have abandoned this discipline in favor of more production-oriented methods, such as DNA.

History of the Forensic Examination of Documents

LA Mohammed, San Bruno, CA, USA

Introduction

Contentions in documents can relate to a whole range of factors including their authenticity, age, source, or content. Factors that must be considered are the substrate of the documents and the manner of their production. The content of the document may comprise the handwriting, typewriting, printing, or a combination of these or other forms of information.

Disputed documents can find their way into the legal system in both the criminal and civil arenas where the outcome of a case may depend on the evidential value of the document. In many cases, documents contribute to the overall evidence. However, in the cases described in this section, the documents involved were pivotal to the resolution.

---

[1] From Wisconsin Paper Council, www.wipapercouncil.org. Edited for space and content.

The Letters of Junius

In the eighteenth century, letters critical of the ruling establishment in England were published in a newspaper. These handwritten letters were anonymous and there was great debate as to who the author was. In the days when punishment for criticism of the King would be imprisonment or death, it was no wonder that the author wished to remain anonymous. Handwriting comparison by Charles Chabot pointed the finger at Sir Phillip Francis. While little is known of Chabot, his methodology reflected a thorough understanding of the principles of handwriting examination.

The Dreyfus Case

The case of Captain Alfred Dreyfus caused a scandal in France at the end of the nineteenth century. This case involved several forged documents, one of which was the infamous "bordereau." Capt. Dreyfus was accused of being a spy and of passing French military secrets to Germany. Despite the evidence of several handwriting experts that Dreyfus was not the author of the suspect documents, he was convicted twice in separate trials. A letter entitled "J'accuse" by novelist Emile Zola to a French newspaper whipped up world opinion and Dreyfus was later pardoned with all his rights restored. The true forger, a Col. Henry, confessed to the forgeries and he later committed suicide.

In the United States, expert testimony on handwriting was accepted in courts in the early nineteenth century. The experts were mainly bank tellers and penmanship teachers. Names such as Daniel T. Ames, William Hagan, and Albert S. Osborn were well known in the field. Ames and Hagan had both written books on document examination, but in 1910, Albert S. Osborn published "*Questioned Documents*," which became the standard treatise in the field. Osborn was a penman of great note, and his book was a comprehensive treatise on all aspects of document examination. The preface was written by Dean John Wigmore who was considered an authority in the law of evidence in the United States. Osborn wrote three more books "*The Mind of the Juror*," "*The Problem of Proof*," and "*Questioned Document Problems*." He was responsible for forming and establishing the American Society of Questioned Document Examiners. He emphasized the value of proper training for a document examiner and described the equipment needed for a fully equipped laboratory.

The Lindbergh Case

The kidnapping of the infant son of famed aviator Charles Lindbergh and the subsequent prosecution of Richard Bruno Hauptmann captivated the United States. Lindbergh's son, Charles Jr, was kidnapped from his room during the night. Fourteen ransom letters were eventually sent to the family. Eight document examiners, including Albert S. Osborn, were retained by the prosecution in this case to compare the handwriting on the ransom notes with the handwriting of the main suspect, Hauptmann. All eight examiners identified Hauptmann as the writer of the ransom notes. The examiners testified with the aid of demonstration charts. Their evidence was so convincing that even Hauptmann said, "Dot handwriting is the worstest thing against me." On April 9, 1936, Hauptmann was executed (**Figures 1–3**).

Hauptmann's widow, Anna, maintained that her husband was innocent and her case was supported by British author, Ludovich Kennedy. The Lindbergh case was reexamined in 2005 at the request of a television show Forensic Files by three contemporary document examiners: Peter Baier, Grant Sperry, and Gideon Epstein. Each conducted his examination independently and concluded with a varying degree of certainty that Hauptmann was indeed the writer of the ransom notes.

The Peter Weinberger Case

In another horrific case, Peter Weinberger was kidnapped from the front porch of his home on July 4, 1956 in what turned out to be a random crime. After the receipt of a ransom note for $200 000, the FBI conducted an examination of the handwriting of over 2 million people (**Figure 4**).

The ransom note contained what were considered to be characteristic letter formations. The FBI trained investigators to

Figure 1   Copy of one of the ransom notes. Source: www.fbi.gov.

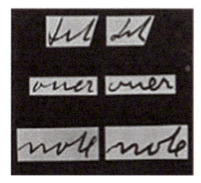

"Did"   "our"   "not"

Hauptmann   Ransom
    writing   notes

Figure 2 Comparison chart used to demonstrate the similarity between Hauptmann's handwriting (left) and the writing on a ransom note (right). The words from top to bottom are "Did," "our," and "note." Source: www.fbi.gov.

Figure 3 A chart showing Hauptmann's signature (top) and a composite of individual letters from a ransom note (bottom). Source: www.fbi.gov.

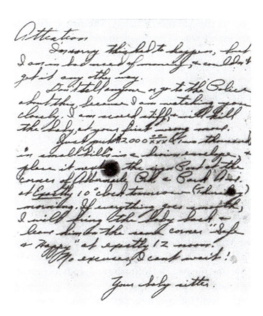

Figure 4 The first of the Weinberger ransom notes. Source: www.fbi.gov.

look for these specific features. Eventually, the handwriting of one person, Angelo De Marca, was identified from the Department of Motor Vehicle records. The body of Peter Weinberger, however, had already been found under some bushes near a road not far from the Weinberger home.

Angelo de Marca confessed to the kidnapping and murder and was executed at Sing Sing prison on August 7, 1958. This case had an impact on the timelines for kidnapping investigations. Instead of a waiting period of 3 weeks, the FBI could now be brought into a case within 24 h.

The Hitler Diaries

The investigation of the Hitler Diaries was a remarkable one given the number of documents that were forged and the simple way they were ultimately exposed as fakes. The German magazine "Stern" paid 2 million marks for 63 volumes of diaries purported to be of Adolf Hitler. In 1982, three

document examiners (one Swiss, one German, and one American) also compared the handwriting from the diaries with handwriting purportedly of Adolf Hitler. They each declared the handwriting in the diary to be authentic. However, the specimen handwriting that was provided to the examiners for comparison as the known handwriting of Adolph Hitler also included samples that had been written by the forger of the diaries. Therefore, while the examiner's handwriting examination was correct, his conclusion that the handwriting in the diaries was Hitler's was wrong. The voluminous material was examined by historians in 1983 and declared to be genuine.

Eventually, in 1983, Dr Julius Grant exposed the diaries as a fraud by the simple fact that the pages in the diaries contained optical brighteners. The optical brighteners, which were apparent when exposed to ultraviolet (UV) radiation, were not used in paper that was manufactured during the dates when the diaries were purportedly written. Also in 1983, the Federal Bureau of Criminal Investigation examined three of the diaries (1934, 1943, and 1944) and found evidence from the inks, bookbinding, paper, and typewriting that confirmed the hoax.

The Mormon Forgeries and Murders

The Mark Hoffman case was a crime that ballooned from forgery to mayhem and murder. Mark Hoffman was a dealer in old books and papers. He was a Mormon and soon realized that he could make a lot of money selling documents pertaining to the Mormon Church. The first document that Hoffman found was "The Salamander Letter." After several years of selling and trading documents, Hoffmann began to be suspected of peddling forged documents. To throw off suspicion, he started a series of bombings in the 1980s in which he was the first to get injured.

In 1985, George Throckmorton, a forensic document examiner (FDE) from Utah, was hired to examine Hoffman's documents. Throckmorton was a Mormon and he wanted another examiner who was not a Mormon. William Flynn, a Catholic from Arizona, joined Throckmorton in the examination. Throckmorton and Flynn noted a peculiar feature that was common to Hoffman's documents. The ink on the documents displayed a cracked or alligator pattern (**Figure 5**).

They researched old ink formulas with which they knew Hoffman was familiar and hit upon one that had the same alligatoring effect when combined with sodium hydroxide. They could now unerringly pick Hoffman-produced documents.

Throckmorton and Flynn devised a combination of tests that could detect Hoffman forgeries. UV radiation was used to disclose a discoloration caused by the treatment of documents with chemicals such as sodium hydroxide. They described the effect as blue haze. UV radiation also disclosed a unidirectional running of iron gall ink caused by the chemicals, which Hoffman used to mimic artificial aging. Chemical treatment also caused "bleed through," which depended to some extent on the paper type.

Microscopic examination revealed the "alligatoring" effect caused by the iron gall ink cracking when treated with hydrogen peroxide and ammonium hydroxide. Solubility tests, the presence of printing flaws from photographic negatives, observation of the lack of stains from old iron gall ink, and

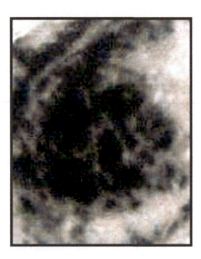

Figure 5 Example of alligatoring in ink seen under the microscope. Source: http://www.trutv.com.

scanning auger microscopy dating were other techniques used to reveal the Hoffman forgeries. These techniques were used in combination and it is this use of multiple tests that provided conclusive proof of the forgeries.

During their 18-month investigation, Flynn and Throckmorton examined over 6000 documents dated between 1792 and 1929. 448 of these were Hoffman documents, of which 268 (60%) were found to be authentic, 68 (15%) were not proven as genuine or forged, and 107 (27%) were proven as forged.

Hoffman eventually pled guilty to two counts of second-degree murder, forgery of the Salamander Letter, and other associated crimes. He was sentenced to four concurrent terms of 5 years to life in the state penitentiary.

The Howard Hughes "Mormon Will" Case

On April 5, 1976, billionaire and recluse Howard Hughes died. No official will of Hughes could be found despite the fact that he owned a vast business empire. Once word of this spread, over 30 wills were submitted to the County Clerk in Nevada. One of these wills became known as "The Mormon Will," as it was delivered by an official of the Mormon Church. The will had been left at the Church addressed to the President of the Church. The handwritten will gave one-sixteenth of Hughes estate to the Mormon Church and another one-sixteenth to an individual named Melvin Du Mar [sic]. Melvin Dummar's story was that he had picked up Hughes hitchhiking in the desert several years before. Dummar initially denied knowing anything about the will. However, his fingerprint was found on one of the envelopes left at the Mormon Church. He later admitted to writing the note to the Church and that he delivered the will to the Church.

The will was examined in court in Las Vegas by FDE John "Jack" Harris. Harris knew almost immediately that the will was as he described "a rank forgery." Harris had access to numerous samples of Hughes' handwriting and signatures and he found many features in the will that did not correspond with Hughes' handwriting. Harris described the writing on the will as slow and laborious and several letter forms did not match. He also pointed out differences in features such as i-dots, t-crossings, and commas. The natural variation seen in the specimen Hughes handwriting was absent in the handwriting on the will.

There were four signatures in the name of H.R. Hughes on the will and another on the envelope. These were also shown to be palpable forgeries. The forgeries appeared to be copied from signatures of Hughes that were illustrated in the book *Hoax*, which was written about the forgery of a biography of Hughes.

There were numerous other discrepancies between the known handwriting of Hughes and the handwriting on the will. Nevertheless, there was a trial that commenced on November 7, 1977 and finished on May 8, 1978. The jury took a day and a half to return a verdict that the "Mormon Will" was a forgery.

The Alger Hiss Case

A Woodstock typewriter, bearing the serial number 230 099, played a central role in the Alger Hiss case. The case for the US government was that Hiss, alleged to be a Soviet spy, used the typewriter to copy secret documents. The case for Hiss' defense was that the US government forged Hiss' typewriter by building an exact replica. During Hiss' trial in 1948, the prosecutor Thomas Murphy described the typewriter as the main witness against Hiss. Hiss' defense engaged the services of Martin Tytell of New York to build a typewriter to show that forgery of a typewriter was possible. Tytell only had to work from specimens of the Woodstock's typing, which made it a very difficult job, as he had to get the defects in the typefaces and alignment in the typing correct. However, he owned a typewriter repair shop that contained thousands of typefaces and he had extensive experiences in typewriter repair. Tytell constructed the "Woodstock" at a cost of $750 000. Prominent FDEs such as Donald Doud and Ordway Hilton considered that Tytell could not have built a perfect replica that would be good enough to get past a trained FDE. Hiss was tried for perjury twice with the first trial ending in a hung jury. He was found guilty in the second trial on two counts of perjury. Tytell's typewriter was built for an appeal by Hiss for a new trial. However, it was denied as the trial judge ruled that there was no evidence that the prosecution had access to a typewriter fabricator with Tytell's skill.

Hiss could not have been tried for espionage, as the statute of limitations had run out. He was sentenced to 5 years and eventually served 44 months. At his sentencing on January 25, 1950, Hiss remarked that "I am confident that in the future the full facts of how Whittaker Chambers was able to carry out forgery by typewriter will be disclosed." Despite the length of time that has passed, the Hiss case remains controversial in the United States. Former President Richard. M. Nixon had been involved early on in the investigation of Hiss when Nixon was a member of the House of Representatives. Hiss' family still actively defends his innocence.

The Unabomber

Between May 25, 1978 and April 24, 1995, Theodore Kaczynski was responsible for sending a series of bombs through the mail to universities and airlines. Because of this, he was dubbed the unabomber—"una" for "university" and "a" for "airlines." Kaczynski, who held a doctoral degree in mathematics, was antitechnology and produced a typewritten manifesto in which he detailed his demands in order to have the bombings stopped. After he was arrested based on a tip from his brother, investigators found three manual typewriters in Kaczynski's rustic home in Montana. One of the typewriters, a Smith-Corona, was identified as the machine that was used to type the manifesto. Kaczynski eventually pled guilty in 1998 to 13 counts of attacks in three states that killed three and injured two. He was sentenced to life and is confined in isolation at a "Supermax" prison in Colorado without any possibility of parole.

The Killian Memos

During the 2004 General Election in the United States, a document was produced that indicated that incumbent President George W. Bush had attempted to evade National Guard duty. The document was a copy, and CBS News hired several FDEs to determine whether or not the document was authentic. The FDEs' opinions ranged from inconclusive to authentic. Peter Tytell, an FDE from New York and a noted typewriter expert, quickly showed that the document was very likely not to be authentic as the typewritten date had a superscript for the "th." In the early 1970s, there were very few typewriters that could type a superscript and the possibility of one being on a far-flung military base was remote. There were also differences in typestyle and spacing, which caused Tytell to conclude that the memos were prepared by a word processing program rather than on an Olympia manual typewriter. A panel appointed by CBS News concluded that there were serious problems about the authenticity of the memos. The panel strongly criticized CBS News. The producer was fired and several top executives resigned.

The Jon Benet Ramsey Case

On the night of Christmas in 1996, 6-year-old Jon Benet Ramsey was put to bed at 9.30 p.m. The next morning her mother, Patricia, went down to breakfast at 5.00 a.m. and in the kitchen found a two-page ransom note demanding $118 000 for the return of Jon Benet. Eight hours later, during a search of the house, John Ramsey found his daughter's body in a basement room. The young girl, according to the autopsy report, had been strangled, suffered severe head injuries, and may have been sexually assaulted. During the search of the home, police officers allowed the family and friends throughout the house, thereby compromising possible forensic evidence.

Attention was immediately focused on the handwritten ransom letter. The amount of $118 000 curiously matched John Ramsey's bonus for that year. The family became the main suspects. Document examiners compared the writing on the note with samples taken from Patricia, John, and Jon Benet's brother, Burke, who was 9 years old at the time. John and Burke as well as John's two adult children from a previous marriage were quickly cleared as possible authors of the note. Patricia became the prime suspect. Several FDEs were asked to conduct examinations and the majority opined that Patricia was probably not the writer, although a minority of FDEs opined that she had indeed written the note.

The handwriting on the note may have been disguised, which led to some of the problems in identifying the writer. However, the general consensus was that none of the Ramsey family members were involved in writing the note. In June 2006, Patricia Ramsey died from ovarian cancer. Two months later, John Mark Kerr who was in prison in Thailand confessed to killing Jon Benet. He was extradited to the United States where DNA evidence quickly showed that he was not the guilty party in this case.

The Jon Benet Ramsey case remains unsolved at the time of writing. Most investigators now believe that an unknown intruder was involved. The evolution of forensic DNA and handwriting examination techniques may be the key to solving the murder of a 6-year-old child on Christmas night in 1996.

The Zodiac Killer

In July 1969, letters were mailed to three newspapers in San Francisco. The writer claimed to be responsible for two attacks on courting couples. In the first attack, the couple was killed and, in the second, the male survived but the woman died. The letters were handwritten in blue felt-tip ink and described facts that only the investigators would know. In each letter, the writer enclosed a coded cipher and demanded that the newspapers publish his letters on their front pages warning that he would go on a murderous rampage if they did not comply. The newspapers complied and sent the San Franciscans into a state of panic (**Figure 6**).

The killings continued with the stabbing of a couple in which the woman died. After shooting to death a cabdriver on October 13, 1969, the killer mailed a letter to the San Francisco Chronicle, which included a bloodstained piece of the cabdriver's shirt. He called himself "The Zodiac." He then threatened to kill schoolchildren either by shooting or with a bomb. However, despite sending several more letters, no more killings were reported.

Figure 6   Cipher sent to the Vallejo Times-Herald. Source: http://www.trutv.com.

The handwriting on the letters (14 of them) was compared to many suspects but no one was identified as the Zodiac. Three main suspects were developed by amateur investigators. Development of partial DNA evidence from the back of a stamp on an envelope excluded all three suspects. The DNA from saliva on the back of the stamp was assumed to be that of the Zodiac. The case remains unsolved.

Admissibility

Questioned document evidence was readily accepted in US courts where the standard of admissibility was the Frye rule of general acceptance. In 1993, the US Supreme Court established what came to be known as the Daubert guidelines in the case of Daubert v. Merrell-Dow Pharmaceuticals. The intent of these guidelines was to make the trial judge the "gatekeeper" of scientific evidence in an effort to keep junk science out of the courts. In 1998, a Daubert hearing to exclude handwriting evidence was held in the case of United States v. Starzecpyzel. The trial judge ruled that while handwriting evidence was not scientific, it was admissible under the Daubert guidelines as technical evidence.

Two trials, General Electric v. Joiner (1997) and Kumho Tire Company v. Carmichael (1999), became the second and third parts of the Daubert trilogy. The Kumho decision ruled that technical evidence was also subject to Daubert guidelines. Daubert hearings were held to exclude the testimony of FDEs in several cases. In some cases, the FDE was limited to testifying to findings but not being able to express an opinion. In other cases, the FDE was excluded altogether.

However, the FDE community was hard at work responding to the criticisms aimed at it in the Daubert hearings. Empirical research in conjunction with the academic community was conducted and the results published. Additional Daubert requirements were addressed and met. In 2002, in the case of United States v. Prime, a Daubert hearing was conducted and the judge ruled that the FDE had met all the Daubert guidelines.

FDEs have met the challenges posed by the development of the ballpoint pen, the typewriter, photocopiers, fax machines, imaging software, and laser and inkjet printers. Research by FDEs, neuroscientists, motor control scientists, and computer scientists is ongoing to investigate and strengthen the foundations of forensic document examination, in particular, handwriting examination.

See also: **Documents:** Analytical Methods; Document Dating; Forgery/Counterfeits; Handwriting; Ink Analysis; Overview of Forensic Document Examination; Paper Analysis.

Further Reading

Ames, D.T., 1992. Ames on Forgery. Fred B. Rothman & Co, Littleton, CO.

Baier, P.E., Michel, L., 1985. The diaries of Adolf Hitler implication for document examination. Journal of the Forensic Science Society 25, 67–178.

Cantu, A.A., 1986. The paper Mate® ink on the howard Hughes 'Mormon will'. Journal of Forensic Sciences 31 (1), 360–364.

Chabot, C., 1871. The Handwriting of Junius 1769. John Murray, London.

Chapman, G., 1972. The Dreyfus Trials. Stein and Day, New York, NY.

Cook, F.J., 1958. The Unfinished Story of Alger Hiss. William Morrow & Company, New York, NY.

Fisher, J., 1987. The Lindbergh Case. Rutgers University Press, New Brunswick and London.

Fisher, J., 1999. The Ghosts of Hopewell. Setting the Record Straight in the Lindbergh Case. Southern Illinois University Press, Carbondale and Edwardsville.

Freese, P.L., 1986. Howard Hughes and Melvin Dummar: forensic science versus film fiction. Journal of Forensic Sciences 31 (1), 342–359.

Grant, J., 1985. The diaries of Adolf Hitler. Journal of the Forensic Science Society 25, 189.

Graysmith, R., 2007. Zodiac Unmasked. Penguin Group, New York, NY.

Hagan, W.E., 1974. Treatise on Disputed Handwriting. Ames Press Inc, New York, NY.

Haring, J.V., 1937. The Hand of Hauptmann. The Hamer Publishing Company, Plainfield, NJ.

Harris, J.J., 1986. The document evidence and some other observations about the Howard R. Hughes 'Mormon Will contest'. Journal of Forensic Sciences 31 (1), 365–375.

Hicks, F.A., 2003. The greatest handwriting mystery of the eighteenth century: the Junius Letters. Journal of the American Society of Questioned Document Examiners 5 (2), 67–77.

Hilton, O., 1979. History of questioned document examination in the United States. Journal of Forensic Sciences 24 (4), 890–897.

Kennedy, L., 1985. The Airman and the Carpenter. The Lindbergh Case and the Framing of Richard Hauptmann. Collins, London, UK.

Osborn, A.S., 1929. Questioned Documents, second ed. Patterson Smith, New Montclair, NJ.

Rhoden, H., 1980. High Stakes. The Gamble for the Howard Hughes Will. Crown Publishers, Inc., New York, NY.

Sillitoe, L., Roberts, A., 1988. Salamander. The Story of the Mormon Forgery Murders. Signature Books, Salt Lake City, Utah.

Wood, J.F., 1930. The Leopold-Loeb case (From the standpoint of the handwriting, pen printing, and typewriting expert). American Journal of Police Science 1, 339–352.

Relevant Websites

http://abcnews.go.com—ABC News.

www.cedartech.com—CedarTech, Pattern Recognition Technology.

www.trutv.com/librar—Crime library, Criminal Minds and Methods.

http://www.washingtonpost.com—Expert Cited by CBS Says He Didn't Authenticate Papers.

http://www.fbi.gov—The FBI, Federal Bureau of Investigation: Famous Cases and Criminals.

http://www.usatoday.com—USA Today. News.

Overview of Forensic Document Examination

DL Hammond, U.S. Army Criminal Investigation Laboratory, Forest Park, GA, USA

Glossary

Black box testing A research/testing strategy used to assess the reliability and validity of forensic methods and/or techniques, which rely primarily on subjective and experience-based decision-making.

What Is a Forensic Document Examiner?

When was a document created? How was it created? Who prepared the document? What device was used to create the document? Is the document genuine? Has the document been altered? Experts in the field of forensic document examination are confronted with these, and other, questions on a daily basis. The field of forensic document examination has developed over time because of the courts' needs to correctly interpret and resolve these types of questions. These issues typically arise in legal matters, both civil and criminal, and often require the unique talents of highly skilled and reliable experts referred to as forensic document examiners (FDEs).

What Are the Duties of an FDE?

An FDE's primary duties include the examination, comparison, and analysis of documents in order to (1) determine genuineness or nongenuineness, to expose forgery, or to reveal alterations, additions, or deletions; (2) provide evidence as to the authorship or nonauthorship of handwritten entries (i.e., cursive handwriting, hand printing, and signatures); (3) provide evidence as to the source of typewriting or other mechanical impressions, marks, or relative evidence; and (4) prepare written reports and provide expert testimony as needed.

For many examiners, the examination and comparison of questioned (i.e., disputed) and known writing specimens for the purpose of determining authorship dominate their daily casework. As a result, FDEs are commonly referred to as handwriting experts. As a general rule, this title is appropriate; however, it does not do justice to the variety of examinations and comparisons that fall within the discipline of forensic document examination.

Exploring FDE Casework

In spite of the continued push for a paperless society, FDEs remain actively employed in local, state/province, federal, and private forensic laboratories worldwide and are routinely called upon to provide forensic support in all types of civil and criminal cases. Homicides, sexual assault, drugs, identity theft, bank robberies, hate crimes, terrorism, financial fraud, child abuse, theft, counterfeiting, medical malpractice, and a plethora of almost any other civil and criminal issues can arise that may require the assistance of an FDE.

Types of Examinations

There are a broad range of examinations and comparisons conducted in traditional forensic document laboratories and may involve almost anything relating to the production of a document. One case may focus on a single examination type (e.g., handwriting comparison), while another case may present the need to take a multifaceted approach (e.g., ink analysis, detection and development of indented writing, and handwriting comparison) and require various examination methods in order to develop the full evidentiary value of the item(s).

Handwriting

Handwriting comparisons (the examination and comparison of questioned and known handwriting, hand printing, and signatures) are the most prevalent examination type encountered and often constitute 80% or more of the day-to-day case load in many modern forensic document laboratories.

Handwriting examinations can either consist of the examination of questioned writing and known specimen writing or be based solely on a comparison of one questioned document to one or more additional questioned documents

---

(e.g., determination of common authorship among a series of threatening anonymous letters). However, the typical handwriting comparison will involve the comparison of a questioned handwritten item(s) to a set of known writings from one or more individuals. In this instance, the analyst will attempt to determine whether there is evidence to support which, if any, of the writers of the known specimens wrote, or did not write, the disputed writing.

Other examinations

Aside from handwritten text and signature examinations, FDEs may use their expertise in a large number of areas including the following:

- The detection and decipherment of indented writing in paper
- Physical matching, reconstruction, and dating of paper, tape, and adhesives
- Differentiating different types of inks
- The detection and decipherment of alterations, obliterations, and erasures
- The examination of type and typewriters (e.g., typestyle classification to establish make/model of typewriter; ribbon and correction ribbon examination; the identification of the source of a typewritten document and the establishment of the date of manufacture of a typewritten document)
- The examination of printers (laser, inkjet, etc.) and printed documents, fax machine, and facsimile documents
- The determination of the sequence of two or more intersecting strokes
- The determination of printing processes associated with counterfeit documents

Types of documents examined

Documents exist in our day-to-day lives and can provide a "paper trail" of our activities. Documents can play an important role in linking an individual to a crime by placing them at a location and perhaps during a specific time period. A document may provide evidence that one person knows or has had contact with another person. The information on a document can also form the basis to determine where or how a document was prepared, who prepared it, and when the document was prepared. Information altered on a document can be detected to verify that the content of a document has been changed or modified to appear to be something else.

Some examples of the types of documents examined include the following:

- Anonymous letters (threatening notes, bomb threats, and robbery notes)
- Financial documents (checks, credit card/debit cards receipts, promissory notes, tax returns, purchase receipts, and bill of sale)

- Deeds, wills, contracts and agreements, and applications
- Log books
- Suicide notes
- Prescriptions
- Time sheets
- Work orders
- Certificates
- Performance evaluations
- Diaries and journals
- School papers
- Post-it notes
- Envelopes and letters
- Address books
- Graffiti
- Lottery tickets
- Counterfeiting (currency, credit cards, ID cards, driver's license, passports, immigration documents, etc.)

Instrumentation

The most common method of analysis in the examination of documents is a side-by-side comparison of items. As a result, the examiner's cognitive machinery serves as the most used "instrument" in the analysis, comparison, and evaluation process. A stereomicroscope is often used to aid and enhance the examiner's ability to distinguish fine detail through the use of low-power magnification (i.e., up to ×40).

Some of the other instruments and tools commonly used may include, but are not limited to, the following:

- Video spectral analysis devices (ink and paper differentiation)
- Hyperspectral analysis devices (ink and paper differentiation)
- Ultraviolet light boxes and handheld wands (ink and paper differentiation)
- Micrometers (paper thickness)
- Electrostatic detection devices (development of indented writings)
- Digital imaging processing software (ink and paper differentiation)

The Origins of Modern Forensic Document Examination

Before the establishment of law enforcement crime laboratories, forensic document examination was dominated by individual practitioners primarily working in private practices. These practitioners, often expert penmen, calligraphers, and others interested in handwriting, were self-taught experts who turned their expertise into one of the first forensic science disciplines.

Arguably, the most influential individual in the development of modern forensic document examination was Albert S. Osborn. Osborn worked tirelessly to promote the field and to extend its acceptance in the legal system of the United States.

Considered by many to be the founding father of document examination, Osborn was a prolific writer, who in 1910 published *Questioned Documents*. Later republished in 1929, this book provided many of the theories and principles that are still relevant and used in practice more than a century later.

The development of the discipline

Before about the middle of the twentieth century, self-education was about the only manner in which one could become an FDE. Albert S. Osborn believed strongly in the development of the profession through the sharing of information among colleagues. Osborn often invited small groups of well-respected colleagues to his home to foster the sharing of information and ideas. These meetings eventually led to the creation of the American Society of Questioned Document Examiners in 1942.

Establishing formal training programs

The American Academy of Forensic Sciences was established in the late 1940s; and by the 1960s, forensic document examination, known at the time as "questioned document examination" or "document examination," was starting to mature and grow. Up until this point, self-education and informal apprenticeships were the only methods for training in forensic document examination. As the need for crime laboratories increased, it became apparent that formal training programs needed to be developed and qualifications for forensic experts established and defined. By the late 1960s, formalized, structured written training programs began to appear. Although still centered on an apprenticeship-based model, the 2-year training programs provided detailed required reading lists, lectures, practical exercises, and knowledge- and competency-based written, practical, and/or oral examinations. In the years since, the model for training in forensic document examination has essentially remained unchanged. In 2005, a modified version of this training model was established and published as a voluntary consensus standard within the international community.

Qualifications of Modern FDEs

Regrettably, a wide variance exists in the qualifications of those currently practicing as FDEs. In spite of the fact that many of the organizations within the profession have set high standards of qualification, courts have established thresholds for the admission of expert witnesses, which fall well short of the modern standards held in the FDE community.

As a general rule, courts will admit someone as an expert witness in a scientific or other field provided that the witness' knowledge in that subject matter (by way of their education, training, experience, or skill) is perceived to be beyond that of the average person. If the "expertise" of a potential expert witness is not thoroughly vetted, the door may be left open to a number of pseudoexperts and charlatans.

Education

Most forensic laboratories and document-related professional organizations require examiners to have a baccalaureate degree from an accredited academic institution. As the interest in forensic science has increased dramatically in recent years, the number of academic institutions offering undergraduate- and graduate-level degrees in forensic science has greatly expanded. Forensic laboratories have been the immediate benefactor, as incoming trainees are entering into careers in forensic document examination with graduate-level degrees in forensic science or with degrees that have a strong background in science. With an ever-growing interest in strengthening the "science" in the forensic sciences, the influx of more traditionally trained scientists should continue to push the field of forensic document examination forward.

Visual Acuity

As most of the tasks conducted by FDEs involve visual examinations and comparisons, a key prerequisite is the ability of the examiner to distinguish fine detail. To assess this ability, applicants must be able to successfully complete several preliminary tests to evaluate their suitability for training. Typical prehire evaluations may therefore include the following:

- Form blindness/form discrimination tests
- Color perception/color blindness tests
- Visual Acuity tests

The absence of even one of these abilities is likely to serve as a basis of exclusion from a forensic document training program.

Training

The modern standard for training in forensic document examination is the successful completion of a broad-based formal 2-year apprenticeship style training program under the tutelage of a qualified principal trainer. The FDE training programs typically cover all aspects of modern forensic document examination methods and procedures. Teaching methods include the following:

- Required reading
- Lectures
- Demonstration (i.e., practical exercises)
- Knowledge and competency assessments (e.g., written, practical, and oral examinations)
- Mock trials

- Supervised casework
- Research projects
- Tours of manufacturing plants

Specialists

Owing to the limited nature of their casework, some laboratories limit the examiner's training to a specific element(s) of forensic document examination. Examples of some forensic document-related specialties include the following:

- Forensic ink chemists
- Handwriting experts/specialists
- Counterfeit specialists

To account for this diversity, one forensic document organization (the American Society of Questioned Document Examiners) recently created a "specialist" membership category.

Posttraining Qualifications

The continuing education and professional development of FDEs do not end at the completion of training but should continue throughout the career of the individual. Skill sets need to be continually assessed, and the examiners should make every effort to keep up with emerging technologies and changes in examination methodologies and procedures.

Certification

Certification provides a mechanism whereby members of the judicial system and other interested parties can easily identify those individuals engaged in forensic document examination, who have demonstrated adequate levels of qualification and competence. While there are several certification boards worldwide that certify FDEs, there are only a few that have been externally accredited.

Some of the key elements of any certification program include the following:

- Credentials review
- Testing
- Requirements for recertification
- Verification of training
- Code of ethics

Unfortunately, individual certification is generally neither a requirement to work in most forensic laboratories nor a requirement that must be met in order to provide expert testimony in most courts. This may soon change, at least in the United States, as there has been a renewed interest in the last few years toward requiring all forensic scientists to obtain individual certification.

Proficiency testing

Proficiency testing can be used as a means to assess the skills and expertise of the examiner for the various tasks associated with forensic document examination. However, proficiency testing is similar to certification in that it is another element of continuing education and ongoing professional development that is often underappreciated, and depending on where one is employed, it may not even be required.

Proficiency tests that are not based on actual casework are preferred. Feedback that is based on tests, where there are true known answers, provides a mechanism for learning. In the absence of true known answers, there always exists the possibility that bad habits or bad methodology or procedures will not be revealed.

Proficiency tests should be challenging. Being able to successfully complete easy tasks does nothing to develop expert performers and may serve only to further the examiner's belief of expertise when he or she may not have any. This false belief can be extended especially if the examiner's exposure to testing is limited. Anytime that a human element is involved, errors are sure to happen. If an examiner, whether an FDE or an examiner in any other forensic discipline, claims to have a "zero error rate," it is probably safe to say that they have not been exposed to enough testing.

Error rates and skill–task assessments

In the past decade, there has been a large increase in the number of studies and tests aimed at assessing the potential error rates associated with the various tasks conducted by FDEs. Slowly, these studies are helping to define the limits of forensic document examination and have helped identify areas where additional research should be targeted.

It is unlikely that these tests will ever be able to provide a definite error rate for a given task. However, over time and through exposure to multiple tests covering a range of problems with varying difficulties, a clearer picture of the nature of the skill and expertise of FDEs will emerge. In time, perhaps, courts will begin to require some form of documentation from all forensic scientists, which illustrates their individual skills based on some form of "black box" testing.

Other mechanisms for professional development and continuing education

An excellent means to further one's knowledge and education within forensic document examination is by being active in professional organizations. There are numerous professional organizations and societies around the world where an FDE can seek membership. Many of these organizations host annual conferences, seminars, and workshops, where emerging techniques and methods of analysis are presented and discussed. Attendees are also exposed to new technologies that may redefine the boundaries of a technique or allow an analysis to be completed faster and/or cheaper. The ability to network within the community is also an important element of being involved in the larger community. Sooner or later, every expert is bound to come across something that is unfamiliar and that requires consultation within the peer group before taking a step forward.

Issues for the Future

Forensic science continues to grow and evolve, as new techniques and capabilities are rapidly emerging. With this growth, more and more emphasis is being placed on the need to conduct research. Fortunately, after years of neglect, funding for research related to forensic document examination is starting to appear. Given the legal challenges over the past 15 years to all of the comparative sciences (e.g., document examination, latent prints, firearms and tool marks, etc.), the renewed emphasis on research will only aid in placing each of these fields on a stronger scientific footing.

Acknowledgment

The opinions or assertions contained herein are the private views of the author and are not to be construed as official or as reflecting the views of the Department of the Army or the Department of Defense.

See also: **Documents:** Analytical Methods; Document Dating; Forgery/Counterfeits; Handwriting; History of the Forensic Examination of Documents; Ink Analysis; Paper Analysis.

Further Reading

ASTM Standard E2388-11, 2008. Standard Guide for Minimum Training Requirements for Forensic Document Examiners. ASTM International, West Conshohocken, PA. http://dx.doi.org/10.1520/E2388-11.

ASTM Standard E444-09, 2008. Standard Guide for Scope of Work of Forensic Document Examiners. ASTM International, West Conshohocken, PA. http://dx.doi.org/10.1520/E0444-09.

Dyer, A.G., Found, B., Rogers, D., 2006. Visual attention and expertise for forensic signature analysis. Journal of Forensic Sciences 51 (6), 1397–1404.

Fisher, J., 1994. The Lindbergh Case. Rutgers University Press, Piscataway, NJ.

Found, B., Rogers, D., 2003. The initial profiling trial of a program to characterize forensic handwriting examiners' skill. Journal of the American Society of Questioned Document Examiners 6 (2), 72–81.

Huber, R.A., Headrick, A.M., 1999. Handwriting Identification: Facts and Fundamentals. CRC Press, Boca Raton.

Kam, M., Gummadidala, K., Fielding, G., Conn, R., 2001. Signature authentication by forensic document examiners. Journal of Forensic Sciences 46 (4), 884–888.

Kam, M., Lin, E., 2003. Writer identification using hand-printed and non-hand-printed questioned documents. Journal of Forensic Sciences 48 (6), 1391–1395.

Kelly, J.S., Lindblom, B.S., 2006. Scientific Examination of Questioned Documents. CRC Press, Boca Raton.

Merlino, M.L., Sprinter, V., Kelly, J.S., Hammond, D., Sahota, E., Haines, L., 2007. Meeting the challenges of the Daubert trilogy: redefining the reliability of forensic evidence. Tulsa Law Review 43 (2), 417–445.

Mnookin, J.L., 2008. Of black boxes, instruments, and experts: testing the validity of forensic science. Episteme 5, 343–358.

Osborn, A.S., 1929. Questioned Documents, second ed. Nelson-Hall Co, Chicago.

Risinger, D.M., 2009. Handwriting identification. In: Faigman, D.L., Saks, M.J., Sanders, J., Cheng, E.K. (Eds.), ,, Modern Scientific Evidence: The Law and Science of Expert Testimony, vol. 4. Thomson Reuters/West, Eagan, MN, pp. 451–643.

Sita, J., Found, B., Rogers, D., 2002. Forensic handwriting examiners' expertise for signature comparison. Journal of Forensic Sciences 47, 1117–1124.

Srihari, S.N., Cha, S., Arora, H., Lee, S., 2002. Individuality of handwriting. Journal of Forensic Sciences 47 (4), 856–872.

Relevant Websites

http://www.aafs.org—American Academy of Forensic Sciences.
http://www.asqde.org—American Society of Questioned Document Examiners.
http://www.astm.org—ASTM International.
http://www.collaborativetesting.com—Collaborative Testing Service, Inc.
http://www.thefsab.org—Forensic Specialties Accreditation Board.
http://www.st2ar.org—Skill-Task Training, Assessment and Research, Inc.

Analytical Methods

J de Koeijer, Netherlands Forensic Institute, The Hague, The Netherlands

Glossary

Multispectral analysis Optical analysis of reflection and fluorescence characteristics at various wavelengths in the ultraviolet, visible, and near-infrared region of the electromagnetic spectrum.

Questioned documents analysis The forensic analysis of documents to determine authenticity, date of production, latent contents, or (common) origin.

Introduction

In the past decade, research in document examination has been largely technology driven. The introduction of new analytical techniques has opened the door to new and improved methods for the analysis of inks, toner, and paper. A second driving force has been changes in the materials and technologies used to produce documents, which have fueled the need for new methods of analysis. The move from soluble dye-based inks to insoluble pigment-based inks is a good example of such a change necessitating a new analysis strategy. Document examiners in the past relied heavily on chromatographic techniques such as thin-layer chromatography (TLC) to analyze inks, but these techniques have become increasingly less applicable, as modern pigment-based inks such as gel pen ink and black inkjet inks cannot be extracted from the paper anymore. The newer so-called "hyphenated" techniques with a mass spectrometer as a detector show much potential in this area of analysis, combining high discrimination power with low detection limits. Techniques such as laser ablation inductively coupled plasma mass spectrometry (LA–ICPMS), laser desorption mass spectrometry, and secondary ion mass spectrometry (SIMS) are now being discovered by document examiners. Also, chromatographic techniques such as thermal desorption gas chromatography–mass spectrometry (TD–GC/MS) and high-performance liquid chromatography–MS (HPLC–MS) have become more and more mainstream and are slowly replacing the traditional analytical methods. Many document examiners, however, often still rely on trusted, nondestructive, relatively inexpensive, and often highly effective techniques such as ultraviolet fluorescence, infrared fluorescence, TLC, Raman spectroscopy (RS), and Fourier transform infrared (FTIR) spectrometry. This chapter discusses both the traditional and the newer trends of analysis and their application to document examination.

The Traditional Methods

The traditional document analysis methods fall into three main categories: optical, spectroscopic, or chromatographic. Whereas the methods in the first two are essentially nondestructive, often needing little sample preparation, chromatography generally needs a destructive form of sampling.

Optical Methods

For decades now, document examiners have relied on optical methods exploiting both luminescent and reflective properties of inks and paper for the examination of questioned documents. While the stereomicroscope may still be considered one of the most important tools for an examiner of questioned documents, multispectral examination of documents in the ultraviolet (UV), visible (Vis), and near-infrared (NIR) region of the electromagnetic spectrum has also become one of the first methods a document examiner will turn to in daily casework. In dealing with the authentication of documents or the examination of added, concealed, erased, or faded entries, the luminescent and reflective properties of inks and paper provide document examiners with the possibility of quick discrimination and enhancement of weak or latent features. Manufacturers of security documents have also picked up on this by adding fibers and inks with special luminescent or reflective properties as security features. These may be checked using the standard multispectral equipment a document examiner will normally have access to (**Figure 1**).

Microscopy, as mentioned earlier, is still an essential part of the examination of a questioned document and is mainly used to study the morphology of the surface of the paper or ink to determine, for example, the writing instrument or printing method used to produce a document, unusual paper fiber disturbance, faint remnants of previous entries, or the sequence

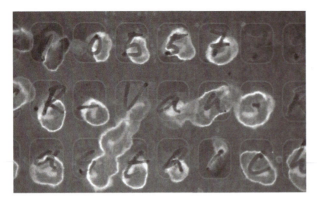

Figure 1 Infrared fluorescent image of the chemical erasure of a bank draft.

in which entries have been placed on the document. Besides the traditional microscopic examinations, miniaturization of security features is also demanding more and more from a microscope in terms of magnification and depth of field. This often forces the document examiner to opt for a digital video microscope, which can deal with these new specifications.

Spectroscopic Methods

Spectroscopy has always been a firm basis for a document examiner to rely on when dealing with the comparison of paper, inks, toners, tapes, etc. The spectroscopic techniques applied to documents may be roughly divided into two main categories: those dealing with elemental analysis and those based more on molecular phenomena.

Elemental spectroscopy

The most commonly used method for elemental spectroscopy is X-ray fluorescence (XRF) spectroscopy or micro-XRF (μ-XRF) if smaller areas are to be analyzed. While XRF is often used for comparison of paper, μ-XRF can also be applied to toner and other pigmented inks. Similar applications are also dealt with at a much higher magnification using a scanning electron microscope with an energy dispersive X-ray detector (SEM–EDX or SEM–EDXRF). In the above methods, bombardment of a sample with highly energetic X-rays, gamma rays, or electrons results in the emission of secondary (or fluorescent) X-rays that are characteristics of the elemental content of the sample.

Molecular spectroscopy

Some of the more traditional molecular spectroscopic methods such as FTIR spectroscopy and microspectrophotometry (MSP) are still being used for the analysis and comparison of documents. MSP, now often found on most routinely used multispectral analysis equipment, is mainly used for the comparison

of inks based on their UV/Vis/NIR reflection or fluorescence spectrum.

FTIR may, depending on the substrate and the accessories at hand, be used in different operation modes, for example, diffuse reflection for powders, (micro)attenuated total reflection for surface analysis, and diamond cells and FTIR microscopes for microanalysis of solids.

FTIR is a form of vibrational spectroscopy in which molecules absorb specific wavelengths of radiation related to the vibrational energy of the molecular bonds present. FTIR therefore delivers a compound spectrum of all excitable molecular bonds in a sample within the applied wavelength range. Their identification can be very difficult due to matrix effects. Large libraries containing FTIR spectra can, however, assist the analyst greatly in this task.

Applications of FTIR spectroscopy in questioned documents are mainly in the analysis, classification, and comparison of organic compounds in toners, tapes, and coatings.

Closely related to infrared spectroscopy but often delivering complementary information is RS where the inelastic scattering of laser radiation produces information on the molecular composition of a sample. Its main application in the analysis of documents is the comparison of inks and toners. Spectra of inks will sometimes improve dramatically when a silver or gold colloid is applied, resulting in surface-enhanced Raman scattering or an even stronger surface-enhanced resonance Raman scattering if the excitation wavelength also matches the maximum absorption of the molecule being analyzed (**Figure 2**).

Chromatographic Methods

Document examiners have in the past relied heavily on chromatographic methods for the discrimination and characterization of writing, stamp, and printing inks. As the use of optical methods is most often limited to the comparison of inks on the same paper, chromatographic methods such as TLC and HPLC are needed for comparing inks between documents. These methods often offer a higher degree of discrimination than the optical methods.

Gas chromatography

Gas chromatography with mass spectrometric detection (GC/MS) is one of the workhorses of a forensic laboratory with applications in illicit drugs, fire accelerants, explosives, toxicology, environmental crime, materials science, and questioned documents. GC/MS is used for the analysis of organic volatile compounds. Separation of the different components is obtained from a partitioning between a gas and a solid phase in combination with a temperature programming of the oven containing the column. A further separation based on the mass-to-charge ratio and detection of the eluting compounds is achieved with a mass spectrometer. The resulting fragmentation patterns provide structural information that can be used

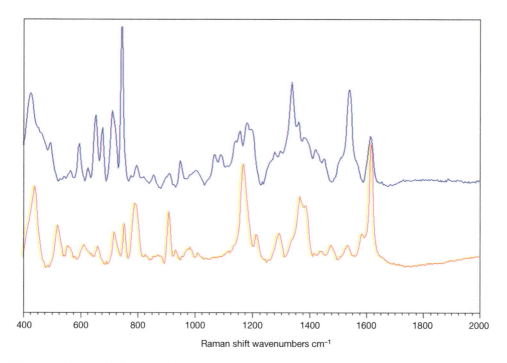

Raman shift wavenumbers cm⁻¹

Figure 2 Raman spectra of two black ballpoint pen inks.

for identification and quantification purposes. Specific fragmentation patterns can also help to identify different species with similar chromatographic behavior. The mass spectrometer can be run in the total ion current (TIC) or selected ion monitoring (SIM) mode. In the TIC mode, the sum of the intensities of all detected masses within a specific time interval is used, while in the SIM mode, one specific mass-to-charge ratio is monitored, resulting in high selectivity and high sensitivity for one specific compound.

While standard GC/MS is aimed at the analysis of volatiles, pyrolysis GC/MS (Py–GC/MS) can deal with nonvolatiles or solids. In Py–GC/MS, a sample is thermally decomposed at high temperatures, after which the resulting volatile fragments are analyzed with GC/MS. Substances such as ink resins, polymers, and paper sizing materials may be analyzed in this manner. Within questioned documents, Py–GC/MS has mainly been used for the analysis of toners and pigment-based inks such as black inkjet inks and gel pen inks. The resulting pyrogram has a high discrimination power, giving a detailed chemical fingerprint of the analyzed substance.

Liquid chromatography
TLC or, more importantly, high-performance (HP) TLC has been the chromatographic method of choice for the past generations of examiners of questioned documents if it came to a chemical comparison and/or identification of inks. An extract from an ink line of 5–10 mm is manually or automatically

spotted onto an (HP)TLC plate and allowed to develop in a suitable solvent mixture. Separation is based on the partitioning behavior of the different dyes between the solid stationary phase of the TLC plate (usually a silica gel) and the liquid mobile phase, which travels up the plate due to capillary action. Comparison of inks is done after side-by-side analysis followed by an evaluation of the resulting separation profile by naked eye, multispectral methods, or with a dedicated TLC scanner with UV/Vis spectral capabilities. Identification of the inks is done by comparison of the separation profile or chromatogram to an ink library of similar analyses, followed by a side-by-side analysis of the main remaining candidates (**Figure 3**).

TLC is also still in use for ink dating applications. Different approaches may be identified:

- The "static" approach, where an ink manufacturer is identified from the combination of dyes used in the ink or from specific tagging compounds, which have been added by the manufacturer. This approach may sometimes lead to information concerning the date of introduction of the ink, which may then be used for dating purposes.
- The "dynamic" approach, where chemical changes in the dyes or their extraction efficiency, is used to determine the (relative) age of the inks. This approach to ink dating, however, has always been quite controversial in the questioned documents community.

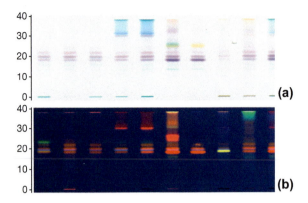

(a)

(b)

Figure 3 Thin-layer chromatographic (TLC) separation of five blue and five black ballpoint pen inks on a LiChrospher Si 60 F254 TLC plate. (a) Real-color image. (b) Artificial-color image composed from the three luminescence channels R: 550/650 nm; G: 500/600 nm; and B: 400/500 nm produced on a Sentinel® Quantitative Hyperspectral Imager by DEMCON Advanced Products, Oldenzaal, The Netherlands. Klein, M.E., Aalderink, B.J., Berger, C.E.H., Herlaar, K., de Koeijer, J.A., 2010. Quantitative hyperspectral imaging technique for measuring material degradation effects and analyzing TLC plate traces. Journal of the American Society of Questioned Document Examiners 13 (2), 71–81.

In HPLC, the stationary phase is not located on a glass or aluminum plate (as in TLC) but in a glass or stainless steel column. The ink extract is injected into the mobile phase, which is pumped through the column under high pressure. After separation, the dyes may be detected with a UV/Vis detector at a fixed wavelength, resulting in a two-dimensional chromatogram (time vs absorbance). If a photodiode array (PDA) detector is used, the absorbance of every eluting component is monitored over a specific wavelength range, resulting in a three-dimensional chromatogram (time vs wavelength vs absorbance). This gives greater capabilities for a more reliable comparison and identification of the separated compounds. Applications of HPLC range from writing, stamp pad, and printing inks to toners and paper additives such as optical brighteners (**Figure 4**).

The Newer Trends

Optical Methods

The two major developments in optical methods are the move from multispectral to hyperspectral or chemical imaging and the gradual increase in the use of digital image analysis.

Hyperspectral imaging

A hyperspectral imager differs from a conventional multispectral imaging device in two important ways. First, the new instrument features a considerable increase in the number of independent spectral bands realized by using either liquid crystal tunable filters or a large number (up to several hundred) of optical filters. This increases the chances of finding differences between compared features.

Second, postprocessing in hyperspectral imaging makes it possible to calibrate the spectral curve for every pixel of the recorded image. This has several important advantages for the way in which the data can be analyzed:

- Spectral curves can be easily extracted from all desired locations in the image, plotted together in diagrams and processed numerically so that any differences between the curves can be established in a quantitative way.
- Optimization of the workflow of a case investigation can be achieved. The tasks of measuring a document sample and of analyzing the results with respect to particular forensic questions have become quite independent of each other. After having measured all available spectral bands of a document in a single, relatively short session, the forensic analysis on the collected data can be performed off-line.
- Image analysis algorithms aimed at retrieving the best information possible from the total image data cube are introduced. Examples of such algorithms are principal component analysis, color deconvolution, and image subtraction and multiplication (**Figure 5**).

Digital image analysis techniques

Since the introduction of flatbed scanners, digital cameras, and software packages such as Adobe Photoshop, digital image analysis has been made available to the general public, and

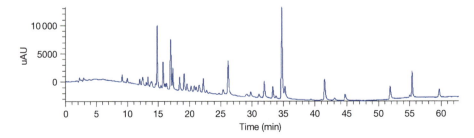

Figure 4 High-performance liquid chromatogram of a blue ballpoint pen ink.

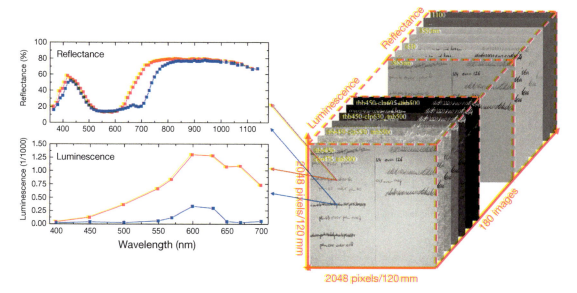

Figure 5 The hyperspectral data cube consisting of the calibrated spectral reflectance and luminescence images of the recorded document area. For each point on the document, the entire reflectance and luminescence curves can be extracted. The illustration indicates the spectral reflectance and luminescence curves for two ink areas as blue and red curves. Generated on a Sentinel® Quantitative Hyperspectral Imager by DEMCON Advanced Products, Oldenzaal, The Netherlands. Klein, M.E., Aalderink, B.J., Berger, C.E.H., Herlaar, K., de Koeijer, J.A., 2010. Quantitative hyperspectral imaging technique for measuring material degradation effects and analyzing TLC plate traces. Journal of the American Society of Questioned Document Examiners 13 (2), 71–81.

hence it has become an important new tool for forensic document examiners. Tasks that were quite complicated for an analog forensic photographer have now become as simple as a mouse click for the modern document examiner. Specialized forensic filters or plug-ins have been designed to assist the document examiner in performing tasks such as follows:

- Contrast stretching or optimization, which can be applied to enhance weak (barely legible) images of, for example, erased or faded writing/printing, writing on charred documents, etc.;
- Color filtering or deconvolution, which can be used to discriminate between two closely related colors, remove background color, or just enhance a specific color;
- Making digital overlays, which can assist the document examiner with the comparison of traced or copied signatures, stamp impressions, etc.;
- Sharpening, which may be applied to increase image detail;
- Morphing, used to remove warping or skew in an image;
- Fast Fourier transform (FFT) analysis, which is a mathematical transformation of an image used to remove or visualize/enhance regular patterns. Removal of specific frequencies is accomplished by transforming the image to the frequency domain where specific frequencies may be selected and erased, resulting in removal of the pattern with that frequency in the original image after performing a reversed FFT. Another useful application is the comparison of paper. FFT spectra of a paper scanned in the transparency mode will contain specific

frequencies from machine components with which the wet paper (pulp) has been in contact during the papermaking process. Such an FFT image can show whether two different sheets of paper were produced on the same machine (**Figure 6**).

Spectroscopic Methods

New developments in spectroscopic techniques have boosted the capability of not only questioned document examination but also forensic science in general. The many new MS-related methods have been a driving force for developments in

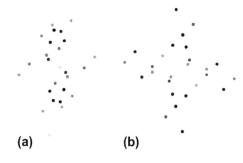

(a) **(b)**

Figure 6 Digitally enhanced fast Fourier transform spectra of two different sheets of paper.

chemical analysis in the forensic domain. Methods such as LA–ICPMS, laser desorption ionization MS (LDI–MS), and isotope ratio MS (IRMS) have become more and more mainstream methods of analysis for the larger forensic labs.

Elemental spectroscopy

A relatively new addition to the elemental analysis used in document examination is laser-induced breakdown spectroscopy (LIBS). This is a form of atomic emission spectroscopy using a highly energetic pulsed laser source to form a plasma of excited atoms emitting light of characteristic wavelengths. This type of elemental spectroscopy has recently been applied to the analysis of paper and pigmented inks. LIBS is extremely rapid, needing little to no sample preparation and with only very minor microscopic destruction of the sample.

Molecular spectroscopy

The surface mapping possibilities of new FTIR and Raman microscopes have introduced a new type of spectroscopy called "chemical imaging." The technique has a strong resemblance to hyperspectral imaging mentioned in the section Optical Methods. Here, a surface is scanned and at every coordinate, a full spectrum is generated. By selecting specific frequencies, an image of the surface details absorbing these frequencies is generated. Applications, although still in their infancy, have

been published in the area of fingerprints, paints, and documents. Work has been done on the sequencing of crossing ink lines and the suppression of background printing.

Mass spectrometry

Mass spectrometric methods have developed explosively in the past decade, showing large potential in forensic science in general and document examination in particular. Methods such as LA–ICPMS and LDI–MS are currently leading the way to smaller samples, less sample preparation, increased sensitivity, and almost unlimited discrimination possibilities.

In LA–ICPMS, a minute sample is taken by ablating the surface with a pulsed laser beam. The aerosol formed is transported into an inductively coupled argon plasma, which generates temperature of ~8000 °C. The ions generated here are then introduced into a mass spectrometer where they are separated according to their mass-to-charge ratio. The strength of sampling by laser ablation is that all types of solid samples can be analyzed regardless of sample size and often without preparation. Up to 70 different elements can be detected and quantified down to the ppb (parts per billion) level with only microgram quantities of sample. Analysis of paper by LA–ICPMS has shown discrimination possibilities at batch level. LA–ICPMS is also suited for the analysis of writing and printing inks, especially pigment-based inks, which do not readily dissolve from the substrate (**Figure 7**).

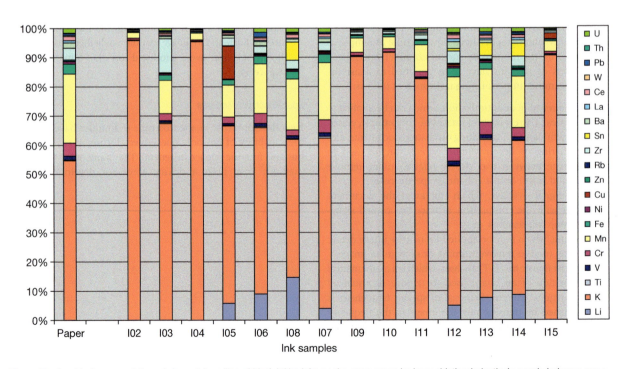

Figure 7 Graphical representation of elemental profiles of black inkjet inks on the same paper by laser ablation inductively coupled plasma mass spectrometry.

LDI–MS and matrix-assisted laser desorption ionization MS (MALDI–MS) are two closely related methods that also use a laser to vaporize and ionize a solid sample. LDI–MS can analyze inks directly on the paper or from an extract deposited on a metal surface. Extreme sensitivity has been shown with LDI–TOFMS (TOF, "time of flight"), where a single ink-containing fiber is enough to analyze its dye composition. MALDI–MS, however, needs more sample preparation, as a matrix that protects the sample molecules from destruction (too much fragmentation) needs to be introduced. To accomplish this, a matrix solution is added to an extract of the ink, which is then allowed to dry on a metal surface before analysis.

By scanning the surface with a scanning microprobe (MA) LDI–MS for specific ions from two inks of different composition, this technique can be used to determine the sequence of intersecting ink lines. Similar results may also be obtained by TOF–SIMS analysis of the surface of such an intersection (see **Figure 8**).

In TOF–SIMS, a pulsed beam of focused ions hits a surface, resulting in secondary ions being emitted from the surface to be detected in the mass spectrometer. TOF–SIMS is a surface scanning technique with the possibility of analyzing ultrathin molecular layers. Detection possibilities include all elements from the periodic table as well as molecular species. Depth profiling is also an option.

New additions to the field of mass spectrometric techniques are the so-called ambient ionization methods where ions are generated under ordinary ambient conditions in their native environment, without any sample preparation or preseparation. Methods belonging to this category are, for example, desorption electrospray ionization MS (DESI–MS) and direct analysis in real-time MS (DART–MS). In DESI, a solvent is electrosprayed to generate charged droplets, which are directed at the analyte surface. The secondary scattered droplets containing dissolved surface ions are then mass analyzed. DART, on the other hand, uses a heated stream of excited and ionized helium or nitrogen gas to ablate and ionize material from a sample so that it may be analyzed by the mass spectrometer. DART produces relatively simple mass spectra characterized in the positive-ion mode by $M^+/[M + H]^+$ and $M-/[M - H]^-$ in the negative-ion mode. Both DESI and DART have been used in document examination for real-time analysis of inks. Besides direct analysis, DESI also allows chemical imaging of a surface, making it possible to detect any changes to a questioned handwritten entry.

Last, but certainly not least, IRMS has claimed its position in forensic science with applications in the areas of explosives, illicit drugs, materials, and the identification of human remains based on their geographical history. In document examination, IRMS has shown potential for the analysis of isotopic ratios in paper, differentiating paper based on its $\delta^2 H$, $\delta^{13} C$, and $\delta^{18} O$ isotopes (**Figure 9**).

Chromatographic Methods

In the challenges of dealing with the frequently asked question to date documents, chromatography has played a major role. After the first attempts using TLC to determine the age of an ink by differences in the extraction rate of the dyes, the focus shifted to the volatiles using solvent extraction and GC/MS. Further developments in this area have led to methods combining solid-phase microextraction (SPME) with GC/MS, TD with GC/MS, and finally HPLC with fluorescence detection. Also in the area of ink comparison, progress has been made with methods such as HPLC–MS(/MS) and capillary electrophoresis (CE).

Gas chromatographic techniques

GC in the examination of questioned documents has mainly been used for ink dating purposes. Recent developments in this area are the use of SPME with TD–GC/MS. SPME uses a fused silica fiber coated with a polymeric phase tailored to absorb certain classes of compounds. The fiber is placed in a closed environment in close proximity to the (heated) sample. After equilibrium is reached between the absorbed analytes on the fiber and the sample matrix, the fiber is placed in the injector of the GC/MS where desorption takes place followed by further analysis.

In TD–GC/MS, the ink sample is placed in a desorption tube, which is then heated. A steady gas flow through the tube transfers the evaporated analytes to a cold trap area where they are collected. Once this process is complete, the cold trap is heated and the gas flow takes the analytes to the GC column for further separation.

Both SPME–GC/MS and TD–GC/MS use mass-independent sampling strategies where the same ink sample is extracted/desorbed at two different temperatures and the ratio of solvent from both analyses is used as an age indicator. Almost all ink dating work has been aimed at the analysis of 2-phenoxyethanol (PE), which is the most common solvent used in ballpoint pens. The analysis strategy is aimed at determining the relative freshness of the ink (<6–12 months old) in contrast to the date mentioned on the document, which may suggest a much earlier date of production.

Liquid chromatographic techniques

A promising method for the analysis of soluble inks is HPLC–MS(/MS). As HPLC–MS interfaces have improved, the range of applications for this powerful separation method has increased dramatically. The combination of HPLC–MS with a PDA detector promises the best of both worlds, with both UV/Vis detection of the dyes and the enhanced MS functionality of detection of noncolored species and their identification.

A new approach to the determination of the age of an ink is the use of HPLC with a fluorescence and a PDA detector. The fluorescence detector is used to quantify PE, while the PDA

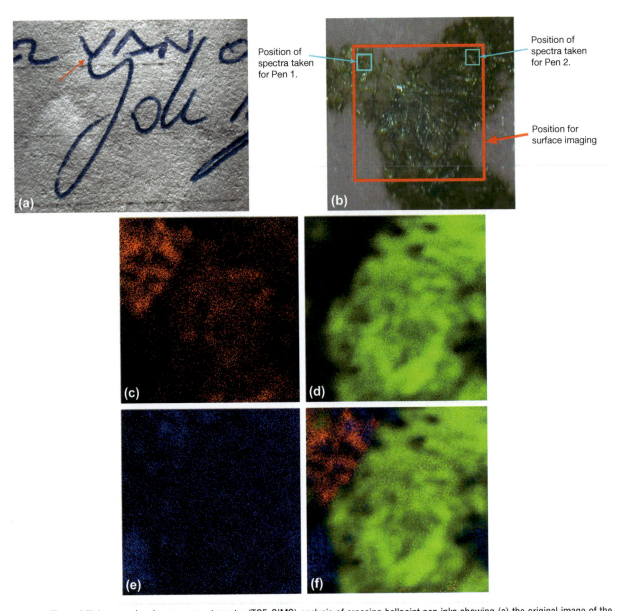

Figure 8 Time-of-flight secondary ion mass spectrometry (TOF–SIMS) analysis of crossing ballpoint pen inks showing (a) the original image of the crossing between text and signature, (b) the areas where the separate inks were sampled and the intersection was imaged, (c) TOF–SIMS imaging of Pen 1 at the intersection, (d) TOF–SIMS imaging of Pen 2 at the intersection, (e) TOF–SIMS imaging of the paper at the intersection, (f) a composite image of the TOF–SIMS analysis of the Pen 1–Pen 2 intersection showing that the ink of Pen 2 is situated on top of that from Pen 1.

detector detects the methyl violet dyes. The dyes can now be used as internal standards for the quantification of PE from two ink samples, one sample taken directly and one after a period of (artificial) aging in the laboratory.

Another promising development in this area is the use of ultra performance liquid chromatography (UPLC) instead of HPLC. In UPLC, smaller stationary phase particles are used. The main advantages of UPLC are higher separation efficiency, faster chromatographic process, and increased sensitivity. The main disadvantage is that specialized equipment is needed to deal with the increased pressure needed to force the mobile phase through the column.

A technique that is used extensively in forensics but has been used only to a limited extent in document examination is

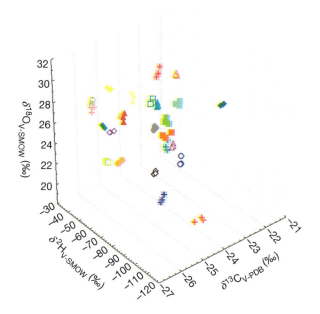

Figure 9   Isotope ratio mass spectrometry analysis of 25 different brands of multifunctional printing paper.

Separation in CE depends on the size and charge of the analyte molecules. Ions migrate in an electric field applied over the capillary in the direction of the electrode of the opposite charge. The migration rate is related to the following sequence: multiply charged small ions, singly charged small ions and/or multiply charged large ions, and, finally, singly charged large ions. One of the main driving forces of CE is electroosmosis causing an electroosmotic flow (EOF). CE has different operation modes, of which capillary zone electrophoresis (CZE) and micellar electrokinetic capillary chromatography (MECC) have been used for the analysis of ink and paper. CZE can be used for the separation of water-soluble ionic species, while MECC can also deal with neutral and even hydrophobic molecules.

MECC is a mode of CE in which surfactants are added to the buffer solution, which then form micelles (cluster of molecules with the polar groups toward the solution). The MECC separation is based on the differential partitioning of an analyte between two phases, that is, a mobile (aqueous) phase and a stationary (micellar) phase. The charge of the micelle is chosen so that the migration force of the micelle is opposite to the direction of the EOF. However, due to the fact that the mobility of the EOF is greater than that of the micelle, the micelle will slowly migrate in the direction of the EOF. Analytes partitioning between the micelle and the buffer solution will therefore elute between the EOF and the micelle. Excellent separation of closely related dye compounds including isomers has been achieved for the analysis of different kinds of writing and inkjet printing inks (**Figure 10**).

CE. This is a separation technique based on the transport of ionic species in an electric field. CE is characterized by its extremely low solvent and sample consumption, its high separation power, and its broad range of applications.

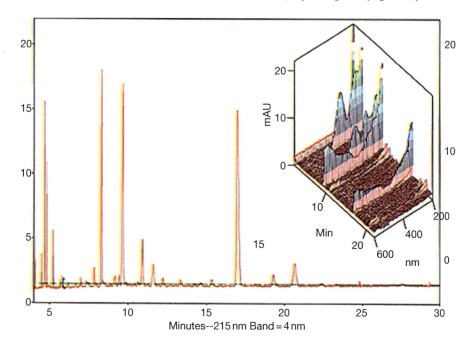

Figure 10   Micellar electrokinetic capillary chromatography analysis of a black inkjet printer ink.

See also: **Documents:** Document Dating; Forgery/Counterfeits; Ink Analysis; Paper Analysis; **Methods:** Capillary Electrophoresis: Basic Principles; Capillary Electrophoresis in Forensic Chemistry; Chromatography: Basic Principles; Gas Chromatography; Gas Chromatography–Mass Spectrometry; Liquid and Thin-Layer Chromatography; Liquid Chromatography–Mass Spectrometry; Mass Spectrometry; Spectroscopic Techniques; Spectroscopy: Basic Principles.

Further Reading

Berger, C.E.H., 2009. Objective paper structure comparison through processing of transmitted light images. Forensic Science International 192, 1–6.

Berger, C.E.H., de Koeijer, J.A., Glas, W., Madhuizen, H.T., 2006. Color separation in forensic image processing. Journal of Forensic Sciences 51 (1), 100–102.

Bojko, K., Roux, C., Reedy, B.J., 2008. An examination of the sequence of intersecting lines using attenuated total reflectance – Fourier transform infrared spectral imaging. Journal of Forensic Sciences 53, 1458–1467.

Brazeau, L., Chem, C., Gaudreau, M., 2007. Ballpoint pen inks: the quantitative analysis of ink solvents on paper by solid-phase microextraction. Journal of Forensic Sciences 52 (1), 209–215.

Bügler, J.H., Buchner, H., Dallmayer, A., 2008. Age determination of ballpoint pen ink by thermal desorption and gas chromatography–mass spectrometry. Journal of Forensic Sciences 53 (4), 982–988.

Coumbaros, J., Kirkbride, K.P., Klass, G., Skinner, W., 2009. Application of time of flight secondary ion mass spectrometry to the in situ analysis of ballpoint pen inks on paper. Forensic Science International 193, 42–46.

Dunn, J.D., Allison, J., 2007. The detection of multiply charged dyes using matrix-assisted laser desorption/ionization mass spectrometry for the forensic examination of pen ink dyes directly from paper. Journal of Forensic Sciences 52 (5), 1205–1211.

Ifa, D.R., Gumaelius, L.M., Eberlin, L.S., Manickea, N.E., Cooks, R.G., 2007. Forensic analysis of inks by imaging desorption electrospray ionization (DESI) mass spectrometry. Analyst 132, 461–467.

Jones, R.W., Cody, R.B., McClelland, J.F., 2006. Differentiating writing inks using direct analysis in real time mass spectrometry. Journal of Forensic Sciences 51 (4), 915–918.

Klein, M.E., Aalderink, B.J., Berger, C.E.H., Herlaar, K., de Koeijer, J.A., 2010. Quantitative hyperspectral imaging technique for measuring material degradation effects and analyzing TLC plate traces. Journal of the American Society of Questioned Document Examiners 13 (2), 71–81.

Ostrum, R.B., 2006. Application of hyperspectral imaging to forensic document examination problems. Journal of the American Society of Questioned Document Examiners 9 (2), 85–93.

Sarkar, A., Aggarwal, S.K., Alamelu, D., 2010. Laser induced breakdown spectroscopy for rapid identification of different types of paper for forensic application. Analytical Methods 2 (1), 1–100.

Van Es, A., de Koeijer, J., van der Peijl, G., 2009. Discrimination of document paper by XRF, LA–ICPMS and IRMS using multivariate statistical techniques. Science & Justice: Journal of the Forensic Science Society 49 (2), 120–126.

Weyermann, C., Marquis, R., Mazzella, W., Spengler, B., 2007. Differentiation of blue ballpoint pen inks by laser desorption ionization mass spectrometry and high-performance thin-layer chromatography. Journal of Forensic Sciences 52 (1), 216–220.

Xu, X., de Koeijer, J.A., de Moel, J.J.M., Logtenberg, H., 1997. Ink analysis for forensic science applications by micellar electrokinetic capillary chromatography with photo-diode array detection. International Journal of Forensic Document Examiners 3 (3), 240–260.

Relevant Websites

http://www.aafs.org—American Academy of Forensic Sciences.
http://www.asqde.org—American Society of Questioned Document Examiners.
http://www.enfsi.eu—European Network of Forensic Institutes.
http://dl.dropbox.com—Forensic Science Resources.
http://english.forensischinstituut.nl—Netherlands Forensic Institute.
http://forensic.to/index.php—Zeno's Forensic Site.

Document Dating

WD Mazzella and DC Purdy, Forensic Document Examination Services Inc., Vancouver, BC, Canada; University of Lausanne, Lausanne, Switzerland

This chapter is a revision of the previous edition article by D.C. Purdy, volume 2, pp. 570–580, © 2000, Elsevier Ltd.

The misrepresentation of dates on documents is not a recent challenge faced by forensic document examiners. In his book, *Questioned Documents*, Albert S. Osborn provided several examples of documents, which were altered or backdated to make it appear as though they were written much earlier. Many frauds still involve document dating problems, and forensic document examiners should diligently search for any clues that suggest a document was prepared some time other than indicated.

Various methods can be employed to backdate or fabricate documents. Such incidents can involve the relatively simple process of overwriting the date on a receipt to far more complex undertakings such as falsifying an entire document. Regardless of the method used, dating suspect documents is a very challenging problem for the document examiner and should be approached cautiously.

The most straightforward method for solving a dating problem considers the type of office equipment and the technologies that were used to produce the questioned document. This method, often called the "static" approach, can prove a document is false if the instruments and materials used to produce it were unavailable when it was supposedly prepared. A subgroup of the static approach involves the analysis of materials that make up a suspect document. For example, specialty papers or writing inks may contain materials that have been added to improve their quality. If it can be established that these materials were introduced on a specific date, any document in which they are found must have been prepared at a later time.

The second method, described as the "dynamic" approach, takes into account certain features in a contested document, which vary over time. Defective letters produced by a worn typewriter or photocopier "trash marks" that originate from dirt on a copier's platen glass are two examples of this type of evidence, which have dating significance. An important related issue concerns the natural aging of components that are present in the ink and paper. The aging of writing media will not be discussed here, as the topic is covered in another chapter of this encyclopedia.

The third method of solving dating problems involves determining the chronology or sequence of events responsible for the production of a document. The sequence of intersecting lines, page substitutions, and adding information to the body of a document can all challenge the alleged history of a contested document.

The following sections describe different areas that can be examined to determine when a document was drawn up or whether its date is false. The results of these tests do not always provide conclusive evidence of fraud. They can, however, draw attention to irregularities that must be reconciled before a suspect document can be relied on as genuine.

Paper Products

Watermarks

Conventional paper watermarks are produced during the manufacturing process by a "dandy roll" cylinder located at the beginning of the papermaking machine where paper is formed into a web. The dandy roll cylinder consists of a woven wire gauze onto which raised designs are soldered or otherwise attached. A watermark is created when the relief areas of the dandy roll press into and displace paper fibers. These unique designs permit sheets of watermarked paper to be traced to their manufacturer.

Paper mills usually maintain accurate records concerning their watermarks. Once the paper manufacturer of a questioned document is known, the company can be contacted to determine the earliest date that a watermark design was used. Any document dated earlier than this time must have been backdated.

The design of a watermark can also change over time, as relief areas of the dandy roll suffer damage through normal wear and tear. Detached or broken wires produce slight but visible changes in the design, which are transferred to the paper. Paper mills usually keep records when dandy roll damage occurred and when repairs were made. This information can be very helpful in narrowing the period during which a watermarked paper was manufactured.

A few paper companies have intentionally changed the design of their watermarks from time to time. Such watermarks are said to contain a "date tag," which will often indicate the year that a sheet of paper was produced. For example, Southworth Paper Company placed a short bar under or over the letters in their watermark to indicate the last digit of the year in which the paper was manufactured (**Figure 1**). If a document bears a watermark that was not in existence when it was allegedly dated, the genuineness of its date must surely be challenged.

Figure 1   The short vertical bar under the letter b of "fiber" in this watermark confirms the sheet of paper was manufactured during 2004.

When using watermarks to date paper, it is strongly recommended that the paper manufacturer be contacted to verify the time period when the noted features were present.

Paper Composition

Over the years, different fillers, surface coatings, or chemical additives have been added during the paper-making process to improve the quality of the product. Other changes in the manufacturing processes have occurred for economic or environmental reasons. These innovations and modifications can establish the earliest date or period a particular sheet of paper was manufactured.

Many North American paper manufacturers stopped producing acidic paper in favor of alkaline or neutral process papers during the late 1980s and early 1990s. A simple pH test can indicate if a questioned document was produced before its purported date. This finding can be corroborated if certain chemicals that were introduced after the date on the document are present in the paper. For example, when mills converted their operations to an alkaline process, many also began using calcium carbonate ($CaCO_3$) as a substitute for titanium dioxide (TiO_2) in order to improve the brightness and opacity of papers. Paper production based on acidic processes is still carried out in other areas of the globe. Consequently, caution should be exercised when interpreting such evidence, and the paper manufacturer should be consulted to confirm when the observed processes and materials were introduced.

Specialty papers can also contain information of dating significance. For example, NCR (no carbon required) paper first appeared in the United States during 1954. The formula for manufacturing this product was changed several times during the 1960s and 1970s. In 1972, NCR developed a coding scheme to identify the source and date of its papers. Trace amounts of various high-atomic weight elements have been added by other manufacturers as a means of tagging their products. The dates of documents produced on specialty papers that contain tags can be verified by taking such information into account.

A more sophisticated technique can occasionally be used to date the paper, which takes into account strong increases in atmospheric radiocarbon concentration caused by nuclear weapons tests conducted during the last 50 years. Such tests reportedly allow papers, less than 50 years old, to be dated within a few months of their dates of production independent of storage conditions.

Envelopes

Envelopes are often discarded once their contents are removed. This is unfortunate because an envelope may contain important information about when it was mailed and possibly when its contents were prepared. The following envelope areas can have dating significance: postage stamps, postage cancellation marks, envelope shape, and printed information.

Postage stamps affixed to envelopes can be examined to determine if they were available when the envelope's contents were prepared. A new postage stamp is released for sale as a "first day cover" on a particular date. Postal officials or a knowledgeable stamp collector should be able to provide the precise date a stamp was issued. Once this date is known, the envelope and its contents must have been mailed some time after this period.

Stamps on many envelopes bear cancellation marks that are applied by the post office. Even if a cancellation mark is not legible, the format of the mark, the way it was struck, and the chemical composition of ink can serve to establish the period when it was applied.

Occasionally, logos or product codes are applied to envelopes while they are being manufactured, which can have dating significance. The impression shown in **Figure 2** was found on the inside of an envelope manufactured by Elco. This

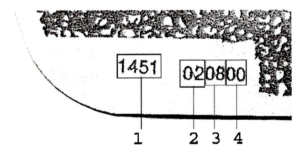

Figure 2   A notation "1451 020800" on the inside of an "Elco" envelope represents (1) personnel number, (2) machine code, (3) month of manufacturing, and (4) year of manufacturing.

notation represents the personnel number (1451), the printing machine code (02), as well as the month and last two digits of the year (0800) the envelope was printed. Numbers (0800) correspond to the month (August) and the last two digits in the year (2000) it was manufactured. The envelope manufacturer should always be contacted to confirm the accuracy of any dating information.

The design and appearance of some envelopes are unique to their manufacturers and may well indicate when they were produced. These include, but are not limited to, the following:

- small irregularities along the edges of the paper related to a damaged die stamp;
- types of adhesives applied to the side seams and the flap areas of the envelope; and
- patterns in adhesive layers associated with the method of application.

Other areas sometimes overlooked are addresses, which appear on an envelope. A particular mailing or return address may not have existed when the document was supposed to have been sent. Postal or zip codes change from time to time and these should always be checked to ensure that they existed during the period in question.

Inks and Writing Instruments

One of the most challenging dating problems faced by the document examiner is estimating when a particular document was signed or written. If a document was supposed to have been written many years ago, it may be possible to prove it was backdated if the type of pen and writing materials used were not available at that time. Important milestone events concerning the development of modern writing materials are shown in **Table 1** along with their dates of introduction.

Table 1 Significant dates of introduction in the history of writing instruments

Year	Historical development
624	Earliest reference to the quill pen
1662	Pencils made in Nuremberg, Germany
1700	Early reference to steel pens
1780	Steel pens made in England by Samuel Harrison
1857	First appearance of "copying pencils"
1945	Ballpoint pen first marketed in New York City
1951	Felt-tip markers introduced
1955	Liquid lead pencil introduced
1963	Fiber-tip pen first produced
1967	Roller ball pen first produced
1979	Eraser Mate erasable pen introduced by Paper Mate
1984	Gel pens introduced by Sakura in Japan
1993	Gel pens introduced in the United States
2006	Frixion ball, based on thermochromic ink, introduced by Pilot

Clues as to when a document was signed can also be found by analyzing the questioned writing ink. A small sample of ink removed from a document can be separated into its solid components by thin-layer chromatography (TLC). The result of this analysis is a chromatogram that isolates the different dyes present in the ink formulation on a coated glass or plastic plate. Success of this method relies on the different physical and chemical properties of the ink and the existence of a sufficiently complete set of ink reference standards.

TLC can also detect the presence of tags, which have been added to some writing inks by their manufacturers. During the 1970s, several US ink producers participated in an ink tagging program organized by the Alcohol, Tobacco and Firearms (ATF) Laboratory in the United States. This scheme urged ink manufacturers to add trace amounts of different materials with distinct properties to their inks. These materials would be changed annually and thereby indicate the year an ink was manufactured. By 1978, approximately 40% of writing inks produced in the United States contained such dating tags. Although this initiative greatly increased the ability of forensic scientists to date domestic writing inks, the continued growth of imported products threatened the success of the program. Although most ink manufacturers withdrew from the tagging program by the early 1980s, documents purportedly written before this period may contain chemical taggants that suggest they were manufactured at a much later date. A US company commenced tagging their products in 2002, but this program ended in January of 2010 when the ink company was purchased by a competitor.

Ink chemists have observed that many writing inks begin to change or age the instant they are applied to paper. Most people have noticed writing inks fade or become lighter with the passage of time. In addition to this obvious physical transition, investigations have shown that the chemical composition of an ink also changes over several months or years. These effects are especially true with respect to the color, solubility, and solvent volatility of the writing inks.

Other testing methods rely on sophisticated analytical techniques such as gas chromatography/mass spectrometry to measure the concentration of volatile components, such as phenoxyethanol, in an ink sample. This technique also requires two samples be taken from the suspect ink entry. After exposing one to heat, both samples are tested and the extent to which their solvent components differ provides an estimate of when the ink entry was written. This method is better suited for entries made within 4–6 months of testing and do apply to some ballpoint ink formulations.

The described methods are beyond all, but a few specialists who possess the equipment, knowledge, and experience needed to analyze and date writing inks. Some controversy still surrounds certain ink testing methods, and further validation studies could resolve these debates. The aforementioned ink dating methods have not been validated by an international intralaboratory double-blind test and, therefore, should be applied with extreme caution.

Commercially Printed Documents

Many documents subjected to forensic examinations take the form of documents with letterheads, contracts, envelopes, notary records, receipts, and other types of printed stationery. Apart from typewriting, handwriting, and other information they may contain, commercial printing on documents can be used to establish whether they were produced during or after a certain period.

Minuscule printing defects such as irregular letter outlines, uneven inking, or small breaks in line work can associate a questioned document with a particular stationery order produced by a commercial printer. Once the company that produced a printed document is identified, more precise information about when the order was delivered and the earliest time the stock was put into circulation can be determined. Access to samples from the order retained by the print shop can also be of value when attempting to date commercially printed documents.

A coded mark within the body of a printed document can also provide important information about a print job. For example, the bottom corner of the form shown in **Figure 3** bears the notation "A-5(80-08) 7530-21-029-4767" that describes the form number (A-5) and digits corresponding to the year and month (80-08) the form was created. The remaining 13 numbers are internal codes that refer to the work order, the location where the form was printed and other internal information. It is always advisable to contact the printer to confirm the interpretation of coded information and to determine if the document contains other characteristics

Figure 3 The alphanumeric code "A-5(80-08) 7530-21-029-4767" within this advertisement on a patient's medical form was used to establish the date the stationery was printed. The date (year/month 80-08) the form was created is embedded in the notation, which appears along the left margin near the bottom of the sheet.

(e.g., dimensions, color/type of paper, and applied adhesives) that might have dating significance.

Typewriting

The typewriting technology used to produce a questioned document is one of the first factors that should be considered when its date is at issue. During the last century, many advances have occurred in the development of the modern typewriter. Some important events and when they occurred are listed in **Table 2**.

The date a typewritten document was prepared can be determined in other ways. One method considers the typestyle that appears on a questioned document. The shape and size of typed letters can indicate the make(s) and model(s) of typewriter(s) that might have been used to produce the typewriting. The results of searching a large collection of typewriter specimens can indicate that the questioned typestyle was introduced to the market on a particular date. Should the typestyle's date of introduction be later than the date on the suspect document, the questioned document must certainly be regarded with suspicion.

The second method of dating typescript takes into account any typeface defects present in the questioned typewritten text.

Table 2   Significant dates of introduction in the development of the typewriter

Year	Technological development
1909	First use of bicolored ribbon (Underwood)
1927	First use of carbon ribbon (Hammond-Varityper)
1944	IBM executive proportional spaced typewriter
1956	Remington Statesman the first proportional typewriter by Remington
1960	First Underwood proportional spaced typewriter
1960	Underwood electric standard typewriter with duplex carbon and fabric ribbons
1961	IBM Selectric I dual pitch single element typewriter
1963	First use of IBM Selectric polyethylene film ribbon
1971	IBM Selectric II dual escapement, half backspace machine
1971	Tech III ribbon cartridge for IBM Selectric
1972	First daisy wheel produced by Diablo Systems
1973	IBM Correcting Selectric II with special lift-off ribbon
1975	Thermal transfer ribbon developed by IBM
1977	First use of polyurethane ribbons (Olivetti)
1978	First dot-matrix printer for personal computer (Epson TX 80)
1962	IBM Electronic 65 and 85 typewriters with triple pitch and right justification
1982	Brother EP-20 seven-pin thermal typewriter
1984	Diablo releases EPM 1—first thermal ribbon transfer printer
1984	IBM Quietwriter with nonimpact thermal printhead
1984	Quietwriter ribbon by IBM
1999	IBM Courier typestyle introduces a special character to represent Euro currency

Typewriters contain many moving parts, which gradually become worn or defective with use. These defective components produce misaligned or damaged letters that become quite apparent when examined with a microscope. Subsequent adjustments or repairs by a service technician can create further changes to the appearance of typewriting produced by a machine. The dates when typewriter damage occurred or disappeared are very significant for dating purposes.

If a typewriter is not cleaned regularly, oil, ribbon particles, dirt, and paper fibers can accumulate within the crevices of certain letters. When dirty typefaces strike the paper through the ribbon, the letters appear filled-in rather than clear letters and numbers. These imperfections will remain until the dirt is removed by cleaning the typefaces. Access to uncontested document produced on the same typewriter over a period of time will reveal when changes to the appearance of the typescript occurred. **Figure 4** shows how the appearance of typeface dirt and damage can expose a fraudulent document.

Typewriter single-strike and correcting ribbons can also indicate the date when documents were produced on a particular typewriter. A used single-stroke ribbon will contain impressions of all the characters struck by the machine in chronological order, as the ribbon was last changed. If the typewriter ribbon used to produce a questioned document is available for inspection, it can be examined to ensure the date of a questioned typewritten document is contemporaneous with the dates of typed documents, which precede and follow it. If it is not, dated correspondence appearing immediately before and after the location of the question passage can serve to determine the approximate period when the contested document was typed.

Questioned Date	Known Dates	
	May 19, 1996	D-1
	July 2, 1996	D-2
	Aug. 6, 1996	D-3
June 12, 1996	Aug. 28, 1996	D-4
	Sept. 26, 1996	D-5
	Oct. 12, 1996	D-6

Figure 4 The questioned document could not have been typed on June 12, 1996. Damage to the digit "9" and the filled-in-body of the "6" occurred after August 6, 1996 and before October 12, 1996.

Correction fluids applied to conceal typing errors can also help date a typewritten document. Wite-Out Company first introduced this product to the market in 1965. In 1984, Liquid Paper introduced colored correcting fluid to mask corrections on different colored paper stock. The presence of these materials on a typewritten document before their respective introductory dates will strongly suggest a document has been backdated.

Correcting fluids are complex substances composed of different resins, plasticizers, pigments, solvents, and binders. The manufacturer of a correcting fluid can be identified by extracting a sample from the document, analyzing it by infrared spectroscopy, and comparing the result to a database of correcting fluid spectra. Once known, the manufacturer can be contacted to determine when a particular correcting fluid formulation was first produced. Of course, a correcting fluid could not have been applied to a questioned document before its date of introduction.

Photocopiers

Photocopied documents that suddenly surface during a litigation are often regarded with suspicion. In some cases, these documents are genuine, but in other instances, they are produced at the last moment with an astonishing story that they were just discovered recently by some strange coincidence. The subject of interest in these cases is not when the original document was produced but rather the date or period it was photocopied. Three facets of photocopied documents that have dating significance include the copier technology used, the presence of copier defects, the properties of the toner and/or paper and, since about 1993, the introduction of security codes into color photocopiers. These codes contain the machine's serial number and indirectly the manufacture date. Some manufacturers also include the time, date, month, and year a document was produced into the security code on each color copy produced by their machines. Please note that the security codes may also be present in digital color laser printers.

Copier Technologies

Just as milestone events in the development of the typewriter are useful for dating purposes, the date of a copied document can be checked against the release date of a particular office technology to ensure that it was available when the document was allegedly produced. Different copier technologies include (1) dual spectrum, (2) stabilization, (3) diffusion transfer, (4) indirect electrostatic, (5) diazo, (6) dye transfer, (7) direct electrostatic, (8) thermographic, and (9) laser. A questioned copied document should be checked to ensure its date follows the introductory date of the technology used to produce it, keeping in mind that introductory dates may vary from region to region.

Examination of Defects

The most straightforward means of dating photocopied documents relies on defects, "trash marks," or small flecks of toner that appear in "white" areas of a copied document. These marks can originate from dirt, foreign material, or defects on the glass, platen cover, or photosensitive drum of the photocopier (**Figure 5**). Scratches to the glass or drum tend to be more permanent and will generate marks on copies produced by a machine until such time, as the defective component is removed and replaced. The nature of other defects, such as those originating from dirt or foreign material on the glass, lid, or internal components, is temporary in that they can be removed by cleaning the copier surfaces. Genuine photocopied documents made by the same copier that produced the questioned document provide an excellent means of confirming its date. Logs and service records maintained by repair technicians are also helpful in that they often contain photocopies produced before and after copier repairs were made.

Toner Analysis

Most photocopier toners consist of a pigment (usually carbon black), a binder, which fixes the pigment to the paper (usually an organic resin such as polystyrene), and additives used to improve the properties of the toner. When any of these components are changed, the event can provide a useful means of dating photocopied documents. Analysis of photocopier toners by infrared spectroscopy and scanning electron microscope equipment with energy dispersive spectrometry can yield

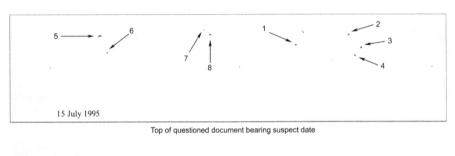

Top of questioned document bearing suspect date

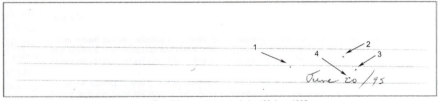

Top of document photocopied on 20 June 1995

Top of document photocopied on 3 August 1995

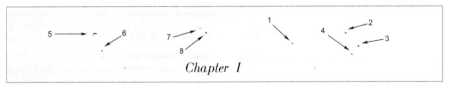

Top of document photocopied on 8 September 1995

Figure 5   The combination of photocopier "trash" marks on the questioned document (top) emerged during the period August 3, 1995 to September 8, 1995 and could not have occurred on July 15, 1995 when copies of the questioned documents were allegedly prepared.

information about the chemical and physical properties of toner. A comprehensive library of toners can be used to establish initial production dates. In some cases, the manufacturer will confirm that a particular ingredient was first used several years after the date the photocopy was supposed to be prepared. This would constitute conclusive evidence that the alleged date of the photocopy was false.

The process used to fuse toner to the paper can vary from one photocopier to another. Older photocopiers use cold pressure fusing wherein toner is pressed into the paper surface. Newer generations use either heat alone or both heat and pressure to fuse toner to the surface of the paper. The date a given fusing process first appeared is the earliest that a photocopy bearing this technology could have been produced.

In 1992, it was reported that indentations are imparted to the surface of toner by damage to the surface of a copier's fusing rollers. Fusing roller defects occur through normal wear and tear. They vary with time and consequently, the indentations they produce in the surface of toner can be used to estimate when a given photocopied document was produced.

Handwriting and Signatures

The writing of many individuals does not change significantly for most of their adult life. However, despite the constant and repetitive nature of developed handwriting, practically everyone has noticed that their signatures and handwriting do change—especially over long periods of time. The development, progression, and eventual disappearance of handwriting features can be very helpful in solving dating problems. Access to a quantity of specimen material produced during a period of time can show that writers change the shape of certain letters or the form of their signatures (**Figure 6**). The quantity of specimens required for this purpose will depend on many factors including (1) how

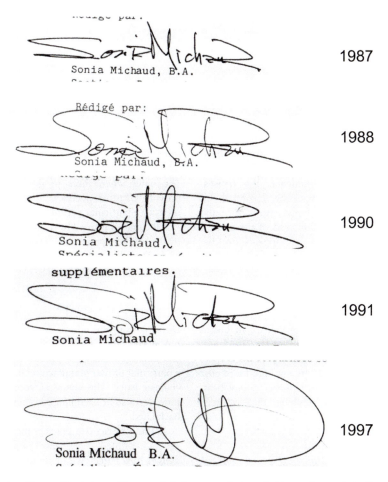

Figure 6 Six signatures produced by a writer during a 10-year period show some features that have a temporal significance.

rapidly the writing changes; (2) what factor(s) influenced the changes; and (3) the number of specimen writings prepared near the period in question and their homogeneity during a fixed period of time. Once the specimens are arranged in chronological order, it is often possible to date a disputed writing within a particular time period.

Rapid changes in a person's writing can result from the sudden onset of a serious illness, the administration of therapeutic drugs, or the consequence of a debilitating accident. Although such sudden transitions can create problems for the document examiner, they also provide a means of determining when a questioned signature or handwriting might have been produced.

Contents of a Document

Proof that a document was backdated or postdated can occasionally be found within its contents. These details are often overlooked by the perpetrator, as his attention is focused on producing a document that contains the right information. Names, addresses, postal codes, phone numbers, trade names, and job titles mentioned in a document might provide evidence that it was produced at a different time.

Events are occasionally mentioned in correspondence that did not occur until months or years after the date appearing on the document. Verb tenses in relation to events mentioned can also indicate a document was prepared after its purported date. When preparing a postdated or backdated document, the writer may not remember what verb tense to use. Such inconsistencies, especially when repeated, provide a good indication that something is amiss.

When preparing business correspondence, the typist's initials are often placed at the bottom of the document. In fraudulent documents, the initials of a typist who is currently employed by a company may be used instead of the person who held the position on the date that appears on the document.

Computer-Printed Documents

Dating computer-printed documents is approached in much the same manner as dating typewritten documents. The debut of computer printer technologies is all associated with a date of introduction. Consequently, any document produced by a daisy-wheel, dot-matrix, inkjet, or laser printer cannot bear a date that precedes the respective periods when these printers first appeared on the market.

Daisy-Wheel Printers

The daisy-wheel printer, using a similar impact technology to the typewriter, bridged the gap between typewriters and later generations of computer printers. Although very popular during the 1970s, a few daisy-wheel printers are still in use. The print elements of these machines contain a full set of characters positioned on the end of long spokes attached to a central hub. As the elements spin on a central shaft, the characters are struck at the appropriate time from behind with a plunger. The action of the character striking the paper through an inked ribbon produces a letter on a document.

Like their typewritten counterparts, documents produced by daisy-wheel printers can be dated by considering irregularities in the alignment of letters or damage to their outlines through wear and tear. The source of other temporal defects can be traced to faulty moving components of the printer. These changes provide a means for dating the work of a particular printer. It should be kept in mind, however, that daisy wheels can be easily removed, discarded, and replaced by a new element. All defects associated with the old daisy wheel will disappear and only those that relate to the printer will remain.

Dot-Matrix Printers

Dot-matrix printers gained popularity during the early 1980s. Early models had nine metal pins arranged along a vertical axis that struck the paper through an inked ribbon, whereas the printhead moved across the page. At the end of a single pass, the paper would advance slightly and the printhead would return across the page in the opposite direction. This process would be repeated until the entire page was printed. Printing produced by dot-matrix printers improved as 12-, 18-, and 24-pin models became available. These produced sharper printing, which was referred to as "near letter quality" or NLQ printing. The dates when these progressive improvements occurred provide a further means of limiting computer-printed document to a particular period.

Documents printed by dot-matrix printers can also be dated by the sudden appearance of printing defects, which are due to broken or bent pins, worn printhead housings, or other manifestations caused by defective printer components.

Ink-Jet and Laser Printers

Documents produced by ink-jet or laser printers could only be produced after these technologies were introduced. A computer-generated document can often be associated to a particular printer manufacturer based on the presence of class characteristics. The chemical composition of ink-jet ink or toner can also be useful for determining if a document has been backdated.

All nonimpact computer printers use computer software to generate printed characters. Printer control language (PCL) defines how letters belonging to a particular typestyle are shaped. For example, until October 1993, no Hewlett Packard PCL was capable of handling 600 dots per inch (dpi) printing. The

Figure 7 Letters "r" produced by HP laserJet III printer (left) and by an HP LaserJet 4 (right) introduced to the market in October 1993 show several conspicuous differences between the internal Courier fonts installed on these printers.

Hewlett Packard LaserJet 4, introduced in October 1993, was distributed with a special internal Courier font developed specifically for 600 dpi printing. This typestyle was different from any prior Courier font used in LaserJet printers (**Figure 7**). Since the LaserJet 4 was introduced in October 1993, any document that contains this special Courier font but dated earlier than this must be backdated.

The mechanics of laser printers are very similar to the processes used by modern photocopier machines. Hence, methods for dating photocopied documents described above also apply to documents produced by laser printers.

An interesting approach to try to date ink-jet printed documents is to measure the area of the dots because the latter diminish within the time, that is, the dot size is reduced according to the technological development. This approach is actually limited to the documents printed on high-quality papers.

Facsimile Documents

Recently, facsimile machines have become a common form of business communication. Although the first fax was designed by Alexander Bain and patented during 1843, the machine has only really gained popularity since the early 1980s. Facsimile documents are often presented as proof that business transactions or agreements took place on a particular date. Not all of these documents, however, are genuine. Fast and convenient for their users, facsimile machines also provide fraud artists with an opportunity to fabricate documents and defraud unsuspecting victims.

The transmitting terminal identifier (TTI) header usually appears at the top of most facsimile documents. This header may contain the page number, the date, the time the message was sent, and other information supplied by the sending machine. Although dispatched by the sending machine, this information is printed by the fax that receives the message. A receiving terminal identifier (RTI) printed by the receiving fax machine can also appear at the bottom of transmitted documents. The TTI and RTI of every suspected faxed document warrant close inspection.

In many cases, the date and time appearing in the TTI of faxed message are correct. It should be noted, however, that these settings can be quickly changed by anyone who has access to the machine and who possesses the knowledge to make the adjustments.

It is possible to identify the make and model of both sending and receiving machines by comparing the TTI and RTI of a received facsimile document to a library or collection of fax fonts. If such a search indicates that one or both facsimile machines were not available when the questioned fax was received, then it casts suspicion on the authenticity of the transmitted document. If long-distance charges were incurred when sending the facsimile transmissions, telephone records should be examined for evidence that a fax was sent on the date and time alleged. Telephone numbers and area codes appearing in the TTI or on the cover sheet should also be checked to ensure that they existed when the document was supposed to have been sent.

The format and content of the fax cover sheet should be examined to determine if it is consistent with that used during the period in question. Details of the transmitted message and cover sheet should also be examined to ensure people's names, titles, or initials are appropriate for the period in question.

Cachet Impressions

The development of rubber stamps followed the discovery of vulcanizing rubber by Charles Goodyear. The first commercial production of rubber stamps occurred in 1864. Since that time, the processes used to manufacture stamps have undergone several improvements as the demand for better quality rubber stamps increased. The first preinked stamp, Perma Stamp, was produced in 1958. These stamps are still a popular item in stationery stores. Although today's stamps are still referred to as "rubber stamps," most stamps are now produced from a plastic-based photopolymer material.

Both rubber and plastic deteriorate over time. The relief edges of a stamp can crack off or break off, an ink/dirt mixture can clog deep crevices, and the relief areas of a stamp can become worn through constant use. These events introduce flaws that are reproduced in the impressions produced by a worn stamp. The approximate period when a stamp impression was made can be determined by comparing its defects with standards from the same stamp arranged in chronological order.

Another method by which stamp impressions can be dated involves changes to the size of some stamps with time. It has been found that stamps can shrink as much as 1.5 mm during a 4-year period. Although this phenomenon is relatively rare, it does provide yet another means of dating stamp impressions.

Glues, Tapes, and Paper Fasteners

Adhesives used to manufacture envelopes, stationery pads, and tapes occasionally undergo changes or modifications to improve their properties. Such changes can be used to establish the earliest date that a document manufactured with a given adhesive was produced. The stationery manufacturer or adhesive company should always be contacted to verify the date when a particular adhesive was first used.

Lift-off tape was introduced by IBM to facilitate the correction of typewriting errors. This innovation, first introduced to the market by IBM on the April 1, 1973, removed unwanted typed characters by overstriking letters through the lift-off tape. This action would lift the letter from the document and allow the typist to correct errors with little disturbance to the paper surface.

Indented Writing

Indented handwritten impressions made in the surface of a document can reveal important information about whether written entries on a piece of paper were made before or after the indented writing occurred. Such sequence determinations are confirmed by subjecting the document to an electrostatic detection apparatus (ESDA) examination.

It is often possible to establish the exact date when indented handwritten impressions on a document were produced. An ESDA examination that establishes the visible writing on a questioned document was made after dated indented impressions can provide an unusual but effective method for confirming the document was backdated.

Handwritten entries in a journal, ledger, notepad, or receipt book usually produce indented impressions on underlying sheets of paper. If it is necessary to date one of the sheets, which was removed, its original location can be confirmed by matching writing on the document with corresponding impressions on the other bound papers. If the dates on adjacent pages are reliable, this simple method enables the document examiner to place the questioned document within a particular time frame.

Guillotine Marks

The exposed edges of receipt books, reams of paper, and stationery pads may contain marks produced by cutters or guillotine blades used to trim these products to size. These stria, often referred to as "guillotine marks," do not run perpendicular to the surface of the paper but run at an angle across the trimmed surfaces. Their locations along the four edges of a document can indicate where a sheet was positioned in the original stack of paper.

Access to several documents from the same stack of paper is needed to establish a cutting pattern against which the contested document is compared. Once the location of guillotine marks on the four edges of the questioned sheet matches the position of sheets from the same lot, any dating information on adjacent sheets can be used to determine when the questioned document was written. If the questioned document is not contemporaneous with information on adjacent sheets of stationery, some plausible explanation should be sought.

See also: **Digital Evidence:** Digital Imaging: Enhancement and Authentication; **Documents:** Analytical Methods; Forgery/ Counterfeits; Handwriting; History of the Forensic Examination of Documents; Ink Analysis; Paper Analysis.

Further Reading

Brunelle, R.L., Reed, R.W., 1984. Forensic Examination of Ink and Paper. Charles C Thomas, Springfield.

Cantu, A.A., 1995. A sketch of analytical methods for document dating. Part I. The static approach: determining age independent analytical profiles. International Journal of Forensic Document Examiners 1, 40–51.

Cantu, A.A., 1995. A sketch of analytical methods for document dating. Part II. The dynamic approach: determining age independent analytical profiles. International Journal of Forensic Document Examiners 2, 192–208.

Dietz, G., 2010. Research in paper structures and its opportunities for forensic tasks. In: 6th EDEWG Conference, Dubrovnik.

Ezcurra, M., Gongora, J., Maguregui, I., Alonso, R., 2010. Analytical methods for dating modern writing instrument inks on paper. Forensic Science International 197, 1–20.

Gerhart, J., 1992. Identification of photocopiers from fusing roller defects. Journal of Forensic Sciences 37, 130–139.

Godown, L., 1969. Forgeries over genuine signatures. Journal of Forensic Sciences 14, 463–468.

Kelly, J.S., 1983. Classification and Identification of Modern Office Copiers. American Board of Forensic Document Examiners, Inc, Houston.

Kelly, J.S., Lindblom, B.S., 2006. Scientific Examination of Questioned Documents. CRC Taylor Francis, Boca Raton, FL.

LaPorte, G.M., Stephens, J.C., Beuchel, A.K., 2010. The examination of commercial printing defects to assess common origin, batch variation and error rate. Journal of Forensic Sciences 55, 136–140.

Mazzella, W.D., Taroni, F., 2005. A simple logical approach to questioned envelopes examination. Science & Justice: Journal of the Forensic Science Society 45, 35–38.

Osborn, A.S., 1929. Questioned Documents, second ed. Boyd Printing Co, Albany.

Purtell, D.J., 1980. Dating a signature. Forensic Science International 15, 243–248.

Starrs, J., 1991. The case of the doctor who doctored the documents. Scientific Sleuthing Review 15, 1.

Totty, R.N., 1990. The examination of photocopy documents. Forensic Science International 46, 121–126.

Tweedy, J., 2001. Class characteristics of counterfeit protection system codes of color laser copiers. Journal of the American Society of Questioned Document Examiners 4, 53–66.

Welch, J., 2008. Erasable ink; something old, something new. Science & Justice: Journal of the Forensic Science Society 48, 187–191.

Weyermann, C., Almog, J., Bügler, J., Cantu, A., 2011. Minimum requirements for application of ink dating methods based on solvent analysis in casework. Forensic Science International 210, 52–62.

Zavattaro, D., Quarta, G., D'Elia, M., Calcagnile, L., 2007. Recent documents dating: an approach using radiocarbon techniques. Forensic Science International 167, 160–162.

Forgery/Counterfeits

T Trubshoe and J McGinn, Department of Immigration and Citizenship, Perth, WA, Australia; Document Examination Solutions, Perth, WA, Australia

Glossary

Biographical data page The page or pages in a passport that contain personal information belonging to the bearer of the document. This information commonly contains full names, date of birth, place of issue, and dates of issue and expiry, as well as a photograph of the bearer.

Covert security features Security features that are included in a document and require a complex understanding of document security and access to sophisticated equipment to enhance. Generally information of a restricted nature with limited disclosure, these features are the final line of security that can be used to confirm or discredit the authenticity of a document.

Optically variable devices Features that show multiple optical effects by changing the angle with which light strikes it and with which it is viewed. These effects can show movement and/or changes in color and cannot be photocopied or scanned.

Overt security features Security features that are included in a document and require a minimal understanding of document security and no equipment to visualize. These features are designed to be difficult to effectively counterfeit and to be easily detected by those persons to whom they are presented.

Planchettes Small colored discs of ∼2 mm diameter that can be incorporated into the manufacture of security paper. The discs can be designed to be viewed under visible and/or ultraviolet light sources and may include additional security features such as microprinting.

Radio frequency identification devices (RFIDs) They are contactless microchips embedded into a document such as a passport or identity card, which allow for the storage and processing of data. Communication with chip readers is via electronic waves, which are able to be read when within a defined proximity to the reader and when authenticated by public key infrastructure (PKI).

Semicovert security features Security features that are included in a document and require a basic understanding of document security and access to basic handheld equipment. These features are designed to be viewed with magnification of ∼10× or simple white and ultraviolet light sources, while still being recognizable by the person to whom they are presented in a minimal time period.

Introduction

History is riddled with attempts to deceive through the forgery of documents, such as by Frank Abagnale Jr throughout the 1960s, made famous through the 2002 movie *Catch Me if You Can*, and by Mark Hoffmann throughout the 1980s with the various Mormon documents.

Although there has been a shift toward transactions occurring electronically, the fact remains that documents continue to be a pivotal requirement in a range of financial and other activities. In any given circumstance, a document can contribute to the facilitation of a transaction, whether for financial gain or some other purpose. Given the resultant value of many documents, it is an attractive proposition for forgers to explore methods of simulating or altering some or all of the information to gain an advantage or benefit.

As a result, there has been significant technological development in the nature and appearance of documents used for a variety of transactions. Governments worldwide have a vested interest in the development of documents to withstand attempts at simulation or alteration, which is undertaken in partnership with a range of organizations and businesses including security document manufacturers, research scientists, and document examination specialists. Documents produced with a high level of security and therefore integrity pose a challenge to forgers; however, it is also recognized that any document is capable, in a given circumstance, of being attractive as a "tool" to facilitate a greater deceit. Documents classified in any quadrant of **Figure 1** may contribute to fraudulent activities.

Although they are devoid of financial value and have limited or no security characteristics, there are documents that enable or support transactions. These are often referred to as

Low value Low integrity	High value Low integrity
Low value High integrity	High value High integrity

Figure 1   The nature of documents in terms of their value and integrity.

"breeder documents," which can enable a forger to gain credibility or potentially provide a mechanism to obtain high-value documents with a high level of integrity. This is particularly relevant with respect to identity documents. For this reason, it should be stated that forgery is not only limited to high-quality documents displaying a high level of security and therefore integrity, but can also include any document that may provide a mechanism to gain this high-value document.

The Nature of Documents Used for Deceit

The distinction between different types of documents used to deceive is important. Counterfeit documents are produced with the appearance of a genuine document and, where appropriate, will display features that attempt to replicate the security characteristics of the said document.

Counterfeit documents are based on a genuine model and are manufactured completely without authority. It is a generalization with some merit that counterfeit documents are a reproduction of a document of some value, either in terms of integrity or financial value.

Fantasy documents differ; these may have the appearance of a document of value or integrity, but they are not based on a genuine and credible base document model. They are fabricated documents commonly marketed as novelty items, although they can be and are used for illicit purposes.

Forged documents are original, genuine documents that have been altered in some way. The alterations may be complex and may relate to the document itself, such as the replacement of pages within a passport, or they may be the inclusion of additional information, such as the inflation of the dollar value of a check.

In considering these basic definitions, experience with fraudulent documents can be generally categorized. Certain documents such as currency are more likely to be counterfeited; documents such as checks are more likely to be forged; and experience has shown that documents such as passports are not confined to either method.

The use of counterfeit or forged documents can be considered broadly under the following sections.

Organized Crime

Given that documents are used to facilitate a range of activities including, but not limited to, the transfer of funds or title, the verification of identity or cross-border movements, and the smuggling and trading of drugs and firearms, it is not unexpected that the production and use of a range of documents is organized. Whether it contributes to a direct fraudulent activity, such as financial fraud, or enables alternative activities such as drug smuggling, people trafficking (or smuggling), or terrorism, there is a high prevalence of organized crime elements involved. These elements are involved in both the production and the distribution of counterfeit and forged documents associated with these illicit activities.

Opportune Crime

Opportune crimes involving counterfeit or forged documents are events that generally occur in isolation, involving limited perpetrators. It is not uncommon for the quality of documents created under these circumstances to be inferior. Perpetrators are reliant on the ability to obtain a successful outcome with little effort. Many opportune crimes are possible through a lack of vigilance on the part of the receiving person or a lack of understanding regarding the nature, appearance, and security value of documents that are presented.

Combating Counterfeit and Forged Documents

There are a number of elements that combine as combative measures to activities involving fraudulent documents.

First and foremost, there is recognition that documents with a high value or purpose are produced with a range of features that allow the receiver, and therefore the person assessing the documents, to judge the genuineness or otherwise of the documents presented. Both organized and opportune crime perpetrators are reliant on various factors such as limited time, minimal training, and various distractions to impact on this person's ability to detect the fraudulent documents.

It can therefore be said that the ability to determine counterfeit or fraudulent documents and activities relies on an understanding of the process of production of genuine documents, together with appropriate training and organizational processes to allow their examination. This includes an understanding of fundamental document security features and characteristics, as well as the limitations associated with their examination.

To enable consideration of whether a document is forged or counterfeited, an understanding of the production of genuine documents must first be gained within the following broad categories:

1. Document security features
2. Quality of manufacture

3. Credible issuing protocols and data registration
4. Verification mechanisms

Some of these aspects are discussed in detail in the following sections.

Document Security Features

The high-quality production of important documents in itself adds a level of integrity. In addition, security features with varying degrees of complexity are introduced into such documents. The purpose of these features can generally be considered as twofold:

● To verify the genuineness of the document and/or
● To allow for identification of intentional alteration, manipulation, or addition.

It could be expected that the complexity of features would bear a direct relationship to the value of the document. However, this is not always the case. There are many valuable documents bearing limited features or features that are easily compromised. In documents used for travel and identity purposes, a range of initiatives over many years have seen quality standards increase to a level that can and does influence the ability of forgers to easily create counterfeit or forged documents. This has, in part, increased the requirement of organized syndicates to produce high-quality fraudulent documents and has generated alternative methodologies for illegal activities, some of which include the use of genuine but fraudulently obtained documents.

Owing to the different situations in which documents are used and the ways in which they are examined, various overt, semicovert, and covert security features are incorporated into their design. By including security features at these different levels, the documents are designed to enable examination with minimal or no equipment at a bank, airport, or retail outlet as well as with sophisticated equipment within laboratories.

Security features and characteristics are introduced into a document during the manufacturing process and where they are used for identity through the issuing process as well. The document's components can roughly be divided into the substrate, printing, personalization, and issuance security, with it being possible to incorporate as many or as few security features in each component as desired.

Substrate

Although secure documents were traditionally manufactured using only paper-based substrates, recent technological developments in synthetic polymers have allowed for a wider range of substrates to be manufactured and a larger number of features to be incorporated.

With paper being the substrate on which the majority of secure documents are still manufactured, various security features are available for incorporation into paper manufacture and therefore available to be evaluated in an examination. Secure documents generally incorporate one or more of the following security features: watermark, security thread, security fibers, and planchettes, and omit the optical brighteners traditionally included in plain or copy paper. With the security features being incorporated into the physical manufacture of paper, postproduction inclusion of genuine security features into commercially available paper is not possible.

Whether as a generic laid pattern or as an intricate image, the watermark is incorporated into paper during the forming stage, where paper fibers are clumped together or pushed apart, to change the density of the paper to create the required design. Using a transmitted light source (light shining through the document from behind), the pattern or image can be viewed as tonal changes in the paper. **Figure 2(a) and (b)** shows the watermark under reflected and transmitted light, respectively. Simulated watermarks, on counterfeit documents, are often the result of printing or embossing and as such are regularly viewed using oblique (light grazing a document from the side) or ultraviolet light.

(a)

(b)

Figure 2 (a) A 100 Peso note displaying a windowed security thread under reflected light. (b) A 100 Peso note displaying a watermark, security thread, and windowed security thread under transmitted light.

Security threads, traditionally associated with high-security documents such as currency and passports, are now being seen in the packaging of computer software and the like because of the increasing counterfeit market that has emerged for these products. Either fully embedded into the paper, or being woven into and out of the paper in a uniform manner (often referred to as a windowed security thread), the security thread, as with the watermark, is incorporated into the paper during the forming stage and is examined using a transmitted light source. **Figure 2(a) and (b)** shows the two types of security threads under reflected and transmitted light, respectively. Printing of these threads, either as a solid line or text, is the most frequently encountered simulation of this feature in the production of counterfeit documents.

Although they are different paper security components, security fibers and planchettes are incorporated into paper and examined in the same way. End product requirements determine the color of the fibers and planchettes used and whether they are to be visible under white light, ultraviolet light, or both. Included in the pulp stage of the paper's manufacture, the resulting fibers and planchettes will be randomly placed throughout and sit within the structure of the paper. Should a counterfeiter attempt to simulate either of these components, it is most often through printing and can result in the appearance of fibers or planchettes occurring in the same position on multiple pages.

Ordinary white copy paper incorporates optical brightening agents in its manufacture to give the paper a brighter white appearance. Under an ultraviolet light source, these agents give off a bright blue/purple fluorescence. It is generally accepted that security paper does not incorporate optical brightening agents in its manufacture and, as such, under an ultraviolet light source the paper remains relatively dull. When counterfeiters use optically bright paper in the manufacture of their documents, it is not uncommon for them to attempt to mask the ultraviolet fluorescence by using ultraviolet-absorbing substances such as lacquer.

Synthetic polymer substrates have become a part of everyday life because of technological advances in financial and identity systems and requirements. From relatively simple store gift cards and telephone cards, to various types of credit cards and currency, synthetic polymer documents have become a popular option in the creation of a low-cost item with a financial value. Identity documents manufactured with these substrates have also increased in popularity, whether as a document in its entirety, such as a driver's license or identity card, or in part, such as a biographical data page within a passport. Various synthetic polymers are used in the manufacture of such documents, with specific polymers chosen because of the particular properties appropriate for the intended use. For example, polyvinyl chloride is most commonly used for credit cards and loyalty cards because of its low cost and ease of mass production; polycarbonate offers

an extended life span and embedded layers for security printing methods and features to be included; and polypropylene is used in the manufacture of synthetic polymer currency.

As with secure paper, numerous security features can be incorporated into the synthetic polymers during their manufacture. These include, but are not restricted to, Multiple Laser Images™, optically variable devices, security threads, and contact chips, or radio frequency identification devices. In addition to the specific polymers mentioned above, composite substrates are also used, allowing security features available to different substrates to be incorporated into the one substrate structure.

The introduction of substrate security features is designed to impact on the ability of forgers to counterfeit the document.

Printing

Depending on the type of document, portions of, or all of, the printing can be created using commercial processes. Currency as an example is a document that is printed consistently and repetitively throughout the course of the series of note with no variable printing required except for the serial number. Identity documents differ in that they too have the consistent repetitive printing throughout the series of the document, but in addition to the commercial printing, desktop printing processes are required to allow for the printing of variable data.

Although not a secure printing process in its own right, the most common commercial printing process used in secure documents is offset lithography. Having a flat and sharp image, this process contributes the majority of the background printing and a great portion of the overprinting on any secure document and is often utilized in the printing of security features. Other commercial printing processes such as letterpress, flexography, gravure, and screen printing are again not specific to secure documents but are often used in areas such as document numbering, laminate printing, and security feature inclusion.

Some key security features can be printed using only the secure commercial printing process of intaglio. This process is available only to secure printers and is used to manufacture a raised print with fine detail and high-quality security capabilities. The latent image is an example of a security feature that will operate correctly only if intaglio is used. Using side light, and relying on the height of the ink to create a shadow and reveal a word or image, the latent image will not be revealed if a flat printing process is utilized. **Figure 3(a) and (b)** shows the intaglio printing of a latent image under reflected and side lights, respectively. The background is printed with a lithographic process.

The printing processes used and the associated security features printed are intended to allow for the detection of counterfeits and to provide the capacity to reveal alterations in forgeries.

(a)

(b)

Figure 3 (a) A 100 Baht note displaying intaglio printing over a lithographic printed background under reflected light. (b) A 100 Baht note displaying an intaglio printed latent image using side light.

Personalization

A number of documents, especially identity documents, require additional printing to allow personalization, thereby individualizing the document. This inclusion of unique information on each document requires printing methods that are readily available, versatile, and cost-effective. These types of printing are commonly referred to as "desktop printing" processes and are readily accessible to the ordinary person. Although a desktop process, the hardware for high-volume requirement can be of a commercial standard. Depending on the type of substrate used to create the base document, various desktop printing processes may be employed.

Traditional processes such as typewriters and dot-matrix machines are no longer expected to be used in modern, high-

Figure 4 A magnified image of the characteristics of thermal transfer printing on a synthetic polymer document.

level identity documents, but they can be regularly seen in older identity documents. Most documents have moved toward using one of four processes, namely, inkjet, laser, thermal transfer, or dye diffusion thermal transfer (often referred to as D2T2), and in the case of synthetic polymer documents, laser engraving.

Typewriters and dot-matrix printers, together with the more commonly used processes inkjet and toner, are confined to printing directly on paper-based documents. The exception is where the information is printed onto the reverse of a laminate and the laminate material is adhered to the substrate. Should a photo have to be included in the personalization, a physical patch photograph needs to be attached alongside the traditional processes, while inkjet and toner can print text and images directly onto the document.

The more modern thermal transfer printing is able to be used on both paper and polymer documents, whereas the D2T2 combination requires a polymer substrate to print correctly. As with inkjet and toner, both of these processes allow for the printing of black and white or colored photos directly onto the substrate. The characteristics specific to thermal transfer printing can be seen in **Figure 4**.

Laser engraving, the most recent of the common personalization processes, can be used only on synthetic polymer documents. Activating a carbon sensitized layer within the polymer substrate, the resulting personal information becomes a component within the document. Because the printing is carbon, it can create only black and white images. This laser-based process is somewhat unique in that it is able to create flat and/or raised printing, adding further security to a document.

Issuance security

Added to protect personal information from being altered or added, additional security covering a portion of, or the entire, document is applied. This will be an action on the part of the issuing authority or organization, with the fundamental purpose of protecting the personal data. As with other components utilized in the document manufacture, issuing security may include quite simple and/or dated features or modern features developed through technological advances and research.

A traditional patch photograph on a paper substrate, for example, may be sufficiently protected by the application of a dry or wet seal stamped partially over both substrates or through attachment by a metal grommet or eyelet. A polymer identity card, on the other hand, may include security features that not only cover the substrate surface but also are bonded in such a way as to make a separation attempt on the layers impossible.

Commonly synthetic polymers, such as laminate security products, protect a document from forgery or counterfeit by ensuring that there is a layer that requires removal to alter information or needs simulation when an original is not available. Numerous types of laminates are manufactured, each encompassing various security features and designs. Laminates can include simple security features such as embossed patterns, ultraviolet reactive ink, and visible printed geometric images in strategically placed sections. More sophisticated laminates can be formed using glass beads to mask a covert image that becomes visible only through correct use of coaxial light or can include holography across the entire surface creating various diffracting images and patterns when viewed from different angles.

The purpose of including issuing security is to render a forgery to the document or a counterfeit of the document detectable.

Issuing Protocols

The role of issuing authorities is important to the overall integrity of a document and the document security continuum. A document can be designed and manufactured to have the highest level of security imaginable, but without appropriate issuing protocols in place it cannot be assumed that the bearer of the document is the owner of the presented identity.

For high-level documents to be obtained, breeder documents comprising birth, death, and marriage certificates, land title certificates, credit cards, and other documents of this nature are required to be shown as proof of identity. Often, the methods available to verify the authenticity of the breeder documents are limited, and the security features incorporated within them are poor, making it difficult for issuing authorities to place a high level of integrity on either the document or the information contained within. As document security features become more sophisticated and systems related to their use more developed, there is a visible increase in the number of fraudulently obtained genuine base documents being used; forged or counterfeit breeder documents are used in their acquisition. An examination of these fraudulently obtained documents would result in the determination of genuineness as to their manufacture, with no way of fraud detection being possible.

International standards, through organizations such as the International Civil Aviation Organization, are widely acknowledged and implemented in the manufacture of high-security documents such as passports and identity cards. With standardization of these documents being in place, capacity building and assistance to aid countries, through international organizations, has turned toward the manufacture and issuing protocols of breeder documents to assist in raising the integrity of the complete security continuum.

The Examination Role

The nature of counterfeits and forgeries is such that the initial encounter with a document requiring examination is rarely within a specialized document examination laboratory. A passport may first be viewed by immigration or customs officers, a credit card by a shop assistant in a department store, currency by a bank clerk, identity documents by a transport authority officer, etc.

The examination of documents to determine their genuineness or otherwise is separated into three levels. Depending on the country or organization, these three levels of examination are described under the following headings: detection, assessment, and specialist.

Depending on the level of examination undertaken, a decision is then made to refer the document for further examination or to determine the outcome as required.

The distinction between counterfeit and forged documents is important. On commencement of any examination, the base document is examined to determine whether it was manufactured through genuine means and contains security features expected in a secure document or a document of that nature. This first level can enable counterfeit documents to be identified on the basis of an evaluation of key but generic document security components, which should be consistent from one document to another in a particular series.

Following the determination of the authenticity of the base document, evidence of forgery to the original document can be identified. At this stage of examination, methods used to alter documents are considered, security features of documents are examined to determine their genuineness or otherwise, and any areas where tampering might have occurred are examined in detail.

To assist in formulating opinions, sample documents, reference databases, and experienced examiners or document examination networks are often engaged.

Detection

For a forged or counterfeited document to be identified, it must first be detected. The detection level of examination is arguably the most important level which is why so much of a document's design focuses on incorporating simple but effective security features that can be examined with minimal training and no equipment.

With timeframes as short as 30 s allocated for the examination of each document, the overt features must be easily examinable to ensure correct operation and to recognize signs of tampering. The detection process may include evaluation of substrate security features such as a watermark, the changing of color and/or image of optically variable devices, the consistency of manufactured components such as number perforations, commercial printing, etc., and the overall quality of the document.

If a document does not raise concern within the short examination period available, it is assumed to be genuine and the processing or transaction proceeds. It is because of the minimal scrutiny that is possible at this point that a forged or counterfeit document, even though crude in appearance, is accepted as being genuine.

Assessment

The assessment level of examination occurs once a document has been detected as being of concern. It is here that a more detailed understanding of document manufacture and security is required, together with equipment capable of examining semicovert levels of security within the document. Depending on the examination environment, the resources utilized may range from being quite simple and consisting only of handheld equipment, such as a magnifier, an ultraviolet light, and a white light source, to quite sophisticated technical equipment, such as a stereomicroscope and a multispectral imaging system.

With more time available for examination, often ranging from hours to days, the document is usually examined in depth by a document examiner or someone whose function includes the examination of documents. With the information that is obtained through the examination, additional avenues of questioning or investigation may be determined.

Documents assessed as being a forgery or counterfeit at this stage may or may not require further examination for judicial or organizational needs.

Specialist

The traditional forensic document examiner, or a specialist in a particular field of document manufacture, undertakes the most in-depth examination of a document to determine its authenticity, which may include a detailed assessment of the covert security features. With many years of specialist training and access to sophisticated technical equipment, systems, and databases, the examiner can undertake an examination that is often limited only by the requirements of the organization. The examination timeframes are not as stringent, so the specialist can undertake complex examinations if deemed necessary.

Technical equipment such as a stereomicroscope and a multispectral imaging system allow the examination of a document in fine detail, under various lighting and filtering conditions. In addition to these core pieces of equipment, electrostatic detection systems, photography accessories, and a selection of other microscopy and spectroscopy equipment are often employed for their respective examinations of impressions on the paper, for the capture of images for evidence, and for the detailed analysis of various components of a document.

Throughout the examination process, observations are made of areas within the document, allowing propositions for the document's condition to be formulated and, where possible, opinions to be expressed.

Conclusion

The production of counterfeit and forged documents is a significant international issue. The use of documents to facilitate illicit acts cannot be understated, nor can the fact that documents remain cornerstones of identity verification be negated.

The development of advanced document security features, in combination with sound issuing protocols and verification methodologies, ongoing emergence of biometric capabilities associated with documents, and an increase in community awareness, are all strategies to be designed to enhance a receiver's ability to accept documents as genuine or positively identify the effects of counterfeit and forged documents.

When a document is determined to be a counterfeit or a forgery, it is possible that, through additional analysis of the document, linkages to other documents, their components, or manufacturers may be made. This type of forensic intelligence can assist in the disruption of document manufacturing syndicates and of organized criminal activities such as people smuggling, drug trafficking, and terrorism.

See also: **Documents:** Analytical Methods; Document Dating; Handwriting; Ink Analysis; Paper Analysis; **Investigations:** Counterfeit Currency; Identity Theft.

Further Reading

Ellen, D., 2006. Scientific Examination of Documents – Methods and Techniques, third ed. Taylor and Francis Group, Boca Raton, FL.

Harrison, W.R., 1981. Suspect Documents: Their Scientific Examination. Nelson-Hall, Chicago, IL.

Kelly, J.S., Lindblom, B.S., 2006. Scientific Examination of Questioned Documents, second ed. CRC Taylor & Francis, New York, NY.

Ng, P.K., Hui, W.S., Chim, J.L.C., Li, C.-K., Poon, N.L., 2004. Methods of forgery in counterfeit travel documents. Journal of the American Society of Questioned Document Examiners 7 (2), 83–90.

Nugent, N., 2008. How to personalize a passport – Part 1. Keesing Journal of Documents and Identity 27, 3–8.

Nugent, N., 2009. How to personalize a passport – Part 2. Keesing Journal of Documents and Identity 28, 11–15.

Ombelli, D., Knopjes, F., 2008. Documents: The Developer's Toolkit. European Union: Occidentalis Editora Lda.

Rettig, R., 2011. Security features in composite material documents. Keesing Journal of Documents and Identity 34, 13–17.

United Nations Office on Drugs and Crime, 2010. Guide for the Development of Forensic Document Examination Capacity. United Nations, New York.

Van Renesse, R.L., 2005. Optical Document Security, third ed. Artech House, Boston.

Relevant Websites

www.icao.int—International Civil Aviation Organization.

www.iso.org—International Organisation for Standardization.

Handwriting

CL Bird, Forensic Science SA, Adelaide, SA, Australia

This chapter is a revision of the previous edition article by M. Vos, S. Strach, & P. Westwood, volume 2, pp. 584–590, © 2000, Elsevier Ltd.

Glossary

Copybook A manual of handwriting instruction that contains models of penmanship to be copied.

Diacritic A mark added to a letter to indicate a particular pronunciation. Also used to refer to the dots over the "i" and "j."

Disguised writing The writing of a person who has deliberately attempted to alter their usual writing habits in order to conceal their identity.

Fluency Quality of smoothness and flow of movement.

Line quality A measure of fluency of handwriting, the degree of regularity.

Natural variation Normal or usual deviations found between repeated instances of any individual's writing.

Retouching Touching up to correct or perfect a written character.

Simulated writing Writing that is produced by attempting to copy the pictorial characteristics of a target writing. It may be created freehand with the use of a physical or mental model or by a tracing process.

Tremor A lack of smoothness in the writing trace, due to lack of skill, deliberate control of the writing implement, or involuntary movement (illness affecting motor control).

Introduction

Handwriting is the process, and outcome, of creating letters, numbers, or symbols using a writing implement, usually following a set of guidelines such that the content may be communicated to another person. Opinions on the authorship of handwriting and signatures have been accepted as expert evidence in courts of law around the world for over 100 years. These opinions may be on writings related to criminal investigations or civil litigation. In the majority of cases, the markings being examined are present on conventional paper documents; however, examinations are not limited to these and may also encompass writings appearing on such surfaces as doors, walls, vehicles, furniture, and skin. Examples of commonly encountered documents on which questioned handwriting may appear are wills, contracts, mortgages, other legal documents, checks, credit or withdrawal vouchers, anonymous or threatening letters, and diaries.

While there are slight differences in the way handwriting and signatures are produced and examined (discussed in more detail below), throughout this chapter when the term handwriting is used, it will usually imply both handwritten text and signatures.

Theoretical Basis for Handwriting Comparison

In relation to other "identification sciences" such as DNA profiling, fingerprints, or tool mark comparisons, handwriting opinion evidence stands alone as the examinations and evidence evaluations are based solely on movement outcomes. The basis for this is that handwriting features embedded within the writing trace are believed to be somewhat characteristic of an individual. Since handwriting is a learned behavior, it is found that the features of the writing can vary normally, can be purposefully distorted, or can be copied by others. The effectiveness of forensic handwriting comparisons is reliant on the relationship between the features observed in the movement outcome and the extent to which those features characterize an individual.

Why Does One Believe Handwriting Can Be Used as an Individuating Feature?

Handwriting is a complex learned behavior that is the product of cognitive, psychomotor, and biomechanical processes directing the movement of the arm, hand, and fingers in order to manipulate the writing implement in three-dimensional space to produce a visual trace on the writing surface. Like any type of complex movement, the handwriting learning process is comprised of three relatively distinct phases of movement acquisition. During the *cognitive phase*, the learner writer is concerned with how to construct letters and symbols. This usually requires a high degree of cognition, as different motor strategies are trialed and successful strategies are preserved. As each step in the movement progression is

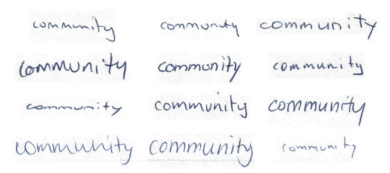

Figure 1   The word "community" written by 12 different people, illustrating interwriter variation.

considered and controlled, writing produced during this phase usually displays poor fluency. The *associative phase* occurs when the writer has determined an effective way of constructing characters and is employing subtle adjustments in order to improve their output. The movement, and therefore the handwriting, becomes more consistent in this period. The associative phase for handwriting movement acquisition extends over months or years. When the writer reaches a stage where movement production becomes "automatic,'" they have reached the *autonomous stage*. Now, their handwriting can be carried out seemingly without attention to the process.

People carry out this skilled movement in different ways to achieve similar goals, and their movement style may be characteristic to some extent. Although the formation of letters is initially dependent on the copybook style learned by the writer, as the skill develops over many years variations may be introduced due to differences in teaching methods, muscular control, sequence of movements employed, esthetic preferences, exposure to writings of others, and frequency of writing. This results in interwriter variation in form (**Figure 1**).

An analogous progression is made through these phases as a person's signature is developed. Initially, writers will consider how they want their signature to look and how to achieve that look. With practice and over time the output may change, perhaps under the influence of the factors mentioned above, until the production of the signature becomes automatic and, to some extent, individual to them.

At the autonomous stage of handwriting movement acquisition, the abstract motor programs controlling the muscles responsible for the movement are generated by stringing together smaller programmed units of behavior, which are eventually controlled as a single unit (**Figure 2**). These motor programs are not muscle specific; that is, the movements required to produce a character, word, or signature are differentially transferable between muscle sets not normally associated with writing tasks. There are numerous spatial and temporal features that are preserved in the movement patterns, resulting in a constancy of form production within a writer, in spite of influences such as body, arm and hand position, writing speed, writing surface, or even limb used for writing.

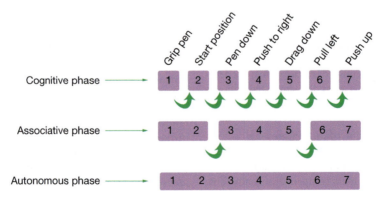

Figure 2   Phases of handwriting movement acquisition. Adapted from Keele, S.W., Summers, J.J., 1976. The structure of motor programs. In: Stelmach, G.E., (Ed.), Motor Control: Issues and Trends, pp. 109–142. Academic Press, New York.

However, no person writes so consistently that every character is exactly the same each time it is written. There will be a small range of variation in features such as proportions, size, slope, and spacing. This intrawriter variation arises from a combination of the writer's motor output varying to different extents due to the nature of the movement's representation in the brain as well as features associated with particular letter combinations, position in a word, style, format of the document, or the writer's mood. External factors and deliberate changes to the movement process can also affect the appearance of a person's writing and will be discussed later in this chapter.

The general propositions of handwriting examinations, which enable handwriting to be a useful form of "opinion identification evidence" in the forensic sciences, are as follows:

- Given a sufficient amount of handwriting, no two skilled writers exhibit identical handwriting features (interwriter variation).
- The natural handwriting of individual writers varies (intrawriter variation).
- Due to the ingrained nature of handwriting production, individuals find it difficult to disguise extended bodies of their writing and to accurately simulate the writing characteristics of others.

Handwriting Comparison Method

Historically, forensic handwriting examination has been based on the underlying belief that training and experience enable the handwriting examiner to distinguish between "class" (or "style") and "individual" characteristics. "Style" characteristics are those that are derived from the general model or copybook system taught, and "individual" characteristics are deviations from the copybook form, introduced into the writing or developed over time either consciously or unconsciously. Class characteristics may be shared with many other people taught the same system of handwriting, while individual characteristics are the primary features that a forensic document examiner (FDE) relies on to differentiate the writings of different people. However, while this theory seems logical, there is no clear evidence that experience increases the validity of findings, FDEs do not claim that they can reliably identify the class and individual characteristics of samples that they examine, and FDEs can subscribe to the theory yet express opinions as to the authorship of foreign writings where the class system is unknown to them. Furthermore, signatures may exhibit no class characteristics, being partially or entirely stylized, but are still examined.

More recently, complexity and feature detection theory has been put forward as an explanation for identification expertise. Complexity theory, while embracing class and class-divergent

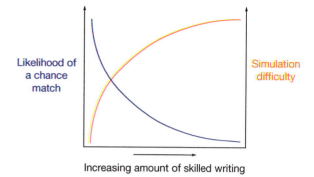

Figure 3 Generalized complexity relationships between the amount of skilled writing available in a sample, the difficulty with which the sample may be simulated, and the likelihood of a chance match with more than one writer.

properties of writings, proposes an inverse relationship between the complexity and amount of handwriting examined, and the ease of successful simulation of that handwriting. In addition, as the amount of skilled writing increases, the likelihood of a chance match also decreases (**Figure 3**). This theory explains the common ground between text-based and signature examinations and informs the assessment of whether sufficient material is available on which to express a valid opinion.

Feature detection theory is based on the rationale that under normal conditions, given a sufficient amount of writing, skilled writers are unlikely to produce handwritten images that are exactly the same in terms of the combination of construction, line quality, form variation, and layout. These features are compared between questioned and comparison writings and used as a basis for a primary opinion on the similarity or dissimilarity of the writings.

Examination of Questioned Writing

When a questioned document is received for handwriting examination, the FDE will examine the writing visually using a handheld magnifier and a microscope. Pictorial and spatial features are noted, including line quality, construction of each character, connectivity, size relationships within and between letters, slope, apparent pen pressure, spacing within and between words, line spacing, margin and baseline habits, diacritics, and punctuation. Pen direction and stroke order can often be assessed from microscopic features, particularly at the commencing or terminating strokes of a character or element. These spurs, ticks, or faint drag lines show the direction of the writing implement just prior to or following its contact with the writing surface. Striations, evident in ballpoint pen writings, can also be used to determine pen direction, as these lines run from the inside to the outside of a curve in the direction of motion (**Figure 4**). The striation pattern present when the pen

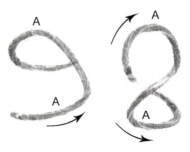

Figure 4 Ballpoint pen writings with (A) striations, which show the direction of pen movement (indicated by the arrows).

is lifted from the paper at the conclusion of a stroke may be preserved on the ball of the pen and transferred to the beginning of the next stroke ("memory effect"). At other times, all of the ink on the ball tip at the terminus of a stroke is deposited on the page, so that the next stroke displays a deficiency of ink at the commencement ("inkless start"). These features may be used to help determine the sequence of strokes in ballpoint pen writings, and thus a writer's habits.

Examination of Known Writing

Known (also referred to as comparison, specimen, or exemplar) writing may be either *collected* from documents written during normal course of business or social activity or *requested* to be written specifically for the purposes of comparison. Features of known handwriting are examined in the same way as questioned writings. These writings must be in a comparable style, for example, if the questioned writing is in a cursive style, the comparison writing also needs to be in a cursive style. There will be few, if any, comparison points if the known writing was in an uppercase print style. Furthermore, the format of a document may impact on the way handwriting appears. If there is a limited amount of space available for writing, the writer may cramp their writing to a greater extent than usual, or if there are printed boxes within which to write individual letters or words (e.g., on an application form), the normal spacing and connectivity may be affected. Wherever possible, comparison writing appearing in a similar format to the questioned writings should be examined. Another important aspect of the examination of known writings is assessing whether the writings are consistent when compared among themselves. Any inconsistencies observed are referred to as contamination and may be due to having been written by more than one writer, the specimen writer having more than one writing style (aside from the expected dissimilarities associated with writings in uppercase, lowercase, and cursive), or the writings having been created by the specimen writer at significantly different times. Contamination appearing in small amounts is excluded from the specimen pool of writing, but if

a significant amount of potential contamination is identified, the FDE should contact the investigator for clarification of proof of authorship. FDEs should be aware that contamination may also be an issue in questioned writings. Inconsistencies due to multiple writers must be carefully considered, while those due to one writer having different writing styles or writing at different times may be addressed with sufficient comparison material.

It should be noted that some examinations will not include known writings but involve the comparison of a number of different questioned documents in order to determine whether common authorship exists. In these cases, feature comparison can proceed as outlined below.

Feature Comparison

Once the specimen material is established as suitable for comparison, and the features of the questioned and known writings have been examined separately, these are compared with each other with the aim to express an opinion as to whether the questioned writing is similar or dissimilar to the specimen writing. That is, whether the questioned writing is consistent or inconsistent with having been produced by the same motor memories as the specimen writing.

Similarities can be defined as pictorial or structural features that appear consistent between the populations of questioned and known writings. Put another way, a character in the questioned writing would be considered similar if it fell within the range of variation exhibited for that character in the known writings. Differences are pictorial or structural features that appear dissimilar between the populations of questioned and known writings. These may be observed in terms of one or a combination of fluency, stroke direction, stroke order, and connectivity. For these features to be described as different, they need to be fundamental to the pictorial or structural character of the writing and not shared between the bodies of questioned and known writings (**Figure 5**).

Evaluation and Opinion

If either similarities or differences are observed between the questioned and known writings, these may each be explained by a number of different propositions.

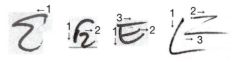

Figure 5 Four forms of the letter E showing different construction and stroke order as indicated by numbers.

Similarities

1. The questioned writings were written by the writer of the comparison writings.
2. The questioned writing is a simulation or disguised form of the genuine writing and no evidence of the process remains.
3. A different writer's handwriting resembles the comparison writing by chance.

Differences

1. The questioned writings were not written by the writer of the comparison writings.
2. The questioned writing is either simulated or disguised and there is evidence of this process.
3. The writer of the comparison samples wrote the questioned writings; however:
   a. They have more than one writing style and these are not all represented in the comparison material, or the comparison writings are not a complete representation of the individual's handwriting, or
   b. Their writing has been affected by unknown internal or environmental factors such as age, illness, intoxication, and so on.

In some instances, the examiner may observe a combination of marked similarities and differences within the questioned writing, such that it will not be clear which of the two proposition sets to consider.

FDEs may find it difficult to support any one of these propositions over one or more of the others. The relationship between complexity, amount of handwriting, and ease of simulation can be used to aid in the process of forming an opinion. For example, if the questioned writing is similar to the specimen writing, but the writing is not complex and restricted to a few words (or elements in a signature), the possibility that the writing has been simulated or that a chance match has occurred cannot be practically excluded (**Figure 6**) and an inconclusive or qualified opinion may be expressed. However, if the questioned writing is similar to the specimen writing and the writing is complex and comprises a paragraph or more, the possibility that the writing has been simulated or that a chance match has occurred can be practically excluded (**Figure 7**) and an unqualified opinion that the writer of the specimen material wrote the questioned writing may be expressed.

If significant differences are found in structural features, this usually results in an opinion that the two writings are unlikely to have been written by the same writer or that there is nothing to link the questioned and specimen writings as having been written by one writer. Although unqualified exclusionary opinions are sometimes justified (e.g., in cases where the questioned writing displays far greater skill than the comparison writer is capable of), they should be used with caution,

Specimen   Questioned

Figure 6 Questioned signature that is similar to the specimen material, but not complex, therefore the possibility that the signature has been simulated or that a chance match has occurred cannot be practically excluded.

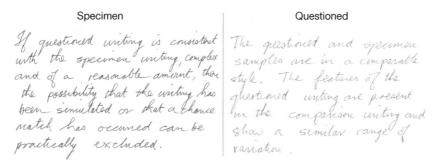

Specimen   Questioned

Figure 7 Questioned writing that is similar to the specimen writing, complex and of a reasonable amount, therefore the possibility that the writing has been simulated or that a chance match has occurred can be practically excluded.

taking into consideration the possibility that the specimen writer has more than one distinct handwriting style.

Dissimilarities in line quality may be generally attributable to one of two groups:

1. Those deemed the result of simulation behavior, where the questioned material is written slowly but shares features with the specimen material that are unlikely to be the result of chance match. In these cases, the likelihood of being able to identify or exclude specific writers (including the person whose writing is "simulated") as a potential author is limited.
2. All other types of line quality dissimilarities, including uneven writing surface, poor pen function, the effect of illness or drugs, or disturbances due to disguise behavior. In these cases too, the ability to express an opinion as to authorship may be limited.

Generally, the examination process and therefore the opinion able to be expressed are affected by the quality and quantity of both the questioned and comparison material. The quantity of the questioned writing cannot usually be controlled. The amount of comparison material should be sufficient so as to represent the writer's normal range of natural variation and is often easily achieved through collected than requested writings. The quality of writings includes the following considerations, which may each impose limitations on the examination:

- The comparability of the writings. The comparison material should be written in the same style as the questioned writing.
- Complexity of the handwriting.
- The relative timing of the writings. Ideally the comparison material should have been written at around the same time as the questioned writing. This is particularly important if the known writer suffers from an illness affecting motor control or is elderly.
- The evidence of an un-natural writing process (see below). This may be due to disguise, simulation, or some other factor.
- The original or nonoriginal nature of the documents.

If the limitations associated with an examination are deemed to be too great, for example, in cases with entries restricted to a few words, severe distortion of the questioned or comparison writing due to simulation or disguise, or a poor reproduction quality nonoriginal document, the FDE will be unable to support any of the possible propositions over the others and will express an inconclusive opinion. This is also the case when both similarities and dissimilarities are observed between questioned and known writings. Qualified and inconclusive opinions noting the possible propositions to explain the observations may still be of assistance to investigators, lawyers, and the courts, as they may have access to other evidence that may lend support to one of the propositions over the others.

Signature Comparison Method

Signature comparisons are approached in much the same way as handwriting comparisons, with the same general process followed. However, as signatures are usually the result of a single, over learned abstract motor program and may be highly stylized, it is often possible to express an unqualified opinion on the authorship of a questioned signature where a handwriting examination of a similar amount would be limited. Again, complexity and feature detection theory can be applied, so that the more complex the signature, the lower the likelihood of a chance match, and the more difficult it would be to successfully simulate.

The general limitations associated with handwriting examinations also apply here. It can sometimes be difficult to assess whether the comparison material available is sufficient to represent the writer's full range of natural variation, and ensuring the comparison signatures are contemporaneous with the questioned signature(s) is particularly important.

Un-natural Handwriting Behaviors

The features of un-natural writing habits can be quite different from normal writing due to their physiological and psychological characteristics. Un-natural handwriting may be considered that which is simulated, disguised, or modified by internal or external factors such as the writing environment (e.g., paper surface, writing implement, and writing surface), illness, and medication or intoxication by drugs or alcohol. Each of these may result in writing displaying poor line quality, tremor, or other distortions; however, medication may lead to an improvement in the writing movement that the examiner should consider.

Simulations may be freehand, traced, or machine generated. Signatures are more commonly simulated than handwritten text. Freehand simulations are "drawn" either based on a physical model or a mental image. In this case, the writer is required to imitate another person's complex mechanisms for controlling muscle contractions while suppressing the characteristics of their own system. The same areas of the brain will be used, but differently configured, with more input from the sensory areas (feedback) and an increased cognitive load. The movement will generally be slower and less fluent than natural handwriting movements, as the writer stops frequently to check letter construction and progress against the model. This writing behavior is likely to be reflected in the static handwriting trace in terms of features that can be readily observed: a lack of fluency, unusual pen lifts, pauses, retouches and internal inconsistencies in pen direction, and letter construction or connectivity.

Tracings may result in writings that are more pictorially similar to the specimen writing, but fluency of the line trace will almost invariably be lacking. There may be evidence of the process on the questioned document if traced guidelines in the form of indented impressions or pencil transfers have been used. Similar marks may be present on the document used as the template, should this be available.

Generally, simulations may capture one or the other of the pictorial or line quality features of the genuine writing, but very rarely both. However, the possibility of a well-practiced simulator or expert penman may need to be considered. Machine-generated simulations are created from source writing using a scanner, photocopier, or other machine. The simulation may be a direct reproduction or be electronically manipulated to alter some aspects, e.g., size or slant.

Like freehand simulation, disguise behavior imposes taxes on the movement system, resulting in a similar disturbance to fluency. When attempting disguise, a writer will again have to suppress their normal writing behavior and introduce new features that they consider significantly different. Typically, changes are made to obvious features such as slope, size, or letter design, while inconspicuous features are left unchanged. Some writers may not realize what characteristics are significant, or find the task of disguise so difficult, that their attempts are unsuccessful, and an examination may lead the examiner to express an opinion that the writing is genuine.

Signatures may be disguised in such a way as to be initially accepted by a third party, with the writer later denying that they wrote it. These will often closely resemble the specimen signatures in all but one or two features and may be able to be associated with the specimen writer. Autosimulation (or self-simulation) may also be employed as a means of disguise, where a writer attempts to simulate their own handwriting or signature. Because of this, the term simulation does not exclude the writer of the target writing as an author. Autosimulated writings may be impossible to differentiate from writings simulated by a different writer.

It is difficult for writers to maintain either type of un-natural writing behavior, so with extended writing some of the writer's normal characteristics are likely to appear. This results in the presence of both similarities and dissimilarities with the comparison writing. Recent research provides empirical data for the difficulty that FDEs have in distinguishing between disguised and simulated writing behaviors. Therefore, it should be noted that where there is evidence of a simulation or disguise process in questioned writing, it is not generally possible to express an opinion as to authorship.

Examination of Nonoriginal Writing

The examination of nonoriginal writing gives rise to a number of issues for FDEs. Examples of nonoriginal documents include photocopies, facsimiles, carbon or carbonless duplicates, photographs, and scans. Most of these reproduction processes will result in a loss of microscopic detail, making features such as pen lifts, retouching, striations, and line quality difficult or impossible to determine. Features associated with disturbances to the substrate, such as traced guidelines to assist copying, or erased pencil marks will also be undetectable. Nevertheless, useful handwriting comparisons of nonoriginal documents can be undertaken. However, the limitations should be taken into account when expressing opinions, so that suitably qualified opinions will usually be expressed along with a statement that the opinions are expressed on the assumption that the questioned document examined is a true and accurate representation of the original document and that if this assumption is proven, by whatever means, not to be true, then the opinion should be reviewed.

Recent Research in Handwriting Comparisons

While other forensic science disciplines such as DNA and drug analysis have solid theoretical and empirical footings, forensic handwriting examination has evolved outside of any mainstream scientific culture. The past two decades have seen the emergence of academic critics of forensic handwriting examination. Their published works have principally focused on the lack of empirical testing of the theoretical basis underlying authorship opinions and perceived shortfalls in data dealing with the accuracy, reliability, and validity of these opinions. In order to strengthen the scientific basis for handwriting comparisons, a number of studies addressing these issues have been undertaken. Tests of FDEs' proficiency compared to that of a control group of lay people have found that handwriting identification expertise does exist, with the expertise characterized by what may be described as the "conservatism" of the professional group compared to the control group. Using blinded studies where participants compare questioned samples to known samples, it has been found that both FDE and lay groups report a similar number of correct associations of questioned writings with known writings. The difference between the FDE and lay groups is in the significantly lower error rate for FDEs. This has been attributed to FDEs expressing more inconclusive opinions, where the control group expresses erroneous false matches.

Statistical studies on the individuality of handwriting have shown that based on the sample sets examined, handwriting is unique and identifiable. A number of software programs have also been developed for automated, computer-based writer identification and verification based on feature extraction algorithms, designed to assist in the examination process. Results from these automated searches require verification by an FDE.

Reporting Opinions

Along with the move toward investigating the scientific validity of the principles underpinning forensic handwriting examination and obtaining empirical data on the skill of examiners, pressure is also on for forensic document examination and other identification sciences to apply a more scientifically correct reporting terminology. Different professional groups of FDEs around the world approach reporting in different ways. The ASTM standards, in use in the United States of America, recommend a 9-point reporting scale ranging from "identification" to "elimination," with varying levels of probability (or degrees of confidence) between them. However, categorical opinions of identity of source are not intrinsically scientific, and recent publications have supported logical, scientific methods for expressing evaluative opinions. This approach (known as the Bayesian approach) requires the forensic scientist to consider their observations in the light of propositions that represent the prosecution and defense, respectively. Opinions ought to be presented in terms of the ratio of the probability of the observations given the prosecution hypothesis to the probability of the observations given the defense hypothesis, which is known as the *likelihood ratio*. This may be expressed along the lines of "the observations are much more probable if the questioned note was written by the writer of the comparison sample than if it was written by someone else." The Board of the European Network of Forensic Science Institutes (ENFSI) has engaged itself to work toward full implementation of this approach within the ENFSI laboratories.

Other Examinations

Although this chapter focuses on handwriting and signature comparisons undertaken by FDEs, there are many other types of examinations that may be carried out in a forensic document examination laboratory. These include analysis of inks (writing and printing), printing processes and paper, stamp and seal impressions, impressions of writing or other marks on the document, and reconstruction and restoration of damaged documents. In some laboratories, an FDE performs all of these examinations along with handwriting comparisons; in others, handwriting comparisons and the other document examinations are completed by different people.

FDEs should not be confused with graphologists. Graphology, also known as graphoanalysis or handwriting analysis, is concerned with the examination of handwriting to reveal psychological or personality traits of the writer. No aspects of this field qualify a graphologist as an FDE.

See also: **Documents:** Analytical Methods; Document Dating; Forgery/Counterfeits; History of the Forensic Examination of Documents; Ink Analysis; Paper Analysis; **Foundations:** Evidence/Classification; Overview and Meaning of Identification/Individualization; Interpretation/The Comparative Method; Statistical Interpretation of Evidence: Bayesian Analysis; The Frequentist Approach to Forensic Evidence Interpretation.

Further Reading

Association of Forensic Science Providers, 2009. Standards for the formulation of evaluative forensic science expert opinion. Science & Justice: Journal of the Forensic Science Society 49 (3), 161–164.

ASTM Standard E1658, 2008. Standard Terminology for Expressing Conclusions of Forensic Document Examiners. ASTM International, West Conshohocken, PA. http://dx.doi.org/10.1520/E1658-08.

Bird, C., Found, B., Ballantyne, K., Rogers, D., 2010. Forensic handwriting examiners' opinions on the process of production of disguised and simulated signatures. Forensic Science International 195, 103–107.

Bird, C., Found, B., Rogers, D., 2010. Forensic document examiners' skill in distinguishing between natural and disguised handwriting behaviors. Journal of Forensic Sciences 55 (5), 1291–1295.

Conway, J.V.P., 1959. Evidential Documents. Charles C Thomas, Springfield.

Ellen, D., 1997. The Scientific Examination of Documents: Methods and Techniques, second ed. Taylor and Francis Ltd, London.

Evett, I.W., 1998. Towards a uniform framework for reporting opinions in forensic science casework. Science & Justice: Journal of the Forensic Science Society 38 (3), 198–202.

Evett, I.W., et al., 2011. Expressing evaluative opinions: a position statement. Science & Justice: Journal of the Forensic Science Society 51 (1), 1–2.

Found, B., Rogers, D., 1995. Contemporary issues in forensic handwriting examination. A discussion of key issues in the wake of the Starzecpyzel decision. Journal of Forensic Document Examination 8, 1–33.

Found, B., Rogers, D., 1998. A consideration of the theoretical basis of forensic handwriting examination. International Journal of Forensic Document Examiners 4 (2), 109–118.

Found, B., Rogers, D., 1999. Documentation of forensic handwriting comparison and identification method: a modular approach. Journal of Forensic Document Examination 12, 1–68.

Found, B., Rogers, D., 2008. The probative character of forensic handwriting examiners' identification and elimination opinions on questioned signatures. Forensic Science International 178, 54–60.

Found, B., Sita, J., Rogers, D., 1999. The development of a program for characterising forensic handwriting examiners' expertise: signature examination pilot study. Journal of Forensic Document Examination 12, 69–80.

Harrison, W.R., 1958. Suspect Documents. Sweet and Maxwell Limited, London.

Hilton, O., 1982. Scientific Examination of Questioned Documents, revised ed. Elsevier North Holland, Inc., New York.

Huber, R.A., Headrick, A.M., 1999. Handwriting Identification: Facts and Fundamentals. CRC Press LLC, New York.

Kam, M., 2010. Proficiency testing and procedure validation for forensic document examination. In: Technical Support Working Group, Requirement Number: 000/IS-001-DREXEL-03-FP.

Kam, M., Fielding, G., Conn, R., 1997. Writer identification by professional document examiners. Journal of Forensic Sciences 42 (5), 778–786.

Kam, M., Wetstein, J., Conn, R., 1994. Proficiency of professional document examiners in writer identification. Journal of Forensic Sciences 39 (1), 5–14.

Keele, S.W., Summers, J.J., 1976. The structure of motor programs. In: Stelmach, G.E. (Ed.), Motor Control: Issues and Trends. Academic Press, New York, pp. 109–142.

Levinson, J., 2001. Questioned Documents: A Lawyers Handbook. Academic Press, Avon.

Marcelli, A., Rendina, M., De Stefano, C., 2011. Disguising writiers identification: an experimental study. Journal of Forensic Document Examination 21, 23–35.

Morris, R.N., 2000. Forensic Handwriting Identification. Academic Press, Avon.

National Research Council of the National Academies, 2009. Strengthening Forensic Science in the United States: A Path Forward. The National Academies Press, Washington, DC.

Osborn, A.S., 1929. Questioned Documents, second ed. Nelson-Hall Co, Chicago.

Risinger, D., Denbeaux, M.P., Saks, M.J., 1989. Exorcism of ignorance as a proxy for rational knowledge: the lessons of handwriting identification "expertise". University of Pennsylvania Law Review 137, 731–792.

Risinger, D., Denbeaux, M.P., Saks, M.J., 1998. Brave new "post-*Daubert* world" – a reply to Professor Moenssens. Seton Law Review 29, 405–485.

Risinger, D., Saks, M.J., 1996. Science and nonscience in the courts: *Daubert* meets handwriting identification expertise. Iowa Law Review 82, 21–74.

Saks, M.J., Koehler, J.J., 2005. The coming paradigm shift in forensic identification science. Science 309, 892–895.

Saks, M.J., VanderHaar, H., 2005. On the "general acceptance" of handwriting identification principles. Journal of Forensic Sciences 50 (1), 1–8.

Sita, J., Found, B., Rogers, D.K., 2002. Forensic handwriting examiners' expertise for signature comparison. Journal of Forensic Sciences 47 (5), 1117–1123.

Slyter, S.A., 1995. Forensic Signature Examination. Charles C Thomas, Springfield.

Srihari, S.N., Cha, S., Arora, H., Lee, S., 2002. Individuality of handwriting. Journal of Forensic Sciences 47 (4), 856–872.

Srihari, S., Huang, C., Srinivasan, H., 2008. On the discriminability of the handwriting of twins. Journal of Forensic Sciences 53 (2), 430–446.

Srihari, S.N., Srinivasan, H., Desai, K., 2007. The relationship between quantitatively modelled signature complexity levels and forensic document examiners' qualitative opinions on casework. Journal of Forensic Document Examination 18, 1–19.

Relevant Websites

http://www.abfde.org/—American Board of Forensic Document Examiners, Inc.

http://www.asqde.org/—American Society of Questioned Document Examiners.

http://www.afde.org/—Association of Forensic Document Examiners.

http://www.asfdeinc.org/—Australasian Society of Forensic Document Examination, Inc.

http://www.enfsi.eu—European Network of Forensic Science Institutes' European Network of Forensic Handwriting Experts.

http://www.graphonomics.org/—International Graphonomics Society.

http://www.safde.org/—Southeastern Association of Forensic Document Examiners.

http://www.swafde.org/—Southwestern Association of Forensic Document Examiners.

Ink Analysis

JA Siegel, Indiana University Purdue University Indianapolis, Indianapolis, IN, USA

Glossary

Densitometry A technique whereby a light-sensitive element measures the depth and concentration of color associated with a solid material.

Scanning Auger microscopy An analytical method whereby the elemental composition of a solid surface such as paper can be determined by the Auger effect, which measures the release of electrons from various elements.

Thin-layer chromatography An analytical chemical method whereby a mixture of substances may be separated by their differential adherence to a solid stationary phase that is coated onto a solid platform such as a microscope slide. The mixture is dissolved in a solvent and spotted at the bottom of the platform and then the platform is introduced into a mobile liquid phase, which carries the spots up the platform, separating the components of the mixture.

Introduction

Most people identify questioned document analysis with handwriting and that remains one of the principal areas of analysis in this type of forensic science. Even though computers and computer printing seem to have taken over the world of documents, handwritten documents and especially signatures are still very important in society. Although some documents are written using a pencil, the vast majority employs some type of ink pen. Analyzing only the characteristics of the handwriting leaves out an important piece of evidence, that is, the ink. Chemical and physical analyses of inks on questioned documents provide valuable information regarding their authenticity. Comparison of the chemical and physical properties of two or more inks can determine (1) if the inks were made by the same manufacturer, (2) in some cases, whether the inks were products of the same production batch, and (3) the first production date of the specific ink formulation involved. When dating tags are detected, it is possible to determine the actual year or years when the ink was manufactured. Dating tags are unique chemicals that have been added to ballpoint inks by some ink companies as a way to determine the year the ink was made.

Relative age comparison tests performed on inks of the same formula, stored under the same conditions and used on the same type of paper (performed by measuring changing solubility properties of inks), can help to estimate the age of ink on questioned documents. This is done by (1) comparing the rates and extent of extraction of questioned and known dated inks in organic solvents by thin-layer chromatography (TLC) densitometry, (2) comparing changes in dye concentrations by TLC and TLC densitometry, (3) comparing the volatile ink components by gas chromatography–mass spectrometry (GC–MS), and (4) using mass spectrometric methods for following the degradation of ink components, mainly dyes or pigments, with time. In cases where known dated writings are not available for comparison with questioned inks, accelerated aging (heating the ink to induce aging of the ink) can sometimes be used to estimate the age of ink using any or all of the above-described techniques. Iron-based inks can be dated by measuring the migration of iron along the fibers of the paper by scanning Auger microscopy.

This chapter describes state-of-the-art procedures for the chemical and physical comparison, identification, and dating of inks on questioned documents.

Composition of Major Types of Writing Inks

Knowledge of the composition of inks is necessary to understand the reasons for the various methods used to analyze inks. In addition, knowledge of the first production date for each type of ink or certain ingredients in the inks is useful for dating inks.

Carbon (India) Ink

In its simplest form, carbon ink consists of amorphous carbon shaped into a solid cake with glue. It is made into a liquid for writing by grinding the cake and suspending the particles in a water-glue medium. A pigmented dye may be used to improve the color. Liquid carbon inks are also commercially available. In the liquid carbon inks, shellac and borax are used in place of animal glue and a wetting agent is added to aid in the mixing of the shellac and carbon. Carbon inks are insoluble in water, very stable, and are not decomposed by air, light, heat, moisture, or microbiological organisms. This class of ink has been available for more than 2000 years.

Fountain Pen Inks

There are two types of fountain pen inks: (1) the iron gallo-tannate type of inks and (2) aqueous solutions of synthetic dyes. Modern inks of type (2) contain synthetic blue dyes to provide an immediate blue color to the ink, which gradually turns black after oxidation on paper. This explains the origin of the name blue–black fountain pen ink. This class of ink is also very stable. This ink is insoluble in water and cannot be effectively erased by abrasion. The most popular fountain pen ink (developed in the 1950s) consists of an aqueous solution of synthetic dyes. These inks are bright and attractive in color, but they are not nearly as stable as the carbon or blue–black inks. Some of the synthetic dyes used fade and are soluble in water. The most modern inks of this type contain pigmented dyes, such as copper phthalocyanine (introduced in about 1953), which makes these inks much more permanent.

Ballpoint Inks

The ballpoint pen was developed in Europe about 1939 and was initially distributed in Argentina about 1943. In 1946, several million Reynolds ballpoint pens reached the market in the United States.

Ballpoint inks consist of synthetic dyes (sometimes carbon or graphite is also added for permanence) in various glycol solvents or benzyl alcohol. The dyes in ballpoint inks can make up nearly 50% of the total formulation. Several other ingredients are usually added to the ink to impart specific characteristics. These ingredients consist of fatty acids, resins, surface active agents, corrosion control ingredients, and viscosity adjustors. The fatty acids (oleic is the most common) act as lubricants for the ball of the pen and they also help the starting characteristics of the ballpoint.

Ballpoint inks made before 1950 used oil-based solvents such as mineral oil, linseed oil, recinoleic acid, methyl and ethyl esters of recinoleic acid, glycerin monoricinoleate, coconut fatty acids, sorbital derivatives, and plasticizers such as tricresylphosphate. Modern ballpoint inks (post-1950) are referred to as glycol-based inks, because of the common use of ethylene glycol or glycol derivatives as a solvent for the dyes. Benzyl alcohol is also commonly used as the vehicle (solvent) by some ink manufacturers. Chelated dyes (introduced commercially in about 1953) are stable to light. Red, green, yellow, and other colored chelated dyes are now used for various colored ballpoint inks.

Pressurized ballpoint inks were developed about 1968. These pens contain a pressurized feed system instead of gravity flow. The physical characteristics of these inks are quite different from the standard glycol-based ballpoint inks. The composition is basically the same, but this ink does not become fluid until disturbed by the rotation of the ballpoint in the socket. Cartridges containing this ink are under the pressure of nitrogen or some other inert gas. The positive pressure on the ink allows the pen to write in all positions and in a vacuum. These pens are used by astronauts during space travel.

Rolling Ball Marker Inks

Rolling ball marker inks were introduced in Japan in about 1968 and shortly thereafter in the United States. These inks are water based and usually contain organic liquids such as glycols and formamide to retard the drying of the ballpoint. The dyes in these inks are water soluble or acidic dye salts. The light fastness of these dyes ranges from good for the metalized acid dyes to poor for some of the basic dye salts. Water fastness is usually poor, except that some of these dyes have an affinity for cellulose fibers in paper, which produces a degree of water fastness. Water-resistant rolling ball marker inks are also available. These inks are totally insoluble in water and can only be dissolved in strong organic solvents, such as pyridine or dimethylsulfoxide.

Fiber- or Porous-Tip Pen Inks

This class of inks was developed in Japan in about 1962 and in the United States in about 1965. Fiber-tip inks are usually water or xylene based and contain dyes and additives similar to those in rolling ball marker inks and fountain pen inks. The water-based inks are obviously water soluble, whereas the xylene-based inks are water resistant and can only be dissolved with strong organic solvents. Formamide or glycol solvents are essential ingredients in fiber-tip inks to keep the fiber tip from drying out. Fiber-tip inks that contain metalized dyes are light fast.

Gel Pen Inks

The most recent development in the writing instrument industry is the introduction of the gel pen by the Japanese. Four brands of gel pen inks have been introduced: (1) the Uniball Signo by Mitsubishi, (2) the Zebra J5, (3) the Pentel Hybrid, and (4) the Sakura Gelly Roll pen. These pens have been marketed by the Japanese since the mid-1980s, and a limited supply of the pens was sold in the United States in about 1993. Two US manufacturers are now producing these pens.

Gel inks contain completely insoluble colored pigments rather than organic dyes. Writing with this ink is very similar to the appearance of the writing with a ballpoint pen. This ink, which is water based, is a gel and not a liquid. It is insoluble in both water and strong organic solvents. This physical property makes it impossible to analyze (by traditional methods) for the purpose of comparing two or more inks of this type.

Ink Comparisons and Identifications

Inks are usually examined for three reasons:

1. To compare two or more ink entries to determine similarities or differences in inks, which can provide information concerning whether entries have been added or altered.
2. To determine if two or more entries were written with the same formula and batch of ink, thus providing a lead as to whether certain entries could have been written with the same pen.
3. To date ink entries to determine whether documents have been backdated. This section deals with the first two reasons for analyzing inks.

Nondestructive methods of comparison should be carried out first, because chemical analysis causes minor damage to the document by removing ink samples for analysis. Typically, the nondestructive methods include (1) a visual and microscopic examination of the writing to assess its color and the type of pen used, (2) infrared reflectance and luminescence examinations to determine whether the inks reflect or absorb infrared light and whether the inks luminesce, and (3) viewing the inks under long- and shortwave ultraviolet light to determine if the inks are fluorescent under these wavelengths of light. Often, these techniques are sufficient to determine if two or more inks are different. However, if these techniques fail to detect any differences in the inks, then further chemical analysis is necessary to determine if the inks being compared really have the same formula.

The most widely used technique for comparing and identifying inks is TLC. This technique separates the dyes in the ink and the invisible organic components in the ink. This allows a direct comparison of the composition of inks being examined on the same TLC plate. To determine the relative concentrations of dyes present in the ink, the dyes separated on the TLC plate are scanned in a TLC scanning densitometer. The method is fast, reliable, and inexpensive. High-performance liquid chromatography has also been used for comparing inks with some success. GC–MS is a very useful technique but the equipment is expensive.

Dating of Inks

As mentioned earlier in this chapter, there is a huge demand for the dating of inks on questioned documents. Any time during an investigation when there is a question about the date of

preparation of a document, an ink-dating chemist is needed. Over the past 30 years, the ability to perform these examinations has become widely known among forensic scientists, document examiners, and attorneys throughout the world. The ink-dating procedures that are described have passed the Frye and Daubert tests on numerous occasions and are routinely accepted in US courts. Testimony has also been admitted using these techniques in Israel and Australia.

First Date of Production Method

After the ink is uniquely/positively identified, the first date of production of that ink or certain ingredients in the ink is determined from the manufacturer of that specific ink formulation. If the ink was not made until after the date of the document, then it can be concluded that the document was backdated. If the ink was available on the date of the document, then the document could have been written on that date.

Ink Tag Method

If an ink tag is identified in an ink, it is possible to determine the actual year or years when an ink was made. Tags were added to some ballpoint inks by the Formulab Company before 1970; however, the use of tags in their inks was discontinued in June 1994. Since the tags are considered proprietary information by Formulab, no further information about the tags can be reported here. Formulab should be contacted directly, if this information is needed.

Ink-dating tags are detected and identified by TLC using a solvent system of chlorobenzene and ethyl acetate (5:1, v/v). Standard samples of the tags should be run simultaneously on the same TLC plate as the questioned inks. The tags, if present, are viewed under longwave ultraviolet light, and the RF values of the tags present in questioned inks are compared with the RF values of the standard tags. The dates the various tags were used must be obtained from Formulab.

Relative Age Comparison Methods

Dating inks by this procedure is based on the scientifically supported premise that, as ink ages on paper, there are corresponding changes in the solubility properties of the inks. Therefore, by comparing the solubility or extraction properties of questioned inks with known dated inks of the same formula on the same type of paper and stored under the same conditions, it becomes possible to estimate how long the ink has been written on the document. Two or more inks of the same formulation can be compared without known dated writings to determine whether the writings were made at the same or different times. This is only true if the inks being compared are still aging (drying), because after the ink has aged out (completely dry), no differences in solubility properties are expected, even if the inks were written at different times. Typically, inks will become totally dry (as measured by these procedures) within 6 years; some inks become dry in less than 6 years.

When two or more matching inks are compared without known dated writings, it is still possible to determine the sequence in which the inks were written. This again requires knowing that the inks are still aging and also knowing how the inks age. For example, some inks extract faster and more completely in organic solvents as the ink ages, whereas others extract more slowly and less completely as they age. To determine which way the ink ages, a sample of the ink is heated at 100 °C for 30 min. The rate and extent of extraction of this heated sample into an organic solvent are compared with an unheated sample of the same ink to determine if the heated (totally aged) sample extracted faster and more completely than the unheated sample, or vice versa.

Accelerated Aging

In situations where known dated inks are not available for comparison with questioned inks, accelerated aging of a questioned ink can be performed to estimate its age. The measurement procedures are identical to those described for R-ratios, percent extraction, and dye ratios. This test involves just one additional step, which is to heat a sample of the questioned ink for 30 min at 100 °C, allow it to cool and equilibrate with the temperature and humidity in the room for 1 h, and then compare the results of the various measurements (using any or all of the R-ratio, percent extraction, and dye ratio methods) with the results obtained from an unheated sample of the same ink.

Significant differences obtained by any one of the methods indicate that the ink is still drying and is therefore less than 6 years old, as no inks have been found to take longer than 6 years to become completely dry using these methods. If it is known that the specific ink in question takes only 3 years to dry, then it can be concluded that the questioned ink is less than 3 years old. This method can also be used to determine which of two or more inks is newer than the other. This is done by observing which ink changes more with heat; the larger the change caused by heat, the newer the ink. This can only be done when all inks compared consist of the same ink formulation on the same type of paper and stored under the same conditions. This statement applies to all of the relative age comparison techniques described here.

Time-Dependent Degradation of Ink Dyes

Research over the past two decades indicates that many dyes and pigments in inks degrade over time in a linear, time-dependent, predictable fashion. This is due to both light and oxygen and thus it is sensitive to the environmental conditions under which the ink is stored. The major recent method for tracking the chemical degradation of inks is by means of laser desorption mass spectrometry (LDMS). This is a variant of matrix-assisted laser desorption ionization mass spectrometry, the chief difference being that no matrix is used.

In 2001, Grim et al. reported the first application of LDMS for the analysis of ink on paper. The technique proved to be an excellent analytical tool for such analytes. The technique uses a pulsed ultraviolet laser that can directly desorb colorant molecules from a penstroke off of paper, carrying a charge, such that they can be analyzed using time-of-flight mass spectrometry. A schematic of a simple LDMS instrument is shown in **Figure 1**. The laser generates 2-ns pulses of 337 nm (UV) light, which impinges on a sample inside the vacuum system of the mass spectrometer. If compounds are present that absorb at this wavelength, they may be desorbed and ionized. Ions formed are accelerated to a constant kinetic energy such that ions of different masses will have differing velocities; thus, the time it will take for them to travel approximately 1 m to the ion detector will be proportional to their mass. No sample preparation is needed. Initial work involved the detection and identification of crystal violet, the dye commonly used in ballpoint pen inks. Like many dyes, this is a cationic dye which, when desorbed, already has a charge associated with it. While unexpected, several related compounds were detected as well. These were shown to be degradation products that form slowly over time, through a process known as oxidative dealkylation, and thus they can provide a "chemical clock" for estimating the

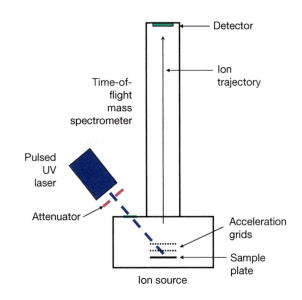

Figure 1   A diagram of a laser desorption mass spectrometry time-of-flight mass spectrometer.

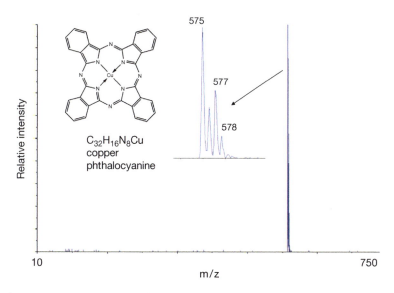

Figure 2 The laser desorption mass spectrometry spectrum from a penstroke of a blue-pigmented ink. The mass and isotopic compositions are consistent with the very popular blue pigment, copper phthalocyanine (structure shown).

time that the ink has been on the paper. A similar process was observed for the red pen ink dyes Rhodamine 6G and Rhodamine B. Since 2000, the pen and inkjet printer industries have been replacing dye-based inks with pigment-based inks. In the case of printers, color photos printed with dyes fade quickly while pigmented inks with a well-chosen paper can yield an archival copy that will remain unfaded and vibrant for hundreds of years. The conversion from dyes to pigments was of particular concern to those who used TLC for pen ink analysis, as pigments are insoluble compounds. However, LDMS efficiently analyzes small amounts of pigments in such samples. An example is shown in **Figure 2**. A penstroke was made on paper from a blue-pigmented pen ink. A small piece of the page was introduced into the ion source of the LDMS. While the ink has many components, only the pigment absorbed the UV laser light, leading to desorption/ionization of just these pigment molecules. The spectrum shown in **Figure 2** is exceedingly simple. No fragmentation is observed, just the intact cation of the pigment. At this point, it is known that the pigment is blue and has a molecular weight (monoisotopic mass) of 575. There are smaller peaks following the major peak, which represents the same molecule with different isotopes present. The isotopic distribution, unique to the elemental composition of the species, is very useful in identifying the pigment. For example, if one carbon atom is C(13) instead of the most abundant form C(12), the mass will increase by one atomic mass unit. If the molecule is a simple organic molecule, isotopic peaks usually decrease in relative intensity as their mass increases. Here, we see an enhanced peak

at m/z 577. This is due to the fact that the pigment contains copper, which has two prominent isotopes with masses of 63 and 65 atomic mass units. The distribution of isotopes is consistent with the formula for copper phthalocyanine, as shown in the figure.

LDMS has been used to characterize artist's colorants and was demonstrated to be useful in an investigation of the authenticity of a page of the Qur'an, purportedly from the 1600s. LDMS showed that the handwritten black, gold, and red inks used in this document contained inorganic pigments such as arsenic sulfide and mercury sulfide, which were used at the time.

See also: **Documents:** Analytical Methods; Document Dating; Forgery/Counterfeits; Handwriting; **Forensic Medicine/Clinical:** Clinical Forensic Medicine—Overview; Domestic Violence.

Further Reading

Aginsky, V.N., 1996. Dating and characterizing writing, stamp pad and jet printer inks by gas chromatography/mass spectrometry. International Journal of Forensic Document Examiners 2, 103–115.

Brunell, R.L., Speckin, E.J., 1988. Technical report with case studies on the accelerated aging of ballpoint inks. International Journal of Forensic Document Examiners 4, 240–254.

Brunelle, R.L., 1992. Ink dating – the state of the art. Journal of Forensic Sciences 37, 113–124.

Brunelle, R.L., 1995. A sequential multiple approach to determining the relative age of writing inks. International Journal of Forensic Document Examiners 1, 94–98.

Brunelle, R.L., Cantu, A.A., 1987. A critical evaluation of current ink dating techniques. Journal of Forensic Sciences 32, 1511–1521.

Brunelle, R.L., Lee, H., 1989. Determining the relative age of ballpoint ink using a single solvent extraction mass independent approach. Journal of Forensic Sciences 34, 1166–1182.

Brunelle, R.L., Reed, R.W., 1984. Forensic Examination of Ink and Paper. Charles C Thomas, Springfield, IL.

Cantu, A.A., 1988. Comments on the accelerated aging of inks. Journal of Forensic Sciences 33, 744–750.

Cantu, A.A., 1996. A sketch of analytical methods for document dating, Part II. The dynamic approach: determining age dependent analytical profiles. International Journal of Forensic Document Examiners 2, 192–208.

Cantu, A.A., Prough, R.S., 1987. On the relative aging of ink – the solvent extraction technique. Journal of Forensic Sciences 32, 1151–1174.

McNeil, R.J., 1984. Scanning auger microscopy for dating of manuscript inks. In: Lamber, J.B. (Ed.), Archeology Chemistry III. American Chemical Society Advances in Chemistry Series No. 205, Washington, DC, pp. 255–269.

Paper Analysis

T Fritz and S Nekkache, IRCGN, Rosny Sous Bois, France

Glossary

Basis weight or grammage The weight of paper in grams per square meter.

Flocks Fiber aggregates.

Forming fabric Element of endless wire screen dedicated to drain off the water present in the paper pulp.

Headbox Element of the paper machine where the pulp is homogeneously distributed on the forming fabric.

Hygrometry rate (relative humidity) The amount of water vapor in the air.

Infrared (IR) Part of the electromagnetic spectrum between about 780 nm and 1 mm.

Look-through appearance The aspect of paper when viewed using transmitted light.

Luminescence The emission of radiant energy that takes place during the transition from an excited electronic state

of an atom, molecule, or ion to a lower electronic state (which includes fluorescence and phosphorescence).

Metamerism Phenomenon where two surfaces show the same color under one illumination but different colors under a different illumination.

Ultraviolet (UV) Part of the electromagnetic spectrum between about 10 and 380 nm. In questioned documents, three different wavelengths are often used: 254, 312, and 365 nm.

Watermark A design or text created in the paper during the manufacturing stage by locally modifying the amount of fibers.

Whiteners Bleaching agents used to bleach paper.

Wire marks Repetitive marks left by the forming fabric(s) on the paper side that is in contact with it.

Paper analysis is often seen as a secondary issue by questioned documents examiners (QDEs), although, as a corroborative proof, it can provide complementary evidence that may be useful to investigators and the courts. Paper analysis can be a valuable complementary tool for enriching traditional questioned document examination techniques. One has always to keep in mind that expertise in analyzing questioned documents requires a multidisciplinary approach, and experience has taught us that downplaying or bypassing paper analysis can lead to irreversible mistakes as occurred in the case of the fake Hitler diaries (see section "Dating"). With the exception of security paper, examinations of paper are a challenge, first, because paper is a product of mass consumption and, second, because manufacturers may use processes that are similar to those of their competitors. However, in many instances, it is possible to provide useful answers to the judicial authority, even in the case of ordinary papers. This chapter aims at presenting the major physical, optical, and chemical techniques used to analyze paper substrates in the forensic environment.

Paper Manufacturing Process

In order to better understand the methods used in the forensic analysis of printing and writing paper, and to provide a better

appreciation of the difficulties met by QDEs when interpreting the result of their examinations and comparisons on paper substrates, the common manufacturing process (Fourdrinier machine) is briefly overviewed. Specialty papers (e.g., thermal paper, adhesive sticker paper, and semiconducting paper) are not considered in this chapter.

Paper is essentially made of hardwood and softwood fibers, which originate from thermomechanical (TMP), chemical, or chemithermomechanical (CTMP) pulp. In some cases, plants (e.g., linter, cotton, and alfa) or synthetic fibers are used. These different families of fibers are mixed in the paper pulp in various proportions depending on the required characteristics of the paper (good resistance or good opacity, for example).

To improve paper characteristics, other nonfibrous raw materials are introduced into the pulp or into the paper itself during the manufacturing process. Thus, we find such additives as starch (to increase the resistance of the paper sheet), whiteners (to bleach the paper), and fillers such as china clay, talc, or calcium carbonate (to improve opacity).

The paper machine consists of two main parts: the wet part and the dry part. The refined and purified pulp is thrown by the headbox onto the wire part. The continuous movement of the forming fabric will orient the fibers in a preferential way called "machine direction." The perpendicular direction is called

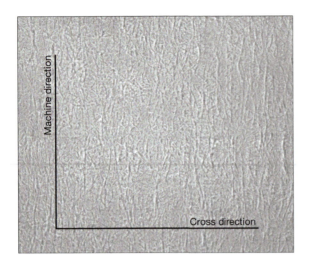

Figure 1 Fiber orientation observation.

Figure 2 Different repartition rate of fluorescent fibers in two paper sheets coming from the same ream.

Figure 3 Different repartition rate of fluorescent fibers in two paper sheets coming from the same ream.

"cross direction" (**Figure 1**). The degree of orientation is directly linked to the difference in speed between the pulp jet and the wire.

Water trapped in the just-formed sheet of paper, which may create asymmetry between the two sides of the sheet, the "wire side" and the "felt side," is drained through the forming fabric. The wire side is the side that presses against the forming fabric, whereas the felt side is the opposite side, which will be in contact with dryer felts in the next sector of the wet part, that is, the press section. In this section, some more water is removed under reduced pressure. In some particular cases, forming fabrics are used on both sides of the paper sheet as in the case of the Fourdrinier machine, completed by a top former at the end of the wet part, and of the twin-wire machine. Although asymmetry remains generally true, the classical distinction of wire side and felt side becomes optically irrelevant.

The sheet of paper then enters the dry part of the paper machine, where the remaining water is evaporated by heat and air. Surface treatment (sizing or coating, for instance) can be used to improve printability or the optical aspect of the sheet. At the end of the process, the sheet is wound onto a jumbo roll. Finally, the finishing consists of the conversion of the jumbo roll into commercial products such as rolls or paper reams. Paper reams are obtained by guillotining several rolls, which may or may not come from the same master roll, and, therefore, may or may not belong to the same production run. Thus, it is possible to get some paper products with minor physical, optical, and chemical differences between them in spite of their originating from the same ream (see **Figures 2 and 3**, where the florescent fibers have a different repartition rate although the two samples come from the same paper ream). When comparing papers to determine whether they may have come from an identified ream, it is therefore important to take a large sample of the ream. Also, the guillotining can provide unique traces that might be useful in identifying the source.

Indeed, during the finishing process, which is aimed at transforming rolls into reams, cutters and guillotine blades are used. Because of their use and their sharpening process, the blades may develop faults. The observation of these faults can assist the QDEs in identifying a common source or even locating a sheet inside its original ream.

Forensic Examination of Paper

Because paper is a complex product that can be used in so many ways, the industry applies numerous techniques to evaluate a range of parameters, such as basis weight, brightness, opacity, and so on. However, industry standards are far from compliant with the forensic environment, which is often required to preserve samples for further investigations (fingerprint identification, for instance). This may limit the extent to which any potentially destructive analysis can be performed, particularly when the item of evidence is small. Moreover, the industry standards only deal with newly manufactured paper, whereas in forensic sciences, the life conditions of the substrate may be unknown and environmental elements may alter the substrate characteristics. Indeed, paper is a heterogeneous material very sensitive to variations under ambient conditions (e.g., temperature, humidity, and sun exposure). Thus, only a subset of applicable industry standards are used or partially used in questioned document examination methods.

Physical Analysis

Physical examinations are used to assess the dimensions of the paper sample (length, width, and thickness) including its basis weight or grammage. Because of the heterogeneous structure of paper, QDEs need to be aware of some singularities before any results can be interpreted:

- The thickness has to be the average value of at least ten measurements per A4 sheet of paper taken with a calibrated micrometer.
- In the same paper production run, the basis weight can vary from one sheet to another. The classically accepted variations by the manufacturer are given in **Table 1**.
- Paper basis weight can vary because of the relative humidity. Thus, comparisons have to be made preferably under the same ambient conditions.

The samples studied by QDEs are often irregular, because the document may be torn. Thus the measurement of area, which is necessary to determine the basis weight, can be difficult. In such case, it may be advantageous to use a calibrated automated process of surface measurement based on an image analysis software (for instance, AutoCAD, Visilog, ImageJ, etc.).

Optical Analysis

Optical analysis relies on the study of color, fluorescence under ultraviolet (UV) light, and look-through appearance, and also on the determination of the wire and the felt sides. It is complemented by infrared (IR) and IR luminescence examinations. However, the classical recommendations in the field of questioned document examination are often limited when it comes to the means of observation and measurement. For instance, it is recommended to judge the color of the substrate only in daylight or to measure it using a microspectrophotometer. Further, "the fluorescence may be compared with a fluorescent scale" (e.g., Ciba Geigy). Fluorescence is essentially linked to the presence of a whitener in the paper composition.

Human perception of color can be tricky, as it is influenced by several parameters such as the size of the sample, the light source (type and intensity), the background and environment, and the length of observation. These methods can be usefully complemented or totally replaced by the use of a specific paper spectrophotometer that is capable of measuring brightness, fluorescence, whiteness, opacity, metamerism, and color difference in compliance with most industry standards. The advantage here is that all the measurements are objective, made with known repeatability and reproducibility. Moreover, the results can be implemented in internal databases for possible further comparisons or for a second opinion. The limits are the presence on the substrate of printed or written entries, because the standard aperture size for measurement is 30 mm. However, professional paper spectrophotometers provide optional measurement aperture sizes with a smaller radius (down to 2.5 mm depending on the brand).

Regarding the look-through appearance, it is accepted by paper manufacturers and QDEs that this parameter may differ between different paper machines (see **Figures 4 and 5** illustrating differences in look-through appearance of papers manufactured by two different paper machines). Thus, instruments exist that are dedicated to measure look-through visuals (illustrating similarities or differences in flock size and orientation of the flocks). However, these types of apparatus are widely influenced by the presence of printed or written material on the substrate or even the surface aspect. It is then easy to understand why they are of little help in forensic applications.

Table 1   Classically accepted variations by manufacturers in a same paper production run

Basis weight ordered	Variations acceptance (%)
Till 32 g m^{-2} included	±2.5
From 30 to 39 g m^{-2} included	±8
From 40 to 59 g m^{-2} included	±6
From 60 to 179 g m^{-2} included	±5
From 180 to 224 g m^{-2} included	±6
From 225 g m^{-2} and more	±7

Figure 4 Differences in look-through appearance of papers manufactured by two different paper machines.

Figure 5   Differences in look-through appearance of papers manufactured by two different paper machines.

Figure 6   Watermark of a security paper.

In this case, the visual observation remains the best method, although automated analysis could be a useful future tool for the QDE.

The look-through examination can lead to the observation of a strong security feature, namely, the "watermark." Watermarks are either symbols or drawings formed into the paper substrate during the papermaking process. Watermarks were first introduced in the thirteenth century, when they were integrated in quality paper, allowing the identification of its source. Its dark areas are created by increasing the quantity of fibers, whereas the light areas are made by decreasing their quantity. Two main processes exist (Fourdrinier machine for single-tone or dual-tone watermarks and cylinder mold processes for multitone watermarks). Because a watermark is the result of a controlled variation of fiber distribution, it is observable by looking through the paper and/or with oblique lighting. For faded watermarks, the observation can be improved by using a radioactive source and photographic paper. This kind of image enhancement is, however, rare in the questioned document examination field. Today, watermarks are essentially used for security papers (**Figure 6**). It is the easiest and most reliable way to identify the paper source accurately.

Concerning the discrimination of the wire side and the felt side, simple visual observations of a sample may be ineffective as paper makers tend to avoid pronounced wire marks in their products so as to improve printability. Also, in some cases, top-former or twin-wire machines can produce paper with wire marks on both sides. Because wire marks are a repetitive phenomenon occurring at the millimeter scale on the paper, an appropriate technique to observe and compare them objectively is to apply "two-dimensional fast Fourier transform" to a scanned image. This technique allows the transformation of a spatial image into a frequency image where wire mark angles

and periods are easily observable. Spectra can be compared directly or by using cross-correlation. The advantages of this method are that it is nondestructive; it is independent of the other paper parameters; and it has good discriminating power. This technique provides exploitable results even for paper with invisible wire marks and/or paper where written and printed entries are present. (See **Figures 7–10** where fast Fourier transform is applied to a scan of virgin paper and then to a paper of the same brand bearing written entries. In both cases, the spectra show the same peaks, which correspond to the characteristics of the wire marks.)

Additional evidence associated with the paper substrate can also be obtained by observation of the sample under various lighting conditions (UV, IR, and luminescence). Indeed, these

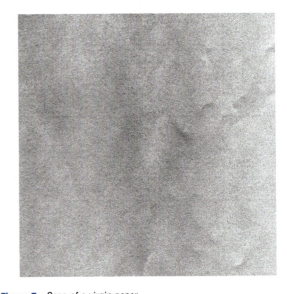

Figure 7   Scan of a virgin paper.

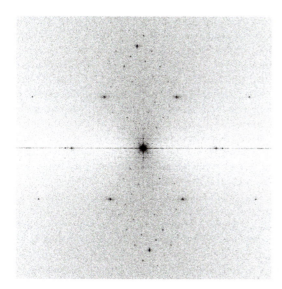

Figure 8 Observation of wire marks by fast Fourier transform applied to the scan of a virgin paper.

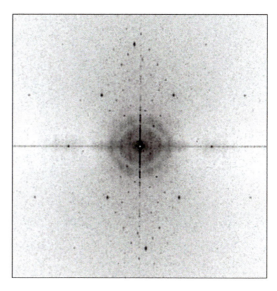

Figure 10 Observation of wire marks by fast Fourier transform applied to the scan of a paper bearing written entries.

La vitesse d'avancée de l'échantillon
L'intensité du traitement
paramètres vont nous permettre de choisir quelle sera l
ent sur la surface, si celui-ci sera plus ou moins important.

s réaliserons plusieurs passages :
Vitesse de passage : 2 ; Intensité de traitement : 50
mesurant ensuite l'angle de contact, avec de l'eau, on relève
traitement n'a donc pas eu d'influence sur la surface. Il fa
r noter une différence augmenter soit l'intensité de la décharge
se de passage.
Vitesse de passage : 2 ; Intensité de traitement : 60
s avons donc ici choisi d'augmenter l'intensité de traitement.
de contact donne une valeur de 52°. Ce passage-ci a donc
de contact. La surface est donc bien devenue plus polair
tés avec l'eau.
Vitesse de passage : 2 ; Intensité de traitement : 60
obtient ainsi après ce troisième passage un angle de conta
est donc quasiment étalée sur le support. L'affinité est d
ante entre l'eau et le polystyrène. Cette valeur est proche
le d'angle possible.

s constatons bien sur le graphique suivant la diminution d
t. Le traitement corona est donc bien efficace pour permettre l
ur le polystyrène et donc une augmentation de l'énergie de

Figure 9 Scan of a paper bearing written entries.

techniques can reveal evidence that cannot be obtained visually from a paper document that was accidentally or purposely erased. These observations are essentially based on the principle of difference of wavelength absorption and luminescence. In the latter case, the emission of radiant energy can display invisible writings. It is obviously possible, when a printed grid is present, to measure line length and spacing. The appearance of these lines under UV, IR, and luminescence is also useful for comparison.

Chemical Analysis

To this day, no unique forensic standard dealing with chemical analysis of paper has been published. The reason lies in the destructive aspect of most of the existing standards pertaining to the industry. Moreover, the precision and accuracy of the results obtained are often considered to be too unreliable to help the QDE answer questions posed by investigators or courts. Paper is indeed a material with significant intrasample variability, and logically, to get reliable results, the number of samples available for examination must be high. In the forensic field, where the questioned document is often a single sheet of paper, one can easily understand that the quantity of the required material is extremely small. However, a technique such as paper micrography can help. This technique allows the identification of the pulp (TMP, CTMP) and the fibers' origin (hardwood, softwood, plants or synthetic, thanks to the length and width of the fibers), as well as the possible presence of vessels, with only a very small sample. This method can even help to identify the types of trees or plants used (e.g., pine, oak, aspen, cotton) thanks to the shape characteristics of fibers and vessels (see **Figure 11** showing birch vessels and pine fibers from a chemical pulp).

In some cases, a quantitative analysis can be carried out to evaluate the proportion of each type of fiber. However, the results have to be taken with caution because of the possibility that manufacturers might have integrated different pulps in the same paper production batch. Sometimes, broken pulp (waste pulp from a previous production) can be integrated during the papermaking process, which can result in differences among the sheets of paper coming from the same run.

Figure 11 Paper micrography: birch vessels and pine fibers from a chemical pulp.

X-ray fluorescence is often quoted in the literature as an efficient method for identification of the elemental composition of paper. In some cases, the technique does produce results that are useful in discriminating between different papers. Recently, it was shown that the combination of XRF, laser ablation inductively coupled mass spectrometry, and isotope ratio mass spetrometry analysis gives a better discriminating power than the use of only one of these techniques.

Finally, it can be said that the chemical analysis of the printed grid, following forensic methods for ink analysis, can usefully complement the measurement and observation of this grid under different light sources.

Dating

"Can you tell the date of this document?" is a question often asked of the QDE. To better understand the problem, one must comprehend that it is well nigh impossible to give a precise date to a paper sample unless it contains typical and referenced watermarks, allowing for an identification of both the manufacturer and the period of production. This particular case is becoming rarer and rarer, as watermarks are essentially reserved today for use in the manufacture of security and quality papers. In spite of this, anachronisms can still be detected and back-dating of documents can be proved by closely inspecting the type of paper, ink, typewriting, or printed information that is present on the questioned document.

Paper composition has evolved through time, thanks to the progress of the industry and the evolution of public demand. The presence of a single specific component in the substrate can be sufficient evidence to prove that a document does not belong to its alleged timeframe. For instance, optical whiteners were discovered by Krais in 1929 but were first introduced in the paper industry only in the 1950s.

One of the most famous and published examples of anachronism ever brought to light is the fake Hitler diaries case. In 1983, the German magazine "Stern" published excerpts from what it claimed to be the authentic diaries of Hitler, allegedly written between 1932 and 1945. While some historians and handwriting experts disagreed about the origin of these diaries, the hoax was clearly revealed by technical analysis of the ink, paper, and binding. For instance, it was demonstrated that the whitener and fibers used in the paper were of post-World War II manufacture.

In fact, for the specific case of dating, it is useful to first understand the real need of the investigators or the courts. Indeed, a document is often asked to be dated just to determine the authenticity of the sample. Hence, it is often possible to demonstrate it by other more straightforward approaches: display of a paper substitution, for instance, or combination of questioned document analysis, handwriting comparison, ink analysis, etc. Indeed, in the questioned documents field, paper analysis remains a corroborative proof.

Miscellaneous

Paper is as much a vector of information as is writing or printing. Some information may be hidden, as is the case with indented writings or indented printer-specific marks (see **Figure 12** where printer-specific marks are revealed by the electrostatic detection apparatus). The detection method to reveal these indented printings depends on their depth. Indeed, deep indented printings are usually well revealed by using an oblique light source. The best method is to use an electrostatic detection apparatus, which is very sensitive to weak marks. In fact, the two techniques complement each other. Owing to the nondestructive nature of this kind of analysis and the evidential importance of the results that can be revealed, it is recommended to begin each questioned document analysis by looking for indented writings or printings.

Figure 12 Printer-specific marks revealed by an electrostatic detection apparatus.

Moreover, the QDE is often asked whether a single sheet of paper came from a specific pad. In this kind of analysis, the QDE has at his/her disposal many methodologies. Of course, all of the aforementioned methods are necessary (physical, optical, chemical, and indented printings analysis), but they can usefully be complemented by the evaluation of physical match of paper cuts, tears, and perforations. For instance, the examination of the edges under magnification can reveal remnants of binding, adhesives, or padding materials.

Paper is a complex and heterogeneous material, often used for criminal purposes such as anonymous letters, forgery, and counterfeiting. The knowledge of the paper manufacturing process and its consequences on the final product is a prerequisite for the discrimination or identification of the paper source. Thus, paper examination techniques need to be considered, as the results may provide corroborative proofs, along with all the other possible techniques utilized in the field of questioned document analysis.

> *See also:* **Documents:** Document Dating; Handwriting; Ink Analysis; Overview of Forensic Document Examination.

Further Reading

Aitken, Y., Kaden, F., Voillot, C., 1988. Constituants fibreux des pâtes, papiers et cartons, pratique de l'analyse. In: Saint Martin d'Hères: EFPG Ecole Française de Papeterie et des Industries Graphiques.

ASTM International. ASTM E 2325–05 STANDARD, 2005. Guide for Nondestructive Examination of Paper. ASTM International, West Conshohocken, Pennsylvania.

Bodziak, W.J., 1998. EDGE characteristics of commercially produced paper stock. Journal of the American Society of Questioned Document Examiners 1 (1), 57–66.

Browning, B.L., 1977. Analysis of Paper, second ed. Marcel Dekker, New York.

Brunelle, R.l., Reed, R.R., 1984. FORENSIC Examinations of Ink and Paper. Charles C. Thomas, Springfield, IL.

Burton, M., Delefosse, M., 1994. GUIDE du papier édition 1992/1993. Paracel – Caractère.

Caywood, D., 1995. WATERMARKS and the questioned document examiner. International Journal of Forensic Document Examiners 1, 299.

Grant, J., 1985. The diaries of Adolf Hitler. Journal of the Forensic Science Society 25, 179.

Krais, P., 1929. ÜBER ein Neues Schwartz und ein neues Weiß. Melliand Textilberichte 10, 468–469.

Lafait, J., Elias, M., 2006. LA couleur: Lumière, vison et matériaux. Belin, Paris.

Miyata, H., Shinozaki, M., Nakayama, T., Enomae, T., 2002. A discrimination method for paper by Fourier transform and cross correlation. Journal of Forensic Sciences 47, 1125–1132.

Pauler, N., 1995–2000. Propriétés optiques du papier. AB Lorentzen et Wettre, Kista.

Popson, T., Crawford, T., Popson, S.J., 2010. Measurement and Control of the Optical Properties of Paper. Technidyne Corporation.

Sabatier, J., Kerneis, J.C., Bauduin, S., 1985. CONTINUOUS look through assessment: an industrial reality. ATIP 39 (1), 9–14.

Steering Committee European Documents Experts Working Group, 2004. Nondestructive Paper Examination. ENFSI, EDEWG.

Vallette, P., De Choudens, C., 1992. LE bois, la pâte, le papier. Centre Technique de l'Industrie des Papiers, Carton et Cellulose, Grenoble.

Van Es, A., de Koeijer, J., van der Peijl, G., 2009. DISCRIMINATION of document paper by XRF, LA–ICP–MS and IRMS using multivariate statistical techniques. Science & Justice: Journal of the Forensic Science Society 49 (2), 120–126.

Relevant Websites

http://www.memoryofpaper.eu:8080/BernsteinPortal/appl_start.disp—Bernstein Portal—The Memory of Paper.

http://cerig.efpg.inpg.fr/—Cellule de veille technologique de Grenoble INP Pagora.

http://www.enfsi.eu/—ENFSI Website.

Key Terms

Desktop printing, Digital imaging, Disguise, Document age, Document examination, Document fraud, Envelopes, Fabrication, Fakes, Fluorescence, Forensic document examination, Forensic handwriting comparison, Forensic science, Forensic signature comparison, Forgery, Fraud, FTIR, Handwriting, Handwriting examination, HPLC, Hyperspectral analysis, Indented writing, Identity documents, Ink, Ink analysis, Ink examination, Kidnapping, LA–ICPMS, LDMS, LIBS, Multispectral analysis, Murder, Nonoriginal documents, Organized crime, Paper, Paper analysis, Paper examination, Paper security, Printed products, Printing and writing substrate analysis, Printing processes, Printing technologies, Proficiency testing, Qualifications, Questioned document, Raman spectroscopy, Reporting, Secure documents, Security features, Signature examination, Signatures, Simulation, TLC, TOF–SIMS, Toner, Toner, Training, Typewriting, Writing materials, XRF.

Review Questions

1. Name at least three factors relating to contentions about documents.
2. What was the Dreyfus case?
3. How was Hoffman discovered to be a forger of Mormon documents?
4. Name three types of instrumentation that are used to analyze documents.
5. Why is microscopy still essential to document analysis?
6. What is hyperspectral imaging?

7. How is digital image analysis used to examine documents?
8. Why would the age of an ink matter in a document analysis?
9. What are the two main approaches for dating documents? Describe them.
10. What is a watermark?
11. Of what use are striation patterns in adhesives on envelopes?
12. Does a document need to have financial value or security characteristics to be involved in fraud? Why or why not?
13. What is the difference between counterfeit, fantasy, and forged documents?
14. What is the purpose of document security features?
15. What is intaglio printing?
16. What is lithographic printing?
17. List the major types of ink and their manufacture.
18. What are the three reasons for ink analysis?
19. Why is paper analysis so challenging?
20. Name several ways paper can be physically analyzed.

Discussion Questions

1. Is handwriting analysis a science? Is it considered such by the courts? Develop a case for it being a science and one against it being a science.
2. In archaeology, the phrases *terminus ante quem* (Latin for "time before which") and *terminus post quem* ("time after which") are used to establish points for relative dating. For example, a coffee stain on a piece of paper means the paper was in place *before* the coffee was spilled (*terminus ante quem*). How do these concepts apply to document analysis? How were they used, for example, in the Hitler Diaries case?
3. How has the use of nonpaper substrates changed the analysis of documents?
4. Why has no forensic standard been published that details the chemical analysis of paper? Is this a strength or a weakness in the profession?
5. Why are they called "watermarks," even in digital documents? How does the advance of technology make the forensic document examiner's work more difficult?

Additional Readings

Agius, A., Jones, K., Epple, R., Morelato, M., Moret, S., Chadwick, S., Roux, C., 2017. The use of handwriting examinations beyond the traditional court purpose. Science & Justice. http://dx.doi.org/10.1016/j.scijus.2017.05.001.

Bryan, V., 2017. Obituary: Bryan Found 1962–2016. Australian Journal of Forensic Sciences 49 (4), 361–365.

Buzzini, P., Suzuki, E., 2016. Forensic applications of Raman spectroscopy for the in situ analyses of pigments and dyes in ink and paint evidence. Journal of Raman Spectroscopy 47 (1), 16–27.

Miller, J.J., Patterson, R.B., Gantz, D.T., Saunders, C.P., Walch, M.A., Buscaglia, J., 2017. A set of handwriting features for use in automated writer identification. Journal of Forensic Sciences 62 (3), 722–734.

NicDaeid, N., Michelle, D., 2016. Miranda: forensic analysis of tattoos and tattoo inks. Analytical and Bioanalytical Chemistry 408 (23), 6247–6248.

Srihari, S.N., Meng, L., Hanson, L., 2016. Development of individuality in children's handwriting. Journal of Forensic Sciences 61 (5), 1292–1300.

Sun, Q., Luo, Y., Xiang, P., Yang, X., Shen, M., 2017. Analysis of PEG oligomers in black gel inks: discrimination and ink dating. Forensic Science International 277, 1–9.

Section 5. Financial

Money is not everything, the old adage goes—until it is yours and someone steals it, that is. The digital nature of money and finance lends itself to computerized theft and it is safer and far more lucrative to steal money with a computer than it is with a gun. In modern (read: Digital) financial crime investigations, specialization is a requirement, not merely a nicety. The technology and ingenuity brought to bear by today's financial criminals would make Charles Ponzi faint. But, likewise, forensic fraud investigators, forensic accountants, and specialists in money laundering are just as able, clever, and persistent in their work.

Counterfeit Currency

KC Harris and K Corbin, US Secret Service, Washington, DC, USA

Glossary

Feathering A term used to describe small ink extensions along the edge of an intaglio printed image. These are caused by some of the ink being forced into the spaces between individual paper fibers from the extreme pressure of the intaglio printing process.

Intaglio A printing technique in which the reversed image is incised into the surface of a printing plate. This technique produces a raised image on the printing surface.

Letterpress A printing technique in which a reversed, raised image on a printing plate is inked and applied to the printing surface.

Offset lithography A printing technique in which the inked image is transferred from a printing plate to a rubber blanket and then to the printing surface.

Optically variable device An image that exhibits various optical effects such as movement or color changes.

Planchettes Distinctive, small disks added to paper stock during the papermaking process. These disks can be made of a variety of materials and may possess properties allowing them to serve as security features.

Thin-layer chromatography A technique used to separate a mixture into its components using a sheet of glass or plastic that is coated with a silica gel.

Genuine Currency

To successfully determine if a banknote is counterfeit, the characteristics of the corresponding genuine banknote must be understood. Genuine banknotes are mass produced to a set of standards and specifications, while no such standards exist for counterfeits. Identifying a counterfeit is done by confirming that it does not meet the specifications of a genuine banknote.

The materials and methods used to produce genuine currency are selected for their difficulty to counterfeit as well as for their durability. Banknotes will go through extensive handling and equipment processing during their lifetime, so it is vital that the materials used be able to withstand these treatments along with routine wear and tear due to circulation. Materials are selected for their distinctiveness and are often manufactured specifically for security documents and are not commercially available. The printing of banknotes utilizes the traditional printing processes such as intaglio, typography, and offset on high-quality rag paper or polymer substrates. The specialized security inks are also selected for their durability and functionality within the overall banknote design.

Genuine Currency Substrates

Traditionally, the substrate chosen for banknotes has been a highly durable, uncoated, ultraviolet (UV)-dull rag paper made from either cotton or linen or a combination of the two. Fillers, binders, and other distinctive materials, such as security fibers or planchettes, can be added during the papermaking process for added security and durability. These materials may be natural or synthetic and help distinguish the security substrate from commercially available paper stock. Security fibers or planchettes may contain materials for overt, covert, or forensic identification.

There are other types of security features that can be inserted during the papermaking process. These features may be embedded entirely in the paper or weave in and out of the paper for a windowed effect. The most common of these is in the form of a security thread, which can also contain additional properties such as UV fluorescence or the appearance of movement as well as machine-readable features to assist with authentication. Security watermarks are another feature that can be incorporated during the papermaking process. Traditional portrait watermarks are created by depositing paper fibers in varying densities to produce a shadowed appearance. Electrotype watermarks are created by reducing paper thickness in determined areas to produce lighter areas and increase the visibility of the desired image within the paper.

As technology has advanced so has the sophistication of the substrates available for use. Polymer substrates have advanced and offer a durability advantage over paper substrates. Polymer substrates are resistant to tears and folds because of its nonporous and nonfibrous composition. Polymer substrates can incorporate the same security features as paper substrates; however, there are additional security features that can be incorporated into polymer that are unavailable to paper. One of these is a transparent window containing an optically variable device.

Genuine Currency Printing Processes

The three printing processes commonly used to produce genuine currency are intaglio, letterpress, (typography), and wet or dry offset. Screen printing may also be utilized to apply specialized features. Any combination of these printing processes can be found on most currencies.

Intaglio

Historically, intaglio printing has been used for engraved artwork, invitations, and banknotes. The image that was to be printed was engraved by hand into a metal plate using lines and dots of varying length and depth. A very opaque, viscous ink is forced into the engravings, while the plate surface is kept clean. The high pressure of an intaglio printing press forces the substrate into the engravings where it adheres to the ink and the image is transferred. This type of printing is desirable for security documents such as banknotes because of its unique characteristics. The thick intaglio ink will produce an image with a raised, embossed texture that is extremely difficult to achieve using other methods of printing. Another unique characteristic of intaglio is the "feathering" it produces along the edges of printed areas. These patterns of ink spread along individual paper fibers, along with the tonal qualities that intaglio is capable of producing, help give the image area a more lifelike appearance (**Figure 1**). Advances in technology have led to the use of computer-assisted laser devices to engrave the intaglio plates.

Letterpress (typography)

Letterpress printing involves applying ink to a raised surface, which is then transferred to the desired substrate by direct impression. One of the characteristics produced by this method is a slight indentation or embossing of the paper from the impression. Another characteristic is the slightly darker and thicker outline of a letterpress image area due to the excess ink being squeezed toward the edge (**Figure 2**). This type of printing is typically used to add unique identifying information to banknotes such as serial numbers.

Offset

Offset lithography is a flat printing process with none of the characteristics typically found in intaglio or letterpress images. This style of printing is commonly used in commercial industry for printing high-volume items such as newspapers. Wet offset produces images on a flat, metal printing plate for single color printing. Chemical differences between the image and nonimage areas allow for the image areas to accept ink and the

Figure 1   Genuine intaglio printing on US currency.

Figure 2   Genuine letterpress (typography) printing on US currency.

Figure 3 Genuine offset printing on US currency.

nonimage areas to resist ink. Unlike most traditional printing processes such as intaglio and letterpress, where the printing plates come into direct contact with the substrate, offset is an indirect printing process. The ink is first transferred from the printing plate to a transfer plate or "blanket" and then to the desired substrate.

The main characteristic of offset printing is that the image area appears sharp and even with very crisp lines and edges (**Figure** 3). There will not be any "feathering" as seen with intaglio or a dark outline due to ink build up as often seen with letterpress. Because it is an indirect printing process, there will not be any embossing of the substrate from contact with the printing plate.

While offset printing is used commercially for a variety of items, it allows for additional layers of security in the printing of documents such as banknotes. More advanced offset presses are capable of exceptionally tight registration between images on the front and back of the document as well as the ability to print extremely fine interwoven lines of varying color saturation. This produces images with qualities that are very difficult for counterfeits to reproduce whether using traditional or digital methods.

Dry offset is another form of offset printing that uses a raised image area but still utilizes the transfer "blanket." Images produced this way may have some of the same characteristics of letterpress, but the substrate will not demonstrate any signs of embossing.

Screen printing

The screen printing process uses a stencil and screen to produce images. Ink is forced through the screen onto the substrate. The ink used is very thick resulting in a slightly raised image; however, the pattern of the screen can sometimes be seen along the edges of images produced with this process and because no considerable pressure is applied, the substrate will not demonstrate any embossing (**Figure** 4). Screen printing is commonly used to apply specialized optically variable features to banknotes.

Figure 4 Genuine screen printing on Euro banknote.

Applied Security Features

The security of a banknote is only as good as the security of the design. There are many options for features that can be incorporated into the design. Holographic features are widely used in many security documents including currency and are a challenge for counterfeiters to simulate.

Currency Authentication

Authenticating any document requires an understanding of the genuine and the security features it should contain. This means the quality of the genuine production process is vital to ensure a product that can be consistently recognized and authenticated as genuine. Natural variation can occur in any production process, but these variations must be understood and documented to eliminate any confusion. If a banknote does not fall within these known ranges of variation, then it can be determined to be counterfeit. Experienced cash handlers scrutinize banknotes for their security features and will recognize variations in quality very easily, while someone less experienced may simply rely on the image. Counterfeiters can take advantage of untrained individuals by creating a counterfeit with high image quality but lacking in many of the other security features that a trained cash handler would check.

Machine authentication of banknotes utilizes specific features in the currency designed to be machine readable. If a counterfeiter's goal is to defeat these types of authentication devices, they will often focus their attention on these machine-readable features and ignore the quality of the image on their counterfeit.

Counterfeit Examinations

Microscopy continues to be the most advantageous method for examining suspect counterfeit banknotes. The magnification can range from 7× to 40× for observation of security features and printing process characteristics allowing for retail establishments to have a small, handheld magnifier, such as a linen tester, to check suspect counterfeits. More complex examinations, such as paper fiber assessments, will require higher magnification from 40× to 100× and are often reserved for the forensic document examiner or counterfeit specialist. Alternate light sources ranging from the near infrared to the UV are also necessary. More extensive examinations can be performed with specialized equipment that requires operator expertise but can lead to valuable forensic and investigative information.

Physical Examination with Light Sources

Physical examination of the suspect counterfeit can first be done using standard and transmitted light and a direct comparison to a known genuine image. Standard reflective light allows for the color and presence of overt security features to be evaluated and compared. Using reflective light at an oblique angle will allow for the viewing of the substrate's topography as well as observation of optically variable features such as optically variable ink (**Figures 5 and 6**).

Transmitted light allows the examiner to view embedded security features such as threads and watermarks, which by design should only be able to be observed with transmitted light (**Figures 7–10**). Any misalignment of front-to-back registered features can also be detected using transmitted light and may be the indication that a suspect banknote is counterfeit.

UV light sources allow the examiner to observe the UV brightness of the suspect substrate. While most commercial papers have optical brighteners added to them, currency paper substrates inherently possess a UV-dull response. Postissuance

Figure 5   Genuine optically variable ink copper color on US currency.

Figure 6   Genuine optically variable ink green color on US currency.

Figure 7   Genuine embedded security thread.

chemical exposure, however, can result in genuine currency paper substrates obtaining a UV response, so this examination should always be combined with other examinations to confirm if a banknote is counterfeit. Security features incorporated into banknotes may also possess UV properties. A UV light source will allow the examiner to determine if UV properties are present but can also reveal simulated security features on counterfeit banknotes (**Figures 11–13**). Since the materials used to print these simulated features will often absorb or reflect UV light, they can be viewed in a distinguishable manner from genuine substrates.

Physical Examination with Microscopy

Microscopy is one of the most valuable tools an examiner can use when conducting physical examinations of suspect counterfeit banknotes. Paper substrate composition, security features, and side-by-side comparisons of the intricate banknote design can all be done with various microscopy sources.

The physical characteristics, for example, color and morphology, of substrate-based security features such as fibers,

Figure 10   Security watermark simulated by printing on counterfeit US currency.

Figure 8   Security thread simulated by printing on counterfeit US currency.

Figure 9   Genuine security watermark.

Figure 11   Genuine ultraviolet response.

Figure 12　Counterfeit US currency showing no ultraviolet response of the security thread simulation.

Figure 13　Ultraviolet response of a printed watermark simulation on counterfeit US currency.

planchettes, and threads can be microscopically examined and compared to the genuine specimen. The location of these features can also be evaluated. While genuine fibers, planchettes, and threads are embedded in the substrate, counterfeit features can be simulated by printing or gluing them to the

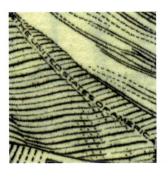

Figure 14　Genuine microprinting on US currency.

Figure 15　Counterfeit microprinting reproduction.

surface. More sophisticated counterfeits will have embedded features, but microscopic examination will reveal difference in the color, morphology, or composition of these counterfeit features when compared to genuine specimens.

Microscopic analysis will also reveal security features that may not have been successfully reproduced by the printing technique chosen by the counterfeiter. Microprinting, for example, is small text that cannot be reproduced by low-resolution digital technology such as scanners and will often be illegible on counterfeits that use that technology to acquire an image. More recently, however, the resolution in affordable digital technology has increased to where some of these devices will successfully reproduce microprinting from the genuine image (**Figures 14 and 15**).

Microscopy is the best tool to determine the printing method used to produce the suspect counterfeit banknote. Different methods of printing have different characteristics that can be observed with magnification. The four printing processes used to produce genuine currency, intaglio, letterpress, offset, and screen have been discussed, but counterfeit versions of these printing processes can be used and will possess similar characteristics as their genuine counterparts (**Figures 16–19**). The following printing processes are also known to be used to produce counterfeits.

Figure 16   Counterfeit intaglio printing.

Figure 17   Counterfeit letterpress (typography) printing.

Figure 18   Counterfiet offset printing.

Figure 19   Counterfeit screen printing.

Figure 20   Counterfeit halftone offset printing.

Figure 21   Counterfeit full-color toner printing.

Halftone offset lithography

If a counterfeiter wants to use offset lithography to entirely produce their counterfeit image, they will sometimes use halftone offset because of its ability to produce tonal variations that regular offset lithography cannot. A screen or computer is used to break up the desired images into a series of dots that range in size and location, and once combined together will create the illusion of a continuous tone. If full color separation is desired to simulate the various shades and colors of the genuine currency, a full color halftone process can be used in which the subtractive color mixture of cyan, yellow, magenta, and black (CMYK) are used in various combinations to create the illusion of the distinct colors contained in the genuine image (**Figure 20**).

Laser technology

Digital devices that use dry toner such as copy machines and laser printers will produce images composed of tiny plastic particles that have been fused to the surface of the substrate. Under magnification, the image will resemble melted plastic with stray toner particles scattered along the edge of the image area (**Figure 21**).

Figure 22   Counterfeit inkjet printing.

Inkjet technology

Inkjet-produced images are composed of ink dots that have absorbed into the paper. These dots will be flat and irregularly shaped. Legacy inkjet devices used basic CMYK components, but newer devices have the ability to use a vast array of color options (**Figure 22**).

Bleached Currency Examinations

Paper currency substrates possess unique characteristics and a unique "feel" that is often recognized as currency. Because of this, some counterfeiters want to use currency paper to produce their counterfeits. They will "bleach" or chemically remove the ink from low-denomination banknotes leaving a blank piece of currency paper for use as a substrate for their counterfeit image. The image of a higher-denomination banknote is printed on the genuine currency paper, which will possess any paper-based, embedded security features of the denomination that was bleached, making it a more deceptive counterfeit (**Figure 23**).

An examination of bleached counterfeits may reveal signs of the process. The process of bleaching involves not only the use of chemicals but also the abrasive process of removing the ink from the paper. A microscopic examination of a bleached

counterfeit may reveal a disruption in the genuine paper fibers from this process as well as the removal of the paper's surface sizing. This will result in the topography and color of the bleached paper being distinguishable from original genuine paper. Residual images of the original banknote may also remain if the bleaching process was not completed correctly. Any postbleaching steps taken by the counterfeiter to improve the bleached paper's texture or printability can be detected microscopically.

Inkjet Examinations

Thin-layer chromatography is a common and rapid technique used to separate the organic components of inkjet inks and provide an easy side-by-side comparison of the dyes in the ink formulations. While a conclusion can be made that the inkjet chromatogram is consistent with a specific manufacturer of inkjet ink, it cannot be used to conclusively link a suspect inkjet printer to a suspect counterfeit banknote and should be supported by other investigative or forensic information.

Counterfeits will commonly use an all-in-one inkjet printer and use the scanning capability to obtain the image from a genuine banknote. When this procedure is used, any defects on the scanner glass or lid such as dirt or scratches can be detected in the printed sheets of counterfeits. These "trash-marks" can help conclusively link a suspect inkjet printer to the counterfeit that was produced from that printer.

Chemical and Instrumental Examinations

Spectroscopy, elemental analysis, and chromatography of components such as the paper and ink of the suspect banknote may also be utilized to compare a suspect banknote to genuine and obtain valuable information that may benefit a counterfeit investigation. Research efforts have focused on characterizing specific inkjet inks using methods such as Raman spectroscopy. While these methods may not be necessary when simply determining if a suspect banknote is counterfeit, they could provide valuable investigative information when needed.

Summary

Paper currency is a method that has been used throughout history to purchase or trade goods and services. As long as paper currency has been used, the threat of counterfeiting has existed. Being able to recognize printing processes and security features used to produce genuine currency will assist an examiner in identifying a counterfeit, as many methods used to produce counterfeit differ from the genuine methods.

Figure 23   Bleached genuine $5 printed as a counterfeit $100 showing retained $5 security thread and security watermark.

See also: **Documents:** Analytical Methods; Forgery/Counterfeits; Ink Analysis; Paper Analysis.

Further Reading

Brunelle, R.L., Reed, R.W., 1991. Forensic Examination of Ink and Paper. Thomas, Springfield, IL.

Committee on Next Generation Currency Design, Nationals Materials Advisory Board, Commission on Engineering and Technical Systems, National Research Council, 1993. Counterfeit Deterrent Features for the Next-generation Currency Design. National Academy Press, Washington, DC. Publication NMAB-472.

Durst, S.J., 1978. History of the Bureau of Engraving and Printing. Sanford J Durst, Washington, DC.

Eu, P., Chiew, B., Straus, S., 2006. World Polymer Banknotes, second ed. Eureka Metro Sdn. Bhd, Malaysia.

Stevenson, D.L., 1994. Handbook of Printing Processes. Graphic Arts Technical Foundation, Pittsburgh, PA.

van Renesse, R.L. (Ed.), 1995. Optical Document Security. Artech House, Boston, MA.

Weatherford, J., 1997. The History of Paper Money. Crown, New York.

Relevant Websites

www.moneyfactory.gov—Bureau of Engraving and Printing.
http://www.frbsf.org—Federal Reserve Bank of San Francisco.
http://www/newmoney.gov—The New $100 Note.

Identity Theft

Z Geradts, Netherlands Forensic Institute, Den Haag, The Netherlands

Glossary

Identity fraud Mostly the same as identity theft.
Identity theft The crime of obtaining the personal or financial information of another person for the sole purpose of assuming that person's name or identity in order to get access and to make transactions or purchases.
Personal identifier A personal identifier is a data element within a data set that singly or in combination can uniquely identify an individual, such as a social security number, name, address, birth date, physical characteristics, demographic information (e.g., combining gender, race, occupation, and location), and hospital patient numbers (definition from IT law wiki).
Skimming Copying the magnetic stripe or contents of the chip of a banking or credit card.

Introduction

The term identity theft is often used for identity fraud or more generally, for identity-related crime. An example is a skimming case where the magnetic strip of a bank card is copied, as well as the pin code, and money is taken from a bank account without the owner of the account being aware of this. Other examples are creating profiles of person on social networks, which are not yet registered, or using stolen passports for opening bank accounts and making financial transactions.

Stealing someone's identity completely is not possible; most often data or information that represents an individual's identity is stolen. In understanding the nature of identity-related crimes, it is also useful to look at lawful and unlawful identity changes. Lawful identity changes are, for instance, writing under a pseudonym on social networks or publishing in books, which are common.

Often a person possesses a certain personal identifier. The personal identifier can be something a person knows, such as a password or pin code, or something a person owns, such as biometric features, for example, fingerprints or iris or a token that generates codes or an identity document. Sometimes they are used in combination.

Identity theft is defined in the US 1998 Federal Identity Theft and Assumption Deterrence Act as when an individual "knowingly transfers or uses, without lawful authority, a means of identification of another person with the intent to commit, or to aid or abet, any unlawful activity."

The literature further differentiates identity-related crimes as-identity collision: a wrong link is accidentally made between personal identifier and individual:

- Identity change: A wrong link is intentionally made between personal identifier and individual (the personal identifier may be a personal identifier to an existing individual or a newly created one).
- Identity obstruction: A personal identifier is accidentally or intentionally erased.
- Identity restoration: A deleted personal identifier is restored by the individual and the linkability of the individual is reestablished.

The phrase "identity theft" is often used in the United States for banking frauds, where people use someone else's credit card or social security number for financial transactions. On the Internet, there are often weak systems for identity verification, such as password-only verification. The weakness of this system is that someone else also can use the service if they possess the password, which can be prevented by using a two-step verification, much like you see on a banking Web site, a password plus a code that is only used once.

In the United States, the number of incidents of personal identity theft number is around 9–10 million per year, or approximately 4% of the US adult population. Seven percent is related to medical identity fraud to claim on someone else's insurance. In the European Union, the number of cases of identity fraud is growing, for example, in the United Kingdom, there were 100 000 cases of identity fraud in 2007 (the rate of identity fraud is growing 10% a year). In some countries, it is easier to commit identity theft than in others with stronger personal identifiers. The more a certain personal identifier is used, the weaker it gets; since each time it is used, there is also a chance it is copied by someone.

There are different ways of illicitly retrieving passwords and other data from persons, such as false e-mails purporting to be from an individual's bank asking for personal data (fishing):

- Guessing or using passwords from other services and testing them.
- Keyboard bugs in both hardware and software, where the software approach can be easily installed as malware.
- Use of insecure network systems such as unprotected Wi-Fi and e-mail accounts. These are a source of valuable information, such as photocopies of passports and sometime passwords of other accounts. Typically, these personal identifiers can be used elsewhere.
- Hacking systems where credit card numbers and passwords are stored.
- Sniffing USB and other communication channels.

The more common types of identity theft are financial identity theft, medical identity theft, business identity theft, and illegal border entry. The direct and indirect costs of identity theft for financial institutions and society are growing.

Identity Related to Biometrics

The following biometric features can be used in passport documents (as described in the ICAO (International Civil Aviation Organization) standards on biometrics): signatures, face, iris, fingerprint, and body height.

In other biometric systems, for example, for access in computers, in fitness centers, or for entry into buildings, other biometric features used include hand shape, vein patterns on hand, weight of a person, and handwriting characteristics.

Identity fraud at borders is possible by using a "look alike," since face comparison software in real-life situations has high error rates. Furthermore, people age, can use makeup, and make other changes to their face, and the quality of image in the passport is limited due to storage on the radio-frequency identification (RFID) chip. Small and important details (such as scars and birthmarks) on the face may not be visible anymore.

If a fingerprint is stored, the fingerprint can be compared; however, in practice, often fingerprints are not very well acquired, and this gives error rates in the comparison. It is also possible to spoof fingerprints. However, by checking the person if the fingerprint has been spoofed and by watching the person entering the biometric system, this can be prevented. Also, countries are aware of privacy concerns of their citizens and might not store this data anymore.

Spoofing an iris is more complicated if a proper life detection algorithm is used. In India, currently there is a project on storing both iris and fingerprint from all their citizens.

Also, other forms of biometrics are used in forensic science, but these are not used in biometric verification systems. DNA is too complicated, and of course, the collection of the DNA sample should also be watched carefully.

The increasing frequency of use in places such as fitness clubs means that they may be stored in low-security systems amenable to attack or abuse by others for identity theft. The drawback of using biometrics is that they cannot be easily revoked or changed if they have been compromised.

Virtual Identities

Since most identity verification is by unmanned digital systems, they become more sensitive to attacks. The person who likes to enter the system can take the time to investigate the system as such, do testing of the system itself, and find specifications on the design.

Virtual identities are not necessarily illegal since people often use nicknames at social networking and gaming software. However, if a crime is committed in the virtual world, for instance, by stealing someone's money in the virtual world in a game or social networking software, it becomes a virtual crime.

Since criminals will use many methods to conceal their real identity, it is difficult to investigate, and this kind of cybercrime often crosses international borders. Often, combinations of harvesting personal identifiers such as credit card numbers with malware or cracking unsecure systems are carried out. Currently, malware developers are aware of virus and malware checking software, so they will try to circumvent the protection by changing the malware rapidly.

Forensic Properties of Verification and Identification Systems

The questions that have to be answered in an investigation include how reliable is the underlying technology? This depends on what kind of technology has been used, how secure is it, and is there any experience with the combination of technologies.

How well is the individual bound to the personal identifier? This is of interest in access control of buildings and RFID cards in public transportation, or as well in mobile phones. These devices and cards can be stolen from a person, and often, it takes some time before a person notices this.

Transparency

How well is it possible to audit if a biometric system actually does what it says? How transparent is the software, open source implementation can be verified easier than proprietary implementations, where it is not verifiable what actually happens in the device. If a manufacturer discloses the exact way the biometric system works, it becomes easier to check.

There might be a data retention law that applies for the system, and of course, there might be an ethical issue depending on a country's standards concerning storage of fingerprints. How long are data kept in the system?

Unintended Audit Trail

In software implementation, often for debugging purposes, interim results or data are stored in the system. However, in practice, it appears that it is not always deleted, which helps in investigations, but is unintended.

Examples of Identity Fraud (Skimming, Wrong Persons in Prisons, Banking Fraud, and Spoofing) and Relating Them to Other Articles

A well-known method for identity fraud is skimming of credit and banking cards. The skimming device is often integrated in an automatic teller machine (ATM) or point-of-sale (POS) terminal by the perpetrator, during out-of-office hours. The copying of the magnetic stripe is easy with a magnetic swipe card reader.

There are several methods for integrating this device without the customers being aware of it. In the early days of this crime, customers were not aware of this kind of crime, so changes to the front of ATM or POS were not detected. For the skimming fraud, it is important to have a copy of the magnetic stripe and the pin code. The pin code can be acquired with a camera or by integrating it in the keypad. Later on, there were complete fronts being used, or the POS was revised that the customers are not aware of it.

Nowadays, skimmers often use good encryption to store the data from the skimmed device since otherwise, other perpetrators might steal it. Often the perpetrators will harvest the data for a longer time, of several days to weeks or months, and then collect the data, or they might also transfer the data wireless to their system.

The crime often gets detected later by the bank following by complaints of customers that money has been taken from their accounts. These kinds of crimes are often international since the money is taken abroad from the customers. Such crimes can also be detected by intelligent data analysis of the ATM traffic.

Most banks in the European Union have switched to chip cards. However, this is not the case elsewhere in the world, so the magnetic stripe will be there for several years, until this vanishes. However, the current standard of EMV (Eurocard, Mastercard, Visa) with the chip also has weaknesses, as is described by Murdoch et al.

For forensic investigation, it is important to collect the manipulated devices and carry out the customary DNA and fingerprint analysis. Also, by making databases of these devices, intelligence can be made from the methods used, and if perpetrators are caught, more cases by the same groups can be solved. The digital analysis of the skimming device is also important since the banking numbers should be found and customers can be informed. This is also an important evidence for court. The storage of the data from the camera can also be important as evidence since sometimes video is stored from the perpetrator themselves.

Other cases are with online banking accounts, where the account information is stolen and money is wired to other bank accounts, which is most often an international crime. The criminals later on try to find the so-called money mules by contacting them (much spam derives from this) and will ask to take the money from the account keeping a certain amount and send it further to an address. Investigation of this kind of crime is by studying the modus operandi of the crime and using intelligent data analysis algorithms at banks. They often result in complicated cases in forensic evidence since it is international, and the perpetrators learn from earlier experiences of how to prevent from being caught.

Future Expectations

In future cases, it is expected that biometric features might become less trustworthy, especially if they are stored in systems that are not secure. Investigations of cloud systems, where all kinds of data are stored, can also be a challenge to track data leaks. The investigation of identity crime will require increasingly more resources for law enforcement, especially if criminals use strong encryption and hiding techniques. Identity theft if used on a large scale is related to cyber terrorism.

In **Figure 1**, the issues are visualized. With the user registration, it is important to have the right person; otherwise the wrong identity propagates through the whole system. The method of identity verification is important, as well as how well does it work and how many false rejects and false accepts does it have. Furthermore, the denied user can still enter the system if the person proves his/her identity. The denied person can use alternative identifiers, such as mother's maiden name, which might be weak.

See also: **Documents:** Forgery/Counterfeits; **Investigations:** Payment Cards.

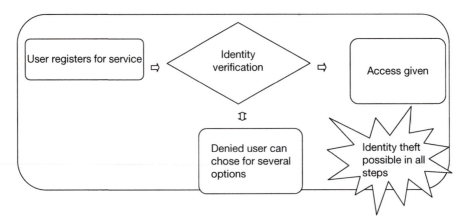

Figure 1   Schematic overview of identity system.

Further Reading

Benson, B., Zimmerman, P., 2010. Handbook on the Economics of Crime. Edward Elgar, Cheltenham, UK.

Florêncio, D., Herley, C., 2010. Phishing and money mules. In: IEEE International Workshop on Information Forensics and Security, 12–15 December 2010, pp. 1–5.

Gorrindo, T., Groves, J.E., 2010. Crime and hate in virtual worlds: a new playground for the Id? Harvard Review of Psychiatry 18 (2), 113–118.

Grijpink, J., 2006. Identiteitsfraude. Justitiele verkenningen 32, 36–56.

Henry, K., Lee, R., 2009. Are you really someone else? The credibility of identity documents. Journal of Forensic and Investigative Techniques 2 (3), 164–190.

Koops, B.J., Geradts, Z., Sommer, P., 2009. Identity related crimes and forensics. In: Rannenberg, K. (Ed.), The Future of Identity in the Information Society. Springer, Berlin, pp. 315–347.

Marcon, J.L., Susa, K.J., Meissner, C.A., 2009. Assessing the influence of recollection and familiarity in memory for own- vs. other-race faces. Psychonomic Bulletin & Review 16 (1), 99–103.

Mastersa, G., Turner, P., 2007. Forensic data recovery and examination of magnetic swipe card cloning devices. Digital Investigation 4 (Suppl. 1), 16–22.

Moore, T., 2010. Cybercrime Investigating High – Technology Crime. Anderson Publishing, Cleveland, MS.

Murdoch, S.J., Drimer, S., Anderson, R., Bond, M., 2010. Chip and pin is broken. In: IEEE Symposium on Security and Privacy, 2010, pp. 433–446.

Rannenberg, K., 2009. The Future of Identity in the Information Society. Springer, Berlin.

Romero, J., 2011. Fast start for world's biggest biometrics ID project. In: IEEE Spectrum 2011, pp. 66–67.

Relevant Websites

https://www.comp.glam.ac.ukhttps://www.comp.glam.ac.uk—O. Angelopoulo et al., Online ID Theft Techniques, Investigations and Response.

http://www.ftc.gov—Federal Trade Commission, Fighting Back against Identity Theft.

http://www.theiacp.org—A Forensic Approach to Effective Identity Theft Investigations.

http://ec.europa.eu—FPEG: The EU Fraud Prevention Expert Group.

https://www.privacyassociation.orghttps://www.privacyassociation.org—International Association of Privacy professionals.

http://www.icao.int—International Civil Aviation Organization.

Forensic Accounting

J Cali, CPA, CFF, CGMA

Glossary

Alter Ego "Second self" under the doctrine of Alter Ego, the owners of the corporation are held responsible for the corporate acts, disregarding the corporate entity.

Answer The formal response by a defendant to a plaintiff's complaint.

Asset Anything tangible or intangible that is capable of being owned or controlled to produce value and that is held to have positive economic value is considered an asset.

Asset approach A general way of determining a value indication of a business, business ownership interest, or security using methods based on the value of the net assets of their liabilities.

Authentication The process of making a written document admissible as evidence.

Benefit of the bargain rule A rule permitting a defrauded purchaser to recover the differences between the actual value received and what the purchaser expected to receive.

Benford's law A law used by auditors to identify fictitious populations of numbers, and applies to any population of numbers derived from other numbers. This law also gives the expected distribution for digits beyond the first, which approach a uniform distribution as the digit place goes to the right.

Best evidence rule The rule requiring that the best evidence available (i.e., an original document or object) be presented unless it is shown that the original has been lost, destroyed, or not subject to the jurisdiction of the court.

Bid rigging A scheme in which a vendor is given an unfair advantage in an open competition for certain goods and/or services.

Bona fide In good faith; without fraud or deceit.

Business enterprise A commercial, industrial, service, or investment entity (or combination thereof) that pursues an economic activity.

Business risk The amount of uncertainty in realizing expected future returns of the business resulting from other factors than financial leverage (also see Financial risk).

Business valuation The act or process of determining the value of a business enterprise or ownership interest.

Capital structure The makeup of the invested capital within a business enterprise; the mix of debt and equity financing.

Cash flow Cash that is generated over a period of time by an asset, group of assets, or business enterprise. It may be used generally to encompass various levels of specifically defined cash flows. Cash flow should be supplemented by a qualifier (for example, discretionary or operating) and a definition for a particular valuation context.

Cash "T" A term used in conjunction with the reconstruction of income. It is an analysis of all of the cash received by the taxpayer and all of the cash spent by the taxpayer over a fixed period of time. The theory of the cash "T" is that if a taxpayer's expenditure during a given year exceeds reported income, and the source of the funds for such expenditure is unexplained, such an excess amount represents unreported income.

Channel stuffing Various schemes that stuff the distribution channel with revenue that may be fraudulent (e.g., bill-and-hold schemes).

Circumstantial evidence Evidence from which the truth or validity of an issue may be proved indirectly.

Class action A lawsuit brought on behalf of a class of persons by one or more persons with claims that are typical of and fairly represent the claims.

Collateral estoppel The rule that a prior judgment in a case involving the same parties (or persons privy to those parties) bars retrial of issues decided in the prior judgment.

Common size statements Financial statements in which each line is expressed as a percentage of the total. On the balance sheet, each line item is shown as a percentage of total assets and, on the income statement, as a percentage of sales.

Compensatory damages Damages to recompense an injured party for an injury and restore the injured party to his or her original position prior to the injury.

Compliant The formal written pleading expressing a plaintiff's claim for relief and initiating a court action.

Computer forensics The procedures applied to computers and peripherals for gathering evidence that may be used in civil and/or criminal courts of law.

Consequential damages Damages that do not result directly and immediately from an act but instead result from the consequences of results of that act.

Correspondent banking A situation in which one bank provides services to another bank to move funds, exchange currencies, and access investment services such as money market accounts, overnight investments accounts, CDs, trading accounts, and computer software for making wire transfers and instant updates on account balances.

Cost approach A general means of determining an individual asset's value by quantifying the amount of money required to replace the future service capability of the asset.

Cost of capital The expected rate of return required by the market to attract funds for a particular investment.

Covenant A promise to do or not to do something.

Cross-examination Questioning of a witness by the attorney for the opposing party.

Cybersmear The practice of sending out a large quantity of electronic messages to bash a stock in hopes of causing the stock price to decline.

Data mining A technique that uses mathematical algorithms to seek hidden patterns or associations in data.

Demonstrative evidence Objects of documents (photos, videos, models, charts, etc.) that illustrate points of testimony but possess no probative intrinsic value.

Demurrer A defendant's allegation that the issues alleged in a complaint are insufficient to require the defendant to respond to them.

Direct evidence Evidence that directly proves a fact at issue, without the need for any inference or presumption, usually based on personal knowledge of the witness.

Direct examination Question of a witness by the attorney for the party for whom the witness is testifying.

Discount rate A rate of return used to convert a future sum into its present monetary value.

Discounted cash flow method A method within the income approach in which the present value of future expected net cash flows is determined using a discount rate.

Discounted future earnings method A method within the income approach in which the present value of future expected economic benefits is determined using a discount rate.

Drill down functionality A feature of software that enables forensic accountants to go below the surface of a financial statement and uncover the source of any number and how it was calculated.

Embezzlement The fraudulent appropriation of money or property lawfully in one's possession to be used personally by the embezzler. An embezzler steals from his or her employer.

Employee fraud The use of fraudulent means to take money or other property from an employer, usually involving some kind of falsification (e.g., false documents, lying, exceeding authority, or violating employer policies).

Evidence The testimony, writings, and material objects offered in court to prove an alleged fact of proposition (also see Circumstantial evidence, Demonstrative evidence, and Direct evidence).

Excess earnings The amount of anticipated economic benefits exceeding an appropriate rate of return on the value of a selected asset base (commonly, net tangible assets) used to create those anticipated economic benefits.

Excess earning method A specific way of determining a business valuation, business ownership interest, or security value, by summing the value of assets derived by capitalizing excess earning and the value of the selected asset base. The method is also frequently used in valuing intangible assets.

Expert report A written report prepared about a dispute by an expert witness.

Expert witness A person, who, because of specialized training or experience, testifies in court to enable the judge and/or jurors, to understand complicated and/or technical subjects.

Fact witness A witness who testifies as to facts.

Financial Crimes Enforcement Network (FinCEN) A bureau of the US Department of the Treasury dedicated to enhance the integrity of financial systems by facilitating the detection and deterrence of financial crime. FinCEN receives and maintains financial transaction data; analyzes and disseminates those data for law enforcement purposes; and builds global cooperation with counterpart organizations in other countries and with international bodies.

Financial risk The degree of uncertainty of realizing expected future returns of the business resulting from financial leverage (also see Business risk).

Foreign Corrupt Practices Act (FCPA) Prohibits corrupt payments to foreign officials for the purpose of obtaining or keeping business.

Forensic accounting The use of intelligence-gathering techniques and accounting/business skills to develop information and opinion for use by attorneys involved in civil litigation and/or criminal proceedings and give trial testimony if called upon; the action of identifying, recording, settling, extracting, sorting, reporting, and verifying past financial data or other accounting activities for settling current of prospective legal disputes or using such past financial data for projecting future financial data to settle legal disputes.

Goodwill The intangible asset created as a result of name, reputation, customer loyalty, location, product loyalty, and similar factors not separately identified.

Grand Jury A panel of 16–23 sworn individuals, which meets on a biweekly and/or monthly basis with the prosecutor to review evidence in order to authorize an indictment. A Grand Jury has the power to accuse but not the power to convict.

Hearsay An out-of-court statement of another party offered during a court proceeding to prove the truth of the matter asserted.

High–low method An approach that identifies the highest and lowest costs, along with their related activity levels. The difference is calculated between the two costs and the two activity levels. The difference in costs is then divided by the difference in activity levels to determine an estimate of the variable cost per unit.

Income approach A general way of determining a business valuation, business ownership interest, security value, or worth of an intangible asset using one or more methods that convert anticipated economic benefits into a present amount.

Intangible assets Nonphysical property such as franchises, trademarks, patents copyrights, goodwill, equities, mineral rights, securities, or contracts that grant rights and privileges and possess value for the owner.

Internal rate of return A discount rate at which the present value of the investment's future cash flows equals the cost of the investment.

Interrogation The process of questioning an individual suspected of being involved in a crime.

Interview The formal questioning of an individual.

Intrinsic value The value an investor considers, after evaluation or consideration of available facts, to be the true of real value that will become the market value when other investors reach the same conclusion.

Invested capital The sum of equity and debt in a business enterprise. Debt is typically all interest-bearing debt or long-term interest-bearing debt. The term should be supplemented by a specific definition in the given valuation context.

Invested capital net cash flows Those cash flows available to distribute to equity holders as dividends and debt investors as principal and interest after funding operations of the business enterprise and making necessary capital investments.

Investment value The value of an investment for a particular investor based on individual investment requirements and expectations.

Judicial precedent A court decision establishing a legal principle that subsequently is followed in cases having similar or identical facts.

Kiting Building up balances in bank accounts by floating worthless checks drawn against similar accounts in other banks.

Lapping The recording of payment on a customer's account some time after the receipt of the payment, so that cash is taken to be covered with the receipt from another customer.

Larceny of cash The theft of cash after the cash has been recorded on the books, such as directly from a cash register or petty cash.

Layering transactions The creation of a set of complex transfers to disguise the original source for the money and to hide and/or destroy the audit trail.

Liquidated damages clause A clause in a contract that specifies a dollar amount that a party will pay if that party breaches the contract.

Liquidation value The net amount that would be realized in a business terminates and its assets are sold piecemeal. Liquidation can be either orderly or forced.

Liquidity A property of an investment that enables it to be quickly converted to cash or payment to settle a liability.

Logs Manual and/or electronic records of the activities that have occurred.

Manipulation The falsification or alteration of accounting records or supporting documents from which financial statements are prepared.

Market approach A general way of determining a business valuation, value of a business ownership interest, security price, or intangible asset's value by using one or more methods that compare the asset to similar businesses, business ownership interests, securities, or intangible assets that have been sold.

Marketability The capacity to quickly convert property to cash at minimal cost.

Materiality The measure of whether something is significant enough to change an investor's investment decision.

Minority discount A discount for lack of control applied to the value of a minority interest.

Minority interest A business ownership interest of less than 50% of the voting interest.

Misappropriation The act of obtaining something of value or avoiding an obligation by deception.

Misrepresentation The intentional omission from the financial statements of events, transactions, or other significant information.

Money laundering The use of techniques to take money coming from one source, hide that source, and make the funds available in another setting so that the funds can be used without incurring legal restrictions or penalties.

Motion A request to a court for a rule or order in the applicant's favor.

Motion in limine A pretrial motion requesting a court to prohibit opposing counsel from offering certain evidence.

Net book value The difference between total assets (net of accumulated depreciation, depletion, and amortization) and total liabilities as they appear on the balance sheet of a business enterprise.

Net fraud A scheme to ensnare unsuspecting Internet users into giving up their resources to online criminal.

Net present value The value of the tangible assets of a business enterprise (excluding excess assets and nonoperating assets) minus the value of its liabilities.

Nonoperating assets Assets unnecessary to the ongoing operations of a business enterprise.

Opinion report A report by an expert, such as a valuation report, which is more subjective and relies more on the professional judgment of the expert than does a fact-oriented report.

Out-of-pocket loss Damages measured as the difference between the actual value received and the actual value conveyed.

Parol evidence Oral evidence.

Payable through account A bank account enabling the respondent bank's clients within the country where the bank is registered to write checks that are drawn directly on the respondent bank's correspondent account in the United States.

Pleadings The formal written allegations of the parties in a lawsuit, which includes the complaint and answer, each expressing their respective claims and defenses.

Present value The value as of a specified date, of future economic benefits and/or proceeds from sale, determined using an applicable discount rate.

Privileged communications Statements made between individuals within certain protected relationships such as attorney and client and priest and penitent.

Pump-n-dump A trading scheme causing thinly traded stock to move up rapidly in price after which the perpetrator sells the stock at a huge gain.

Punitive damages Damages awarded in excess of actual damages sustained in order to punish reprehensible conduct and deter future wrongdoers.

Qui tam action A lawsuit filed by a whistle-blower under the Federal False Claims Act against a company or contractor on behalf of the Federal Government.

Rate of return An amount of an investment's income or change in value, either realized or anticipated expressed as a percentage of that investment.

Redirect examination Testimony in which the direct examiner gives the witness the opportunity to clear up any confusion that may have been caused by the

cross-examination and complete any answer that the witness could not complete during cross-examination.

Rejoinder A defendant's pleading in answer to a plaintiff's reply.

Reply A plaintiff's pleading that is required or permitted to respond to a defendant's setoff or counterclaim.

Residual value The value at the conclusion of the discrete projection period in a discounted future earnings model.

Res judicata The rule that a final judgment by a court of competent jurisdiction on the merits of a case is conclusive as to the rights and facts at issue that bars and subsequent action involving the same cause of action brought by the same parties.

Respondent The person against whom an appeal is made to a higher court.

Return on equity A percentage amount earned on a company's common equity for a given period.

RICO laws Racketeer Influenced and Corrupt Organization laws are a set of laws specifically designed to target illegal acts by organized crime groups.

Rules of evidence The rules governing the admissibility of evidence and the weight that evidence is given.

Scienter The guilty knowledge of the defendant.

Skimming An off-book technique to remove cash before it is properly recorded.

Smurfing A money laundering technique in which individuals working for the money launderer deposit random amounts of cash less than $10 000 into numerous named accounts at various financial institutions to evade and/or avoid reporting requirements.

Sniffer A program used to secretly capture data moving across a computer network and to disclose and analyze these data packets.

Source and application of funds method Also called the "expenditure method," this is a technique approved for use by the Internal Revenue Service that shows increases and decreases in a taxpayer's accounts for a given period.

Subpoena A command presented to a witness to appear at a specified time and place in order to testify.

Subpoena duces tecum A command to produce specified documents or other items to the court.

Summary judgment A judge's disposition of a controversy without a trial when there is no dispute about a material fact and the case involves only a question of law.

Surrebutter A plaintiff's reply to a defendant's rebutter.

Surrejoinder The plaintiff's response to a defendant's rejoinder.

Tangible assets Physical assets such as cash, accounts receivable, inventory, property, plant, and equipment.

Tort A civil wrong or wrongful act, whether intentional or accidental, from which injury occurs to another.

Trier of fact A court, regulatory body, or government agency, a grand jury, or an arbitrator or mediator of a dispute.

Trust A legal relationship that is established by one person when assets have been placed under the control of another person for the benefit of the beneficiary for a specific purpose.

Valuation The process of determining the worth of a business, business ownership interest, security, or intangible asset.

Valuation approach A general way of calculating a value indication of a business, business ownership interest, security, or intangible asset that uses one or more valuation methods.

Valuation date The specific point in time as of which the valuator's report of value applies.

Vertical analysis The approach, often referred to as common size statements, that presents every item in a statement as a percentage of the largest item in the statement.

Voir dire examination The preliminary questioning by an attorney (or court) of juror candidates to determine whether they are qualified to serve as a juror.

Washing checks The process of chemically removing the original payee and the amount from a check in order to substitute another payee or amount.

Work product rule Rule that protects personal memoranda, written statements of witnesses, and other materials prepared by an attorney in anticipation of litigation from disclosure to other parties involved in litigation. The work product rule was developed to prevent an attorney's work from being used against a client and undermining the attorney–client privilege.

Writ of certiorari An appellate court's order requiring a lower court to certify the record and send it for review by the higher court.

Writ of elegit An order to seize a portion of a debtor's lands and all his/her goods (except work animals) toward satisfying a creditor, until the debt is paid off.

Writ of fieri facias An order directing the sheriff to take and auction off enough property from a losing party to pay the debt (plus interest and costs) owed by a judgment debtor.

Writ of replevin A court order to regain personal property held or retained by another. It usually involves the process that a bank or lending institution takes to recover collateral (cars, trucks, mobile homes, boats, campers, furniture, etc.).

Zipf's law A natural phenomena in which the frequency of any word is inversely proportional to its rank in the frequency table. Thus, the most frequent word will occur approximately twice as often as the second most frequent word, three times as often as the third most frequent word.

Introduction

With all of the recent corporate accounting scandals at Parmalat, Xerox Corporation, and Satyam Computer Services, and all the high-profile corporate frauds at Enron, World Com, and HealthSouth followed by Bernie Madoff's colossal ponzi scheme, the media have made forensic accounting into a growing industry.

While all the recent media attention given to forensic accounting may give one the impression that this is something new, in reality, the practice of forensic accounting has been around since the sixteenth century. Court records from Antwerp, Belgium, show in 1554 Hercules DeCordes, a "bookkeeper," was recognized as an expert witness when he testified about the accounting records he maintained.

In 1946, Maurice Peloubet, a New York CPA, was the first person to coin the phrase "forensic accountant." It is the forensic accountant who is tasked with the daunting responsibility of reconstructing the complex financial puzzle after the discovery of fraud, embezzlement, or elaborate ponzi scheme. It is the forensic accountant's mission to rebuild the entire financial system to uncover the fraud scheme(s) employed. This is accomplished by painstakingly reviewing financial transactions such as inventory records, payroll disbursements, canceled checks, bank and credit card account records, wire transfers, cashier check purchases, expense reports, and nonfinancial information such as e-mails, text messages, phone logs, purchase orders, vendor files, personnel records, and passport activity.

In most situations, the forensic accountant will appear in court to present his or her work; therefore, the forensic accountant must have knowledge pertaining to the rules of evidence for courtroom proceedings and must demonstrate that due professional care and proper chain of custody was maintained for all paper and electronic evidence entrusted to him. On completion of the forensic accounting engagement, the forensic accountant must be able to present his or her findings in a written report that is clear, concise, and presents the facts in a persuasive manner.

In short, it is the forensic accountant's role to determine what happened, explain how it occurred, and offer a fair and reasonable evaluation for computation of damages. In some cases, the forensic accountant may be called upon to develop a series of recommendations to prevent and deter future losses.

Forensic Accounting for Criminal Investigations

Today, local, state, and federal law enforcement agencies seek the use of forensic accountants to investigate financial crimes such as

- arson for profit,
- bank fraud,
- embezzlement,
- health-care fraud,
- insurance fraud,
- money laundering,
- mortgage fraud,
- organized crime business enterprises,
- ponzi schemes,
- securities and commodities fraud,
- tax evasion, and
- terrorist financial networks.

The father of forensic accounting for law enforcement was none other than Mr. Frank Wilson.

Frank Wilson was a certified public accountant working for the Internal Revenue Service when, in 1930, he was assigned to a federal task force investigating the notorious Chicago gangster, Al Capone.

In searching records, Wilson found an accountant's cash receipts ledger showing net profits from gambling, with Al Capone's name on it.

It was this single document that allowed Wilson to prove that Al Capone had indeed earned "illegal income," which he had failed to report, that was subject to federal income taxation.

Although there had been many attempts to convict Capone for various other illegal activities, he was never found guilty. In fact, he thought Wilson's investigation and the tax evasion charges were a joke.

In response to these charges he stated the following:

"The income tax law is a lot of bunk. The government cannot collect legal taxes from illegal money."

In 1931, on the strength of the forensic accounting analysis of Capone's personal and business accounting records by Wilson, Al Capone was indicted for federal income tax evasion for the years 1925–1929, in addition to the failure to file tax returns for the years 1928 and 1929.

Wilson's detailed forensic accounting methods determined that Capone owed $215 080.48 in federal income taxes from his "illegal gambling profits."

Capone was found guilty of tax evasion and Judge Wilkerson sentenced him to 10 years in Federal Prison and 1 year in the county jail.

Wilson's work on the Capone investigation set the foundation for modern-day forensic accounting and financial investigation applications in law enforcement.

It was Frank Wilson, CPA, who was able to prove to the world that it takes a forensic accountant to catch a crook!

Forensic Accounting Tools

In order to analyze the subject's financial transactions, the forensic accountant may have to search for it. When facing these circumstances, the forensic accountant should begin his or her search with public record databases. Government entities in cities, counties, and states compile a wealth of information on both individuals and corporations.

On state Web sites, the forensic accountant will find a vast array of information on every corporation registered with the state, including the names of the officers and registered agents for corporations, limited liability companies, limited partnerships, and general partnerships in addition to fictitious name registrations and lien filings that are readily available online.

The City or County Property Appraiser has important information pertaining to the ownership and transaction history for every parcel of real and taxable personal property in the county. Additional real estate information is also available from a service called *Zillow*, which provides free real estate information about homes for sale, home prices, home values, and recently sold homes for any location in the United States.

All records pertaining to every legal proceeding are presented in court dockets, which are maintained by the office commonly referred to as the clerk of the court. The clerk of the court's Web site can provide the details and copies of actual documents related to the court proceedings for the following: arrest and conviction records, traffic citations, affidavits and motions filed by plaintiffs and/or defendants, marriage licenses, divorce decrees, final rulings, disposition of property, and a host of other court-related documents related to the assessment and payment of fines, fees, and court costs.

Every city and/or county has an official records custodian. The information contained on the records custodian's Web site will provide the forensic accountant with the details for every "recorded document," such as deeds, declarations of domicile, foreign judgments, domestic partnership registration, liens, evictions, foreclosures, writs of replevin, writs of elegit, and writs of fieri facias.

Forensic accountants who are also members of the law enforcement community have access to a number of specialized investigative Web sites and databases.

The first of these systems is maintained by the Federal Bureau of Investigation (FBI), and it contains a comprehensive database of criminal justice information in a computerized system known as the National Crime Information Center, more commonly referred to as NCIC. The information in NCIC may assist the forensic accountant in locating and returning stolen property.

The second system, known as the Financial Crimes Enforcement Network (FinCEN), was developed by the US Department of the Treasury. FinCEN's mission is to enhance the US national security, deter and detect criminal activity, and safeguard financial systems from abuse by promoting transparency in the United States and international financial systems. FinCEN can provide forensic accountants with a variety of financial information pertaining to an individual and/or a corporation, such as the location of bank and stockbroker accounts, details of wire transfers, cash transactions, and suspicious activity involving financial institutions, casinos, insurance brokers, security dealers, check-cashing stores, foreign currency dealers, jewelers, and precious metal brokers.

It is important to note that any information the forensic accountant obtains from FinCEN is considered to be protected information as defined by the "safe harbor" provisions of the Bank Secrecy Act. As protected information, any documents provided by financial institutions to FinCEN are not subject to discovery and cannot be disclosed to a third party or used as exhibits during trial. This advisory is provided to inform financial institutions of the recent court decision concerning the "safe harbor" provision of the Bank Secrecy Act as applied to reports of suspicious transactions.

It is extremely important for the forensic accountant to organize and catalog all material received during the course of the financial investigation. In an effort to facilitate the collection and classification of data, a Background Investigation Checklist is provided in **Exhibit 1** and a Financial Investigation Checklist is provided in **Exhibit 2**.

Surveillance and Investigation Tools

Pen registers and mail covers are two surveillance and investigation tools commonly used by law enforcement agencies that are extremely useful to the forensic accountant.

A pen register is an electronic device that records all numbers dialed from and to a particular telephone line. The term has come to include any device or program that performs similar functions to an original pen register, including programs monitoring Internet communications. Information obtained from a pen register can provide the forensic accountant with knowledge of foreign bank accounts and key data that can be used to produce a genogram.

Exhibit 1   Background Investigation Checklist

Full Name
Prior Name
Aliases
Social Security Number (SSN)
Date of Birth (DOB)
Vehicle Information
Driver License History
Litigation History
Criminal History/Arrest Record
Sex Offender Status
Bankruptcy Filings
Tax Liens/Judgments/Garnishments/UCC Filings/Liens
Internet Search (Google, Face Book, My Space)
Associations/Personal/Business
Marital Status/Martial History/Divorce Decree
Former/Current
- Employer
- Coworkers
- Neighbors
- Spouses
- Landlords
Education Verification
Immigration Status
Employment History
Professional Licenses
Gun Registrations

Exhibit 2   Financial Investigation Checklist

Real Estate Ownership
Vehicle Registrations
Boat/Aircraft Ownership
Business/Corporation Ownership
Stock/Bond Investments
Retirement Funds (IRA, 401K, 403B, 457)
Domestic Bank Accounts
Foreign Bank Accounts
Insurance Policy Ownership
Litigation/Insurance Settlements
Inheritance
Gambling/Lottery/Powerball Winnings
UCC Filings/Liens
Employment History
Professional Licenses
Collections (Art, Antiques, Sports Memorabilia, etc.)
Government Benefits
Bankruptcy Filings
Tax Liens
Judgments/Garnishments
Credit Reports
Safe Deposit Boxes (Cash, Jewelry)
Gun Registrations
Marital Status/Martial History/Divorce Decree

A genogram is a pictorial display using symbols and lines to illustrate a person's relationships with other individuals. These graphic displays can be used by the forensic accountant at trial to help the judge and jury understand the intricate workings of a complex money laundering or fraud scheme.

"A mail cover is a law enforcement investigative technique that captures any data appearing on the outside cover of sealed or unsealed class of mail, or by which a record is made of the contents of any unsealed mail. Mail covers are allowed by law to:

1. obtain information to protect national security;
2. locate a fugitive;
3. obtain evidence of the commission or attempted commission of a crime;
4. obtain evidence of a violation or attempted violation of a postal statute; or
5. assist in the identification of property, proceeds, or assets forfeitable under law."

A mail cover does not involve the reading of the mail but only information on the outside of the envelope or package that could be read by anyone seeing the item anyway. Mail covers can provide the forensic accountant with vital information pertaining to income from unknown sources as well as an individual's lifestyle and spending habits. An example of a mail cover is presented in **Exhibit 3**.

Forensic Accounting for Civil Litigation

With all the media attention pertaining to the practice of forensic accounting related to sensational fraud examination cases or ponzi schemes, it is easy to overlook the important role

Exhibit 3   Damage Calculation Formula

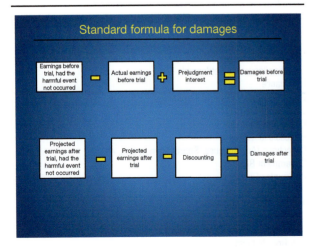

that forensic accountants play in examining and analyzing financial transactions for civil litigation matters such as follows:

- divorce,
- bankruptcy,
- lost profit computations,
- personal injury,
- wrongful death, and
- business interruption claims:
  - mergers and acquisitions,
  - gift and estate tax valuations,
  - life-care plans,
  - buy–sell agreements, and
  - qui tam actions.

The forensic accountant's role in the majority of civil litigation matters is to determine the economic value of damages an injured party has suffered. All things being equal, the injured party would like the damage calculation to be as large as possible, whereas the defendant would like the damages to be as small as possible.

In these cases, the basic assumption for the computation of damages is determined under the principle that compensation should place the injured party in the same position economically that they had before the harmful event took place. Because the computation of damages is based on the premise of "what if nothing had occurred," the forensic accountant engaged by the injured party will employ a series of assumptions and valuation methods to arrive at the highest possible damage estimate. Conversely, the forensic accountant representing the defense must find the means to form a creditable challenge to these assumptions in a professional manner to persuade the judge and/or jury to accept the much lower level of damages presented by the forensic accountant for the defendant.

When an injured party suffers an economic loss and seeks to recover damages, the forensic accountant needs to prepare a "study of losses." In accordance with the established legal framework, the "study of losses" will include the quantification of the reduction in earnings/revenue, the calculation of interest on past losses, and the application of financial discounting to future losses. In computing damages, the forensic accountant must also take into consideration that the injured party has a duty to take the necessary steps to mitigate or reduce the damages.

The standard formula for the computation of damages developed by the Federal Judicial Center's *Reference Manual on Scientific Evidence* is presented in the following table:

The key element in determining economic value of the damages is the measurement of the loss. Losses must be measured over the time period in which the injured party can recover from the wrongful harm; therefore, the forensic accountant must first define the loss period in order to begin the loss measurement process. The measurement process is

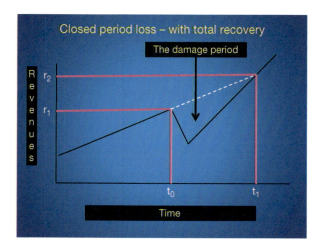

Figure 1 Closed period loss damage analysis.

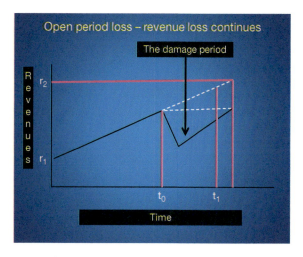

Figure 2 Open period loss damage analysis.

commonly defined by one of three generally accepted methods: the closed period loss, the open period loss, and the infinite period loss.

In the closed period loss, the injured party over time has been able to recover completely and has realized a position that he or she would have obtained if the loss had never occurred. The closed period loss is illustrated in **Figure 1**.

In the open period loss scenario, the injured party has been able to realize a partial recovery; however, the damages are so strong that the party will never realize the position he or she was in before suffering the loss. The open period loss is illustrated in **Figure 2**.

In the infinite period loss situation, the loss is so devastating that the injured party is never able to recover. The infinite period loss is illustrated in **Figure 3**.

Forensic Accounting to Discover Hidden Assets

In divorce, bankruptcy, and partnership liquidation cases, it is not uncommon for one of the parties involved to employ elaborate means to deliberately conceal assets. In these cases where there is a suspicion that assets are disappearing or the asset values seem to be artificially too low, the forensic accountant is called in to verify valuations and locate and recover any hidden assets.

There are two techniques that can be used to perform a forensic analysis to reconstruct unreported income: the direct method and the indirect method.

The direct method mirrors the steps of a traditional audit by examining

- financial statements,
- general ledgers,
- bank accounts,

- sales invoices, and
- canceled checks.

The direct method has one major drawback. In order to complete a direct method analysis, it involves the cooperation of the individual and/or organization under investigation to provide the forensic accountant access to the financial information.

On the other hand, the indirect method utilizes an array of covert means such as subpoenas, currency transaction reports, suspicious activity reports, social security wage reports, phone taps, trash pulls, mail covers, real property records, corporate officer records, occupational license filings, driver license records, vehicle registrations, and the testimony of confidential informant(s).

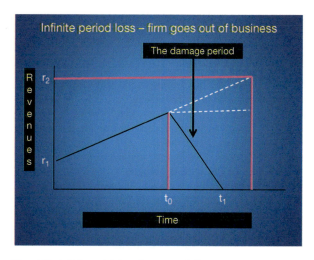

Figure 3 Infinite period loss damage analysis.

Of the two methods, the indirect method is the most commonly used to reconstruct historical financial results to identify income from unknown sources.

The indirect method for reconstructing income actually encompasses four distinct methodologies:

- cash "T" method,
- expenditure method (sometimes called source and application of funds method),
- bank deposit method, and
- net worth method.

The cash "T" method is the simplest indirect method to determine income from unknown sources. The forensic accountant simply compares all cash received to all cash spent. If cash spent exceeds cash received from known sources, then excess may represent income from unknown sources.

The expenditure method is a three-step technique that scrutinizes the suspect's financial transactions throughout the year.

Step 1: List all of the suspect's expenditures.
Step 2: Subtract all the known sources of funds, including all cash on hand at the beginning of the year.
Step 3: Analyze the difference to determine if the suspect has income from unknown sources.

The major advantage of the expenditure method is that it is easy for people, especially for judges and jurors, to understand.

The bank deposit method is a six-step method that is used when income is deposited in bank accounts and most of the expenses are paid by check. This method was approved by the courts almost 70 years ago. This income reconstruction technique has survived a multitude of legal challenges and has been used successfully to solve numerous financial crimes.

Step 1: Determine net deposits to all bank accounts
         Add: Deposits to all business, personal, and children bank accounts
         Less: Transfers, redeposits, transfer of funds and checks made payable to "CASH"
         Equals: Net deposits to all accounts
Step 2: Determine total outlays Add: All business expenses paid by either cash or check
         Add: All personal expenses paid by either cash or check
         Less: Depreciation, depletion, and bad debts
         Equals: Total outlays
Step 3: Determine net bank account disbursements net deposits in all bank accounts
         Plus: Beginning balance all accounts
         Less: Ending balance all accounts
         Equals: Net bank account disbursements
Step 4: Determine cash disbursements total outlays
         Less: Net bank disbursements
         Equals: Cash disbursements

Step 5: Determine total receipts net bank disbursements
         Plus: Cash disbursements
         Equals: Total receipts
Step 6: Identify funds from unknown sources total outlays
         Less: Net bank disbursements
         Equals: Cash disbursements
         Plus: Net deposits to all accounts
         Equals: Total receipts
         Less: Income from known sources
         Equals: Income from unknown sources

The net worth method is a five-step process that uses the changes in balance sheet items to estimate income.

To use this method of income reconstruction, the forensic accountant must calculate the suspect's net worth at both the beginning and end for each period under investigation. The goal is to identify differences between income from known sources and increases in net worth for each time period under investigation.

In 1954, the US Supreme Court ruled in the tax evasion case of M.L. Holland that the Internal Revenue Service's use of the net worth method to identify hidden income was sound. Since that ruling was issued in 1954, the courts have permitted the Internal Revenue Service to make an inference that the taxpayer's income was underreported when the net worth (after the necessary adjustments had been made) increase was greater than the reported taxable income.

Step 1: Calculate the suspect's net worth (current year) known assets
         Less: Known liabilities
         Equals: Net worth
Step 2: Calculate the suspect's net worth (prior year) known assets
         Less: Known liabilities
         Equals: Net worth
Step 3: Calculate year to year change in net worth current year
         Less: Net worth prior year
         Equals: Change in net worth
Step 4: Determine total outlay of funds change in net worth
         Add: Known/nondeductible living expenses and capital losses
         Equals: Total outlay of funds
Step 5: Determine income from unknown sources total outlay of funds
         Less: Income from known sources
         Equals: Income from unknown sources

Conclusion

The culmination of the forensic accountant's work takes place when he or she enters the courtroom and takes the stand as an expert witness. The forensic accountant, in his or her expert witness testimony, must be able to explain complex financial transactions related to specified unlawful acts or the computation and valuation of damages stemming from civil litigation in a manner that is understandable to the judge and members of the jury.

See also: **Investigations:** Counterfeit Currency; Identity Theft; Payment Cards.

Further Reading

Cali, J., 2011. The Forensic Accountant and Fraud Examiner's Tool Kit, second ed. CPA, CFF, CGMA, St. Louis, MO.

Cali, J., 2011. Forensic Accounting Reference Guide Indirect Methods for Reconstructing Income, second ed. CPA, CFF, CGMA, St. Louis, MO.

Crumbley, D.L., Heitger, L.E., Smith, G.S., 2007. Forensic and Investigative Accounting, fourth ed. CCH, Chicago, IL.

Federal Judicial Center, 2000. Reference Manual on Scientific Evidence, second ed. Federal Judicial Center, Washington, DC www.fjc.gov.

Peloubet, M.E., 1946. Forensic accounting: its place in today's economy. Journal of Accountancy 81 (6), 458–462.

Payment Cards

LR Rockwell, Forensic and Intelligence Services, LLC, Alexandria, VA, USA

This chapter is a revision of the previous edition article by R.N. Morris, volume 2, pp. 981–990, © 2000, Elsevier Ltd.

Glossary

Bank identification number (BIN) The first six digits of each payment card account number that numerically identify the issuing bank.

Card not present (CnP) transactions Transactions in which the physical payment card is not present.

Network-branded payment cards Payment cards that bear the logos of and function on the credit networks run by Visa, MasterCard, American Express, and Discover.

Payment cards A group of closely related financial products commonly known as credit cards, debit cards, and prepaid cards.

Payment Cards and Criminal Activity

Payment cards are often targets of fraud schemes, which are a type of white-collar crime. The victims of payment card fraud are primarily the banks that issue the cards, as these financial institutions typically absorb fraud losses on behalf of their customers (the cardholders). While individual cardholders are also victimized by this activity, the cardholders' losses are typically far lower than the losses suffered by affected financial institutions.

What Are Payment Cards?

The term payment cards refers to a group of closely related financial products commonly known as credit cards, debit cards, and prepaid cards. In this chapter, only network-branded payment cards—that is, those cards that bear the logos of and function on the credit networks run by Visa, MasterCard, American Express, and Discover—will be discussed. Other payment cards (such as store credit cards, store gift cards, transit cards, and cards that run exclusively on debit networks) will not be discussed, as they are less commonly used in fraud, money laundering, and terrorist financing schemes.

- Credit cards: These payment cards follow a "pay later" business model and allow cardholders to access a line of credit at point-of-sale locations. The financial obligations incurred during credit card transactions must be repaid, with varying rates of interest, as per the issuing bank's cardholder agreement. Each credit card is branded by and functions on a credit network.

- Debit cards: These payment cards allow customers to "pay now" for point-of-sale purchases by drawing funds directly from the cardholder's checking or savings account. Most debit cards are not only branded by and run on a credit network, but can also be branded by and run on one or more debit networks. Because debit cards were originally used almost exclusively at automated teller machines (ATMs) that functioned on the money access card (MAC) debit network, the cards are frequently called ATM or MAC cards.

- Prepaid cards: These payment cards follow a "pay before" business model by drawing value from funds provided to the prepaid card program or a designee in advance of the cardholder's purchases. Prepaid cards are ideal for unbanked or underbanked financial services customers who do not have or do not qualify for credit or debit cards, but nonetheless require access to payment cards in order to make online purchases, reserve and pay for hotel stays, and rent cars. The prepaid cards discussed in this chapter are not only branded by and run on a credit network, but can also be branded by and run on one or more debit networks. Prepaid cards are sometimes called stored value cards and are often incorrectly called prepaid credit cards or prepaid debit cards.

Network-branded payment cards have a specific visual appearance. Each card must bear the network brand (Visa, MasterCard, American Express, or Discover), which typically appears on the front of the card in the lower right-hand corner. On debit and prepaid cards issued in the United States, the word "DEBIT" must appear above the network brand. Payment cards must also identify and contain contact information for the issuing bank. (Visa and MasterCard cards are issued by a wide variety of financial institutions, American Express is issued by a select group of banks including American Express, and Discover cards are issued only by Discover.) Debit and prepaid cards that also function on debit networks carry the logos of the relevant debit networks on the back of the card. Each card also bears one or more holograms and a signature block for the cardholder's signature. Data are encoded on a magnetic stripe (found on the back of the card), a chip (visible on the front of the card), or both.

Payment cards provide access to payment card account information in digital and analog formats. Payment cards issued in the United States and Canada are typically magnetic stripe cards. These cards use a magnetic stripe, located lengthwise across the back of the card, to electronically store account information. The stripe contains the account number, the name of the authorized user, and the card's expiration date, as well as discretionary data, separators, and other computer characters. Payment cards issued in Europe, Australia, and some parts of Canada are typically smart cards. Smart cards use an EMV-compliant (for Europay, MasterCard, and Visa) chip embedded in the card to store account data and provide an additional layer of security. These cards, which are commonly known as chip-and-PIN (personal identification number) cards, require the cardholder to enter a four-digit PIN at point of sale. The PIN is verified by the chip and is considered to be more secure than signature-based verifications, which can be easily forged and are often not verified at point of sale. Analog account information is stored on the front of each card in the form of raised letters that identify the authorized user, the account number, and the card's expiration date. Magnetic stripe cards also display a card verification value (CVV) number, the location of which varies by credit network, which is used for additional security during certain types of transactions. A more detailed physical description of magnetic stripe payment cards will be provided later in this chapter.

It is not necessary to possess the physical payment card to access the value associated with the card. The physical cards are merely vehicles that allow merchants to efficiently access the account information necessary to process transactions; all that is needed to access the value associated with a payment card is the account information. When a payment card is present at a point-of-sale transaction, the card's magnetic stripe or EMV chip is typically read by hardware designed for this purpose. The transaction is not completed until the account information travels through the appropriate credit network and an authorization—stating that the cardholder has enough value associated with the card to cover the transaction—is obtained. In a transaction involving an EMV card, the user's PIN (or security number) must also be provided and verified. In some cases, merchants may conduct transactions using devices that allow them to capture an imprint of the card's raised letters on carbon

paper. In these situations, authorization is typically acquired after the act of the transaction. This method is often used if any of the infrastructures required to communicate with the credit network is unavailable. Transactions in which the physical payment card is not present are aptly known as card not present (CnP) transactions. These transactions, which typically occur online or telephonically, take place without reading or imprinting the payment card used. Depending on the level of security in these transactions, they may require as little information as the cardholder's name, the account number, the name of the credit network, and the card expiration date, all of which are visually available on the card. Many of these transactions also require the card's CVV number, which is also visually available on the card.

Network-branded payment cards share certain physical characteristics. Knowledge of these characteristics may be helpful to a document examiner. A discussion of pertinent physical characteristics follows.

Plastic

A payment card is a sandwich of plastic—specifically, polyvinyl chloride (PVC)—and is die cut from a larger sheet. The white core plastic contains the printed material, program and issuer names, logos, ownership information on the back of the card, etc., which is covered by an overlay for protection. Depending on the card manufacturer, the core may be a solid sheet of white PVC or two thin sheets of sandwiched white PVC. Not all PVC is the same. For example, two PVC plastic manufacturers may use the same compounds in their plastic, but the printability characteristics and whiteness can be different.

Overlay

The core is protected and sealed by a translucent overlay, the composition of which can vary among card programs. The ultraviolet (UV) characteristics of the overlay are critical because of UV fluorescent ink images printed on the core. The overlay must allow the UV light to pass through it and react with the UV-printed ink image so it will fluoresce.

Size

The nominal size of the card is 3.370 inch (85.60 mm) wide, 2.125 inch (53.98 mm) in height, 0.030 ± 0.003 inch (0.76 ± 0.076 mm) thick, and the corners are rounded with a radius of 0.125 ± 0.012 inch (3.175 ± 0.305 mm). Typically, the core is 0.027 inch (0.686 mm) thick and the thickness of each overlay sheet is 0.0015 inch (0.0381 mm). This size card is described as an ID-1 card by International Standards Organization (ISO) Standard 7810.

Ink

Both offset and screen printing techniques and inks are used to print cards. UV curing inks or drying agents are added to the ink to expedite the drying process. A color shift occurs in the ink during lamination.

Signature Panel

The signature panel appears on the back of the card. The signature panels are as varied as the card programs and issuers. Some are plain, offering little or no security; others are sensitive to solvents, or have complex printed backgrounds or other high-security features. The panel may contain the account number indent printed within it. The signature panel is attached to the individual card after it is die cut from the sheet.

The signature panel may be one of the following:

- a preprinted hot stamp panel attached to the card;
- several layers of screen-printed ink applied to the card, consisting of a base layer with printed information over it identifying the card program;
- special paper or printed material and inks sensitive to solvents that will react with the stripe if an attempt is made to alter the written signature; and
- a high-security printed panel with a variety of printing traps to prevent duplication by using a scanner.

Magnetic Stripe

The magnetic stripe is applied to the card as part of the lamination process and may contain two or three tracks of information. If the stripe width is approximately 7/16 inch (11.11 mm), three tracks of information can be encoded, and if the stripe width is approximately 5/16 inch (7.94 mm), two tracks of information can be encoded.

Encoding consists of a series of zeros and ones, a binary format, where each number, letter, or character is a unique combination of "0" and "1." ISO Standards 7811–2 and 7811–4 establish the number of bits per character. The standard also requires an odd parity for each character bit set, regardless of the character. Odd parity is achieved by adding a 1 or 0 to a bit set, insuring it has more ones than zeros. Other technologies, such as watermark and magnetic, are beyond the scope of this chapter.

The following is a brief description of the characteristics of a magnetic stripe data format based on ISO standards.

Track 1

This is known as the International Air Transportation Association track. The character configuration is seven bits per character, including the parity bit, and the maximum information content is 79 alphanumeric characters, which includes the start sentinel, end sentinel, and longitudinal redundancy check

Figure 1 The International Air Transportation Association track or track 1.

character (LRC) at a recording density of 210 bits/25.4 mm per inch. The card magnetic stripe data format for track 1 is illustrated in **Figure 1** and is described below. The encoded information is subdivided into fields read from right to left, as if the reader were looking at the back of the card.

- A: *Starting clocking bits*. Before data are encoded, a string of clocking bits is encoded and each bit equals zero. Clocking bits provide a timing mechanism for starting the reader synchronization process before the reader head gets to the start sentinel.
- B: *Start sentinel*. The start sentinel (%) is a defined number of bits informing the magnetic stripe reader that the following encoded information will be data.
- C: *Format code*. The format code consists of two digits telling the magnetic stripe reader how to interpret the data encoded in the data field. ISO established a standard of F2F (frequency–double frequency) for payment card magnetic stripes.
- D: *Primary account number (PAN)*. The PAN field is the first data field read by the magnetic stripe reader and can have a maximum of 19 digits. The card program and issuer establish the PAN and its format in the data field. The format of the PAN is not the same in this field for all tracks on all payment cards.
- E: *Field separator*. Following the PAN is a field separator ({). Its purpose is to notify the magnetic stripe reader that all encoded data called for in the preceding field are encoded and a different information field is about to begin. On track 1, it signals the end of a numeric data field, the PAN, and the beginning of an alpha data field, the name of the card owner. On tracks 2 and 3, it signals the end of the PAN and the beginning of the next, numeric data field. The PAN field has frequently fewer than the allotted 19 digits. If the encoded number is 16 digits, the issuer or program may still require the use of the full 19-digit field by leaving the unused digits blank.
- F: *Cardholder name*. The next field on track 1 is the cardholder name, and its allotted size is a maximum of 26 alpha characters. How much of this field is used and the order in which the name is encoded (last name first, first name second, initials third, etc.) are established by the card program and/or issuer.
- G: *Field separator*. A field separator follows the card owner's name. Its function is the same as described in "E" above.
- H: *Additional data and discretionary data field*. The next field is a numeric field containing encoded information, the

expiration date, service code, pin offset, "CVV," etc. Each card program and/or issuer can dictate the information encoded in this field. The ISO standard establishes the number of characters allotted to each specific entry; for example: the expiration date, four digits; the restriction or type, three digits; the pin offset or parameter—optional—five digits, etc. Some issuers require the expiration date and "member since" or "valid from" date. In this situation, the date field will be eight digits rather than four digits. To do this, the program obtains a variance from the standard. The card program and issuer establish what numeric information is encoded in this field, what it means, and how it is used.

- I: *End sentinel*. The end sentinel is encoded after the discretionary data field. The end sentinel informs the magnetic stripe reader that the data fields of the stripe are now encoded and no further data are encoded.
- J: *LRC*. The encoding of an F2F format for payment cards calls for an odd parity on each track. Each character has its own parity bit already; the LRC insures that the string of bits also has an odd parity.
- K: *Ending clocking bits*. After the LRC, there is another series of clocking bits to verify the timing of the synchronization process.

Track 2

This was developed by the American Bankers Association for the automation of financial transactions and its encoded information is numeric only, limited to 40 characters, including the start sentinel, end sentinel, and LRC. The character configuration is 5 bits per character, including the parity bit, at a recording density of 75 bits/25.4 mm per inch.

Track 2 is located below track 1 on the magnetic stripe (**Figure 2**). There is a small separation between the two encoded tracks to prevent magnetic field interference during encoding and reading. Since a detailed description of each field for track 1 is given above, and the explanation is the same for track 2, only the function for each field is given:

- A: clocking bits
- B: start sentinel—HEX-B
- C: PAN
- D: field separator—HEX-D
- E: additional data or discretionary data field
- F: end sentinel—HEX-F
- G: LRC
- H: ending clocking bits

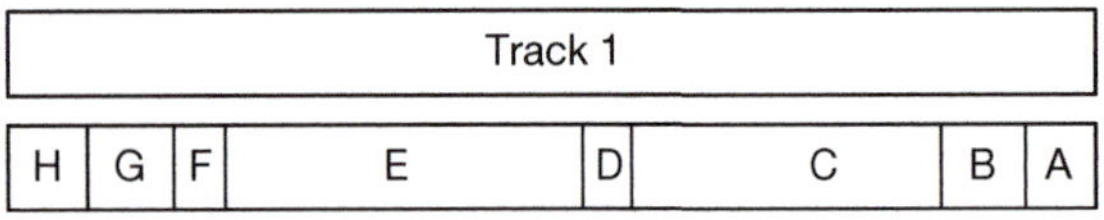

The hexadecimal (HEX) is a numeric system based on powers of 16. Valid hex digits range from 0 to 9 and A to F, where A is 10, B is 11, ..., F is 15. In the above, HEX-B would be the encoded binary equivalent of "11," and HEX-D is the binary equivalent of "13," etc.

Track 3

This was developed by the thrift industry and is a numeric data-only track with 107 characters, which includes the start sentinel, end sentinel, and LRC (**Figure 3**). The encoded density of track 3 is 210/25.4 mm bits per inch with 5 bits per character. The information encoded in the use and security data and additional data fields is updated after each transaction, allowing a card encoded on track 3 to be used in online and offline systems. Since a detailed description of each field for track 1 is given above, only the function will be given for each field in track 3, as they, too, overlap:

- A: clocking bits
- B: start sentinel—HEX-B
- C: format code
- D: PAN
- E: field separator—HEX-D
- F: use and security data, and additional data field
- G: end sentinel—HEX-F
- H: LRC
- I: ending clocking bits

Optical Variable Device

The optical variable device (OVD), or hologram, is hot stamped to the overlay on the front or back of the card. These image foils may be two or three dimensional (2D or 3D). Some companies have trademark names for their OVD products, such as Gyrogram, Optoseal, Kinegram, and Exelgram.

Embossing

Embossing is the production of the 3D characters that rise above the front of, and are recessed in the back of, the card. The ISO Standard 7811-1 mandates the type/style for the account number as a Farrington 7B OCR type. The remaining material, alphanumeric, on the card can be any type of design as long as its size conforms to that allocated by the ISO standard.

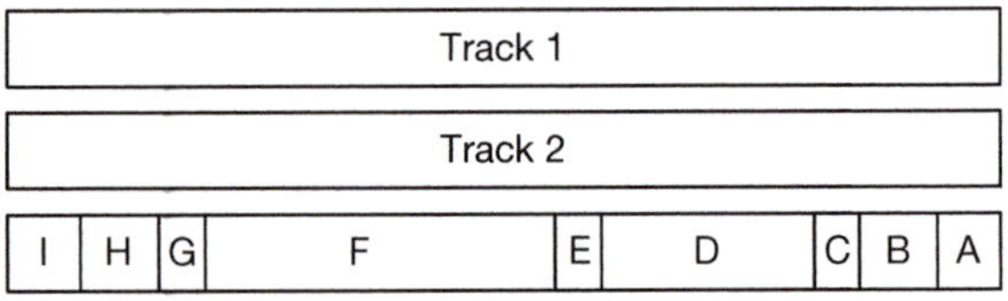

Figure 2   The American Bankers Association track or track 2.

Figure 3   Track 3.

Payment Card Fraud

Payment card fraud is, simply, the unauthorized or fraudulent use of a credit, debit, or prepaid card. Payment card fraud can be accomplished simply by stealing the victim's payment card account information, and does not necessarily involve counterfeiting or physically stealing the victim's payment card. According to a survey conducted in December 2010, credit and debit card fraud have affected 29% of worldwide financial service customers.

Fraud schemes involving payment cards typically involve the theft and subsequent use of payment card account information. In some cases, the account information is stolen by the same individual or criminal group that ultimately uses the card. It has also become common for an individual or group to steal payment card account information and then sell this information to other individuals or groups, who then use the payment card information to make purchases. Stolen account information that is available for sale can range from a single account number to a package containing the cardholder's name, the account number, the card's expiration date, the CVV number, the cardholder's social security number, the cardholder's address, and the cardholder's mother's maiden name, among other items. These bits of information can also be purchased individually.

Criminal groups and individuals can use many methods to steal payment card information and commit payment card fraud. Several examples of payment card fraud schemes are listed below:

- *Account takeover*: This occurs when an existing credit, debit, or prepaid card is intercepted by or redirected to a criminal. Criminals often accomplish this by changing the address on an account and then reporting the cardholder's real card stolen. Replacement cards are then mailed to the address provided by the criminal.
- *Application fraud*: This occurs when criminals use a stolen identity to obtain a payment card in someone else's name. This type of fraud is most frequently associated with credit cards.
- *Bank identification number (BIN) attack*: This fraud scheme occurs when thieves identify a functioning card's account number and expiration date, then change the last four digits of the account number using a number generator. This scheme is not likely to work if the issuing bank has used a random number generator to create account numbers instead of issuing sequential card numbers, all of which most likely would use the same expiration date. BIN refers to the first six digits of each account number that numerically identify the issuing bank.
- *Force post fraud*: In this scheme, thieves use a network-branded prepaid gift card with a zero-dollar balance to purchase items. Purchases under a specified dollar amount

at certain merchants are often force posted, meaning that the transactions are not authorized at the time of the sale. (This process significantly speeds up the point-of-sale process at merchants such as fast food vendors and coffee shops.) Because some of these cards—specifically, network-branded cards that are sold in present dollar amounts—are typically sold and used anonymously, it is often difficult or impossible to track the criminal(s).

- *Hacking*: This occurs when a hacker is able to extract payment card account information from network transactions or access databases of stored payment card information. Hacking into such data sources can allow thieves access to millions of credit card numbers at a time. In July 2005, hackers used this method to steal the information associated with 45.6 million payment cards from TJX-owned retail stores TJ Maxx, Marshalls, and HomeGoods.
- *Phishing*: These schemes, which rely on social engineering techniques, trick cardholders into voluntarily providing personal information, including but not limited to payment card information.
- *Skimming*: In these schemes, a device called a skimmer is used to capture payment card data from payment cards' magnetic stripes. Skimmers have been used to capture card data in restaurants, at gas pumps, ATMs, and countless other locations. Skimmers are frequently used by Eastern European organized criminal groups operating in the United States.

Of the fraud methods discussed above, hacking and skimming likely present the greatest danger to payment card customers and financial institutions. Although popular opinion holds that online transactions are the most likely to result in stolen payment card information, these two fraud methods make brick and mortar merchants even more vulnerable than online retailers: In 2007, the majority of stolen payment card information was taken from brick and mortar retailers and restaurants. According to an analysis conducted by VISA, 83% of payment card information breaches occurred at merchants processing fewer than 1 million payment card transactions each year, with most thefts at restaurants.

Once a criminal possesses payment card information, there are several ways the information can be used to make fraudulent purchases of goods and services. The payment card information can generally be used as it is to conduct CnP transactions through online retailers or brick and mortar merchants if transactions are conducted over the telephone. If the criminal is unable to purchase the desired items or services using a CnP transaction, the stolen payment card information will need to be encoded on a magnetic stripe card.

Stolen payment card information can be encoded on any card that uses a magnetic stripe, including expired or canceled network-branded credit, debit, and prepaid cards; prepaid gift cards; hotel room key cards; or any other card with a magnetic stripe. The goal of these cards is not to look and feel like legitimate payment cards, but simply to interact with standard magnetic stripe readers found at points of sale. All that is needed to convert existing magnetic stripe cards into cards carrying stolen payment card information is a magnetic stripe writer, which can be purchased online for between $200 and $500 USD. A local drug-trafficking gang operating in a US city used this technique to hide the proceeds of their crime from law enforcement agents. Members of the group purchased reloadable network-branded prepaid cards, which they used to launder the proceeds of illegal drug sales. To prevent law enforcement from recognizing and seizing the cards, the gang members used a magnetic stripe writer to encode the contents of each prepaid card's magnetic stripe onto a hotel room key card, effectively turning the hotel room key cards into duplicates of legitimate prepaid cards that contained laundered funds. Because each of the gang members wore several of the hotel key cards/prepaid cards on lanyards, law enforcement officials initially mistook the cards for mementos of gang members' sexual encounters.

Thieves can also create counterfeit cards, which is a significantly more complicated process. Card counterfeiters must create a passable, but not a perfect, product. To be successful, counterfeit cards need only to pass a cursory inspection at point of sale. Because there are hundreds of card programs and tens of thousands of issuers, legitimate cards have a wide variety of appearances, making identification of counterfeit cards very difficult. A discussion of the production of counterfeit cards follows.

Counterfeit Plastic

Counterfeiters fabricate counterfeit cards using the same general techniques and similar equipment as a genuine manufacturer; however, there are typically distinct differences between legitimate cards and counterfeit cards. For example, counterfeit cards may be fabricated as individual cards, not as part of a large sheet of cards. Furthermore, counterfeiters are not obliged to adhere to the same quality and physical standards of a genuine card manufacturer. The card manufacturer must make a product that will last for years; the counterfeiter's card need only last for a couple of passes.

Counterfeit Printing

Some of the processes used to print counterfeit cards are offset, rainbow, screen, hot stamping, typographic or letterpress, thermal mass transfer, thermal dye diffusion, computer printers using transparencies that are then bonded to a plastic card, laser engraving, etc. Frequently, multiple printing processes are used to make a single counterfeit card. Linkage of cards based on the printing process used to print each area of the card is critical. Counterfeiters can, and do, share negatives and computer image software. They can, and do, make changes in the images they acquire, or they use a different combination of images and different printing process to print those images.

Counterfeit Holograms

The OVDs on counterfeit payment cards can be any of the following types: 2D and 3D holograms, hot-stamped images on diffraction foils, computer-generated images using commercially available silver and gold paper, etc. Image analysis and linkage of OVDs is critical to establishing a common source of these devices.

Counterfeit Signature Panels

The type of signature panel, or the printing methods used to make it, is very important in linking cards. The method of printing the panel or applying it to the card must be determined.

Counterfeit Embossing

Linking cards by the embosser or punch and die used to emboss material on the card is very effective. Embossers and embossing have unique characteristics that make them identifiable. The examination of embosser type is a 3D study: In **Figure 4**, the "X" coordinate is the width of the typeface, the "Y" coordinate its height, and "Z" is the depth of the impression in the plastic.

Figures 5 and 6 show an embossing punch and die and describe each of its surfaces. Each surface shown can leave a record of its presence on the plastic overlay surface of the card. These defects, together with the class characteristics of the punch and dies, and the machine, collectively are what make embossing identifiable.

When the card is examined, it is important to observe the presence of any defects on the overlay of the card (**Figure 7**).

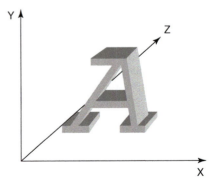

Figure 4　The examination of embosser type is a 3D study. See text for details.

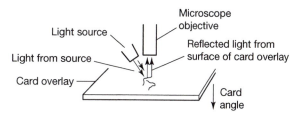

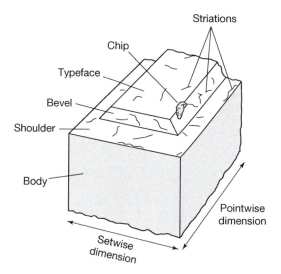

Figure 5 The parts of the embossing punch. This punch has a chip in the typeface and bevel, and striations on the typeface, bevel, and shoulder. These individual characteristic defects are recorded on the surface of the plastic during the embossing process.

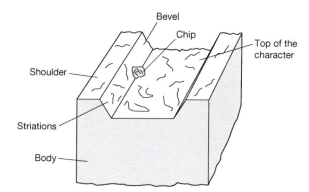

Figure 6 Defects (a chip and striations) in an embossing die.

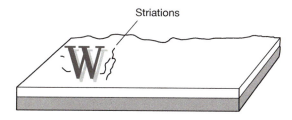

Figure 7 Surface defects on the overlay of an embossed "W." These defects may be found on the front and back of the card, either on or near the embossed character, or inside it.

Figure 8 The relative angle of the light source to the card and the microscope objective for an examination of the overlay surface.

Printed material on the core plastic, such as the text or planchettes added to the background printing, makes it difficult to focus on the top of the overlay. Since the overlay is only about 0.0015 inch (0.031 mm) thick, it is difficult to focus on its top surface and ignore the optical noise under it on the core. To illuminate the top surface properly, the angle of the light must be very small, as shown in **Figure 8**. The use of a stereomicroscope and fiber-optic light source is best for this examination. Varying the angle of the card and light to the objective in small increments allows the examiner to see the greatest overlay surface detail possible. The purpose of this examination is to reflect light off the surface of the overlay, because this is the surface where the striations and defects are located. The use of a comparison microscope is essential when comparing the striations on separate cards or a card with the punch and die from a suspected embossing machine.

Two other methods used to assist in the examination of the card overlay surface are the vacuum deposition of a thin, opaque, layer of metal over the surface of the card where the embossing is located. The evaporation of this thin film is applied to the card surface before the embosser examination begins. This thin metallic film covers the surface of the overlay where the embossing is located and acts as a first surface mirror, highlighting the defects. Because this thin film is opaque, the problem of optical noise caused by the background on the core is overcome. A second method is the use of Mikrosil casting material. While this is a good material to show chips and larger defects in the plastic overlay surface, it does not seem to work as well for very fine microscopic detail defects.

Not all of the embossed material on a card has to have been embossed on the same embosser or with punch and dies on the same machine.

Counterfeit Magnetic Stripes

In certain instances, it is possible to determine that two encoded magnetic stripes were encoded on different encoders, based on the characteristics of the encoder as recorded on the card's magnetic stripe. A special encoder analyzer is needed to perform this examination. It is not just what information is encoded on the stripe but an analysis of that encoding to determine something about the characteristics of the encoder that is used that is important. If the encoded information on the stripe of two different cards is the same, a linkage by encoded information is possible.

See also: **Documents:** Analytical Methods; Forgery/Counterfeits; Ink Analysis; **Investigations:** Counterfeit Currency; Forensic Accounting.

Further Reading

Ianacci, J., Morris, R.N., 1999. Access Device Fraud and Related Financial Crimes. CRC Press, London.

Levi, M., Handley, J., 2002. Criminal Justice and the Future of Credit Card Fraud. Institute for Public Policy Research, London.

Morris, R.N., 1998. Embosser type œ a 3-dimensional type examination. International Journal of Forensic Document Examiners 4 (2), 128–133.

van Renesse, R.L., 1998. Optical Document Security, second ed. Artech House, Boston, MA.

Counterfeit Goods

MM Houck, Consolidated Forensic Laboratory, Washington, DC, USA

Glossary

Authentic goods Goods produced by a manufacturer who purports to make them.
Counterfeit A product produced to be taken as the authentic product.

Fourth shift Products produced illicitly in the same factory that produces the authentic products, using inferior materials or even the same materials as the authentic.
Knockoff A product produced to be similar to an authentic product.

Introduction

Authentic goods are produced by a manufacturer who purports to make them. Authentic goods, or "authentics," can be either licit, legitimate products on the open market or illicit, illegal products sold clandestinely, such as heroin or methamphetamine. Authentic goods present opportunities to criminals and others to simulate them through unauthorized production methods for financial gain. These unauthorized products generally take one of two forms. The first is a *counterfeit*, a product produced to be taken as the authentic product, for example, a nonauthentic purse being sold *as a genuine* Hermes purse. Other forms of counterfeiting include forgeries (as in art, documents, or signatures), fakes (a real object that has been changed in some way to convince others that it has or has not been altered), and plagiarism. Note that an authentic illicit product can still be counterfeited: Tablets containing no active ingredients can be disingenuously sold as genuine but illegal ecstasy, for example. The second form is a *knockoff*, a product produced to be *similar to* an authentic product. For example, a purse designed to *look like* a Hermes purse but with obvious traits or characteristics missing and does not purport to be an actual Hermes purse.

Media traditionally portray counterfeits of luxury goods, such as expensive watches, purses, and shoes, as sold in flea market stalls or out of automobile trunks. In reality, luxury counterfeits compose only about 4% of the total counterfeit market. Any good or product can be counterfeited and no product is too inexpensive to escape notice (**Figure 1**). Pharmaceuticals, aircraft parts, shoe polish, foodstuffs, construction materials, military materiel, movies, alcohol, music, and toothpaste are all examples of genuine products that have been counterfeited. Each year, customs officials seize hundreds of thousands of counterfeit goods and destroy them (**Table 1**).

Figure 1 An authentic *Sharpie* brand pen next to a counterfeit "Shoupie" brand pen. Source: Creative Commons 3.0, open source.

Counterfeits, for many reasons, are not produced to the same standards as authentics. The main reason is economic: If a product can be manufactured illegally for a fraction of the final sales price and the risk of arrest, conviction, and imprisonment is minuscule, the financial reward appears to be worth the minor chance of punishment. The economics of counterfeit production are staggering. In one example, a group imported fake watch parts from China at a cost of $0.27 per watch. The group sold the assembled watches to wholesalers for between $12 and $20 per watch, a profit of between 4344% and 7307%. The wholesalers sold the watches to street dealers and vendors for $20 to $35 per watch, for a profit of between 67% and 115%. The watches were sold by the vendors at bargained prices with customers, sometimes selling as high as $250. Globally, this represents an enormous economic loss to

Table 1   Commodities seized by US Customs and Border Security, Department of Homeland Security, and their dollar value in US$ in 2009

Percentage of total	US-seized counterfeits	Millions US$
0.38	Footwear	45.7
0.12	Electronics	33.6
0.08	Wearing apparel	18.7
0.08	Handbags	15.4
0.06	Optical media	12.7
0.05	Computers	9.5
0.04	Cigarettes	8.6
0.04	Watches	7.8
0.04	Jewelry	6.8
0.02	Pharmaceuticals	5.7
0.08	All others	23.4

Source: United States Department of Homeland Security.

businesses, somewhere around $600 billion annually. By comparison, Walmart's market value is around $168 billion.

The lack of quality in counterfeits constitutes the greatest risk to the end user, as it results in product failures, lack of effectiveness or intended effect, or health risks and even death. For example, somewhere between 10 000 and 200 000 people die every year from counterfeit pharmaceuticals, either because of a lack of intended effect (the counterfeits did not have the purported active ingredients) or the counterfeit contained poisonous materials (such as road paint or concrete, which has been found in counterfeit pharmaceutical tablets). Many hundreds of thousands are hurt or suffer health problems due to counterfeits or knockoffs, as in the incidents of melamine found in Chinese milk (the melamine created a positive result on a necessary quality check), which led to sickness in 300 000 children in 1 year, or strontium in housing drywall made in China (2 to 10 times greater than US-made drywall).

Most counterfeit goods are produced in China and counterfeiting is thought to account for 8% of China's gross domestic product; 66% of US Customs seizures are of goods from China. Hong Kong (14%), Jordan (4%), and other countries (16%) are also top counterfeit producers. Some counterfeits are produced in illegal or makeshift factories, but others are produced in the same factory that produces the authentic products, using inferior materials or even the same materials as the authentic (so-called fourth shifts). Hazardous conditions are common in counterfeiting production sites, as is child labor, forced labor, and human rights abuses, not to mention low pay, usury, and violence.

Counterfeiting is not only a criminal and public health issue but also one of national security. The United States Department of Commerce released a study in 2010 that found counterfeit parts are involved in nearly 40% of the Pentagon's parts supply chain. The problem is on the increase, rising from 3868 incidents in 2005 to 9356 incidents in 2008. Instances of counterfeit body armor and automotive parts affect law enforcement officers and their safety as well. Between amateurish and professional efforts, it is generally estimated that every US $1 in $12 500 is counterfeit. The US $100 "supernote" counterfeit currency is thought to be an attempt by a foreign power to destabilize the US economy with extremely well-made counterfeit currency. This is not a new idea. The Nazi SS planned to destabilize the British economy during World War II with Operation Bernhard, by dumping £134 billion in excellent quality counterfeit pound notes over England; the plan was scrapped when it was found that the *Luftwaffe* did not have enough planes to deliver the bills.

Profits from all counterfeit goods fund organized crime or terrorism at some point. Drug cartels, terror groups, and triads generate enormous profits to fund other legal and illegal enterprises. Money laundering is key to the success of criminal enterprises and complicit consumers who knowingly purchase counterfeits through flea markets or bodegas unwittingly assist in the generation of legitimate funds for criminals and terrorists. Because of this, counterfeiting has been called a "consumer problem" and is seen as a matter of educating the public on the criminal issues surrounding the production of counterfeits and not merely the economic loss to luxury goods companies.

Counterfeits as an Insight to Classification

Evidence is initially categorized much as in the real world, that is, based on natural taxonomies (*Genus species*) or the taxonomy created by manufacturers. Forensic science adds to this taxonomy to further enhance or clarify the meaning of evidence relevant to the goals and procedures of the discipline. Forensic science's taxonomies are based on—but different from—production taxonomies. Manufacturing of economic goods, for example, creates its taxonomy through analytical methods. Set methods ensure a quality product fit for purpose and sale. The taxonomy is based on the markets involved, the orientation of the company production methods, and the supply web of raw and process materials. Explicit rules exist on categories created by manufacturers and recognized by consumers.

Forensic analytical methods create augmented taxonomies because the discipline uses different sets of methods and forensic scientists have different goals. Their taxonomies are based on manufactured traits, aftermarket qualities, intended end use, and also "as used" characteristics. The "as used" traits are those imparted to the item after purchase through either

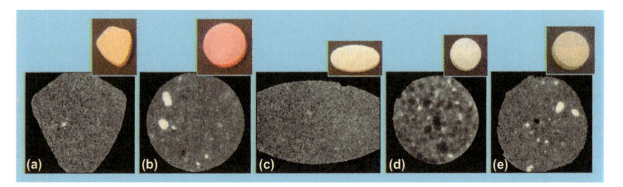

Figure 2 Simvastatin tablets imported via the Internet, color images and near-infrared spectroscopic images (active ingredients are seen as bright spots). (a) Merck, Inc. (manufacturer); (b) Mexico; (c) Thailand; (d) India; and (e) Brazil. Reproduced from Veronin, M., Youan, B.C., 2004. Magic bullet gone astray: Medications and the internet. Science 305, 481.

normal or criminal use. Forensic science has developed a set of rules through which the taxonomies are explicated. For example, forensic scientists are interested in the size, shape, and distribution of delustrants, microscopic grains of rutile titanium dioxide incorporated into a fiber to reduce its luster. The manufacturer has included delustrant in the fiber at a certain rate and percentage with no concern for shape or distribution (but size may be relevant). The forensic science taxonomy is based on manufacturing taxonomy but is extended by incidental characteristics that help us to distinguish otherwise similar objects.

Both production and forensic taxonomies lead to evidentiary significance because they break the world down into intelligible classes of objects related to criminal acts. Counterfeits also add to these taxonomies, although they are neither purely manufacturer nor forensic based. Implicit in the recognition of a counterfeit good, however, is the definition of the authentic product; unless an authentic definition exists, a product cannot be produced clandestinely. For example, **Figure 2** shows simvastatin tablets, in color and near-infrared spectroscopic images, imported via the Internet. The variations in composition, constituents, shape, and consistency would all lead to exclusion from the legitimate source (Merck, Inc., the actual manufacturer) in a comparison examination scheme. Although (b), (d), and (e) are round tablets, differences in their manufacturing parameters—essentially quality control—lead to distinct differences that are easily seen with a visual examination under near-infrared light (the bright spots are active ingredients). Therefore, the manufacturing supply chain and production processes provide the basis for differentiation. Moreover, it is possible to create a definition of the

authentic product from descriptions of the counterfeits (based on what is present, what is lacking, the qualities and quantities of these traits, and others). Manufacturers may be hesitant to provide product descriptions to forensic scientists because of perceived threats to "trade secrets." Knowledge of authentic products is important not only for examination of counterfeits but also to enhance the forensic scientist's understanding of the authentic products under study.

See also: **Documents:** Forgery/Counterfeits; **Investigations:** Counterfeit Currency.

Further Reading

Bender, K., 2006. Moneymakers: The Secret World of Banknote Printing. Wiley-VCH, New York.

Dutton, D., 1979. Artistic crimes. British Journal of Aesthetics 19, 302–341.

Eberlin, L., Haddad, R., Sarabia, N., et al., 2010. Instantaneous chemical profiles of banknotes by ambient mass spectrometry. Analyst 135, 2533–2539.

Gilreath, J., 1996. Guilt, innocence, faith, forensic science, and the Lincoln forgeries. History Cooperative 17 (1). www.historycooperative.org/journals/jala/17.1/gilreath.html.

Grossman, G., Shapiro, C., 2009. Foreign counterfeiting of status goods. Quarterly Journal of Economics 103 (1), 79–100.

Hopkins, D., 2003. Counterfeiting Exposed: Protecting Your Brand and Customers. Wiley, New York.

Kersten, J., 2009. The Art of Making Money: The Story of a Master Counterfeiter. Gotham, New York.

Naim, M., 2005. Illicit. Doubleday, New York.

Philips, T., 2005. Knockoff: The Deadly Trade in Counterfeits. Kogan Page Business Books, London.

Wilson, B., 2008. Swindled: The Dark History of Food Fraud, from Poisoned Candy to Counterfeit Coffee. Princeton University Press, Princeton, NJ.

Key Terms

Arson for profit, Authentics, Bank Secrecy Act, Banking fraud, Biometrics, Business interruption claims, Chip and PIN, Civil litigation disputes, Classification, Comparison, Counterfeiting, Counterfeits, Credit cards, Currency, Currency transaction reports, Cybercrime, Debit cards, Divorce, Economic damages, EMV, Fakes, Financial motive, FinCEN, Fishing, Forensic accounting, Forensic auditing, Fraud, Fraud examination, Fraud investigation, Fraud schemes, Hacking, Hidden assets, ID fraud, ID theft, Identity theft, Income from unknown sources, Income reconstruction, Inkjet technology, Insurance fraud, Intaglio, Knockoffs, Letterpress, Life care plans, Lost profit computations, Microscopy, Money laundering, Mortgage fraud, Offset lithography, Offshore accounts, Optically variable device, Patriot Act, Payment cards, Payment cards and criminal activity, Ponzi scheme, Prepaid cards, Qui tam actions, Screen printing, Securities fraud, Security, Security thread, Security watermark, Skimming, Smart cards, Specified unlawful acts, Spoofing, Stored value cards, Suspicious activity reports, White-collar crime.

Review Questions

1. What are most currencies made from?
2. What is a security fiber?
3. What is offset printing?
4. What is "bleaching" in relation to currency counterfeiting?
5. Why is it impossible to completely steal someone's identity?
6. What is the difference between identity theft and identity collision?
7. How many instances of identity theft are there in the United States each year?
8. What is "phishing" in relation to identity theft?
9. Why is DNA not suitable as a transactional biometric?
10. What is a "skimmer"?
11. Is forensic accounting a recently created profession? When was it first used?
12. List five or more crimes that may need the services of a forensic accountant to investigate.
13. How was the notorious gangster, Al Capone, brought to justice?
14. What are some of the sources of information a forensic accountant might use?
15. What is a pen register?
16. What is the cash T method?
17. What is a payment card? List at least three types. How can they be used for criminal activities?
18. List four methods of payment card fraud.
19. What is the estimated world trade in counterfeit goods?
20. What is the estimated number of deaths per year from counterfeit pharmaceuticals?

Discussion Questions

1. Think of a crime that involves two of the following: counterfeit currency, identity theft, payments cards, and counterfeit goods. What evidence would be needed to investigate the crime? What kinds of experts would be needed?
2. Is forensic accounting a forensic "science"? Why is it relevant to the broader perspective of forensic science in laboratories?
3. If forensic laboratories assist law enforcement agencies and if financial crimes are on the rise, should forensic "laboratories" include examiners in identity theft, financial crimes, and accounting? Why or why not?
4. Was it appropriate to convict a criminal like Al Capone on tax evasion when he was implicated in so many other crimes for which there was little evidence? Is that fair? Or is that a case of "he must be guilty of something"?
5. Why are counterfeit goods such a problem for society? How are they related to criminal financial activities? How could a forensic expert identify a counterfeit item?

Additional Readings

Durtschi, C., Rufus, R.J., 2017. Arson or accident: a forensic accounting case requiring critical thinking and expert communication. Issues in Accounting Education Teaching Notes 32 (1), 89–105.

Froud, D., 2016. The global implications of US EMV adoption. Computer Fraud & Security 2016 (2), 5–7.

Kennedy, J.P., Haberman, C.P., Wilson, J.M., 2016. Occupational pharmaceutical counterfeiting schemes: a crime scripts analysis. Victims & Offenders 1–19.

Murthy, S., Kurumathur, J., Reddy, B.R., November 2016. Design and Implementation of Paper Currency Recognition with Counterfeit Detection. In: Green Engineering and Technologies (IC-GET), 2016 Online International Conference on (pp. 1–6). IEEE.

Smith, A.F., Skrabalak, S.E., 2017. Metal nanomaterials for optical anti-counterfeit labels. Journal of Materials Chemistry C 5 (13), 3207–3215.

Spink, J., Moyer, D.C., Rip, M.R., 2016. Addressing the risk of product fraud: a case study of the Nigerian combating counterfeiting and sub-standard medicines initiatives. Journal of Forensic Science & Criminology 4 (1), 1.

Sullivan, B.A., Chan, F., Fenoff, R., Wilson, J.M., 2016. Assessing the developing knowledge-base of product counterfeiting: a content analysis of four decades of research. Trends in Organized Crime 1–32.

Section 6. Professional Issues

Whether they work in a laboratory or not, digital and document examiners face similar health and safety issues, and some additional ones other forensic specialists do not. For example, digital forensic experts may need to review hours of video of child pornography or hundreds of images from a hard drive of abuse or neglect. These all take a psychological toll on even the strongest person. Nevertheless, these are crimes, some of the most heinous in society, and need to be addressed.

For forensic experts outside the "traditional" laboratory, special attention needs to be paid to the health and safety factors they face. Without the surrounding institution to provide for them, these experts must go it alone to provide the necessary protections of life and health, physical and mental.

Crime Scene to Court

K Ramsey and E Burton, Greater Manchester Police Forensic Services Branch, Manchester, UK

Glossary

T1/2/3 CSI Skill tiers defined for crime scene investigation officers, with 1 being the most basic level of training (usually volume crime offenses only), 2 being the range of volume, serious and major crime investigations, and 3 being trained in crime scene management / the coordination of complex investigations.
CBRN Chemical, biological, radiation, and nuclear incidents.
L2 Level 2 investigations, specific skills required for covert operations, deployment and substitution of items, forensic markers, for example.
CCTV Closed circuit television (cameras or evidence from).

HTCU Hi-tech crime unit (examination of hardware/software/data/images from any system or device).
VSC/ESDA Video Spectral Comparison—the analysis of inks, primarily in fraudulent documents; Electrostatic Detection Analysis—the examination of (writing) indentations on paper.
NaBIS National Ballistic Intelligence Service (UK).
LCH Local Clearing House (firearms).
NCA National Crime Agency (UK).
CPS Crown Prosecution Service (UK).
NOS National Occupational Standards.
CPD Continuous Professional Development.

Introduction

A multitude of disciplines evolved within forensic science during the twentieth century, resulting in highly specialized fields of evidential opportunities to support criminal investigations. Many of the more traditional disciplines, for example, footwear analysis and blood pattern interpretation, now have well-established principles and methodologies that have been proven in a criminal justice context; developments in these areas are largely confined to technical support systems and information sharing through databases. The very rapid rate of development of DNA profiling techniques during the 1980s and 1990s led to the emergence of national and international DNA databases; however, the pace of change has now significantly reduced. Conversely, the end of the twentieth century and the early part of the twenty-first century have seen an explosion of new forensic evidence types that are less established in court—disciplines such as CCTV, mobile phone, computer analysis, and the use of digital images and social media are collectively referred to as e-forensics.

Owing to the highly specialized nature of each forensic discipline and the varied rate of evolution, forensic science effectively represents a composite of interrelated, and often distinct, opportunities to support criminal investigations.

Most current models of forensic service delivery, especially where part of a wider organization, for example, police forces and enforcement agencies, have arisen over time by bolting on additional elements and clustering together within related fields. If the current capability of forensic science were to be designed from scratch as an effective entity, it is certain that a more integrated, and hence effective, structure would be proposed.

In addition, there has been a professionalization of forensic science in the workplace and increasing requirements for regulation; as recently as the 1980s, crime scene investigation, for example, was widely undertaken by police officers and was largely restricted to recording/recovering visible evidence; this was used in a limited capacity to support that particular investigation without scope for wider intelligence development. Now, crime scene investigation is predominantly undertaken by specialist staff employed to exclusively undertake these duties.

To practice in a forensic discipline, specialized training, qualifications, and competency levels are required. The range of evidence types that have potential to support investigations has widened considerably. Some disciplines lend themselves to cross-skilling.

Public expectations of what forensic science can deliver have been heightened by highly popular mainstream television programs, both documentary and fictional. Often, the expectation of what can be delivered exceeds what is either possible or financially sensible. This leads to a requirement on service providers and users to make informed (evidential and financial) decisions regarding the best use of forensic evidence in support of investigations.

This article considers options to optimize the use of forensic evidence types recovered from crime scenes in the context of the different models available to criminal justice systems; the concept of integrated case management is outlined and discussed.

Task

To bring together all potential forensic evidential opportunities, holistically review their significance to the investigation, prioritize the progression of work, deliver the best evidence to the court for testing (complying with all continuity, integrity, and quality requirements), and ensure the best value for money when determining spend on forensic evidence.

Internationally, there are variable constraints and opportunities due both to the different criminal justice models and the commercial market situation at state/regional and country levels.

Models

1. All forensic evidence sourced within a law enforcement agency, for example, a police laboratory
2. All forensic evidence provided by external specialists contracted to a law enforcement agency
3. Composite of (1) and (2)

Forensic Strategies

The recovery of evidence from the crime scene is only the start of the forensic process. Once the evidence has been collected, packaged, and preserved, it needs to be analyzed in order to provide meaningful information to the investigation and subsequently the courts.

Forensic examinations are carried out in order to implicate or eliminate individuals and also in order to establish what has occurred during the commission of an offense or incident.

Deciding what analysis is required can be a complex process. Some of the issues for consideration include the following:

- Is it necessary to examine all the evidence that is recovered?
- Should every possible test be carried out?

In an ideal world, it would be preferable to carry out every possible analysis; however, in reality, it is likely that this will be neither practicable nor financially viable. In addition, carrying out every possible analysis would overload forensic laboratories.

When making decisions about what forensic analysis should be carried out, it is vitally important that consideration is given to both the potential prosecution and defense cases. An impartial approach must be taken to assessing examination requirements. It is often not necessary to carry out an examination of every item of evidence recovered, but examinations should be directed to where value could potentially be added to an investigation.

A forensic strategy should be developed around every case where forensic evidence plays a part and may relate to an overall case or to an individual item of evidence. A forensic strategy should be developed in a holistic manner taking into account all potential evidence types and should direct and coordinate the forensic examinations/analyses that are required.

Forensic strategies can be developed in different ways by one or more of the following:

- Investigating officer
- Crime scene investigator (CSI) or Crime scene manager
- Forensic scientist/forensic specialist
- Forensic submissions officer (this is a role that can be variably named; this role relates to an informed individual within a police force or law enforcement agency who uses knowledge and expertise to advise on forensic analysis and who has decision-making authority and control of the budgetary spend; may also be known as forensic advisor, scientific support manager, etc.)
- Legal representative
- Pathologist

Forensic strategies are generally initially developed and applied by individuals involved in the prosecution aspects of a crime. Although this is the case, it is vitally important that a balanced and unbiased approach is taken to the development of a strategy and consideration given to information that may support the defense case as well as the prosecution case. Examinations that are likely to add value or provide information to an investigation (irrespective of whether it will support or weaken the prosecution case) should be carried out and all results must be disclosed to the defense team. Defense should also be given the opportunity to carry out any review of strategies, examination processes, and/or results that they require and be provided with access to any items of evidence that they want to examine themselves in order to build the defense case.

In order to develop the forensic strategy and make appropriate decisions about which forensic examinations will be of value to the investigation, the following are necessary:

- To be able to gather as much information as possible about the circumstances of the case
  - circumstances of evidence recovery
  - accounts given by victim(s), witnesses, suspect(s), etc.
- To have an understanding and knowledge of forensic science and its application to investigations

A forensic strategy meeting is a useful way of ensuring that all relevant parties are aware of the full circumstances of the case and enables a "multiagency" discussion about the processing of all exhibits to optimize evidential potential in a comprehensive and coordinated manner.

It can often be the case that police officers do not have a full understanding or knowledge of forensic science, likewise forensic scientists historically have had a relatively poor understanding of police and investigative processes; this can lead to miscommunication and confusion in relation to the application of forensic science to meet investigative needs. A joint approach to the development of forensic strategies helps to improve the communication and understanding on a case-by-case basis.

A formal forensic strategy meeting is often required only in more serious cases; however, the general approach can be applied to any investigation. Even in the most simple of cases, it is often beneficial for discussions to take place between the investigating officer, the CSI, the forensic advisor/budget holder/decision maker, and the prosecutor. Alternatively, generic strategies can be implemented, for example, for a particular crime type or *modus operandi*.

When making an assessment regarding the potential examination of a particular item and the development of a forensic strategy, the requirements of the investigation are the primary concern and consideration should be given to the following issues:

- The type and nature of the item/exhibit
- The context of the item
  - Exactly where and when it was recovered
  - Condition of the item, that is, wet, damaged, etc.
- The integrity of the item
  - Has it been appropriately recovered, handled, packaged, and preserved?
  - Is the security and continuity of the item intact?
- The potential evidence that may be obtained from the item, for example, DNA, fingerprints, fibers, footwear marks
- The information these evidence types may provide to the investigation
- Whether this potential information is likely to add value to the investigation
  - Is it possible that new information will be provided?
  - Is it possible that an account given by a witness, victim, or suspect will be supported or refuted?
  - Will the information help to establish what has occurred?
- Whether there is a conflict between potential evidence types, and if so, which evidence type will be of most value under the circumstances
  - For example, swabbing/taping for DNA may damage fingerprints, but where the DNA is likely to be at low levels and requires specialized low-template DNA analysis, the presence of DNA may not necessarily prove contact with an item, whereas fingerprints will always prove that contact has occurred
- The chances of success, that is, obtaining a result/information of value to the investigation (this may be inclusive or exclusive)

Much work has historically been completed in relation to developing and understanding the success rates relating to DNA profiling; however, relatively little work has been undertaken to fully understand the success rates associated with other forensic evidence. This is largely due to the fact that other evidence types, such as fibers, gunshot residue, and footwear marks, are generally more complex to interpret than DNA. In relation to DNA profiling, success rates are generally based on the chances of obtaining a DNA profile; however, with the other evidence types, the value of the outcome is very much dependent on the circumstances of the investigation. For example, when searching an item of clothing taken from a suspect for glass, the absence of glass or the presence of glass could both be of value to the investigation depending on the circumstances. The presence of glass on the clothing that matches control sample(s) from the crime scene is only of value if its presence cannot be accounted for in any legitimate way; conversely, the absence of glass on the item of clothing may lead to a conclusion that the suspect was not involved in the offense, depending on the circumstances of the offense and arrest.

In addition to being able to understand and evaluate the chances of being able to obtain a meaningful result, it is also vital that the value of the overall contribution to the entire case is understood. This involves being able to understand the value and contribution of the forensic examination to the detection of the offense as well as the outcome of the court process. This is an even more difficult issue to evaluate and understand than the chances of being able to obtain a forensic test result.

Because the value of forensic evidence is so dependent on the individual case circumstances, decisions about examinations must be made on an individual case basis. There have been recent developments in some agencies/forces to better understand the chances of success of different types of forensic evidence and the value to investigations; this will help to better inform decisions about evidential potential and examination viability as well as assisting to achieve value for money. This approach is best described as *forensic effectiveness*.

The forensic strategy should also take into account the timescales associated with the investigative process and the criminal justice system, and it should be ensured that forensic analysis can meet the requirements of the criminal justice process, including court dates and any requirements to disclose appropriate information to the defense team(s).

Each police force/law enforcement agency will have its own approach to the submission of exhibits for forensic examination/analysis; irrespective of whether the analysis is carried out in an internal police laboratory, external commercial company, or government owned laboratory, these approaches can be applied to all examinations and all evidence types.

These approaches help to ensure that decisions are made based on scientific knowledge, viability, and evidential value taking into account all aspects of the investigation. They will help to ensure that the best evidence is obtained while considering value for money and that it can be applied to any investigation irrespective of the seriousness of the offense or the scale of the investigation.

Integrated Case Management

The concept and use of forensic strategies in directing investigations is not new, but is often limited by the evolved structure of forensic disciplines within investigative agencies. Classically, DNA and fingerprint evidence from volume crimes will be independently submitted at the same time by different routes and this often results in wasted effort/spends and duplicated results. The development and use of forensic intelligence has been variable. Emerging thinking includes organizational redesign of forensics to better integrate with related functions such as intelligence collection, targeted deployment of resources, and prioritized forensic submissions.

The concept of integrated case management draws together informed operational deployment (e.g., of crime scene investigators) followed by a more holistic approach to submissions for testing. The strategy takes greater account of supporting intelligence and desired outcomes. Regular reviews and trigger points are included for the staged submission of potential evidence, and communication with investigators is enhanced so allowing for a more responsive and directed investigation.

Ultimately, the production of *intelligent identifications* can be better achieved by having an integrated process that links the enforcement priorities, available resources, potential forensic evidence, intelligence, and prosecutor requirements; this model provides flexibility to respond to changing demands and gives an increased likelihood of efficient and effective spend on forensic support to investigations. There is no single way to achieve this, but an illustration of how to rethink some of the traditional silo-based forensic disciplines is provided in **Figure 1**.

Summary

The single biggest challenge to the forensic science community during the twenty-first century is to modernize delivery of integrated services in support of investigations. This must

- build on the previous development of each discipline;
- accommodate the new and emerging technological disciplines;
- meet the regulatory requirements;
- reflect the changing workforce and skills; and
- deliver the best evidence to courts in support of investigations.

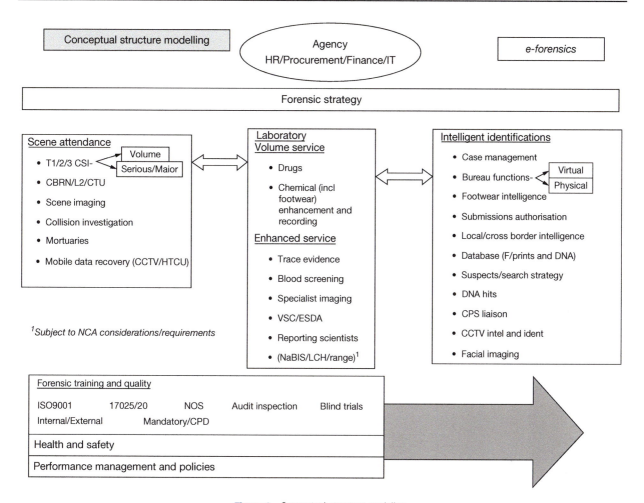

Figure 1 Conceptual structure modeling.

See also: **Foundations:** Forensic Intelligence; History of Forensic Sciences; Principles of Forensic Science.

Further Reading

Faigman, et al., 2006. Modern Scientific Evidence: The Law and Science of Expert Testimony.

Fisher, B.A.J., Fisher, D.R., 2012. Techniques of Crime Scene Investigation, eighth ed. CRC, Boca Raton, FL.

Houck, M., Crispino, F., McAdam, T., 2013. The Science of Crime Scenes. Elsevier.

Innocence Project, 2011. http://www.innocenceproject.org/Content/Facts_on_PostConviction_DNA_Exonerations.php.

Kirk, P.L., 1974. In: Thornton, J.L. (Ed.), Crime Investigation, second ed. Wiley, New York. (1985 reprint edn. Malabar, FL: Krieger Publishing Company).

NAS, 2009. Strengthening Forensic Science in the United States: A Path Forward. NAS Report: Committee on Identifying the Needs of the Forensic Sciences Community. National Academies Press, Washington, DC.

White, P., 2010. Crime Scene to Court: The Essentials of Forensic Science. Royal Society of Chemistry, Cambridge, ISBN 978-1-84755-882-4.

Forensic Laboratory Reports

J Epstein, Widener University School of Law, Wilmington, DE, USA

There is no precise formula, dictated by law or science, as to what a forensic laboratory report must contain when it reports test results or analysis outcomes. Its content may be determined by the individual examiner's predilections, internal laboratory policy, the law of the jurisdiction, accreditation organization standards, or the reason(s) for its production. What can be said with certainty is that by understanding the current criticism of the practice of producing forensic laboratory reports and trends in standards for reports, and by considering the use to which the report may be put in the court process and the legal and ethical commands regarding reporting and, more generally, the duties of the forensic scientist, a model for forensic laboratory reports can be identified.

Before discussing these factors, it bears mention that the term "report" itself lacks clarity, as it may refer to the complete case file documenting the examination or just to the compilation of results. For this chapter, the term "report" denotes the latter—the document prepared for the consumer (the investigator, counsel, or court official who directed that the examination and testing be conducted). Even this report may vary in degree of detail, as there can be the summary report advising the requesting party of the outcome; a more formal report prepared for disclosure to the court or opposing counsel as part of pretrial discovery; an amplification of the initial discovery-generated report when it is determined that the expert will in fact testify; and a report that will be presented in lieu of actual testimony. Additional documentation may include an administrative or dispositional report detailing the receipt or return of the item(s) sent for analysis.

What must also be acknowledged is that the expert's role in the adjudicative process is in some ways defined by whether the system is adversarial, with the expert being called by the party seeking to establish a point, as in the United States; or inquisitorial/"common law," where the expert is a court witness, presumed to be neutral, and without allegiance to a particular party, as in France, Belgium, and Germany. These demarcations are not always adhered to, as American law permits a trial judge to appoint and take testimony from a "court" expert under Federal Rule of Evidence 706, and in some cases involving offenses of fraud and falsification, France permits competing experts. These differing roles, however, do not alter the necessary components of a forensic laboratory report (and, as is detailed below), both ethical and legal considerations as well as a commitment to the role of science may require the report to be neutral and to acknowledge any limitations and/or weaknesses.

Contents of a Report—A "Science" Standard

At least in the United States, there has been substantial criticism of forensic laboratory reporting. This is found in *Strengthening Forensic Science: A Path Forward*, the 2009 report of the National Research Council of the National Academy of Sciences. After reporting that forensic laboratory reports lack precise terminology, it concluded that most laboratory reports do not meet the standard it proposed:

> As a general matter, laboratory reports generated as the result of a scientific analysis should be complete and thorough. They should describe, at a minimum, methods and materials, procedures, results, and conclusions, and they should identify, as appropriate, the sources of uncertainty in the procedures and conclusions along with estimates of their scale (to indicate the level of confidence in the results). Although it is not appropriate and practicable to provide as much detail as might be expected in a research paper, sufficient content should be provided to allow the nonscientist reader to understand what has been done and permit informed and unbiased scrutiny of the conclusion.

This criticism does not stand in isolation. A 2011 British court decision also expressed concern over the sufficiency of detail and documentation in a forensic (latent print) prosecution. After noting the failure of the examiner to contemporaneously record "detailed notes of his examination and the reasons for his conclusions[,]" the court added that [t]he quality of the reports provided by the Nottinghamshire Fingerprint Bureau for the trial reflected standards that existed in other areas of forensic science some years ago, and not the vastly improved standards expected in contemporary forensic science.

The U.S. National Research Council (NRC) standard is more detailed than that of various forensic organizations. American Society of Crime Laboratory Directors/Laboratory Accreditation Board (ASCLD/LAB), for example, requires that only written reports be generated for "all analytical work" and must contain conclusions and opinions and a clear communication of "the significance of associations made...."

Other standards address the need for full documentation, but do not distinguish between a laboratory's bench notes and the final product. For example, International Organization for Standardization's ISO/IEC Standard 5.10.5 requires that "the laboratory shall document the basis upon which the opinions and interpretations have been made" without specifying where that information is to be recorded. Similar language is used for ballistics reports, as recommended by the Scientific Working Group on firearms (SWGGUN) requiring that "[w]hen opinions and interpretations are included, the laboratory shall document the basis upon which the opinions and interpretations have been made. Opinions and interpretations shall be clearly marked as such in the test report."

Yet, the more detailed mandate urged by the NRC Report is not unique. Scholars and agencies have articulated similar or at least substantial standards. A publication of *The Royal Society of Chemistry* in 2004 suggested the following information as appropriate for inclusion in an expert report:

- a summary of the event to contextualize the scientific test(s);
- an outline of the scientific work conducted;
- a listing of items examined;
- description of the work performed;
- a statement interpreting the findings; and
- an overall conclusion.

The Royal Society of Chemistry (RSC) text also urges that the report identify the assistants in the testing and the role each played and include appendices with tables or similar displays of test results.

For DNA analysis, the Federal Bureau of Investigation's standards for DNA laboratories require reports to include a description of the evidence examined and of the technology, results, and/or conclusions, and a "quantitative or qualitative interpretive statement."

One final scientific issue regarding the contents of a report is the concern over bias. Research has shown that information received by the analyst might affect his/her judgment, as when the examiner receives domain-irrelevant information such as the fact that the suspect whose fingerprints are being examined "confessed to the crime" or when the verification is not "blind." Documentation of such information in a laboratory report (or the bench notes) is one responsive action, as is an internal laboratory policy to reduce analyst or verifier exposure to potentially biasing information.

Contents of Report: Legal Standards

That which science requires is to some extent mirrored in legal requirements for expert reports. These vary from nation to nation, and within nations, when states or regions have their own authority to legislate criminal practice.

In the United Kingdom, Rule 33.3, Criminal Procedure Rules 2010 mandates contents of a full report, that is, one for submission in court, as follows:

1. the findings on which they have relied in making the report or statement;
2. details of which of the findings stated in the report or statement are within their own knowledge, which were obtained as a result of examinations, measurements, tests,

etc., carried out by another person and whether or not those examinations, measurements, tests, etc., were carried out under the expert's supervision;
3. the identity, qualifications, relevant experience, and any certification of the person who carried out the examination, measurement, test, etc.;
4. details of any statements of fact, literature, or other information on which they have relied, either to identify the examination or test requirements, or which are material to the opinions expressed in the report or statement or on which those opinions are based;
5. a summary of the conclusions and opinions reached and a rationale for these;
6. a statement that if any of the information on which their conclusions or opinions are based changes then the conclusions or opinions will have to be reviewed;
7. where there is a range of opinion on the matters dealt with in the report or statement, a summary of the range of opinion, and reasons for the expert's own opinion;
8. any information that may cast doubt on their interpretation or opinion; and
9. if the expert is not able to give an opinion without qualification, what the qualification is.

Much less specific is the legislated mandate for federal criminal prosecutions in the United States. Under Federal Rule of Criminal Procedure 16, the Government must permit the defense to inspect and to copy or photograph the results or reports of any scientific test or experiment and must produce before trial a written summary of any proposed expert testimony that describes the witness's opinions, the bases and reasons for those opinions, and the witness's qualifications. Defense counsel in criminal cases has a reciprocal disclosure requirement. Despite the seeming generality of these terms, American courts have at times interpreted them to require some greater detail in the reports, such as underlying documentation.

In the United States, an additional requirement derived from the Constitution's guarantee of Due Process of Law may affect what must be included in a laboratory report issued by a police or other government agency. The prosecution must disclose information that is "favorable to the accused" and "material either to guilt or to punishment" as well as "evidence that the defense might have used to impeach the Government's witnesses by showing bias or interest." This extends to "evidence affecting credibility[.]" This information is generally denominated "Brady material."

The applicability of these rules to official (police or state) laboratories is settled. The US Supreme Court has held that the disclosure obligation extends to police agencies working with the prosecution, and this has been extended to forensic examiners. Hence, in a report or some other communication, a forensic examiner in government employ must ensure that "Brady material" is disclosed.

What remains to be defined are the terms "exculpatory" or "impeachment" information. The core of each is easily described. Evidence is "exculpatory" if it tends to reduce the degree of guilt or question proof of culpability; "impeachment" information is proof of a bias or interest, or otherwise information that could be used to contradict or attack the credibility of the analyst or report. This type of disclosure parallels that of forensic laboratory reports imposed by the United Kingdom's evidence code. The code requires inclusion in the report of "a summary of the range of opinion and reasons for the expert's own opinion; any information that may cast doubt on their interpretation or opinion; and if the expert is not able to give an opinion without qualification, what the qualification is."

Reports: Stand-Alone Evidence or Support for a Testifying Expert

Whether a laboratory report may stand on its own as evidence in a trial, or instead must be accompanied by testimony of the forensic analyst, is a function of the law of the jurisdiction in which the case is tried. In the United States, a prosecution expert's report may not be admitted on its own, as this is deemed to violate the defendant's right to confront adverse witnesses. The Supreme Court in Melendez-Diaz versus Massachusetts held that a certificate of analysis fell within the core class of testimonial statements because it was a solemn "declaration or affirmation made for the purpose of establishing or proving some fact." In the 2011 follow-up of the Melendez-Diaz decision, the Court further held that another lab analyst may not come in to testify to the report's contents, at least where the other analyst neither supervised nor observed the initial testing. (This applies only to prosecution expert reports, as in the United States only the defendant has a guarantee of the right to confront witnesses. Admissibility of a defense forensic report without examiner testimony would be determined by the state's rules of evidence, but is generally unheard of.)

At the same time, the confrontation right does not mean that the analyst must testify. A state may create a notice and demand statute under which the prosecution notifies the defendant of its intent to use an analyst's report as evidence at trial, after which the defendant has a specified period of time in which to demand the expert's live testimony. A defendant's failure to "demand" waives the need for the analyst's presence and allows the use of the report. As well, an accused may always agree to stipulate to the report's content, eliminating the need for any live testimony.

The Melendez-Diaz approach is not followed uniformly on an international basis. Canada permits proof by means of an expert report, without live testimony, where the proponent of the report has provided it to the opposing party and the trial court recognizes the author as a legitimate expert. The court retains discretion to mandate the expert's appearance for cross-examination. Australia's Evidence Act of 1995 similarly authorizes expert proof by certificate, but the opposing party may require the offering side to "call the person who signed the certificate to give evidence." In the United Kingdom, expert reports are themselves admissible as evidence, subject to the judge's discretion in requiring the analyst or examiner to appear.

Ethical Considerations and Forensic Reports

The decision of what to include in a forensic laboratory report, beyond that required by law or by science, may be informed by ethical considerations. Forensics organizations often have ethical codes, but they may be silent as to the particulars of report writing. Illustrative is the Code of the American Board of Criminalistics, which only asserts general obligations such as "[e]nsure that a full and complete disclosure of the findings is made to the submitting agency[.]" Other codes may not mention reporting at all but instead address only the delivery of information without distinguishing between the written report and a courtroom presentation of evidence. An exception is that of the Australian and New Zealand Forensic Science Society, Inc., which requires that a report be nonpartisan when results are ambiguous. "Where test results or conclusions are capable of being interpreted to the advantage of either side in a legal proceeding, each result or conclusion should be given weight according to its merit."

Ethical considerations may also be imposed by law. In the United Kingdom, the expert is deemed to hold only one allegiance, that to the court, regardless of the party who retained the individual. Specific ethical obligations are imposed for written reports. First, where there is a range of opinion, the expert must summarize the various positions. Second, if the opinion rendered cannot be given without qualification, the expert must disclose that and state the qualifying aspects or concerns.

Conclusion

Within and across nations, there is no clear standard for forensic reports intended for court use, except where prescribed by law. What should be manifest is that the more detailed the report, and thus the more it is capable of rigorous assessment by an independent expert evaluator, the more credibility will be attributed to both the results and the examiner.

See also: **Legal:** History of the Law's Reception of Forensic Science; Legal Aspects of Forensic Science; Legal Systems: Adversarial and Inquisitorial; **Management/Quality in Forensic Science:** *Sequential Unmasking:* Minimizing Observer Effects in Forensic Science; **Professional:** Ethics.

Further Reading

Codes of Practice and Conduct for Forensic Science Providers and Practitioners in the Criminal Justice System 44–45 (United Kingdom). http://www.homeoffice.gov.uk/publications/police/forensic-science-regulator1/quality-standards-codes-practice?view=Binary.

Dror, I.E., Cole, S., 2010. The vision in 'blind' justice: expert perception, judgment and visual cognition in forensic pattern recognition. Psychonomic Bulletin & Review 17 (2), 161–167.

Dror, I.E., Rosenthal, R., 2008. Meta-analytically quantifying the reliability and bias-ability of forensic experts. Journal of Forensic Sciences 53 (4), 900–903.

National Research Council, 2009. Strengthening Forensic Science in the United States: A Path Forward. National Academies Press, Washington, DC. http://www.ncjrs.gov/pdffiles1/nij/grants/228091.pdf.

Quality Assurance Standards for Forensic DNA Testing Laboratories, Standard 11.2. http://www.cstl.nist.gov/strbase/QAS/Final-FBI-Director-Forensic-Standards.pdf.

Reviewing Historical Practices of Forensic Science Laboratories (29 September 2010). http://www.ascld.org/.

Rothwell, T., 2004. Presentation of expert forensic evidence. In: White, P. (Ed.), Crime Scene to Court: The Essentials of Forensic Science, second ed. RSC, Cambridge, pp. 430–432 (Chapter 15).

Spencer, J.R., 2002. Evidence. European Criminal Procedures. Cambridge University Press, New York, pp. 632–635 (Chapter 15).

Relevant Websites

http://www.criminalistics.com/ethics.cfm—American Board of Criminalistics, Rules of Professional Conduct.

http://www.forensicdna.com/Media/Bias_FS.htm—An extended list of articles on the issue of bias in forensic examinations.

http://www.afte.org/AssociationInfo/a_codeofethics.htm—Association of Firearms and Toolmarks Examiners, AFTE Code of Ethics.

http://www.anzfss.org.au/code_of_ethics.htm—Australian and New Zealand Forensic Science Society.

http://www.iso.org/iso/home.html—International Organization for Standardization.

http://www.swggun.org/swg/index.php?option=com_content&view=article&id=25:transition-from-ascldlab-legacy-to-isoiec-17025&catid=10:guidelines-adopted&Itemid=6—SWGGUN, Transition from ASCLD/LAB Legacy to ISO/IEC 17025.

http://www.ascld.org/—The American Society of Crime Laboratory Directors.

http://www.ascld-lab.org/—The American Society of Crime Laboratory Directors Laboratory Accreditation Board.

http://webarchive.nationalarchives.gov.uk/; http://www.justice.gov.uk/criminal/procrules_fin/contents/rules/part_33.htm—United Kingdom, Criminal Procedure Rules 2010.

Health and Safety

N Scudder and B Saw, Australian Federal Police, Canberra, ACT, Australia

Glossary

Clandestine laboratory ("Clan Labs") Setting up of equipment or supplies for the manufacture of illegal compounds such as drugs or explosives.

Confined space An enclosed or partially enclosed space that is not intended or designed primarily for human occupancy, within which there is a risk of one or more of the following: (1) an oxygen concentration outside the safe oxygen range; (2) a concentration of airborne contaminant that may cause impairment, loss of consciousness, or asphyxiation; (3) a concentration of flammable airborne contaminant that may cause injury from fire or explosion; (4) engulfment in a stored free-flowing solid or a rising level of liquid that may cause suffocation or drowning.

Dynamic risk management The continuous assessment of risk in the rapidly changing circumstances of an

operational incident, in order to implement the control measures necessary to ensure an acceptable level of safety.

Hazard The potential for a substance to cause adverse effects.

Hierarchy of control measures Ranking of measures taken to prevent or reduce hazard exposure according to effectiveness, from the most effective measures that eliminate hazards to the least effective, which achieve only limited protection.

OHS policy A policy document indicating an organization's commitment to OHS, its intentions, objectives, and priorities and identifying roles and responsibilities.

Risk The likelihood of injury or illness arising from exposure to any hazard(s) and the magnitude of the adverse effect.

Occupational Health and Safety Policy

The legislation in many countries places the onus of responsibility on employers to provide a healthy and safe working environment under occupational health and safety (OHS) legislation and common law. Employers should ensure that all managers, supervisors, and staff are aware of their OHS responsibilities. Management leadership can positively influence OHS outcomes for an organization.

Workplace health and safety is an ongoing process. Subject to the legislative requirements of each jurisdiction, in most instances a documented OHS policy is required. The development of such a policy requires the commitment of both staff and management. Once commitment has been achieved, the OHS policy should be developed with involvement from all stakeholders and promulgated.

The OHS policy should:

- articulate the organization's commitment to OHS;
- indicate that sufficient resources (both financial and personnel) will be provided to promote and maintain OHS standards and meet OHS requirements;
- outline the organization's intentions, objectives, and priorities of OHS;

- describe in broad terms the means by which the objectives will be met;
- identify the roles and responsibilities of management, supervisors, and staff in meeting OHS requirements; and
- be signed off by the most senior manager of the organization, reflecting the importance of the policy.

The OHS policy should be reviewed periodically to ensure its currency.

The OHS policy is, however, only one part of an appropriate OHS strategy for a forensic organization. The OHS policy must be underpinned by risk assessments and incident/accident reports that enable the organization to assess its OHS exposure, to meet legislative requirements such as reporting obligations, and to respond to risks appropriately.

An organization can develop a list of the main hazards that its staff are likely to be exposed to in the course of their duties, utilizing OHS reports, incident/accident reports, and previous risk assessments. Prioritizing the main health and safety issues allows the organization to develop appropriate action plans to meet the objectives of its OHS policy.

Forensic organizations may consider integration of some OHS requirements with their quality assurance system. Many laboratories effectively use their quality system to embed OHS requirements in their documented procedures, to review OHS hazards as part of a periodic audit program, or to manage elements of their OHS action plans through their corrective action system. OHS, like quality, can then be viewed as an important yet integrated component of an effective management system.

Risk Assessments

Once potential OHS hazards have been identified, forensic organizations should evaluate the likelihood of injury from the interaction to the hazard and the magnitude of the adverse effect. The process of risk assessment will be very useful for managing potential OHS hazards within the facility and the expected external work environment. The purpose of the risk assessment process is to ensure that all workplace hazards have been identified, recorded, assessed, controlled, and reviewed. The desired outcome of this process is to eliminate, as far as practicable, the risk of injury or illness to personnel, damage to property, and damage to the environment. The process of developing risk assessment is often better suited to the known work environment. An OHS assessment of an office or laboratory can quickly identify specific hazards that may require attention. Obviously, this works well for the office and laboratory environment within one's control; however, each external scene will be different.

It is important that the range of potential hazards in external crime scenes and work environments is considered. While some risks can be grouped and managed collectively, the specific hazard and risk mitigation and control will vary from scene to scene given the circumstances. Given this, forensic practitioners should have an ability to undertake dynamic risk assessments or "risk on the run" as it is known in some jurisdictions.

Dynamic Risk Management

Dynamic risk assessments are conducted by a forensic practitioner as part of the attendance and examination process. In some instances, such as attendance at a clan lab, a person may be designated as the Site Safety Officer and have carriage of this as well as health and safety for all personnel at the site. Practitioners should be trained to assess the risk given the circumstances at the time, considering the actual hazards present at a crime scene.

A designated forensic practitioner or Site Safety Officer should undertake a quick reconnaissance of the crime scene to ensure the safety of forensic practitioners and others working at the scene. A review of the scene should be repeated whenever the situation at the scene changes. This could involve a visual inspection without entering the crime scene, and asking a number of questions. For example:

- Does the crime scene involve structures that are now unstable?

- Has confirmation been obtained from the Fire Brigade or other emergency responders that power, gas, and water to the site have been turned off?
- Is there adequate shelter so that practitioners can rest without succumbing to environmental stressors such as heat, cold, wind, or rain?

It is important to close the loop, and incorporate any strategic elements of each dynamic risk assessment in OHS policy and planning. After each incident, any relevant information obtained during the dynamic risk assessment should be recorded and collated for strategic analysis.

Hierarchy of Control Measures

Within OHS, there is a "hierarchy of control" designed to mitigate or resolve a risk deemed unacceptably high.

The hierarchy of control is a sequence of options, which offer a number of ways to approach the hazard control process. Various control options may be available. It is important to choose the control that most effectively eliminates the hazard or minimizes the risk in the circumstances. This may involve a single control measure or a combination of different controls that together provide the highest level of protection that is reasonably practicable.

1. Eliminate the hazard.
2. If this is not practical, then substitute the hazard with a lesser risk.
3. If this is not practical, then isolate the hazard.
4. If this is not practical, then use engineering controls.
5. If this is not practical, then use administrative controls, such as safe work practices, instruction, and training.
6. If this is not practical, then use personal protective equipment (PPE), such as gloves, eye protection, boots, and respirators.

It is important that management and staff discuss and consult, where possible, during all phases of the hazard identification, risk assessment, and risk control process.

Examples

1. If an organization is considering purchasing a piece of analytical equipment, and two products have the same capabilities but substantially different noise levels during operation, the organization may consider the noise level of the equipment during procurement and opt for the quieter system. This example demonstrates the principle of eliminating the hazard at source, which is the most effective control measure, when compared to training and provision of PPE such as hearing protection.
2. In the case of a fire scene of a building, applying a hierarchy of control approach, it is first necessary to consider the elimination or substitution of hazards. In a fire scene, this is

not possible. It is, however, possible to isolate the scene to prevent danger to the public and to maintain the integrity of the scene. Power, water, and gas to a building should be disconnected prior to entering the site. A structural engineer's opinion may be necessary prior to entry to the building. Safe entry and exit to the site can be established. Other administrative controls, such as briefing practitioners and maintaining records of the entry and exit of personnel, may be applied. Finally, practitioners can be prevented from entering the fire scene unless utilizing the appropriate PPE.

Specific Laboratory Hazards

The likely hazards within a laboratory environment include the following.

Chemicals

Chemical exposure may occur through inhalation, skin absorption, or direct ingestion and, once absorbed, are either stored in a particular organ or tissue, metabolized, or excreted. The effect of a chemical on a person is dependent on a number of factors such as duration and frequency of exposure, concentration of the chemical, and an individual's metabolism. A synergistic effect may occur when the undesirable effects of one substance are intensified if exposure has occurred to another substance.

Some nanomaterials exhibit different chemical properties compared with what they exhibit on a macroscale. As this is a relatively new field, there is insufficient knowledge regarding the hazards posed by nanomaterials. The potential hazards associated with nanomaterials may include increased reactivity because of their increased surface area-to-volume ratio, the ability to cross some of the body's protective mechanism, and the lack of the body's immunity against such small particles. Because of this lack of knowledge, the suggested control strategy to be used when working with nanomaterials should be "as low as reasonably achievable" (ALARA) approach to reduce exposure.

The effects of chemicals on the body may be categorized as follows:

- Poisonous or toxic chemicals are absorbed into the body and exert either an acute or short-term effect, such as headache, nausea, or loss of consciousness, or a long-term effect such as liver or kidney damage, cancer, or chronic lung disease.
- Corrosive chemicals burn the skin, eyes, or respiratory tract.
- Irritants can inflame the skin or lungs, causing conditions such as dermatitis or bronchitis.
- Sensitizers may exert long-term effects, especially to the skin (such as contact dermatitis) and to the respiratory tract (such as occupational asthma) by inducing an allergic reaction.

- Explosive or flammable substances pose immediate danger of fire and explosion, causing damage to the body through direct burning, or through inhalation of toxic fumes emitted during combustion.

Safety data sheets (SDSs), also known as material safety data sheets (MSDSs), are designed to provide relevant information regarding the identity, physical characteristics, safe storage, use, disposal, first aid treatment, and spill management of substances that are handled in the workplace. The information includes whether the substance is deemed to be a hazardous and/or a dangerous goods item. At a minimum, the SDS should be consulted before the first use of a chemical or other substance within a laboratory, or if practitioners are unfamiliar with the product. Copies of SDS should be retained according to legislative requirements. In some jurisdictions, electronic SDS management systems can allow an efficient way of accessing up-to-date SDS information.

Sharps

Sharps are objects that have sharp edges or points that have the potential to cut, scratch, or puncture the skin. Sharps can cause physical injury and have the potential to introduce infectious and toxic agents through the wounds created in the skin. Examples include hypodermic syringes and needles, knives, or broken glassware.

All forensic practitioners have a responsibility to handle and package sharps safely. Particular care should be given to ensuring that sharps are appropriately labeled when packaged. Sharps such as knives could, for example, be packaged in clear plastic tubes, making it easier for a person opening the item to identify the contents and the direction the sharp items is facing. Forensic labs should be encouraged to develop policies that encourage forensic practitioners and others who submit items to develop safe-packaging procedures.

Biological Material

Examples of "biological material" commonly encountered in forensic examinations include body tissue, blood, and body fluids (urine, saliva, vomit, pus, seminal fluid, vaginal fluid, and feces). Biological material is potentially hazardous as it may contain infectious agents such as viruses, bacteria, fungi, and parasites that cause a variety of communicable diseases.

Hair, fur, and items of clothing that have been in close contact with humans or animals may also harbor parasites such as fleas or nits.

When examining plant material such as cannabis, consideration should be given to the presence of *Aspergillus* sp. mold. If the *Aspergillus* spores are inhaled into the lungs, a serious, chronic respiratory or sinus infection can result. If mold is visible, the cannabis should be treated as a biological and respiratory hazard.

It is impossible to determine the prevalence of infectious or communicable diseases in the environment in which forensic practitioners work. Consequently, practitioners should adhere to recommended procedures for handling biological material and adopt an approach known as the "standard precautions." This approach requires practitioners to assume that all biological material is a potential source of infection, independent of diagnosis or perceived level of underlying risk.

Vaccinations should be offered for practitioners. The types of vaccinations given may depend on whether work is confined to the laboratory or whether work is performed in the field, as well as whether forensic practitioners are likely to be deployed overseas where other diseases may be more prevalent.

Firearms

Forensic practitioners may retrieve firearms from crime scenes. All personnel who may be required to handle firearms, either in the field, in the laboratory, or in support roles such as property or exhibit stores should be trained in how to render a firearm safe. As with the "standard precautions," it is important to consider all firearms as potentially loaded and adopt the practice of never pointing a firearm in the direction of another person, even after it has been rendered safe.

Firearms examiners, who undertake firearms investigations including test firing and bullet recovery, will be exposed to hazards such as noise and lead. They should have their hearing and blood lead levels monitored on a regular basis, to ensure that hearing protection is being worn and is functioning correctly, and any exposure to lead from the firearms is quickly identified and addressed.

Computer Forensics Laboratory

Computer forensic examiners specialize in obtaining, analyzing, and reporting on electronic evidence stored on computers and other electronic devices. Crimes involving a computer can range across the spectrum of criminal activity, from child pornography to theft of personal data to destruction of intellectual property. Potential hazards involve static postures, occupational overuse, and stress from viewing graphic images.

Some suggestions to minimize the stress from viewing graphic images are as follows:

- psychological assessment before and after viewing graphic material, and periodically;
- exposure to only one medium, for example, visual material only, rather than examining both sound and visual material simultaneously;
- specifying limits as to the amount of time spent examining explicit material in a day, and
- ceasing any examination of explicit material the end of their shift, to allow themselves time to refocus attention away from this stressor.

Electrical/Machinery

Forensic laboratories use a wide range of electrical equipment and machinery. Practitioners need to ensure that any inherent risk from electric shock is mitigated. The use of residual current devices (safety switches) is an appropriate strategy, as is visual inspection and periodic testing and tagging of power cords, to detect obvious damage, wear, and other conditions that might render it unsafe by a person qualified to do so under the legislation in effect in the jurisdiction.

Fume Cupboards

Fume cupboards are integral to minimizing the risk of exposure to chemical and biological hazards. Not all fume cupboards are suitable for all hazards. Fume cupboards should be maintained and inspected periodically. During maintenance, attention should be given to the following:

- The fume cupboard itself, including flow rates and replacement of absorbents or filters.
- In the case of externally vented fume cupboards, the ductwork and location of external vents. This is particularly important during any building maintenance or refurbishment.

Fume cupboards must be used for all operations that have the potential to release hazardous fumes, mists, or dusts.

- Before commencement of work, ensure that the fume cupboard is clean and free from contamination.
- Ensure the minimum of equipment is stored in the fume cupboard and is placed toward the back of the cupboard to reduce disturbance to the air flowing into the fume cupboard.
- Lower the sash as far as practicable during use to improve fume containment.

Recirculating fume cabinets rely on filtration or absorption to remove airborne contaminants released in the fume cabinet before the exhaust air is discharged back into the laboratory. They are suitable for light to moderate use with a known range of substances. The range of substances for which each cabinet can be used is limited by the need for compatibility with the chemicals in use as well as with the particular type of absorbent or filter fitted to the cabinet.

Robotics

The introduction of automated robotic platforms has significantly enhanced the efficiency of forensic analysis. The use of robotics is becoming more common and is very useful for a range of repetitive laboratory tasks. Besides saving time, robotics overcomes the need for repetitive work involved in pipetting, eliminating musculo-skeletal injuries.

Hazards associated with robotics include the risk of exposure to the chemicals used in the work, electrocution, and cutting, stabbing, or shearing from the moveable parts of the robot. The interlocks on the robots should not be bypassed.

X-rays

X-rays are used in analytical and imaging instrumentation. Potential exposure to X-rays is generally localized to specific parts of the body, usually the hands or fingers. Depending on the X-ray energies delivered, effects may range from erythema (redness) at point of exposure, blood changes, cancer through to death. Depending on the legislative requirement in each country, practitioners working with X-ray equipment may be required to use dosimeters to assess radiation dose.

Lasers

Lasers span the visible and nonvisible electromagnetic spectrum and have many applications in forensic science, including Raman spectroscopy. Lasers are generally classified according to the level of risk they represent. Damage from laser beams can be thermal or photochemical. The primary sites of damage are the eyes and skin. Hazards associated with laser work may include the following:

- fire,
- explosion,
- electrocution, and
- inhalation of contaminants from laser interactions.

    Precautions for use of lasers include the following:

- Display the class of laser in use.
- Appropriate protective eye wear with side protection and appropriate attenuation for the wavelength(s) in use must be worn.
- Interlocks on the laser should not be bypassed.
- Keep the laser beam path away from eye level whether one is seated or standing.

High-Intensity Light Sources

High-intensity light sources such as the Polilight® provide a range of colored light bands and white light for forensic work.

- Care should be taken that high-intensity white light is not directed onto any object at short distances from the end of the light guide, as this can cause severe heat damage to the object and may result in a fire.
- The light beam should never be directed at eyes, as the light can cause permanent damage.

Manual Handling

Manual handling refers to any activity that involves lifting, lowering, carrying, pushing, pulling, holding, restraining, or the application of force. Only a very small number of manual handling injuries are caused by the lifting of heavy weights alone. Actions such as reaching, twisting, bending, or maintaining static postures contribute to injury affecting the muscle or skeletal systems of the body. These musculo-skeletal injuries predominantly involve the neck, back or shoulder or arm muscle, tendon, ligament, or joints.

Injuries may be caused from activities such as maintaining static postures while working at fume cupboards, repetitive keyboard and mouse work, pipetting, prolonged use of comparison microscopes.

Some preventative strategies include the following:

- Seeking further assistance to have the activities assessed to minimize the manual handling risks inherent in the activity.
- Planning tasks so that rest breaks are scheduled.
- Choosing the best tools for the tasks.
- Alternate hands while using a mouse, if possible.

There is a move to make instruments smaller and more portable for use at crime scenes. While this has significant benefits, including potentially reducing the number of exhibits collected, moving equipment can also raise manual handling concerns.

General Laboratory Management

Housekeeping is important in laboratories. It is important to maintain clear passageways and have proper labeling of chemicals, clean and uncluttered work areas, and appropriate storage. The handling of powders is a potentially hazardous operation, and good housekeeping can help minimize airborne contamination from spilled materials. Having a planned preventative maintenance program and regular inspections of the workplace, plant, and equipment are essential for the smooth running of the laboratory.

Handling of Exhibits in Court

Each evidential item must be appropriately packaged and sealed, if this is not already the case, before it is exhibited in court. Items such as clothing, which are normally stored in paper, may need to be repackaged in clear plastic allowing the item to remain sealed and minimizing the risk of cross-contamination when handled in court. Caution should be exercised against opening exhibits in court, in case any hazards such as mold or irritant fumes are released.

Hazards in the Field

Forensic practitioners are often required to work or train in the field. Consideration should be given to managing hazards, which may affect practitioners, including the following:

- environmental hazards such as heat, cold, humidity or wet weather, the terrain, and fauna or flora at the scene;

- the type of operation, for example, working in a clandestine laboratory often involves quite specific hazards;
- the possible presence of offenders or other security risks such as booby traps at a scene; and
- the availability of first aid and emergency response domestically and overseas.

The risks from these hazards should be considered within the scope of the exercise or operation. Some possible responses to hazards, which may be considered in a dynamic risk assessment, include the following:

- Designating a location for emergency equipment, such as a crime scene vehicle, and ensuring that disinfectants, antiseptics, and a first aid kit are easily accessible.
- Planning an emergency exit from the scene and ensuring that this is communicated to all personnel present.
- Establishing a decontamination point if there is exposure to chemical or biological material.
- The use of appropriate PPE including sunglasses, sunscreen, and hats when working outdoors.
- Depending on the external temperature, work activity, duration, and PPE worn, practitioners should have access to shade for rest and adequate fluids if required during hot weather to prevent heat stress. The wearing of PPE including chemical suits and respirators requires longer and more frequent periods of rest break for recovery in hot temperatures and humid environment.
- In cold weather, provision should be made to have adequate warm clothing and a sheltered area.
- The risk of animal or dog bites while attending a crime scene should not be discounted. If practitioners are searching in vegetated areas, the risk of snake or tick bites should be considered, along with possible exposure to plants such as poison ivy or stinging nettles.

Confined Spaces

Forensic practitioners may have to enter confined spaces. Due to the high risks associated with entering the confined space, many jurisdictions mandate that entry into a confined space must not be made until a confined-space permit has been issued. Practitioners must receive specific training before work or entry into confined spaces.

Chemical, Biological, Radiological, and Nuclear Incidents

Forensic practitioners may be required to attend a chemical, biological, radiological, and nuclear (CBRN) incident. CBRN incidents where forensic practitioners may attend and conduct examinations include the following:

- chemical (warfare agent, toxic industrial chemical);
- biological (weaponized agent, natural disease);

- radiological (discrete or wide area contamination); and
- nuclear.

Depending on the response agency protocol in place, forensic practitioners may be working closely with the Fire Brigade and other emergency first responders. Entry must not be made into the "warm" or "hot" zone of the scene without consultation with the other emergency first responders.

Clan Labs

Clan labs pose a significant threat to the health and safety of police officers, forensic practitioners, the general public, and the environment. There are many hazards associated with clan labs including:

- flammable materials and/or explosive atmosphere;
- acutely toxic atmospheres;
- leaking or damaged compressed gas cylinders; and
- traps and hazards deliberately set to cause injury or death to police and other responders.

As a result of the frequency at which clan labs are encountered and the severe and variable risks associated with the investigation, many jurisdictions have developed specific policies and procedures concerning clan lab investigations.

For forensic practitioners, to deal with clan labs requires a high level of fitness as well as technical expertise. Practitioners have to understand the following:

- illicit drug chemistry;
- how to neutralize the risks of explosions, fires, chemical burns, and toxic fumes;
- how to handle, store, and dispose of hazardous materials; and
- how to treat medical conditions caused by exposure.

Practitioners must also wear full protective equipment including respirators and may be required to move equipment at the clan lab in the process of collecting evidence. The storage and handling of unknown chemicals from clandestine laboratories or seizures should also be considered. Preliminary identification should take place, before its storage or disposal.

When unknowns such as "white powders," chemicals (in liquid, solid, or gas state), or biological materials are encountered in the field, it is prudent to be cautious and obtain up-to-date intelligence to shed more light on what is at the scene. It may be an explosive material or contain anthrax spores or ricin or something as innocuous as talc.

Some precautions include the following:

- wearing the appropriate level of protective clothing/equipment for the activity;
- avoiding direct contact with the substance, even if only in small quantities;

- not smelling or tasting anything from the scene;
- noting physical characteristics such as color, form, and consistency;
- where it is safe to do so, looking for hazard symbols on packaging or labels if available; and
- seeking specialist advice if unable to identify the substance.

Potential Hazards during an Overseas Deployment

Forensic practitioners can be required to work overseas to assist with large-scale disasters. An example was the Thailand Tsunami Victim Identification process involving forensic practitioners from 30 countries working to recover and identify bodies. Forensic practitioners need to be mindful of hazards likely to be encountered during an overseas deployment depending on the location, magnitude of the operation, and how many practitioners are deployed. Some hazards to be considered include the following:

- climatic demands;
- remote and sometimes dangerous terrain;
- different cultural sensitivities;
- security requirements;
- different levels of infrastructure support at the locality;
- logistics, including the transport of large quantities of equipment, manual handling, setting up, and packing up;
- different hygiene levels;
- diseases that can be transmitted by insect and/or animal vectors;
- the possibility of infectious diseases; and
- asbestos and other hazards in buildings.

Work-Related Stress

Practitioners at work may experience work-related stress. There are some specific stressors unique within forensic work. Forensic practitioners may experience workplace-related stress due to their attendances at morgues, violent crime scenes, disaster victim identification, or requirements to view explicit or graphic material or images.

Indicators of stress include changes in eating habits, tiredness due to changes in sleep patterns, frequent absences from work, reduced productivity, concentration, motivation, and morale. Physical symptoms may include headaches, abdominal pains, diarrhea, constipation, high blood pressure, insomnia, anxiety state, and depression.

Many organizations offer programs to provide assistance to employees, including counseling to help practitioners to deal with work-related stress or resilience training to manage work–life balance.

See also: **Management/Quality in Forensic Science:** Principles of Quality Assurance; Risk Management; Principles of Laboratory Organization.

Further Reading

Clancy, D., Billinghurst, A., Cater, H., 2009. Hazard identification and risk assessment – Understanding the transition from the documented plan to assessing dynamic risk in Bio Security emergencies. World Conference on Disaster Management, Sydney, Australia. http://www.humansafety.com.au/getattachment/da338cb7-29b0-4d3a-8a06-d7dc0b569a87/C20.aspx.

Furr, K., 2000. Handbook of Laboratory Safety, fifth ed. CRC Press, Florida.

Green-McKenzie, J., Watkins, M., 2005. Occupational hazards: law enforcement officers are at risk of body fluid exposure. Here's what to expect if it happens to you. Law Enforcement Magazine 29 (9), 52–54, 56, 58.

Hanson, D., 2007. Hazardous duty training officers to tackle hazmat emergencies. Law Enforcement Technology 34 (4), 80–85.

Haski, R., Cardilini, G., Bartolo, W., 2011. Laboratory Safety Manual. CCH Australia Ltd, Sydney.

Horswell, J., 2000. The Practice of Crime Scene Investigation. CRC Press, Florida.

Jackel, G., 2004. The high cost of stress. AUSPOL: The Official Publication of the Australian Federal Police Association and ALAJA 1, 4–37.

Mayhew, C., 2001a. Occupational health and safety risks faced by police officers. Australian Institute of Criminology. Trends and Issues in Crime and Criminal Justice 196, 1–6.

Mayhew, C., 2001b. Protecting the occupational health and safety of police officers. Australian Institute of Criminology. Trends and Issues in Crime and Criminal Justice 197, 1–6.

Rothernbaum, D., 2010. Exposed: an officer's story. Clan Lab Safety Alert 7 (2), 1–2.

Smith, D., 2005. Psychosocial occupational health issues in contemporary police work: a review of research evidence. Journal of Occupational Health and Safety, Australia and New Zealand 21 (3), 217–228.

Tillman, C., 2007. Principles of Occupational Health and Hygiene: An Introduction. Allen & Unwin, Crows Nest.

Whitman, M., Smith, C., 2005. The culture of safety: No one gets hurt today. Police Chief LXXII (11), 20–24, 26–27.

Winder, C., 2011. Hazard Alert: Managing Workplace Hazardous Substances. CCH Australia Ltd, Sydney.

Witter, R., Martyny, J., Mueller, K., Gottschall, B., Newman, L., 2007. Symptoms experienced by law enforcement personnel during methamphetamine lab investigation. Journal of Occupational and Environmental Hygiene 4, 895–902.

Relevant Websites

http://www.ccohs.ca/oshanswers/occup_workplace/labtech.html—Canadian Centre for Occupational Health and Safety (CCOHS).

http://www.cdc.gov/niosh/—Centers for Disease Control and Prevention (CDC).

http://www.forensic.gov.uk/html/company/foi/publication-scheme/health-and-safety/—Forensic Science Service, Health and Safety.

http://www.police.qld.gov.au/Resources/Internet/rti/policies/documents/QPSForensicServicesHealth_SafetyManual.pdf—Health and Safety Manual, Police Forensic Services, Queensland Police.

http://www.hse.gov.uk/services/police/index.htm—Health and Safety Executive (HSE).

http://www.londonhealthandsafetygroup.org/archive.html—London Health and Safety Group.

http://www.osha.gov/—Occupational Safety & Health Administration.

http://www.ccohs.ca/oshanswers/occup_workplace/police.html—What do Police do?.

Child Pornography

E Quayle, University of Edinburgh, Edinburgh, UK

Glossary

COPINE scale A rating system created in Ireland and used in the United Kingdom to categorize the severity of child pornography.

Digital child pornography This may refer to images that have been created by a computer program or images that are of a real child, which have been altered by a computer program.

Social networking Web sites These have been defined as Web-based services that allow individuals to create a public or semipublic profile within a system, define a list of other users with whom they share a connection, and view and access content from their list of connections and those made by others within the system.

The International Centre of Missing & Exploited Children A leading global movement to protect children from sexual exploitation and abduction.

User-generated content The production of content by the general public rather than by paid professionals and experts in the field. Also called "peer production" and mostly available on the Web through blogs and wikis.

Introduction

The past decade has seen a substantial increase in the number of international research publications, policy documents, and legislative changes in relation to still and moving sexualized images of children, variously called child pornography, abuse images, or child exploitation materials. This increased interest in part reflects the growing number of people in the criminal justice system convicted of crimes related to the production, distribution, and possession of child pornography. Data to support this are largely drawn from the United States, Europe, and Australia, although it is unclear whether increased availability of the Internet in Asia, Africa, and South America will change this. While child pornography is not new, it is the case that, with each technological advance, one has seen an increase in the availability of such materials, and this has been most noticeable in relation to the advent of the Internet. In this context, it is one of a number of cybercrimes, a term used to describe a wide range of offenses, including offenses against computer data and systems (such as "hacking"), computer-related forgery and fraud (such as "phishing"), content offenses (such as disseminating child pornography), and copyright offenses (such as the dissemination of pirated content).

There are historical accounts of child pornography and its distribution, which appeared to be facilitated by the popular use of photography. The criminalization of such material, however, made access both difficult and dangerous, although there was a period of approximately 10 years when in some European countries (Denmark and Sweden) all pornographic materials were decriminalized. It has been argued that recognition of child pornography as a societal problem dates to the late 1970s, and this is certainly reflected in the increase of legislation from this time in countries such as the United States. The advent of Internet technology lowered the cost of the production of these images, dramatically increased their availability, and reduced the risk of detection that was associated with the criminalization of production and possession. The move internationally to legislate against the production, dissemination, and possession of these images has meant an increasing focus on the "Internet sex offender" and an expansion of activities that might potentially be criminalized (e.g., in relation to text or audio files).

International Law

In recent years, one has seen the development of supranational and international policy documents, which set out to define "child pornography" and four policy documents that are central to this issue. The European Union's Framework Decision on combating the sexual exploitation of children and child pornography entered into force in 2004 and required member states to take steps to ensure compliance by 20 January 2006. Here, child pornography is defined as pornographic material that visually depicts or represents (1) a real child involved or engaged in sexually explicit conduct, including lascivious exhibition of the genitals or the pubic area of a child, or (2) a real person appearing to be a child involved or engaged in the conduct mentioned in (1), or (3) realistic images of a nonexistent child involved or engaged in the conduct mentioned in (1). As one can see, the definition in the EU Framework Decision talks about a "real" child, "real" person, and "realistic" images, which may prove unlikely to cover virtual images or cartoons. The Council of Europe's Cybercrime Convention came into force in July 2004, and Article 9 defines child pornography as pornographic material that visually depicts a minor engaged in sexually explicit conduct, a person appearing to be a minor engaged in sexually explicit conduct, or realistic images representing a minor engaged in sexually explicit conduct. This relates to all people under the age of 18 years, but it is possible for a lower age limit of 16 years to be set. The third document is the United Nation's Optional Protocol to the Convention on the Rights of the Child on the Sale of Children, Child Prostitution, and Child Pornography, which came into force in January 2002, and defines child pornography as any representation, by whatever means, of a child engaged in real or simulated explicit sexual activities or any representation of the sexual parts of a child for primarily sexual purposes.

In all three, a child is defined as someone under the age of 18 years and includes both photographs of actual children and representations of children, which would appear to include computer-generated images. However, the issue of age is subject to several reservations and complicated by the age of sexual consent established under national law. The UN definition is broad and, as it refers to "any representation," would also include textual material, cartoons, and drawings. The most recent relevant instrument establishing a definition of child pornography is the Council of Europe Convention on the Protection of Children against Sexual Exploitation and Sexual Abuse. While this definition is restricted to visual materials, it does not require that a real child be used in their production (as is the case in the United States). However, member states may opt not to criminalize the production and possession of virtual child pornography.

This UN definition was used in a study of the 184 Interpol member countries. The results indicated that at the time of publication, 95 countries had no legislation at all that specifically addresses child pornography, and 41 countries do not criminalize possession of child pornography, regardless of intent to distribute. However, in law, offenses related to child pornography are not all treated as the same. This has been referred to as a chain of liability. At the top of the chain are those who produce abusive images or content, and these will be made up of, although not exclusively, those who will have sexually abused the children in the images. Many of them will produce images within a domestic setting where production is part of a spectrum of abusive practices. The second group that sexually exploits consists of those who distribute child pornography over the Internet, either commercially (for financial gain) or noncommercially, where the images themselves function as a form of currency or possibly as a means to raise their status in a group or to confirm their allegiance and sense of belonging to a group. The final group includes those who sexually exploit the child through the possession of images downloaded from the Internet. However, it is the enforceability of international law perhaps that demonstrates the biggest weakness of its applicability to child pornography. Although it is easy for countries to sign treaties and conventions and make pledges to tackle child pornography, it is also very easy for countries to simply ignore them.

Harm

One assumption underpinning the interest in abuse images is that of harm. This may be expressed as harm toward the child who was photographed, but equally harm has been argued to take place when someone views the image of the child, even without any contact having taken place. The reasoning is that there is the potential for additional harm, as looking at images may increase the likelihood of the commission of a contact offense against a child at some point in the near, or distant, future. Such arguments have become enshrined in the laws of many countries with, for example, the US Department of Justice prosecuting possession under the rationale that (1) possession leads to contact offenses, (2) demand drives supply, and (3) the availability constitutes continued and indirect abuse of the child depicted. Some researchers have challenged assumptions of harm, arguing that the majority of images depict children not engaged in acts that are harmful in themselves.

Few studies have examined these images, which in part may be due to the difficulties in researchers gaining access without committing an offense, along with the ethical challenges posed by repeat viewing. It might seem that the seriousness of the problem has largely been measured in terms of the number of offenders in the criminal justice system and the proportion of those who have already committed a contact offense or who are deemed at risk of committing one. Where the images in their possession have been explored, this is most often in relation to what it might tell us about the offender: the nature of their sexual interests and fantasies, their sexual orientation, and the intensity of their interest or preoccupation. All of this reflects a legitimate concern with the offender and the nature of the offense, but, unlike the research on solicitation or grooming, does little to help us understand what has happened from the perspective of the child.

Typologies of Child Pornography

Challenges to a systematic analysis of child pornography stem from difficulties in describing the content in any meaningful way outside of the age or gender of the child or children. The adoption by the UK Sentencing Advisory Panel (SAP) of the COPINE scale as an objective measure of content was probably not a reflection of the integrity of the scale but rather the absence of anything else. The original COPINE scale had 10 levels ranging from indicative images (e.g., pictures of children in bathing costumes or underwear) to ones depicting extreme sexually abusive acts such as sadism or bestiality. In 2002, in England and Wales, the SAP published their advice to the Court of Appeal on offenses involving child pornography. The SAP believed that the nature of the material should be the key factor in deciding the level of sentence and adapted the COPINE scale to five levels. They dropped levels 1–3 completely, arguing that nakedness alone was not indicative of indecency. The five levels were described as follows:

- Level 1: Nudity or erotic posing with no sexual activity
- Level 2: Sexual activity between children or solo masturbation
- Level 3: Nonpenetrative sexual activity between adult(s) and child(ren)
- Level 4: Penetrative sexual activity between adult(s) and child(ren)
- Level 5: Sadism or bestiality

In spite of concern over its use and the confusion as to whether it is the original scale or the SAP guidelines that are being referred to, having some objective measure does allow us to make comparisons between samples and have some sense of both preferred materials, and also (although rarely referred to) the types of sexual activity that the depicted child has been exposed to. However, it has been argued that the kinds of images that have the capacity to be described as child pornography are increasing. In addition to photographs that depict the sexual abuse of children, images and texts in countries such as Australia and Canada risk breaking the law for any depiction of minors in a sexualized context. A revised typology of child pornography has been proposed that makes reference to content (as with the COPINE scale), biological development of the child within the image, level of purported consent given by the child, veracity of the image, and the particular genre portrayed.

While analyses of images by law enforcement agencies would suggest that the typical child depicted is a prepubescent girl, an analysis of a sample of seized images within one UK law enforcement database would suggest that the odds of the abuse images being of females versus males were about 4–1, and the odds of the images being of white children versus non-white children were about 10–1. Of those white female children, approximately 48% were pubescent. It may be that, in many instances, one can at best approximate the content of image collections, given the potential volume of images collected, and the limited forensic resources of most specialist police units, and it has been suggested that the volume, complexity, and

inaccessibility of digital evidence have deterred a systematic analysis of the relationship between downloaded material and potential risk.

Internet Sex Offenders

Interest in the content of child pornography images parallels concern that what is downloaded from the Internet is a good indicator of pedophilic interest and that the content of images may prove to relate to who might also commit contact offenses and how such offenses might find expression. In relation to this, the ongoing concern with how similar, or different, people who access online child pornography (Internet sex offenders) are from contact offenders (those who commit a sex offense against a child in the off-line environment) dominates much of the current research. It is apparent that a proportion of people who commit an online offense involving child pornography share similar characteristics to those who offend in the off-line environment. In a large United Kingdom sample of psychometric test results from child pornography offenders, clusters were identified, which were labeled normal, inadequate, and deviant. The authors felt that their results were similar to the clusters found in contact offender groups. A Canadian meta-analysis of published studies indicated that approximately half of the online offenders admitted to committing a contact sexual offense and 12.2% had an official history of contact sexual offenses.

However, differences between Internet and contact sex offenders do exist and appear to be related to demographic characteristics such as age, level of education, and measures of intelligence as well as psychological variables such as cognitive distortions, emotional dysregulation, empathy, and impression management. A meta-analysis of 27 samples from published studies found that online offenders tended to be Caucasian males, who are younger than the general population and more likely to be unemployed. Both online and off-line offenders had an increased incidence of physical and sexual abuse than the general population. In comparison with off-line offenders, online offenders had greater victim empathy, greater sexual deviancy, and lower impression management. These authors concluded that youth and unemployment are risk factors for online sexual offending and that this was consistent with typical crime patterns.

Risk

Research on the offense histories of Internet offenders and the likelihood of future offending would suggest that, with a longer period postoffense, more offenders are detected for new offenses, with recidivism for contact sexual offenses predicted by criminal history, and in particular violent offense history and the age of the offender at the time of their first conviction. Importantly, Canadian researchers also examined failures on conditional release, in particular where offenders put themselves in "risky" situations, such as being alone with children. The finding that one-quarter of this offender group was charged with failures was consistent with the findings from other sex offender groups. Such failures included breaches of conditions about being alone with children, accessing the Internet, and contacting children and downloading child-abuse materials, as well as other violations, which were nonsexual or indicated noncompliance. This is of interest because while 34% of offenders had a charge for any type of further offense, only 4% were charged with any new contact sexual offense and 7% were charged with new child pornography-related offenses. Recidivism has also been found to be low in other recent studies in the United States and Europe.

Studies of risk that have explicitly examined the content of child pornography images have produced what looks like conflicting information, with data suggesting an inverse relationship between the severity of the victimization within the images and the likelihood of recidivism. However, these results appear different to a United Kingdom sample of contact offenders and noncontact offenders, all found in possession of child-abuse images and all of whom were arrested after 2000. Contact offenders were found to have a significantly higher percentage of level 3 and level 4 still images than noncontact offenders. Noncontact offenders could be distinguished by the larger number of level 1 images downloaded. Possession of level 1 and level 3 images was the best predictor of noncontact and contact offending, respectively. With contact offenders, the more severe the contact offense, the higher the SAP level of the images possessed. The content of the images, including gender and age of the children, was directly associated with those of the contact offense victims. Contact offenders tended to view content with a smaller victim range and were polymorphic with regard to gender. This is the first evidence of congruence between images sought and collected and the type of offense committed against a child.

These studies raise additional concerns about how images are used to determine the sentence given to the offender, and whether the sentence should be based on principles of harm or on the likelihood of recidivism. It is apparent that, in reality, these might yield very different decisions.

Digital Child Pornography

One further challenge relates to digitally altered or pseudo-images and virtual child pornography. Important issues have been raised about how different an image has to be for it to constitute a pseudo-image, the possession of which is likely to attract a lower sentence. In the United States, the constitutionality of virtual child pornography remains a critical issue. In Ashcroft versus Free Speech Coalition in 2002, a majority of the Supreme Court struck down portions of the Child Pornography Prevention Act of 1996, stating that virtual child pornography created without real or identifiable minors was unconstitutionally overbroad. One of the primary producers of such imagery is Japan where there is a huge market in *manga*, and other forms of animation, that many believe are sexually exploitative. In countries outside of Japan, there has been a bid to criminalize the possession of nonphotographic visual depictions of child sexual abuse. Recent legislation in the United Kingdom has criminalized nonphotographic pornographic images of children; that is, fantasy visual representations of child pornography in the form of, for example, computer-generated images, cartoons, or drawings. Opponents of these measures, such as the American Civil Liberties Union, have argued that people's thoughts are their private thoughts and that prohibition of pseudo-child pornography is a violation of free speech rights.

User-Generated Content and Sexting

One final consideration is self-generated, or user-generated, child pornography. In a nationally representative US survey, 4% of teenagers aged 12–17 years who own a mobile phone reported that they have sent sexually suggestive nude or nearly nude images of themselves to someone else via text messaging and 15% have received such images. This increases to 8% and 30%, respectively, in those who are 17 years old, with teenagers who pay their own bills more likely to send sexual images. This activity is frequently referred to as "sexting": the practice of sending or posting sexually suggestive text messages and images, including nude or seminude photographs, via cellular telephones or over the Internet. Typically, the young person takes a picture of himself or herself with a mobile phone camera (or other digital camera), or has someone else take the picture; this is then stored as a digital image and transmitted via mobile phone as a text message, photo-send function, or electronic mail. Additionally, the subject may use a mobile phone to post the image to a social networking Web site.

These materials have been referred to as "self-produced child pornography." Self-produced child pornography refers to images that possess the following criteria: They meet the legal definition of child pornography and were originally produced by a minor with no coercion, grooming, or adult participation whatsoever. The definition does not focus exclusively on the young person who makes the image but also on those juveniles in the distribution chain who may coerce production, or later possess, distribute, or utilize such images. It highlights that the term sexting has been used variously to describe: one minor sending one picture to a perceived significant other; a minor taking and/or distributing pictures of himself/herself and others engaged in sexually explicit conduct; a minor extensively forwarding or disseminating a nude picture of another youth without his/her knowledge; a minor posting such pictures on a Web site; an older teen asking (or coercing) another youth for such pictures; a person impersonating a classmate to "dupe" and/or blackmail other minors into sending pictures; and adults sending pictures or videos to minors or possessing sexually explicit pictures of juveniles, as well as adults sending sexually suggestive text or images to other adults. These are all different activities, only some of which would be deemed illegal in many jurisdictions.

There are many recent cases in the United States where young people have been prosecuted for taking photographs of themselves while engaging in lawful sexual activity and the harms that might follow from a possible child pornography conviction. It has been concluded that one cannot ignore that there are also generational factors at work in the prosecutions of teens for sexting and "autopornography" and that the prosecutorial and judicial personnel who are acting in these prosecutions are typically two or more generations removed from the teenagers whose sexual expression is condemned and whose future outlooks are drastically affected. The argument is that such efforts might be seen to be generally futile and that the future and its values belong to those whose lives lie mostly ahead of them. However, there does appear to be a legitimate concern to distinguish between sexting as a serious offense, which poses a danger to others, and when it is simply the product of a legitimate sexual relationship.

> *See also:* **Forensic Medicine/Clinical:** Child Abuse.

Further Reading

Akdeniz, Y., 2008. Internet Child Pornography and the Law: National and International Responses. Ashgate, Aldershot.

Babchishin, K.M., Hanson, R.K., Hermann, C.A., 2010. The characteristics of online sex offenders: a meta-analysis of online sex offenders. Sexual Abuse: a Journal of Research and Treatment 1–32.

Eke, A.W., Seto, M.C., Williams, J., 2010. Examining the criminal history and future offending of child pornography offenders: an extended prospective follow-up study. Law and Human Behavior 1–13.

Glasgow, D., 2010. The potential of digital evidence to contribute to risk assessment of internet offenders. Journal of Sexual Aggression 16 (1), 223–237.

Goode, S.D., 2010. Understanding and Addressing Sexual Attraction to Children: A Study of Paedophiles in Contemporary Society. Routledge, London.

Hebenton, B., Shaw, D., Pease, K., 2009. Offences involving indecent photographs and pseudo-photographs of children: an analysis of sentencing guidelines. Psychology, Crime and Law 15 (5), 425–440.

Humbach, J.A., 2009. 'Sexting' and the first Amendment. In: 37 Hastings Const. L.Q., pp. 433–486.

Leary, M.G., 2010. Sexting or self-produced child pornography? The dialog continues – Structured prosecutorial discretion within a multidisciplinary response. In: 17 Va. J. Soc. Pol'y & L., pp. 486–566.

Quayle, E., Jones, T., 2011. Sexualized images of children on the Internet. Sexual Abuse: a Journal of Research and Treatment 23 (1), 7–21.

Quayle, E., Ribsil, K. (Eds.), 2012. Understanding and Preventing Online Sexual Exploitation of Children. Routledge, London.

Seto, M., 2010. Child pornography use and Internet solicitation in the diagnosis of pedophilia. Archives of Sexual Behavior 39, 591–593.

Stapleton, A., 2010. Knowing it when you (don't) see it: Mapping the pornographic child in order to diffuse the paedophilic gaze. Global Media Journal: Australian Edition 4 (2), 1–21.

Taylor, M., Holland, G., Quayle, E., 2001. Typology of paedophile picture collections. The Police Journal 74 (2), 97–107.

Teens and Sexting. Pew Research Centre. Available online at: http://www.pewinternet.org//media//Files/Reports/2009/PIP_Teens_and_Sexting.pdf.

UNODC, 2010. The Globalization of Crime: A Transnational Organized Crime Threat Assessment. United Nations Office on Drugs and Crime, Vienna. http://www.unodc.org/documents/data-and-analysis/tocta/TOCTA_Report_2010_low_res.pdf.

Wolak, J., Finkelhor, D., Mitchell, K., Ybarra, M., 2008. Online 'predators' and their victims: Myths, realities, and implications for prevention and treatment. American Psychologist 63 (2), 111–128.

Relevant Websites

http://www.ceop.police.uk/—Child Exploitation and Online Protection Centre.

http://www.unh.edu/ccrc/internet-crimes/—Crimes Against Children Research Center, University of New Hampshire.

http://www.ecpat.net/WorldCongressIII/index.php—World Congress against Sexual Exploitation of Children and Adolescents.

Key Terms

Abuse images, Best evidence, Bias, Brady material, Child pornography, Child pornography legislation, Confrontation, COPINE scale, Digital child, Digital evidence, Discovery, Ethical considerations, Forensic, Forensic laboratory report, Hazard, Health, Holistic approach, IIOC (illegal images of children), Integrated case management, Internet sex offender, Investigations, Occupational health and safety (OHS), Pornography, Risk, Safety, Sexting, Strategy, Submissions, Testimony, User-generated content.

Review Questions

1. Are the models offered for forensic service provision suggested by Ramsey and Burton the only ones available? What other models might there be?
2. What is a "forensic strategy"? What questions are part of developing one? Why is it important to a case and to a laboratory?

3. Why is integration of forensic cases "the single biggest challenge to the forensic science community"?
4. What is currently in forensic reports? How do these differ from other scientific reports? How do they differ from published articles in peer-reviewed journals? What *should* be in forensic reports? Make a table listing each component and compare.
5. Who is the "audience" of forensic reports? The police using the technical information to investigate the case or other scientists who must review the technical information? Is it both? How does this affect the content of forensic reports? Should it?
6. How do the legal requirements of the contents of a forensic report differ between the United Kingdom and the United States?
7. Can forensic reports stand on their own (that is, without an expert's testimony)? What determines this?
8. Are there ethical obligations to the format and content of a forensic report? If so, what are they?
9. What is "Brady material"?
10. What is "OHS"? What should this policy articulate?
11. What is a risk, in OHS terms? How is it prevented or mitigated? What is the hierarchy of control measures?
12. List some specific psychological hazards of viewing child pornography. What are their risks and how are they managed?
13. Why is good housekeeping important in a forensic laboratory?
14. Why is stress a health and safety issue? What types of analysis are particularly prone to mental or stress issues?
15. What does it mean to void dire an expert?
16. What is direct testimony? What is cross-examination? How do they differ? Who asks which questions?
17. Who is the "trier of fact"?
18. How is the wording of a report different from the wording of testimony? Should it differ? If so, how?
19. What is the biggest weakness to prosecuting child pornography cases?
20. What is the COPINE scale?

Discussion Questions

1. How are the risks for forensic accountants different than for forensic specialists who work in a laboratory environment? What risks do they face?
2. What OHS issues do document examiners face? What would those issues depend on? What about, for example, ink analysis?
3. How would you integrate a forensic accountant (outside your agency) into a forensic strategy? What about a crime involving prepaid cards—who do you call?
4. What sort of education is required to become a forensic accountant? What about the analysis of counterfeits? Or financial crimes? What agencies might one work for?
5. The trier of fact could be the judge or a jury. Should expert testimony differ depending on which one it is? Judges were previously attorneys and have college education, while juries are a cross section of a population. Does this matter to the content of testimony? Why or why not?

Additional Readings

Gottschalk, P., 2016. Private policing of financial crime: fraud examiners in white-collar crime investigations. International Journal of Police Science & Management 18 (3), 173–183.
Thornton, J.P., 2017. Conflict of interest and legal issues for investigators and authors. Jama 317 (17), 1761–1762.
Van Akkeren, J., Buckby, S., Tarr, J.A., 2016. Forensic accounting: professional regulation of a multi-disciplinary field. Australian Business Law Review 44, 204–2015.

INDEX

I

J

K

Edwards Brothers Inc.
Ann Arbor MI. USA
February 14, 2018